Catholic Pirates and
Greek Merchants

● ○ ●

PRINCETON MODERN GREEK STUDIES

This series is sponsored by the Princeton University Program in Hellenic Studies with the support of the Stanley J. Seeger Hellenic Fund

Firewalking and Religious Healing: The Anastenaria of Greece and the American Firewalking Movement by Loring M. Danforth

Dance and the Body Politic in Northern Greece by Jane K. Cowan

Yannis Ritsos: Repetitions, Testimonies, Parentheses edited and translated by Edmund Keeley

Contested Identities: Gender and Kinship in Modern Greece edited by Peter Loizos and Evthymios Papataxiarchis

A Place in History: Social and Monumental Time in a Cretan Town by Michael Herzfeld

Demons and the Devil: Moral Imagination in Modern Greek Culture by Charles Stewart

The Enlightenment as Social Criticism: Iosipos Moisiodax and Greek Culture in the Eighteenth Century by Paschalis M. Kitromilides

C. P. Cavafy: Collected Poems translated by Edmund Keeley and Philip Sherrard; edited by George Savidis

The Fourth Dimension by Yannis Ritsos; Peter Green and Beverly Bardsley, translators

George Seferis: Collected Poems, Revised Edition translated, edited, and introduced by Edmund Keeley and Philip Sherrard

In a Different Place: Pilgrimage, Gender, and Politics at a Greek Island Shrine by Jill Dubisch

Cavafy's Alexandria, Revised Edition by Edmund Keeley

The Films of Theo Angelopoulos: A Cinema of Contemplation by Andrew Horton

The Muslim Bonaparte: Diplomacy and Orientalism in Ali Pasha's Greece by Katherine E. Fleming

Venom in Verse: Aristophanes in Modern Greece by Gonda A. H. Van Steen

A Shared World: Christians and Muslims in the Early Modern Mediterranean by Molly Greene

After the War Was Over: Reconstructing the Family, Nation, and State in Greece, 1943–1960 edited by Mark Mazower

Notes from the Balkans: Locating Marginality and Ambiguity on the Greek-Albanian Border by Sarah F. Green

Catholic Corsairs and Greek Merchants: A Maritime History of the Mediterranean by Molly Greene

MOLLY GREENE

Catholic Pirates and Greek Merchants

● ○ ●

A Maritime History of the Mediterranean

PRINCETON UNIVERSITY PRESS
PRINCETON AND OXFORD

Library of Congress Cataloging-in-Publication Data

Greene, Molly, 1959–

Catholic pirates and Greek merchants : a maritime history of the Mediterranean /

Molly Greene.

p. cm. — (Princeton modern Greek studies)

Includes bibliographical references and index.

ISBN 978-0-691-14197-8 (hardcover : alk. paper)   1. Mediterranean Sea—History, Naval.

2. Navigation—Mediterranean Sea—History.   3. Mediterranean Sea—Commerce—

History.   4. Mediterranean Sea Region—Commerce—History.   5. Merchants—Greece—

History.   6. Pirates—Mediterranean Sea—History.   7. Knights of Malta—History.

8. Mediterranean Sea Region—History, Naval.   9. Mediterranean Sea Region—Relations.

10.   International relations—History.   I. Title.

D973.G735 2010

387.09182′20903—dc22   2010002665

British Library Cataloging-in-Publication Data is available

This book has been composed in Minion Pro

press.princeton.edu

Printed in the United States of America

1 3 5 7 9 10 8 6 4 2

To Hannah and Henry, my two diamonds

● ○ ●

Contents

● ○ ●

Illustrations

● ○ ●

Preface

● ○ ●

This project had its origins in an article published many years ago by a man with the delightful name of Roderic Cavaliero. In 1959, his "The Decline of the Maltese Corso in the 18th Century: A Study in Maritime History" appeared in *Melita Historica*, the journal of the Maltese Historical Society. "Melita" is the Latin name for this tiny island in the very center of the Mediterranean.

Nearly forty years after its publication, I read his account one summer morning in the New York Public Library, and my pulse began to race. Unlike many who come to the study of Malta, I was not so interested in the knights. But Cavaliero's account of the knights' quarrels with the pope and with the French kings, among others, revealed a seventeenth-century sea swarming with Greek ships. Even better, the article hinted that these ships would show up not only as dry numbers on some sort of port registry; the likelihood was that we would hear their stories as well. They entered the historical record because they were the subject of fierce disputes between the Grand Master of the Order and various powers in and around the Mediterranean. The question at the center of all of these disputes was the same: were the Greeks, or were they not, legitimate targets in the Maltese pursuit of the *corso*, as the war against the Muslim infidel was known? It was the Greeks themselves who raised this question, because they complained to all and sundry in their ongoing battle to protect their shipping from Maltese attacks. Cavaliero's article confirmed for me what I had begun to suspect during the course of writing my first book, namely, that the history of Greek shipping extended much farther back, and was more complicated, than the limited story of the eighteenth-century story that is usually told. On the other hand, I was very surprised to learn that the Greeks had gone all the way to the pope in their pursuit of justice. Trained as an Ottoman historian, I was familiar with the narrative that it was the Phanariots, the Orthodox Christian *Noblesse de Robe*, who were the protectors of Greek maritime endeavor. The connection to Rome suggested the existence of another world.

It makes sense that it was Cavaliero, a historian not of the Greeks or of the Ottoman Empire but of the knights and Malta, who opened up this vista for me. Often it takes outsiders to a field to reveal to us what we have missed because of the power of our own received narratives. At the same time, Cavaliero did not share my interest in the Greeks, and his article only hinted at their stories. But it was enough. Through him, I was able to follow the trail to the records of a court in Malta known as the Tribunale degli Armamenti. And the Tribunale has not disappointed. It has provided a wealth of stories that give a voice to the otherwise anonymous Greek captains, sailors, and merchants who sailed the seas of the eastern and central Mediterranean in the seventeenth century. Their accounts, in turn, are a beginning step in the reconstruction of the maritime world of the early modern Mediterranean.

Acknowledgments

● ○ ●

I have received help and support from many quarters in the writing of this book. The staff at the National Archives of Malta has been unfailingly helpful and responsive. During several trips to Malta I was able to photocopy whatever I needed and, once back in Princeton, further inquiries were always answered promptly. I would particularly like to thank Charles Farrugia, who met me at the Banca Giuratale, or Municipal Palace, in Mdina on my first trip to the archives in the summer of 1999. He gave me a tour of that beautiful building, built in 1730, then introduced me to the Banca Giuratale's holdings. These include the records of the law court known as the Tribunale degli Armamenti, which is at the center of my book. While in Malta I benefited from the counsel of Professor Victor Mallia-Milanes of the University of Malta. His own work has been a source of inspiration for me, and he was kind enough to meet with me on several occasions to discuss my project. I spent several very productive and delightful weeks at the Hill Monastic Manuscript Library at St. John's University in Collegeville, Minnesota. The Malta Study Center in the Hill Manuscript Library possesses an unrivaled collection of documents from the island and is without doubt the premier center for the study of Malta in the United States. Dr. Theresa Vann was very generous with her time while I was there. I am particularly grateful for her guidance in understanding some of the intricacies of the legal procedures and conventions that surface in the documents, and she too has graciously answered numerous email inquiries. Another archival trip took me to Rome to work at the Vatican Library. The library is an outstanding resource for the history of the Eastern Christians. Its riches, I believe, have only begun to be explored. While in Rome I had the pleasure of staying at the American Academy of Rome, and I thank Professor Anthony Grafton for helping to make that happen. I thank the Academy for its gracious hospitality, which included candlelit dinners every evening. Archival work can be a lonely endeavor, and it was wonderful to return to the Academy at the end of every day. I have also been the recipient of generous financial support during the course of this project. The Program in Hellenic Studies at Princeton University and the University Committee on Research in the Humanities and the Social Sciences supported my initial foray into the archives in Malta. A National Endowment for the Humanities fellowship allowed a year of leave during the 2003–4 academic year and further archival research. More recently, the Society of Fellows at Princeton awarded me an Old Dominion Fellowship, which gave me the time to finish writing the book during the 2007–8 academic year.

I have benefited from the intellectual input of many individuals, as well as from responses at academic gatherings where I have presented my research in progress. I would like to thank the Davis Center at Princeton University, the Yale Legal History Forum at Yale University, Aaron Rodrigue and the Mediterranean Studies Forum at Stanford University, Christine Philliou and the Society of Fellows at Columbia University, Jessica Goldberg and the Economic History Forum at the University of Pennsylvania, and the Institute for Economic Research on Civilizations at the University of Southern California. The discussions that followed my presentations at these various venues were all valuable in refining my thinking on the Greeks and their confrontation with the Knights of Malta. More informal exchanges have been just as important. I thank Roxani Margariti, Maria Fusaro, William Chester Jordan, Jeremy Adelman, Linda Colley, John Paul Ghobrial, Will Hanley, Lauren Benton, Eyal Ginio, Francesca Trivellato, and Yaacob Dweck for reading the manuscript and discussing my work with me. A series of conversations with Gerasimos Pangratis on the C Floor of Firestone Library during the summer of 2008 were, quite frankly, amazing. Very special thanks go to Alan Stahl, curator of numismatics at Firestone Library at Princeton, and to Pietro Frassica, professor of French and Italian at Princeton. Both provided invaluable assistance with some of the stranger twists and turns of the Italian language in the documents. Jebro Lit and Alexander Bevilaqua kindly read over my French and Italian translations, respectively, to check for errors. So many people have assisted me that I fear I will inadvertently fail to mention them all. If this is the case, please know that you have my thanks and appreciation. As always, I thank the director of the Program in Hellenic Studies, Dimitri Gondicas, and the chair of Princeton's History Department, William Chester Jordan, for continuing to provide me with a very happy home. I am indeed a fortunate soul.

Introduction

● ○ ●

In 1634 the English traveler Henry Blunt left the Egyptian port city of Alexandria on a French ship. Not more than twenty miles from shore he witnessed the following attack:

> we saw a spectacle of a straine beyond the Spirit of these times; it was thus: a Maltese vessel gave chase to a Greek vessel in search of Turkes or Turkish goods; the Greeks laded with Turkish goods, made up to us, who carry no Flag, he judged Turkes; but when at hand, we appeared as Christians, and from us no help to be had, He yeeled: upon the Vessell were foure Turkes; three suffered themselves to be taken prisoners; the fourth (we all looking on) ran up to the Sterne, where taking a peece of cord, he tyed his feet, and one of his hands together; then threw himself head-long into the sea; in which resolute end, he showed by what a short passage, many a years misery may be prevented.[1]

Just a few years earlier, in 1627, a Greek Orthodox metropolitan on the island of Mytilene in the eastern Aegean sat down and penned a letter to the grand master of the Order of the Knights of St. John on Malta. In it he complained that two Maltese galleons had attacked a vessel captained by one Iacomes reis while it was returning to the port of Rosetta, also on the Egyptian coast.[2] The Maltese beat them, tortured them, stole all their goods, stripped them of their clothing, and took the ship as well, even though it belonged to Christians. The vessel was co-owned, the cleric continued, with half belonging to this Iacomes, while a certain Kyritze Avvagiano, also of Mytilene, owned the other half. The stolen goods belonged to a merchant named Xatzitriandafylo and consisted of sixteen sacks of linen, six hundred okkas of legumes, some textiles, some belts, and some spices. They also made off with the merchant's personal goods.[3]

A few of the knights themselves have left accounts of their forays into the Greek world. Alonso de Contreras, whose picaresque account of his exploits with the knights is one of the most famous, recounts the following from the Aegean archipelago: "I came across a little brigantine, which was carenned on one side for cleaning its hull. There were ten Greeks aboard, and I had them come aboard my frigate."[4] He then began pressing them to reveal the presence of Turks on board, and when they denied there were any, "I started to torture them and not lightly, either. All stood it, even a boy of fifteen whom I had stripped naked and trussed up."[5]

●   ○   ●

These three accounts—from an English traveler, from an Orthodox cleric, and from a knight himself—could be multiplied hundreds of times over and they still would account for only a small fraction of the assaults on Greek shipping and Greek commerce in the seventeenth century. Yet the setting, the victims, and the protagonists are almost entirely unknown in the annals of piracy. For North Americans, the word "pirate" immediately conjures up images of the Caribbean. Even more informed, scholarly surveys of piracy during the golden age of piracy, as the seventeenth century is known, dip into the Mediterranean only to mention the Barbary Corsairs. This was the name given to the crews operating out of the flourishing North African cities of Tripoli, Tunis, and above all Algiers. At the height of their powers in the early seventeenth century they were able to reach as far as the Canary Islands and the coasts of the British Isles, and captured North African pirates languished in the jails of the sea towns in southwestern England.[6] Although the Barbary Coast attracted adventurers from across Mediterranean Europe, as well as many Englishmen, they have been remembered as Muslim pirates. Thus, within the already tiny space that is allotted to the Mediterranean in studies of early modern piracy, there is no mention of anything other than Muslim violence, and it is a western Mediterranean story.

Further east, there is another story to be told. In the eastern Mediterranean, some of the more fearsome pirates—and, from the point of view of local merchants, the most fearsome—were Christian, Catholics from the impoverished coastlines and islands of southern Europe, particularly places in Spanish-held Italy such as Naples, but also the many ports of the French Mediterranean coastline.[7] But the capital *par excellence* of Catholic piracy was the island of Malta. Whereas the Jolly Roger is instantly recognizable as a pirate flag—as *the* pirate flag, actually, to North American audiences—the flag of the Knights of Malta, a white cross on a red background, is likely to summon up vague associations of Christian crusaders, but not much more than that. Yet this flag struck fear into the hearts of Ottoman merchants—Muslim, Jewish, and Orthodox Christian—when it appeared in Ottoman waters, as it did with great frequency beginning in the 1570s and continuing on for the next two centuries.

This rather laconic report, sent to the Grand Duke of Tuscany in 1597, is entirely typical of the attacks carried out during the course of a Maltese "cruise," as these forays into the eastern Mediterranean were known. In this case the cruise was carried out with the Knights of St. Stephen, who operated out of the port of Livorno:

> On the 10th in the said Gulf of Macri, they captured two vessels—
> the first a caramoussal laded with corn, manned by forty Turks,
> who dragged the boat onto land and fled, and the Tuscans found
> on it fifteen Jews, seven female, the rest male; whilst the other was
> a small vessel with a cargo of timber, manned by seven Greeks. The
> Tuscans found four Turks aboard, took the Greeks on board the
> galley, and sank both the said ships.[8]

The Knights of Malta were the latest reincarnation of the Knights Hospitaller of Jerusalem, whose origins lay in the First Crusade. Pushed out of Jerusalem when it was retaken by the Muslim armies of Saladin, the Catholic military order eventually reestablished itself on the island of Rhodes in the early fourteenth century. It was on Rhodes that the knights developed a navy and began maritime attacks on Muslim power, both commercial and military.[9] In 1522 they once again lost their base to a Muslim sovereign when the Ottoman sultan Süleyman wrested the island from them. After eight years of wandering the Mediterranean, the Hapsburg emperor Charles V granted them the islands of Malta and Gozo, as well as the fortress of Tripoli on the North African coast (soon lost), and they would remain there, as the Knights of Malta, until 1798.

Along with the Knights of St. Stephen, another Catholic military order that operated out of Livorno, and assorted groups from Spanish Italy, these self-identified Catholic crusaders wreaked havoc in Ottoman waters in the seventeenth century and, to a lesser extent, in the eighteenth.

The protagonists, then, were Catholics operating in the context of the eternal struggle, as they saw it, against Islam. Given this exalted mission, it is not surprising that they did not see themselves as mere pirates. Instead they called themselves corsairs, a term specific to the Mediterranean.[10] In this particular phase the battlefield was the eastern Mediterranean. The consolidation of Ottoman power in the fifteenth and sixteenth centuries rendered the eastern Mediterranean relatively safe for Ottoman shipping during this period, and maritime activity flourished along the shores of the Aegean and on the main sea-lane connecting Egypt (conquered by the Ottomans in 1517) and the imperial capital. After the Ottoman defeat at Lepanto in 1571 and the relative weakening of the empire's naval power, Catholic pirates switched their main area of activity from the western to the eastern basin of the inland sea.[11]

Having established the protagonists and their venue, it remains to discuss the victims. First we must resolve an apparent contradiction. Although Catholic piracy justified itself in terms of Christian-Muslim enmity, Greek Orthodox Christians were attacked in all three cases described above. The three stories are indicative of an essential truth about Catholic piracy in the early modern eastern Mediterranean, which is that it claimed Orthodox Christian victims as often as it did Muslims, although the treatment was not identical. It was rare for the former to be enslaved and taken to Malta or Livorno; more usually they lost their goods and their ships, but not their personal freedom.[12] The Greek Orthodox were the most prominent Christian victims of the Knights of Malta and other Catholic marauders, for two reasons: first, most of the islands and coastlines favored by the pirates—the Aegean, Crete, Cyprus, and the coastal areas of the Balkan Peninsula—coincided with Greek population centers. Second, the Greek Orthodox were the principal maritime carriers of the Ottoman Empire. After the conquest of Syria (1516) and Egypt (1517), the empire spanned the southern and northern shores of the eastern Mediterranean, and the Greeks played a vital role in connecting the two. When the Maltese attacked an Ottoman vessel coming from Egypt, as was the case in the first two of our stories, the captain of the ship was most likely to be a Greek.

● ○ ●

The rise of Catholic piracy in the seventeenth century can only be understood in the context of the fundamental changes that took place in the Mediterranean arena toward the end of the sixteenth century. More than anything else, it was the retreat of the state that allowed piracy to flourish in both the eastern and the western halves of the sea. From the first decades of the sixteenth century to the spectacular clash at Lepanto in 1571, Ottoman sultans and Spanish monarchs battled each other for supremacy in the inland sea.[13] Somewhat paradoxically, perhaps, the wars held piracy in check, for a time. The forces that would come to be so powerful in the seventeenth century—the North African *beyliks* and the knights on Malta—were already taking up their positions, but in the sixteenth century they functioned largely as auxiliary forces in the wars being fought between the two empires, the Hapsburg and the Ottoman.[14] But after 1571, or at the latest 1581 (historians have debated just how consequential the loss at Lepanto was for the Ottomans), both the Spanish and the Ottomans turned their back on the Mediterranean and focused their energies elsewhere, the former on the New World and the latter on their various land borders. This was the signal for the pirates, both Muslim and Christian, to head out to sea on their account.[15] The shift has been described most poetically by Fernand Braudel in a section of his *The Mediterranean and the Mediterranean World in the Age of Philip II* entitled "One War Replaces Another":

> So when we say that war in the Mediterranean came to an end in 1574, we should make it clear which kind of war we mean. Regular war, maintained at great expense by the authoritarian expansion of major states, yes, that certainly came to an end. But the living materials of that war, the men who could no longer be kept in the war fleets by what had become inadequate rewards and wages were driven to a life of roving by the liquidation of international war.[16]

But piracy never exists in a vacuum, and this held true for the Mediterranean as well. North African piracy was sustained in part by the

ability of its practitioners to play one European power off against another. Despite later colonialist rhetoric about "lawless" Muslim piracy,
the reality is that the North Africans and the Europeans had sustained
diplomatic relations for two centuries prior to the French invasion of
Algeria in 1830.

The relationship between the central Ottoman state and the *beyliks* of
Algiers, Tunis, and Tripoli is harder to discern. This is not a coincidence.
An essential dynamic of the piracy game on both sides was a willingness
on the part of states to use the pirates for their own benefit, while at the
same time denying any connection to them.

Similarly, it is difficult to point to a clear relationship of alliance between the Maltese and any one European power, not even the Vatican.
What can be said is that a certain constellation of power facilitated the
ability of the Knights of St. John and other Catholic powers to operate in
the eastern Mediterranean. This constellation consisted of the decline of
Venice and the rise of France as the strongest Catholic power in the Ottoman Empire. Venice, as we shall see, had a long-standing hostile relationship with the knights, and as long as it was a force to be reckoned
with in the eastern Mediterranean, it stood in the way of the Catholic
powers. But over the course of the sixteenth and seventeenth centuries
the Venetians steadily lost territory to the Ottomans.[17] With territorial
losses came a decline in influence. One must add to this Venice's inability to hold on to maritime and commercial supremacy in the Mediterranean at large.

France stepped into the breach. Here we should issue several caveats
before going any further. First, there is a tendency in certain quarters to
usher the French (and the Dutch and the English) into the Mediterranean before the Venetians have fully closed the door. In this way of telling the history of the early modern period, the French took over from
the Venetians. This is problematic for many reasons, one of which is that
it denies agency to local actors. It is also inaccurate in that it skips over
the entire seventeenth century when no one, whether France, the Ottoman Empire, or anyone else, was strong enough to provide security in
the Mediterranean. This is one of the principal reasons why the seventeenth century is the age of piracy.[18] When discussing the French, we
must bear in mind that the century was "an interregnum of the lesser
powers," not the age of European dominance, which would come later,

in the eighteenth century.[19] Second, there is a tendency to speak of "the French," as if France were a coherent entity with a clearly identifiable policy in the eastern Mediterranean. This was not at all the case.

Keeping these things in mind, we must nevertheless admit that the French were far more conciliatory than the Venetians toward the knights, and toward piracy in general. Many of the knights were French, whereas Venice forbade its citizens and subjects from joining the order.[20] France's subjects from the French Mediterranean coastline were some of the most active pirates in the eastern Mediterranean. French officials in the Ottoman Empire occasionally scandalized and outraged the Ottomans by their willingness to consort with the pirates. All of this worked to the advantage of the knights.

● ○ ●

The Knights of Malta and their Greek victims are at the center of the story this book tells. In the specialized field of Mediterranean studies, Catholic piracy has received a fair amount of attention. This book aspires to depart from the existing narrative in two ways. First, I would like to talk about piracy in a new way, and second, I would like to tie it to a larger narrative. Since these two goals are intertwined, I discuss them simultaneously.

Mediterranean piracy still stands apart from the general story of the global piracy that flourished in the seventeenth century. No doubt part of this isolation is because historians of piracy are almost always concerned with the new vistas opened up by the European journeys of exploration. The Mediterranean is the world left behind; if it is mentioned at all, it is as the point of origin for practices the Europeans took with them as they sailed into new oceans and seas.[21] Historians of the Mediterranean, for their part, have overwhelmingly treated piracy, Muslim and, especially, Catholic, as the last remnant of a dying religious worldview, the hold of pseudo-Crusaders whose days were numbered by an emerging secular international order. Indian or Atlantic Ocean piracy, by contrast, can seem much more consequential, as it was part and parcel of an emerging European world system.

This view of Catholic piracy is part of a larger narrative concerning the Mediterranean as an international space in the early modern period.

Briefly, the story runs as follows. By a rather extraordinary coincidence, both the Spanish Hapsburgs and the Ottoman sultans emerged as world powers at opposite ends of the Mediterranean at roughly the same time. In 1453 Mehmet the Conqueror shocked Christian Europe with his conquest of Constantinople, capital of the Eastern Roman Empire. In 1492 the Spanish crown extinguished the last Muslim state on the Iberian Peninsula with the conquest of Granada. As a result, the sixteenth century saw the spectacular revival of the age-old conflict between Christianity and Islam, and new battles were fought in the Mediterranean, the traditional battleground for the dueling civilizations since the seventh century. Then the Spanish and the Ottomans turned away from the Mediterranean, newcomers from northern Europe arrived, and gradually the international relations of the region normalized. The Maltese, the Tuscans, and other Catholic pirates were no more than ineffectual anachronisms. It is important to note here that in this narrative view, the European newcomers play the role of modernizers; through their arrival they brought an end to the ancient antagonism between Christianity and Islam.[22]

This book tells a different story. First, it takes the word "maritime" in the title seriously. Despite a tremendous amount of writing about Mediterranean commerce in the early modern period, surprisingly little has been written about the realities of traveling across the sea and the norms and customs that structured such crossings, aside from the overly schematic meta-narrative of a transition from a religiously defined to a more secular order. Second, I am inspired by new trends in global history. Global history has directly set itself against an older tradition of scholarship which imagines that the Atlantic and the Indian Oceans were the smooth surfaces over which European laws, norms, and ultimately European-derived international relations were inexorably extended. Instead, global historians suggest a more conflictual and chaotic process deriving as much from the anonymous workings of countless numbers of international sojourners, be they sailors, merchants, diplomats, pirates, or soldiers, as from the imperializing projects of the European maritime powers.[23] This is one of the major reasons (there are others) why I focus on the Greek Orthodox victims of piracy rather than on the pirates themselves. I am interested in how they navigated their way across a sea infested by countless pirates of greater or lesser stature. This moves us away from the traditional story told about Mediterranean piracy in the early modern period, which usually considers it from the point of view of the state and its struggle for hegemony.

The story I tell is not one of a transition from a religiously defined international order to a more secular order. It is the story of an enduring ambiguity that certainly lasted through the early modern period and arguably is still with us today. This ambiguity revolved around two competing visions of the Mediterranean, one territorial, the other religious. Did individuals move across the inland sea as the subjects of various sovereigns? Or was this a world of Muslims, Christians, and Jews? The answer has always been, a little bit of both.

Given the narrative outlined above, I, too, start in the sixteenth century. I argue that despite high levels of religious antagonism, the Ottomans and the Venetians both found it in their respective interest to organize the space they shared—from Venice in the west to Istanbul in the east and Alexandria in the south—on the basis of agreements drawn up between the two states. Together they created a regime of subjects and sovereigns, of Ottoman and Venetian subjects, that competed robustly with a Mediterranean divided into religious blocs. In other words, despite being representatives of the "old" Mediterranean, supposedly driven by religious passion, they actually created an international order that was more secular than what would follow in the seventeenth century.[24]

Moving into the seventeenth century, I argue that it was certain new European forces, not the old antagonists of a previous age, that gave religious affiliation a new importance in the organization of Mediterranean life. In this discussion I take strong exception to the view that the Knights of Malta were an anachronism, a throwback to the days of the Crusades. Instead, they were part of a revival of Catholic power in the eastern Mediterranean. In addition to the knights themselves, this revival rested on two pillars of strength. The first was France, which showed itself to be far more willing than Venice had ever been to defend and advance the interests of Catholicism in the eastern Mediterranean. The second pillar, equally important, was the Catholic Counter-Reformation. Beginning with the founding of the Greek College of Rome in 1576, the Vatican revitalized its presence in the eastern Mediterranean as it sought to bring the Greek Orthodox back into communion with Rome.

These three forces combined, sometimes in unexpected ways. For reasons I explore in the course of this book, one of the results was to create a sort of unintentional experiment (if a rather bitter one) whereby Ottoman merchants—and particularly the Greek Orthodox—could test the efficacy of religious affiliation as a way of resolving commercial problems and, more broadly, as a way of moving across Mediterranean space.

This experiment, which is the primary focus of this study, is an important one to follow, for it changes the story of the early modern Mediterranean. What we shall see is that the protagonists in our story—the French, the Vatican, the Ottomans, Ottoman merchants, and Catholic pirates—do not line up along some hypothetical dividing line, with some wedded to an emerging secular order while others cling to a Mediterranean divided into religious blocs. Instead, all of our actors reveal ambiguity, confusion, and contradictory thinking in terms of how the Mediterranean was and should be organized.

A study of this seventeenth-century experiment reveals something else as well. Despite the modernizing thesis of an increasingly "normalized" Mediterranean in the seventeenth and, especially, the eighteenth centuries, historians of the region still tend to fall back on religious affiliation—Muslims, Christians, and Jews—as a useful way of thinking about the organization of this maritime world, particularly in commercial matters (this division itself is a reflection of that same ambiguity I have been discussing).[25] If we look carefully, however, it becomes clear that these terms were highly contested, in respect to both their actual content and the significance they should be accorded. S. D. Goitein, the famed historian of the medieval Mediterranean, called it "a friendly sea," despite its division between Christianity and Islam.[26] A key factor in ensuring the unity of the sea, he wrote, was that the law was personal rather than territorial. This study revisits Goitein's argument, but for the early modern rather than the medieval Mediterranean. By early modern times the situation had changed, but not beyond all recognition. An increasing emphasis on territorial identity—that is, the claims of sovereigns over their subjects—had come to coexist uneasily with an older tradition of personal law that followed an individual across the sea.

● ○ ●

In conclusion, let us return to the stories with which we began this introduction. Now it is time to explain why the conflicts that erupted between the Greek merchants and the Knights of Malta in the seventeenth century are the ideal venue for our exploration of the contested international order in the Mediterranean.

At the most general level, the Greeks, and Greek merchants in particular, dragged the ambiguity of the Mediterranean in their wake. The Greeks were enduringly liminal. They were Christians but of a rather dubious kind from the Catholic point of view, and many were also Ottoman subjects. Not surprisingly, then, issues of identity and representation followed Greek merchants around the ports of the Mediterranean, including Malta, and we will be considering these questions throughout this study.

Their particular difficulties with the Knights of Malta also represent a great opportunity for the historian. To understand why, we must return briefly to Alonso de Contreras, the Knight of Malta who bragged of torturing the Greeks he encountered in the archipelago. In another attack, he recounts how he was busy robbing a "Turk" whom he had captured at sea when two Frenchmen came up and shouted that the spoils should be divided three ways.[27] An argument ensued, and they eventually took it to the captain in charge of the expedition, who decided that the best course of action would be to put the matter to the "Senores del Tribunal del Armamento" in Malta for a decision.[28] A few pages later Contreras gives us the tribunal's decision. The four hundred sequins gained from the sale of the slave (the unfortunate victim had evidently been taken back to Malta and sold) was to go into a common pool, but Contreras was given an extra financial bonus.[29]

What was this tribunal? The Tribunale degli Armamenti, as it was known in Italian, the language most in use by the knights in Malta, was a tribunal set up by the grand master of the order, Alofius de Wignacourt, in 1605. The pirates, in other words, had a court. As we can see from its appearance in the Contreras story, one of its primary purposes was to resolve disputes among the pirates themselves. But it performed another function as well. Victims of the Maltese who felt they had been unfairly attacked by the knights could appear before the court. Muslims and Jews were uncontestably the enemy, and thus it is not surprising that they never show up in court documents. But the Greeks, who occupied a more ambiguous position, did make the long trip to Malta to plead their case.

Historians are not unaware of the Tribunale's existence. Yet no study of the court exists, despite scattered references to it in the literature. This reflects two assumptions, one specific to the knights, the other a more general view of piracy.

"Corrupt," "arbitrary," "lawless"—these terms are routinely deployed in discussions of the knights. Why, then, study their court, which was, it must be admitted, not a model of probity? This view fits in with common historical treatments of piracy. Pirates, it is asserted, are outside the law.[30] In fact, as global historians are now arguing, the dense historical record left behind by the English pirates as they moved out across the globe at this time—including but not limited to famous men such as William Kidd and Blackbeard (Edward Teach)—shows that pirates strived mightily to present their behavior as lawful, whether in prize proceedings or in criminal trials. Pirates, like other mariners, were important actors in the continuous negotiations that went into the construction of legality and illegality. And, like everyone else, they took full advantage of the legal ambiguity that characterized most encounters at sea.[31]

When viewed this way, the Greek encounter with the Tribunale is an ideal way to uncover the norms, laws, and conventions that structured encounters at sea. In addition to the Tribunale, recent work by historians has brought to light several seventeenth-century court cases from other venues, stretching from Turin to Istanbul, and these too are included in the discussion.[32] By putting these legal encounters at the center of the story, my intent is to take these battles seriously as a place where new international norms were being tested in the Mediterranean. All participants in the commercial and political life of the sea, not just the expanding powers of Europe, played a role in this process. One of the great advantages of privileging these court cases is that they show us the role played by ordinary people, as opposed to states, in the construction of international order.

● ○ ●

This study aims to locate the particular quarrel between the Greeks and the knights in the larger context of the Mediterranean as an international maritime space. To that end, the book is divided into seven chapters that cover, roughly, the sixteenth and seventeenth centuries. The first two chapters are devoted to the period up until 1570, while the other five consider the seventeenth century. The sixteenth century, while not receiving as much space as the later years, does figure prominently in the historical arguments that are being made.

Chapter one describes the maritime order that the Ottomans and the Venetians constructed together in the sixteenth century. Despite high levels of hostility and numerous wars, both sides found it to be in their best interest to facilitate trade between themselves. And because together they controlled all of the territory stretching from Venice to the shores of Anatolia, the net effect was to create a wide-ranging commercial zone that was organized around agreements between the two states. I call what they created a world of subjects and sovereigns.

Chapter two examines the Maltese challenge to the Veneto-Ottoman order. Unlike previous studies of the Knights of Malta, which tend to dismiss their self-justifications even as they acknowledge their formidable maritime power, this chapter takes the knights' objections to Venetian commerce with the Ottomans seriously. The knights' view of the proper balance of commerce and war in the early modern Mediterranean drew on plausible and time-honored conventions in international maritime relations, and their view of the Mediterranean was grounded in the imperatives of religion. Thus, the chapter also includes a general consideration of the place of religion in this sixteenth-century commercial zone that was a joint Veneto-Ottoman creation, with particular attention paid to the situation of the Greeks as Christian Orthodox.

The seventeenth century was the golden age of piracy, across the globe and in the Mediterranean as well. Chapter three lays out the piratical landscape of the Mediterranean at this time, then tightens its focus on the Catholic pirates operating in Ottoman waters after 1571. Unlike in other parts of the globe, piracy in the Mediterranean was most enduringly the preserve of indigenous groups, and this was true on both the Muslim side and the Christian side. The North Africans were the most formidable Muslim pirates, while the Maltese were the most fearsome on the Christian side. For this reason the pirates of the Mediterranean have often been considered an anachronism, the dying embers of a fading religious conflict, in comparison to the English, Spanish, and other European pirates, who sailed to the four corners of the globe and thus helped forge a new global order. This chapter takes issue with that assessment when it comes to the Catholic pirates. Instead, it puts the pirates in the larger context of the renewal of Catholic power in the eastern Mediterranean. When viewed this way it is clear that the pirates were part of a coincidence of forces that all worked together to increase the importance of religion and religiously based networks in facilitating both mobility and security in the eastern Mediterranean.

Chapters four through seven constitute the heart of the book. Together, they form a detailed study of one group of Ottoman merchants and their confrontation with Catholic power—principally but not exclusively the Knights of Malta—in all its manifestations in the seventeenth century. That group, for reasons I discuss at length, is the Greek merchants, some Catholic but most Orthodox, of the Ottoman Empire. Alone among Ottoman merchants, the Greeks challenged Maltese attacks on their shipping in court. This challenge produced an extensive archival record that is in Malta today. Chapter four describes the archival material and the world of Ottoman commerce it reveals. Chapters five and six concentrate on the legal challenge itself. In chapter five we consider the local institutions in the eastern Mediterranean that the Greeks turned to in order to prepare their claim for presentation in Malta. Chapter six looks at the content of the lawsuits themselves, both those in Malta as well as several others that have surfaced in the historical record. I outline the conflicting maritime conventions and traditions that are revealed through the presentation of arguments. Chapter seven follows the Greeks as they take their complaints against the Maltese all the way to Rome. This brings us to a consideration of the Counter-Reformation and the larger world of Catholic power that must be grasped if one is to understand the realities of the seventeenth-century Mediterranean.

CHAPTER 1

Subjects and Sovereigns

● ○ ●

A chronicler of the Order of the Knights of St. John, Abbé de Vertot, re-corded the following conversation in 1671 between the Ottoman sultan Mehmet IV and the notorious Knight of the Order known as Chevalier de Téméricourt.[1] Téméricourt had been captured by the Barbary cor-sairs and taken to Mehmet at Edirne. Mehmet asked him if it was indeed he who had battled with a single vessel five large vessels from Tripoli.

> "Twas myself," replied the knight.
> "What countryman are you" said the Sultan
> "A Frenchman" replied Téméricourt.
> "You are a deserter then" said Mehmet, "for I am in strict peace with the king of France."
> "I am a Frenchman," Téméricourt replied, "but besides that qual-ity I am likewise a knight of Malta, a profession which obliges me to expose my life against all the enemies of the Christian faith."

This exchange perfectly underlines a question that has dogged the Mediterranean since the Muslim armies seized the southern shores of the Roman sea in the seventh century A.D. What is the Mediterranean? Is it a collection of states bound by freely concluded treaty obligations to one another? Or is it a cultural or even a civilizational frontier where two hostile religions face each other in perpetual enmity? The answer has always been an awkward mix of both. *no awkward*

Several factors have combined to ensure that this ambiguity has been a permanent fixture of Mediterranean life. There is the settled topogra-phy of a (mostly) Christian northern shore and a (mostly) Muslim south-ern rim. Given that ideological and political warfare between Christian-ity and Islam was a central feature of European and Near Eastern history for many centuries (and is still with us today), it was inevitable that the Mediterranean border between the two civilizations would be a zone of permanent hostility. Téméricourt explained his actions within the context of this tradition.

But next to that we must place the long history of states that faced each other, from positions of relatively equal strength, across the inland sea. Recognizing the impossibility of conquering, definitively at least, the other side, political leaders chose to treat with the enemy.[2] It was in the Mediterranean that European sovereigns first routinely signed treaties with non-Christian states, stretching all the way back to the twelfth century.[3] Mehmet IV considered Téméricourt not first and foremost a Christian but a subject of France. The long history of Muslim-Christian diplomacy in the Mediterranean was seriously challenged, and in some cases rather skillfully forgotten, by European colonialism. Whereas the Ottoman Empire had been a full participant in European diplomacy in the sixteenth century, by the nineteenth century it was repeatedly frustrated in its attempts to join the Concert of Europe. But for many centuries before that, treaties between Christian and Muslim states had played a fundamental role in organizing Mediterranean life.

Finally, certain features of the Mediterranean environment—a sea that was relatively easy to navigate, the mountain chains and the deserts that cut off Mediterranean cities from their hinterlands, the large cities with their thirst for grain—pushed the two shores together for many centuries, despite their religious differences.

The conversation between Mehmet IV and Téméricourt involved a sultan and a corsair.[4] As such, it nicely reflects the historiography on corsairing in the Mediterranean. The problem has been considered exclusively from the point of view of the relationship between the corsairs, whether of Malta or Barbary, and authorities, whether the doge of Venice or the Ottoman sultan. Some studies, such as those on the Medici princes of Livorno and the Knights of St. Stephen, the order they founded, emphasize cooperation between the state and its corsairing allies. Others, such as a recent study on the relationship between Venice and the Knights of St. John on Malta, emphasize the animosity between the two parties. In either case, the relationship between states and corsairs is at the center of the story.

But this is not a book about politics, or at least not a book about state actors. Rather, this book investigates the consequences of that ambiguity for the conduct of business, and the strategies that merchants adopted to deal with an uncertain world. More specifically, it considers the position of Greek Orthodox merchants in the Mediterranean world in the sixteenth and seventeenth centuries.

Why this particular moment, and why these particular merchants? The sixteenth century is a century of paradox. It was marked by almost continuous religious and political conflict at the highest levels. From their respective corners of the inland sea, the Ottomans and the Hapsburgs clashed repeatedly in their struggle to gain the upper hand in the Mediterranean. The Ottomans and the Venetians also fought three wars in the sixteenth century alone as Venice steadily lost ground in the eastern Mediterranean to the ascendent empire. Despite this, a complex partnership between the Ottoman Empire and the Venetian Republic created a world of subjects and sovereigns, an interimperial space within which merchants could move with relative ease, transparency, and confidence. The terms *subject* and *sovereign* are chosen deliberately, to emphasize that the commercial world rested on interstate agreements buttressed by intensive diplomacy.[5]

In light of the frequent wars between the two states and the emphasis in the literature on the supposed commitment of Muslim states—the Ottomans included—to the relentless pursuit of jihad and their unwillingness to accept permanent borders, it may be surprising to see the Ottomans described as partners with a Christian power in the creation of an international commercial order. But this is indeed what they were. It is worth pointing out that in the exchange between Mehmet and Téméricourt, it is the Muslim sultan who insists on obligations stemming from a treaty concluded between two states.

The transition from the sixteenth century to the seventeenth saw a sharp deterioration in the ability of both the Ottomans and the Venetians to police the eastern Mediterranean and thus to regulate maritime commercial life in the way they had earlier. It is fair to say that no one was in charge for much of the seventeenth century. This transition offers an excellent opportunity to look at the adjustment of merchant strategies as the power of the state receded.

It is also the case that, despite certain historiographic assumptions, the contrast between the sixteenth and the seventeenth centuries is surprising. In the eastern Mediterranean at least (further west the situation was rather different), it was violent entrepreneurs—corsairs and pirates—from the Christian West that disrupted the interimperial space in the name of religion. The tendency in the historiography has been to see Europe as a secularizing force in the international relations of the Mediterranean. One of the ways this is accomplished is by divorcing European states proper, such as France, from the activities of the corsairs.[6] It is also common to dispense with the corsairs by calling them anachronistic.[7] The many links between national governments and the Knights of St. John or the Knights of St. Stephen, operating out of Tuscany, make this divorce problematic. But there is another point as well, one that has been completely overlooked until now. The response of the Greek Orthodox merchants who were prominent targets of (especially) the Knights of Malta suggests the revival of a diplomatic network that linked the Near East to Catholic Europe. Representatives of the papacy, as well as French officials in various capacities, proved themselves willing to act on behalf of Greeks as fellow Christians; these networks were not available to Muslims or Jews. As Ottoman and Venetian control over the eastern Mediterranean declined under the pressure of newly emerging powers, the religious identity of a merchant became more, not less, important.[8]

In a world that is often defined by the clash between the Christian West and the Muslim East, the Greek Orthodox have always been the people in the middle: Christian but not Western, Easterners but not Muslims, Greek Orthodox merchants occupy a particularly interesting position in the early modern period that is the focus of this study. In the sixteenth century, Greek merchants were truly an international community. Spread out from Livorno to Alexandria, they operated as the subjects of various sovereigns, particularly the Venetians and the Ottomans. They lend themselves very well, therefore, to a demonstration of the real differences between Ottoman and Venetian merchants that were a product of a world of subjects and sovereigns. The diplomatic agreements that created this world were negotiated on behalf of all the sovereigns' subjects, regardless of religious identity. By so doing, the agreements helped to create and give real legal weight to what I call "Ottoman" trade and "Venetian" trade. This point requires particular emphasis when it comes to the Ottomans. The legal position of European merchants operating in the Ottoman Empire has received a great deal of attention in the literature, but merchants from the East have rarely been considered in their international context.[9] The failure to do so has obscured the extent to which the Ottomans were the co-architects, along with Venice, of a commercial regime based on treaties concluded between sovereign states.

The Greek Orthodox are also ideally placed to demonstrate the increasing importance of religious identity in commercial life in the seventeenth century. In many ways this was a very different universe. The boundaries of the Greek commercial world had shrunk, and most Greek Orthodox merchants were now subjects of the Ottoman sultan. Corsairing activity soared, on both the Muslim and the Christian sides, and navigating the Mediterranean became much more dangerous. For the Greeks, the main threat issued not from Muslim corsairs but from corsairs coming out of the Catholic world. Most Greeks were no longer subjects of Venice, and in their confrontation with the corsairs their Ottoman identity had to be hidden rather than displayed. Instead, the Greeks decided that the best strategy for defending their trade was to assert their identity as Christians. But this claim could be, and indeed was, contested precisely because of their liminal status. As Ottoman Greeks they highlighted—indeed, they embodied—the tension in the Mediterranean between the claims of religion and the reality of state sovereignty. They were both Christians and Ottoman subjects. When a Greek Christian went to Malta in 1616 to try to obtain redress for wrongful attack (because he was a Christian), the accused Maltese captain immediately seized the opportunity to paint his adversary as an enemy, owing to the close association between the Greeks and the Muslim world. He complained, "The Greeks are always coming here to Malta to cry and pretend to be miserable, having been sent by the Turks to recover their goods."[10]

The Sixteenth-Century Moment

In the sixteenth century, Greek merchants developed a truly international presence in the eastern Mediterranean. Italian commercial decline and Ottoman strength combined to create new opportunities and wider horizons for this commercial class.

How Greek was this world of Greek shipping and commerce? This question has not been asked, but the assumption that it was is demonstrated by the very shape of the historiography. Almost all of the literature on this sixteenth-century world is in Greek and written by Greeks, while others have passed over it in silence. I hasten to add that no one has lumped together under one roof all the different communities—from Venice to Candia to Istanbul—and called the sum total "Greek shipping" or "Greek commerce."[11] Rather, the literature tends to consist of city-based studies, such as studies of the Greek community of Istanbul or the Greek community in Venice. Yet the very fact that they are all called Greek and have been of interest almost exclusively to Greeks very strongly suggests that all these disparate groups had something in common and, more important, that what they had in common outweighed any differences. One of the very rare instances in which a historian attempts a definition of Greek shipping demonstrates both the nationalist unease underlying this assumption of Greekness as well as the difficulty of saying what Greek shipping was. In his recent study of Ionian commerce in the sixteenth to eighteenth centuries, Nikos Vlassopoulos introduces his subject by saying that while most Greek merchants and shipowners were established in Venice,

> this did not stop them from *acting as Greeks* [my emphasis], carrying Greek agricultural goods and other products throughout the Mediterranean and the Black Sea, from using Greek captains and sailors on their ships. It was natural for them to fly the Venetian flag. We also see how it was natural, indeed unavoidable, for them to be co-owners with native and Jewish merchants and financiers. Starting from Venice, they learned the art of navigation from Venetian seafarers. It was in Venice that they found ships to buy and sailors to equip them. But the art of commerce they had within them, it was in their very nature.[12]

Vlassopoulos is a popular historian, and on this ground one could dismiss his rather romantic depiction as simply the result of nationalist blinkers. But the difficulty he confronts is real. Although "Greek shipping" and

"Greek merchants" are standard terms in the historiography of the Mediterranean, the content of these terms has been little investigated. In fact, there was no such thing in the sixteenth century. Greek merchants moved throughout the eastern Mediterranean not as Greeks but as Ottoman or Venetian subjects.[13] Being Greek Orthodox was of little consequence in terms of the legal and diplomatic institutions that structured international trade. This situation would be reversed in the seventeenth century.

Let us start by surveying the eastern Mediterranean, from Istanbul to Crete to Venice, to describe the most important of these commercial communities.

Istanbul

The Ottoman victory in 1453 signaled the end of Italian domination of the eastern Mediterranean and the Black Sea, and cleared the way for the emergence of a strong Greek commercial class in the Ottoman Empire.[14] Differential tax rates privileged Ottoman merchants over the Venetians and the Genoese, who had long enjoyed a free run in the Byzantine Empire. Greeks (and Jews) rapidly emerged as the empire's new tax-farmers, bankers, and merchants. Now that the Ottomans controlled the entrance to the resource-rich Black Sea, Greek merchants spread out along the shores, displacing or absorbing the formerly dominant Genoese, and took over the provisioning of the capital. By 1600 the Greeks were in control of much of the commerce of the eastern half of the Balkan Peninsula.[15]

The Greek community in the Ottoman capital was enormously complex. Geographically, it drew on populations from every corner of the Greek world, from Venice in the west to Trebizond in the east. Some came voluntarily, to seek their fortune in a city where the Ottoman leadership was spending enormous sums to create an imperial capital out of the ruins of the former Byzantine Empire. Others were forced to migrate to Constantinople as part of Mehmet the Conqueror's plan to repopulate the city. Still others, the more desperate, came seeking refuge, fleeing some difficulty they had encountered in their homeland. The end result was a city with a large Greek population—over one-third of the total, according to a survey taken in 1477.[16]

The community was also socially diverse. Istanbul was teeming with Christian slaves, possibly one out of every five residents of Constantinople, and many were from the Aegean and Mediterranean coastline.[17] Yet Greeks such as the infamous Michael Kantekouzenos, who held some of the most profitable tax-farms in the empire, enjoyed a place at the very pinnacle of society. During the war for Cyprus (1570) he spent his own wealth to build galleys for the use of the state.[18] The elites that clustered around the Orthodox patriarchate, the leading institution of Greek society under the Ottomans, were a prominent feature of the community.

Despite this diversity, from the beginning the Greeks were closely associated with commerce, with shipping, and indeed with all the trades having to do with the sea.[19] The neighborhood of Galata, just across the Golden Horn to the north, quickly reemerged as the new commercial center of the city, just as it had been under the Byzantines, and it was very much a Greek neighborhood. Its population was more Greek than Muslim, and the institutions associated with Christian life, from churches to taverns, lined the streets in ways that would have been considered scandalous in the walled city of Istanbul.[20] Michael Kantekouzenos had his residence in Galata, as did many other members of the Greek elite.[21] Istanbul and, in particular, Galata were at the very heart of this community.

Mehmet the Conqueror and his successors aspired to make Istanbul the new center of East-West trade, and the activities of the city's Greek merchants reflect those aspirations. From the Black Sea, now reserved for Ottoman merchants alone, the Greeks brought timber, furs, dried fish, and caviar to Istanbul. On the return trip they carried the luxury goods of the Mediterranean—such as wine from Crete—to the Black Sea ports, where the goods were picked up and sent on to the cities of Central Europe.

From Istanbul, Greek merchants carried the goods of the Black Sea to Western Europe, mostly Italy. The Italian cities, chronically short of grain throughout the sixteenth century, also depended on Greek merchants to bring them precious foodstuffs from the eastern Mediterranean. For the trip home the Greeks loaded their ships with a wide variety of finished products from the West, such as wool fabrics, glassware, and paper.

Discussions of the Greek commercial revival tend to stop here, but this picture, while not incorrect, is incomplete. It fails to capture the full extent of Greek commercial fortunes in the sixteenth century. There is an international story here as well as an Ottoman one.

Italy

Ottoman merchants in general, including the Greeks, were not only happy to replace Italian merchants at home, they were also very interested in trading in Italy, and the Ottoman state supported them in these efforts. This interest predated the Ottomans—it stretches back to the late medieval period—but the consolidation of Ottoman power gave them powerful backing that they had lacked before.[22] The presence of Ottoman merchants in Italy in the sixteenth century, and its larger significance, was remarked upon years ago by Peter Earle:

> This development marks a stage in the resurgence of the commercial vitality of Islam and indeed of the eastern Mediterranean as a whole, which lies between the late medieval pattern of Italian and Catalan domination of eastern Mediterranean commerce and the pattern from 1600 onwards of domination by the new maritime powers of the Atlantic and the North Sea.[23]

This aspect of the sixteenth-century Mediterranean still tends to be overlooked, particularly in general narratives. Part of the reason is certainly the continuation of old stereotypes about Muslim xenophobia; Muslims (including merchants, including Ottoman Muslim merchants) are thought to have been reluctant to travel to Christian lands.[24] Probably taking their cue from the Ottoman historiography, studies on the Ottoman Greeks have failed to appreciate their push into Italy.

It was not just the surge of interest from the East, however, that explains the presence of Ottoman merchants in Italy. Italian commercial decline—which was only partly due to external pressures—also created an opportunity for others to enter the fray. Venice and Ancona were the two most important destinations for Ottoman merchants in the sixteenth century, and in both cases we are looking at an indigenous merchant class in transition. Faced with increasing difficulties in the East, as well as rising costs as home, the Venetian elite slowly but surely turned its face away from the Levant and the world of commerce and began to invest closer to home, in industry and in real estate.[25]

Incredibly, this proud maritime city actually began to recruit foreign merchants to settle in the city and to maintain those commercial ties to the East that Venetian citizens had once so jealously monopolized for themselves. Writing from Istanbul at mid-century, the Venetian bailo remarked that Venetians had largely abandoned the city and that those who remained tended to rely on the Jews as intermediaries, thereby "earning half of what they would if they did it themselves."[26]

The case of Ancona is less well known, but a similar phenomenon was at work there as well. The Anconites had never been merchants; it was the Florentines who passed through Ancona on their way to the East to sell their textiles.[27] The route began in Florence, passed through Ancona and Ragusa, and ended up in Istanbul. In the empire, Florentine merchants bought up Balkan and Eastern goods for sale back home. By the 1520s all this had changed. Ancona was now the meeting point between East and West. Florentine merchants, who had seen their city suffer through political crises, economic failures, plagues, and invasions, no longer maintained agents in the Ottoman capital.[28] Instead, they traveled no farther than Ancona, where they sold their cloth directly to Ottoman merchants. From being a small city that handled transit trade only, Ancona blossomed into a cosmopolitan port of call.

Livorno had a rather different historical trajectory than that of Ancona and Venice. Most important, its development as a port did not begin until the second half of the sixteenth century, whereas the connections between Ancona and Venice and the East stretched back to the medieval period. Nevertheless, Livorno's sixteenth-century rulers also found it necessary to recruit merchants from the eastern Mediterranean in order to develop their port.

At one level, the Italian recruitment of foreign merchants in the early modern period is relatively well known, and the reasons for it have been explored. But the story has only been considered as a Jewish story, part of the larger history of the ripple effect of the Jewish diaspora following the expulsion from Iberia in 1492.[29] And it is quite true that as Venice, Ancona, and Livorno competed for foreign merchants in an attempt to gain prosperity for themselves and deny it to their neighbors, all three cities were most interested in attracting Jewish merchants. But this is only part of the story; there was a significant Ottoman dimension as well.

Although the Italian state authorities were most interested in the Jews, this does not change the fact that concessions were offered to others as well. In the case of Venice, the interest in Jewish merchants must be folded into the larger story of Venice's confrontation with the Ottoman Empire. Venice's vital interests in Levantine trade, combined with the republic's gradual but steady loss of territory to the Ottomans, meant that Venice had little choice but to grant, and enforce, commercial reciprocity between the Most Serene Republic and the empire. In 1419—long before the active recruitment of Jewish merchants began—the capitulations granted by Sultan Mehmet included rights for Ottoman merchants trading in Venetian-ruled areas.[30] Early in the sixteenth century, the Venetians relaxed their monopoly on trade with the Levant. For many centuries this trade had been reserved for citizens of Venice; now Venetian subjects living in the overseas Stato da Màr and Ottoman subjects as well were permitted to trade between Venice and the ports of the eastern Mediterranean.[31]

Historians have emphasized how Jewish merchants were quick to take advantage of this new privilege, but it is also true that Ottoman merchants, both Christian and Muslim, became regular visitors to the Serenissima in the sixteenth century. Despite a number of Ottoman-Venetian wars, Ottoman merchants in great numbers routinely traveled to the city on the lagoon, and Venice made efforts to accommodate them.[32]

The justly famous Greek colony in Venice was the most important center of Greek life outside the Ottoman Empire in the early modern period. As a sign of its increasing prominence, in 1514 the community was given permission to buy land to build its own church. Quarrels delayed the purchase, but it was finally concluded in 1526, and a small church was erected the following year. The building of the church proper, dedicated to St. George (it still stands in Venice today), commenced in 1539 and was finished in 1573. The church remained the nucleus of the community throughout the following centuries.[33]

Records of the Greek Fraternity if Venice show the presence of more than four hundred merchants and sailors in the city between 1536 and 1576.[34] The real number would have been much higher; the four hundred represent only those who chose to make a donation to the fraternity, in support of the church or some other aspect of communal life.

The Greek community drew on Greeks from a wide swath of the eastern Mediterranean, and its composition also responded to particular events. The third Ottoman-Venetian war (1537–40), for example, produced a stream of refugees from the Aegean town of Nauplion as sovereignty passed from Venice to the Ottomans.[35]

But most Greek Ottoman merchants in the city seem to have come from northwestern Greece, the area bordering the Ionian and the Adriatic Seas.[36] Their complaints to the Venetian Senate surface several times during the course of the century, indicating an enduring connection. A 1510 report to the Senate noted the presence in Venice of "some merchants of Ioannina and other places under the rule of the Turks." They were complaining about taxes being levied on them in the harbor of Corfu as they transited through the Ionian Islands on their way to Venice.[37]

Half a century later, things had not improved. Christians of Ioannina, together with Jewish and Muslim merchants from the same city, once again told the Senate that import duties and storage rates in Corfu were too high.[38] Customs officials, they said, also demanded bribes and illegitimate taxes.[39] They also objected to repeated demands that they swear they had not entered into any partnerships with Venetian subjects, given that they had already sworn this in Venice.[40]

More than twenty years later, the customs administration continued to be a source of frustration for merchants coming from the Ottoman Empire. Even though the Senate had declared that goods transiting through Zakynthos or Corfu need not pay customs duties, officials were demanding duties of 12 percent, as well as other "contributions."[41]

In Venice itself, legal documents (most granting power of attorney) indicate at least forty merchants from Epiros (northwestern Greece) in the city between the years 1550 and 1567. All but one of these merchants were from Ioannina.[42] Obviously, forty merchants from Epiros do not add up to the most flourishing center of Greek life outside the Ottoman Empire, which is what Venice was. There was a whole other side to the Greek community in Venice, but the dynamics that created that community were rather different from those we have been discussing to date, namely, the combination of Ottoman strength and Italian commercial decline. Therefore we will leave Venice now but return to it shortly, for a further consideration of the city's Greek community.

To the south, the city of Ancona was also wooing merchants from the East. Once the Florentines stopped going to Istanbul, it was Ancona that became the meeting place of East and West. The history of the concessions granted demonstrates the wide range of the Ottoman merchants—Muslims and Christians as well as Jews—who were interested in trading with the city. In 1514 Dimitri Caloiri of Ioannina obtained reduced customs duties for Greek merchants from the three Balkan towns of Ioannina, Arta, and Vlona. Just a few months later "Turks" in Ancona negotiated a similar deal for Slavs and for several Muslim merchants, Christian converts to Islam whose origins lay in the Dalmatian aristocracy. Finally, in 1518, the efforts of a Jewish merchant of Vlona lowered the duties paid at Ancona for all "the Levantine merchants, subject to the Turk."[43]

Given the 1514 reference to Ioannina, Arta, and Vlona, it seems likely that Ancona attracted those same merchants from northwestern Greece who also traded in Venice. There was a settled community in the city that appears to predate the concessions of 1514. Natalucci, the seventeenth-century historian of the city, records the existence of two hundred Greek families at the opening of the sixteenth century. They were able to secure the use of the Church of St. Anna from the bishop of Ancona and were given permission to hold their services according to the Greek rite and with a Greek priest who would be directly under the pope.[44] It is not clear whether the community was composed of refugees fleeing the Ottoman advance or of Greek Ottoman merchants interested in trading in Italy; Natalucci presents them as refugees. The early date of the community, combined with the fact of permanent settlement, suggests he is right. However, he also notes that although the community lasted until the eighteenth century, its greatest period of vitality was the sixteenth century. Whatever its origin, the community clearly drew on the same dynamics that sustained Greek commercial communities elsewhere.

In 1532 Ancona was incorporated into the Papal States. On the eve of his occupation of Ancona in 1532, Pope Clement VII was disturbed by the large number of "Turkish" merchants in that city. They came, notes the seventeenth-century Anconite historian Giuliano Saracini, "with their large ships loaded with merchandise and stayed in the city with security, thanks to the privileges negotiated by Sultans Bayezit,

Selim and Süleyman." Such a large presence provoked the worry, writes
Saracini, that they could take not only Ancona and the province of Ancona, but perhaps Italy in its entirety." The pope insisted on fortifying
the city and on stationing papal troops there too, against the wishes of
the inhabitants.[45]

Yet just two years later a new pope, Paul III, made it clear that the
city's welcoming attitude toward Ottoman merchants would continue.
He issued a safe-conduct for "all merchants of whatever nation, profession or sect, even if Turks, Jews or infidels," allowing them to come with
their families and goods to stay and trade in Ancona.[46] The Turks and
Greeks of the Ottoman Empire apparently found his offer attractive; a
Venetian traveling through Ancona the following year noted that Ancona was "full of merchants from every nation and mostly Greeks and
Turks."[47] Lodging in the Palazzo della Farina was provided for "Turkish"
merchants during the period of the city's annual fair, which happened in
November and December.[48]

The papacy's subsequent abrupt turnaround with regard to the Jews is
well known. In 1556 Pope Paul IV revoked the promise of safe-conduct
that his predecessors had made to the New Christians who had returned
to Judaism in Ancona, and more than two dozen were burned at the
stake for judaizing.[49] A series of bulls throughout the second half of the
sixteenth century kept the status of the Jews in Ancona, and indeed
throughout the Papal States, uncertain.[50] It was only at the end of the
century that Clement VIII returned to the conciliatory policy of Paul III;
in 1594 he issued a bull "in perpetuity" that allowed merchants of all
countries and nations who were trading with the Levant to come freely
and securely to trade and live in Ancona. The Jews of the Levant and the
existing Jewish community of Ancona were specifically permitted to
enjoy the privileges granted to them in earlier decades.[51]

The extent to which all these events have been told as a story of the
Jews becomes clear when we realize that we do not know what effect these
harsh Counter-Reformation measures had on Ottoman merchants—both
Muslim and Christian—more generally.[52] The scattered references here
and there suggest an unfriendly atmosphere for Ottoman merchants as
well in Ancona. Some Muslim merchants were swept up in the persecu-
tions that followed Pope Paul's measures in 1556. When the city of Pesaro,
seeking to benefit from Ancona's troubles, tried to draw merchants away,

its charter of commercial privileges was addressed to "Turchi, Armeni, Greci and Mori," as well as "Ebrei." The date was 1555.[53] The dramatic drop in references to Ottoman merchants in Ancona in the second half of the sixteenth century is in itself an indication that the Ottoman presence in the city had dwindled. One of the references that does exist points in the same direction: an imperial rescript from 1564 forbade Ottoman merchants from sailing to Ancona. They could trade only in Venice and Dubrovnik.[54] In 1569 the papal bull known as the Coena Domini, issued every year on the Feast of the Lord's Supper, decreed that no prince could give shelter to non-Catholic persons.[55] Surely the pope would have applied this to his own state as well, and thus we can imagine that Ancona was no longer the welcoming place, for the Greeks at least, that it had been. Finally, we do have one documented example of objections raised not just to the settlement of Jews but to "Moors" and "Turks" as well. In 1572 Emmanuel Philibert of Savoy issued a charter inviting foreign merchants, including Jews and Muslims, to settle in Nice. As with other rulers, this was part of his plan to promote Nice as a major commercial center. But 1572 was not 1552, and Savoy was close to Spain. Both the pope and Philip II objected to freedom of trade and residence being granted to Jews, Turks, Moors, and Persians. They managed to prevail, and Nice never became the bustling entrepôt that Emmanuel Philibert had imagined.[56] These anecdotes suggest that Counter-Reformation Ancona was not a welcoming place for Ottoman merchants of all religious backgrounds.

Venetian Decline

The Italian cities that attracted Ottoman merchants in general also played host to a large number of Greek traders. At first glance this would suggest that Greek commerce was part of the larger story of Ottoman strength following the conquest of Constantinople. This conclusion, while not incorrect, is incomplete. Greek merchants in the sixteenth century were operating on a wider stage than their Ottoman Muslim counterparts. The Greeks benefited not only from Ottoman strength but also from the slow ebbing of Venetian power over its colonial subjects. That is why we see important centers of Greek commerce not only within the Ottoman Empire and in those Italian ports that attracted Ottoman merchants. Greek commerce was also strong throughout the Venetian-held eastern Mediterranean, particularly in Candia, the capital of Venetian Crete. In Venice itself, the Greek community was the result not so much of Ottoman-Venetian reciprocity, although that played a role, but of the tenacious efforts of colonial subjects—from Corfu, from Zakynthos, from Nauplion, from Crete—to break into the previously exclusive circles of the lucrative Levantine trade.[57]

Let us continue our tour of the eastern Mediterranean, then, and turn to the Venetian Stato da Màr; we shall also return to the metropolitan city itself. In the Ionian Islands and on Crete, Greek commerce was flourishing.

At the beginning of the sixteenth century Venice still ruled over many of the islands and coastlines of the Aegean, including the important island of Crete. All of the islands in the Ionian Sea were under Venetian control. Yet, while continuing to enjoy political sovereignty, the Venetians no longer possessed the maritime superiority that would allow them to control the trade of their possessions as they once had. Venetian commercial preeminence in its colonial possessions had rested on two pillars: first, all goods originating in the republic's colonies had to be shipped to Venice, either for consumption there or for reexport to the rest of Europe; and second, this lucrative trade was the exclusive province of Venetian citizens. Noncitizens were forbidden to participate. Thus, a Cretan merchant named Costa Michel managed to ship a cargo of pepper to Venice early in the fourteenth century, but when he reached the city the pepper was seized because his name did not appear on a list of Venetian citizens.[58] This wall, while still standing, was in a state of near collapse at the beginning of the sixteenth century, and over the course of the next one hundred years it would disappear altogether. Crete, Venice's jewel in the crown, which had once provided the metropole with grain and wine, had so reoriented its trade toward Istanbul by 1600 that, in the words of one Greek scholar, "it belonged more to the Ottoman economic world than to the Venetian."[59]

The travails of Venetian shipping and commerce in the sixteenth century are well known and have generated an enormous literature. Here I will discuss them only in the briefest of terms and with a view toward what Venetian decline meant for its Greek subjects.[60]

The great merchant galleys that had criss-crossed the Mediterranean, in some cases for centuries, abruptly dropped out of use shortly after 1500. These galleys had played an essential part in ensuring Venice's domination of the Mediterranean and the city's control of East-West trade. From English wool to Indian pepper, the galleys brought all the goods of the world to Venice, where they were loaded onto yet other galleys for shipment to equally far-flung ports. Now, the increasing capability of the round ship combined with the decreasing availability of luxury goods and the threatening presence of the Spanish and Ottoman warfleets to render the galley system unworkable.[61] After 1479, no Venetian galley went to the Black Sea, and the last galley to Flanders sailed in 1533.[62]

That left the round ship, which had traditionally moved more cargo in terms of tonnage in and out of the port. It survived most of the sixteenth century, but only with substantial support from the state, such as subsidies for shipbuilders and punitive taxation of the foreign ships that were competing so effectively with Venice.[63] This reprieve did not halt the progressive turning away from the sea that was characteristic of the Venetian nobility in the sixteenth century; many were still shipowners, but they left the actual captaincy of the ships to others.

In short, Venice and the Venetian merchant no longer ruled the seas. The city's competitors in the sixteenth century were various: the English, the Spanish, the Ragusans, and the Genoese all moved in on traditional Venetian territory. Genoese competition for the sweet wine of Crete led to a 50 percent drop in freight rates on the Crete-to-England route. Closer to home, Ragusans were bidding cargo away, even in Venice's backyard, the Adriatic.[64]

The Greeks are strangely absent from the list of competitors[65]— strangely because so many Greeks still lived under Venetian rule, and one might reasonably ask whether Venice's difficulties opened up possibilities for the republic's subjects. In fact, they did. In the sixteenth century, Greek commercial communities flourished in the Ionian Islands— particularly Zakynthos, Keffalonia, and Corfu—and on Crete. Long resentful of the Venetian monopoly on trade, Greek merchants moved quickly to capitalize on Venice's weakness. They were helped by a dramatic though little mentioned shift in the relationship between ruler and ruled in the Venetian domains.

The lucrative routes of international trade had previously been reserved for Venetian citizens. The Greeks, subjects but not citizens, were excluded, which is why Costa Michel had his pepper seized on arrival in Venice. By the sixteenth century this distinction was no longer important, and was not enforced. Venetian writing at the time makes it clear that the critical distinction now was between "foreigners," on the one hand, and "Venetians" and "subjects of Venice" on the other. Although the distinction between Venetians and subjects was usually (but not always) retained, they were one group in respect to rights and privileges, while the foreigners were another.[66] It is striking that even scholars who study the Greeks under Venetian rule have very little to say about the declining importance for commercial history of the distinction between "*sudditi*" and "*cittadini*." This stands in stark contrast to the attention lavished on the changing status of the Orthodox Church under the Venetians.[67]

All four Ionian Islands were fertile and produced products coveted by the northern Europeans. They had the additional advantage of close proximity to the Balkan Peninsula, which produced its own agricultural surpluses.[68] The Greeks took control of the goods that, in prior centuries, the Venetians had gathered up and shipped to Venice for reexport throughout Europe. They sold them to northern, particularly English, merchants, or else shipped them to London themselves.

The Ionian Islands had long produced currants for the export market. Once the Venetians no longer sent galleys to Flanders, this trade continued, but it was now carried in private ships owned and manned almost exclusively by Ionian islanders. Two families from Zakynthos were particularly prominent in this trade, and both maintained an agent in London to handle the business. The Seguro family, a branch of which had settled in Venice in the 1530s, owned its own ships and routinely sailed to England throughout the sixteenth century.[69] A Venetian report from the middle of the century makes it clear the Seguros were one of the most prominent families on the island: "En ce lieu, ils sont les premiers, ils sont unis à tous les autres citoyens par de liens de sang, ils possèdent la moitié de cette île."[70] The Seguro family had contacts in the East and shipped grain from the Ottoman Empire to Venice.[71]

The Sumacchi family also hailed from Zakynthos, and their commercial activity stretched from Crete to England.[72] They exported Cretan wine and Ionian currants to London, both for their own account and on behalf of a number of Venetian merchants, some of them very prominent.[73] The Sumacchis were so prominent in the export of currents to London that when a Venetian merchant named Acerbo Velutelli lost his (brief) monopoly on this trade, he accused the Sumacchis of being behind it.[74] The son, Michael Sumacchi, was very active in the insurance market in Venice toward the end of the century. In just one three-year period he was named as an insurer in forty-one documents.[75]

The Sumacchi and Seguro families were unusual only in the degree of their success. By the last quarter of the sixteenth century, the majority of the "Venetians" resident in London were in fact Greek subjects of the republic.[76]

The sea voyages to London were perhaps the most striking accomplishment of the Ionian islanders. But, taking advantage of the fact that Venice could no longer compel all commerce to pass through its port, the islanders also sailed throughout the Mediterranean. Notarial records from Corfu show that as early as the closing years of the fifteenth century they were sailing to Venice, of course, but also to Apulia, Ancona, Ferrara, Dalmatia, the Morea, Crete, Cyprus, Thessaly, Messina, Malta, Constantinople, and North Africa. Within the space of just one year (1539) Corfiot notaries recorded over two hundred acts concerning various aspects of seaborne commerce, such as the formation of partnerships, ship purchases, and freight agreements.[77] In the case of the Mediterranean trade, the islanders carried a wide variety of goods, such as grain from the Ottoman hinterland, which they collected from various mainland ports, not just the specialized products of the Ionian Islands.

In many ways, the commercial community in Crete resembled its counterparts in Zakynthos and Corfou.[78] In the sixteenth century, Greek Cretan merchants and shipowners, subjects of Venice, came into their own. They took over the trade between the metropole and the provinces, they sold the famous sweet wine of Crete in faraway markets, such as London, and many of them settled in Venice, where they appear as members of the Greek Fraternity. The island even supported its own shipbuilding industry.[79]

Crete merits special discussion because, in addition to the above, it had a very pronounced orientation toward the Ottoman East. This is not surprising. The island sat in the heart of Ottoman territory, a fact Venice was painfully aware of.[80] After the loss of Cyprus in 1571, it was Venice's easternmost possession. Thus, the commercial community in Crete can be seen as a bridge in the transition from the Venice-oriented world of the Ionian Islands to the Greek community in Istanbul.

Sixteenth-century Crete has generated an immense amount of literature owing to the creative blending of Italian Renaissance and Greek high culture, which produced what is known as the Cretan Renaissance. Ironically, even as urban culture engaged ever more deeply with the West, the island's commercial connections to the East were growing. This development has largely been ignored by scholars of Venetian Crete (who prefer to focus on its ties with the West), but it was well known to Venetian merchants and officials at the time. Already at the beginning of the sixteenth century a Venetian merchant noted that Cretans brought the island's wine, honey, cheese, silk, and cotton to the ports of the eastern Mediterranean, as well as to North Africa, Puglia, and Naples.[81] Foscarini, writing toward the end of that same century, said, "Many go from here to Constantinople and to the *mar maggiore*, and quite a few go to Alexandria where they drink no other wine than Cretan wine."[82]

Another provveditore generale of Crete, Mocenigo, wrote in 1589, "The Cretans sail with their boats in times of peace to Syria, to Alexandria, to Constantinople, to the archipelago and to other places in Turkey in every sort of boat and skiff; they are skillful and daring men."[83] This same official noted that many Cretan shipbuilders had decamped to Istanbul, where they were much better paid than in the beleaguered shipyards of Venice and its colonies.[84] Istanbul was a popular destination, in fact, for many Cretans; the majority of the Greeks living in Galata in the sixteenth century were from the island.[85] From the other side of the fence, as it were, the Venetian ambassadors in Constantinople watched the stream of goods coming into the imperial capital from Crete's fertile hinterland.[86] Throughout the sixteenth and seventeenth centuries the Venetian authorities fought a losing battle to force the Cretans to grow wheat, to ensure that the island could withstand a prolonged Ottoman siege. They even went so far as to forcibly uproot vines.[87] But the Ottoman market was too tempting and the Cretan produce too exquisite to interest anybody in growing wheat. A Dutch mercenary fighting on the island in the middle of the seventeenth century marveled:

> Here I have seen the wine-stocks grow thicker than anywhere else, which is a great argument of the excellent soil, with which this island is blessed, and besides that the vast bigness of the bunches, weighing mostly 8 or 10 pounds a piece, and those so delicate that after I had once tasted of those could not for some years after so much as taste the Spanish. And not only grapes, but also every other fruit the land affords is passing good and delicate, in so much that not only the Turkish Emperor but all the Princes and Potentates near this island have their fruits from hence for table use and banquets.[88]

Some of what we know of the Greek Ionian merchants comes to us from records still extant on the islands of Corfu, Zakynthos, and Keffalonia. But the greatest bulk of the historical record was generated in Venice, where the Greek Fraternity of Venice was founded in 1498.[89]

The Greek Fraternity of Venice came into being when the Greeks approached the Council of Ten and, citing their recent military contribution in the conquest of Dalmatia, asked that they be allowed to organize legally as a confraternita or scuola. The motivation behind this request was the desire to secure the community's religious freedom and to clarify its legal situation. Up until this time the Greeks had chafed under the control of the Latin clergy. Now, with their own confraternita, they gained the right to draw up their own charter, to elect their own priests, and to make any decisions they saw fit, provided they did not contravene the laws of the republic. They were granted the right to worship in the church of Agios Vlasios, and they chose St. Nicholas as their protector.

Despite some difficulties with the authorities, both secular and religious, the confraternity slowly took root. The Church of St. George was finished in 1573; it would remain the nucleus of the community for centuries to come.

Merchants, sailors, and shipowners dominated the membership of the confraternity, as well as its leadership. This was a reflection of Venice's importance as a commercial center and of the Greeks as a prominent commercial community in that city. Of the thirty six individuals who held the post of president (*gastaldos*) between 1498 and 1558, at least sixteen were merchants. Between 1558 and 1570 eleven individuals held that position (some more than once), and all of them were merchants.[90] Merchants and shipowners were the most prominent contributors to the fund for the construction of the Church of St. George. When those monies proved insufficient, a tax was imposed in 1546 on every Greek ship that weighed anchor in Venice.[91]

The records of the Greek Fraternity also show something else. Most of the Greek merchants in Venice in the sixteenth century—and certainly the prominent and wealthy merchants who founded the Greek Fraternity—were from either the Ionian Islands or Crete.[92] In the early years of the fraternity many members hailed from the Ionian island of Leukada, but that number dropped steadily in the sixteenth century following the Ottoman conquest of the island.[93] Although the fraternity was in theory open to all Greeks, its membership drew almost exclusively on those Greeks who were Venetian subjects.

In other words, the Greek merchant community in Venice, as embodied in the Greek Fraternity, had a particular quality that set it apart from the other foreign merchant communities of the city. The community was the result not only of Venetian decline in general, which opened up the city to foreigners, but also of declining Venetian control over its colonial possessions, which created opportunities for the colonial subjects, who were overwhelmingly Greek.[94]

The Greek Ottoman merchants from northwestern Greece whom I mentioned earlier rarely appear in the Greek Fraternity records. Of the more than forty Epirots trading in the city in the 1550s and 1560s, only one paid dues to the fraternity for any significant length of time (fifteen years).[95] They were a peripatetic lot. Most did not declare a permanent residence in the legal documents that concern them, and of those who did (ten), just six said Venice. When one considers their traveling habits, plus the fact that many did not even speak Italian, it is clear that their world had little in common with the well-connected and privileged merchants of the Greek Fraternity.[96]

The Greek Fraternity members moved easily between the metropole and the provincial capitals from which they had originally come.[97] This was the case whether they chose to settle in Venice or to maintain their base in their city of origin. They pursued commerce at multiple levels,

from the local—carrying goods between the Ionian Islands and Venice—
to the regional (between the eastern Mediterranean and Venice) and the
international (carrying the wine of Crete or the currants of Corfu to
England). The most important commodity they dealt in was grain,
which they fetched from the ports of the Ottoman Empire and brought
to grain-starved Italy.[98]

Markos Defaranas (1503–75) was a merchant, but he has interested
historians more because he was a celebrated poet. In the course of investigating his literary production historians have uncovered information
about his commercial life. Born in Zakynthos, Defaranas arrived in
Venice in his early thirties and became a member of the Greek Fraternity in 1534. By the late 1530s he was working as a secretary (*scrivan*) on
the *Luna*, a ship that sailed regularly between Venice, Crete, and Cyprus.
He then advanced to being a shipowner and continued his trips across
the eastern Mediterranean, as well as the smaller orbit between the ports
of the Ottoman Balkans, the Ionian Islands, and Venice. All this time he
continued to reside in Zakynthos, despite his membership in the Greek
Fraternity. In 1550, however, he became a permanent resident of Venice
and sailed that summer with the Venetian *muda* (official convoy) to Alexandria. On another trip to Alexandria in the mid-1550s the ship was
blown off course all the way to the North African coastline and he,
along with the rest of the crew, was enslaved. Defaranas spent fifty-six
days in Alexandria before being ransomed by unidentified Christian
merchants. In 1558 his name appears on the list of sea captains in the
city. This list was compiled by the Venetian government, which wanted
to know how many ships were available for the transport of wheat and
salt to the city.[99]

The Samariaris family was originally from Methone, in the western
Morea, but when that city fell to the Ottomans the family moved to Zakynthos. Markos Samarianis appears as a member of the Greek Fraternity from the early 1520s. He was a shipowner and grain merchant who
used his family connections to the Morea to secure grain for Venice. A
prominent member of the confraternity, he contributed generously to
the construction of the Church of St. George and served in many high
positions.[100] He was a grain merchant who used his family connections
in the Morea (his sister was married and living in Patras) to secure grain
for Venice.

The Vergis family from Corfu appears in Venetian records as early as 1511, when Matthew Vergis sailed from Venice to Constantinople. Other journeys—to Crete, to Cyprus, to Alexandria—were made in the following decade. Throughout the sixteenth century different members of the Vergis family regularly supplied Venice with wheat from various Ottoman ports and with salt from Cyprus and far-away Ibiza. In 1559 another Matthew Vergis had a ship built in Venice that measured 900 botti.[101] In 1569, on a trip back from Southampton with this ship, loaded with cloth, salt, and tin, Vergis was captured by Huguenot pirates and taken to the port of La Rochelle. He and his crew were freed thanks to the efforts of Queen Elizabeth.[102]

These individual and family stories were replicated over and over again throughout the sixteenth century. They all point to the fact that Venice's Greek subjects moved easily throughout the Venetian and Ottoman East. In some cases they took advantage of Venice's preexisting connections with cities in Western Europe and traded as far west as England.

Everywhere and Nowhere: The Chimera of Greek Commerce

Having completed our first tour of the eastern Mediterranean, let us travel it once again. This time, however, we will consider these merchant communities from the legal and diplomatic point of view. Seen from that angle, were there any Greeks at all?

Ottomans

Peter Earle's description of the Ottoman presence in Italy does not include a consideration of its legal and institutional underpinnings. It was the product of diplomatic agreements between the Italian city-states and various representatives from the Ottoman East.[103] These agreements were negotiated on behalf of all Ottoman subjects, without regard to religious identity. In this way the agreements helped to create and gave real legal weight to what is best called "Ottoman merchants" and "Ottoman shipping."

Let us look first at the wording of the three agreements negotiated between the authorities in Ancona and Ottoman merchants in the 1510s. In 1514 privileges were extended to Greek merchants from the Balkan towns of Ioannina, Arta, and Vlona. The language indicates that Greek merchants were recognized as a distinct entity. The document granting these privileges, which were extended by the municipal council, is entitled *Capitula solutionum cum mercatoribus grecis de Janina, Larte et de Velona sub die 3 januaris 1514*.[104]

And yet within just two months, these privileges were extended to "tutti i sudditi del Gran Signore," following an embassy of Turkish merchants sent by the Sultan. This document was entitled *Pro mercantiis subditorum Magno Turco*.[105] The privileges were not for the Turkish or Muslim merchants of the empire but rather for the merchandise of the subjects—"subditorum Magno Turco"—of the sultan. This strongly suggests that Greek merchants were subsumed into this larger category and that the prior language simply reflected the coincidence that all the petitioners happened to be Greek. Finally, the 1518 agreement lowered the duties paid at Ancona for all "the Levantine merchants, subject to the Turk."[106]

We know that the Ottoman sultans played a role in negotiating the privileges that obtained in Ancona, and it is also clear that the sultans were willing to act on behalf of their subjects in general, not just Muslims. By the 1520s the annual fair of Recanati, a small port just to the south of Ancona, was attracting many Ottoman merchants.[107] In 1526 the Anconite authorities took it upon themselves to warn the sultan that Recanati was unable to provide the security necessary for Ottoman merchants to arrive and to trade peacefully. In response, Süleyman ordered his subjects not to trade there, and he forbade Ottoman captains from sailing there.[108] In the wake of the persecution of Jewish merchants in Ancona in the 1550s, Süleyman twice sent ambassadors to try to obtain the release of Jews who were his subjects. The Jewish community in the Ottoman Empire organized a boycott of Ancona that lasted eight months and ended only when Rome assured the sultan that his subjects were no longer being persecuted.[109] We can see why Natalucci, the historian of Ancona, would state, quite matter-of-factly, "The Sultan protected his subjects who frequented Christian lands and often intervened on their behalf."[110]

Agreements between the two states regulated the presence of Ottoman merchants in Venice as well. These agreements, which were negotiated at the highest levels, are known as the capitulations. Most of the literature on the capitulations has emphasized the privileges that were
unilaterally granted to European merchants in the cities of the Ottoman
Empire. This emphasis is understandable for two reasons. Traditionally,
Europeans were more interested in trading in the East than were Easterners in the markets of Western Europe. Second, by the nineteenth
century the Europeans had achieved enormous influence in the Ottoman Empire, and thus historians have always been interested in tracing
the origins and growth of the European presence in the empire.

But such a preoccupation has meant that the Venetian-Ottoman capitulations have not been sufficiently distinguished from the capitulations concluded with other European states. They are, in fact, quite
different, and their importance lies elsewhere. They were bilateral agreements that consistently emphasized commercial reciprocity and thus
provided the legal basis for an integrated commercial zone that stretched
from Venice in the West to Aleppo in the East.[111] Muslims, Jews, and
Christians moved relatively easily across this world. The 1419 capitulations included rights for Ottoman merchants trading in Venetian-ruled
areas. In 1430, just after the Ottoman conquest of Thessaloniki, the Venetians and the Ottomans agreed that Ottoman merchants had the same
rights in Venetian territories as did Venetians in the Ottoman Empire.[112]

The capitulations were buttressed by frequent diplomatic missions. In
the first half of the sixteenth century not a year went by that a representative of the sultan did not show up in Venice, and the authorities began
to worry about the expense involved in hosting such frequent visitors.[113]
Many of the sixteenth-century missions came to discuss purely diplomatic or military issues, but some also took up commercial matters.
Often, of course, the individuals involved in these cases were some of
the most prominent names of their time, men like Joseph Nasi, the Sephardi Jew and banker to the sultan, or Solomon Ashkenazi, a Jew of Venetian origin who became physician to the grand vezir.[114] And commercial transactions on behalf of high-ranking Ottoman officials would of
course receive attention if things went awry. But Ottoman representatives also involved themselves in cases concerning ordinary individuals,
people about whom we know very little other than the fact of this official

intervention. In 1583 two emissaries, Ömer and Ibrahim, traveled to Venice to ask that a lawsuit against one Marino Scaruoli, a Greek from the Morea, be reviewed. They were successful in their request, although they were not able to obtain Scaruoli's release because the judges then brought new charges against the Ottoman subject.[115] A few years earlier, in the mid-1570s, an Ottoman çavuş (messenger) named Hasan came to Venice at the request of two Jews, Salomone todesco di Giacobbe and rabi Salomone Carai di rabi Giuseppe, to help them in their claim against a co-religionist, one Antonio Girardi. Antonio had pledged some jewels to his creditors in case of nonpayment. Now they were having difficulty collecting, and Antonio's guarantors were also not cooperating.[116] At mid-century another çavuş, this one named Ca'fer, went to Venice and retrieved money and goods on behalf of some Ottoman Muslims. He obtained 4,200 gold pieces that had not been paid for the sale of some spices and picked up twenty-one bales of velvet that were in the possession of a Venetian but belonged to an Ottoman merchant named Ani Çelebi.[117]

It is certain that at least part of this reciprocity was merchant-driven. Merchants, in other words, did not hesitate to remind both states of their duty to protect those involved in peaceful trade between Venice and the empire. In 1546 the Ottoman grand vezir Rüstem Pasha felt obliged to write to the doge Francesco Dona asking for the proper protection of Ottoman traders who went "constantly from the well-protected lands of the sultan to those parts for trade."[118] From our point of view, the most interesting aspect of the grand vezir's letter is that he refers to the frequent petitions of complaint by Ottoman merchants.[119]

Diplomacy was an important part of the Venetian-Ottoman partnership, facilitating the conduct of commerce from the Adriactic to the Bosphorus. It stepped in when things went awry.[120] Even more important to remember, however, is that the capitulations created a routine of normalcy that allowed Ottoman merchants to conduct business in Venice (and the Venetians to conduct business in the Ottoman Empire) without, in most cases, the intervention of political authorities. Merchants from the empire routinely sold goods (often through the brokers provided for them by the Venetian state), contracted debt, and rented lodgings, sometimes for extended periods.[121] Cemal Kafadar's study of the death of one Ottoman merchant in Venice is a good illustration of

the ordinary routines that, simply because they are ordinary, often remain invisible. Hüseyin Çelebi bin Haci Hizir bin Ilyas was a camlet
merchant from Anatolia who died in Venice in 1575. The documents
generated by his death show that his uncle, Ahmed bin Kassab, was able
to settle his affairs in an orderly manner and to arrange for a proper
burial. Ahmed paid off the debts Hüseyin owed to another Ottoman
merchant, to a broker, and to his landlady for back rent. He was also able
to sell his nephew's remaining effects. Great care was lavished on his
nephew's body. The uncle hired a washer and a water-pourer and purchased frankincense, camphor, and rosewater to scent the corpse. The
body was then wound in a shroud and placed in a coffin. After prayers
were performed (*alla turchescha*, as the Italian document notes) and
alms given, a convoy of five gondolas carried the coffin, members of the
Muslim mercantile community, and the uncle to the place where the
nephew would be buried.

Venetians

It is not surprising that Ottoman merchants included Greeks as well as
Muslims and Jews, but the Greek hiding behind the Venetian in seemingly unproblematic discussions of "Venetian commerce" and "Venetian
trade" has remained almost invisible. New scholarship is beginning to
take apart the meaning of "Venetian" in the particular circumstances of
the sixteenth century. Two points are of consequence for my argument.
First, a complete picture of Greek commerce in the sixteenth century
must include not just the well-known ascent of the Ottoman Greeks, for
Greeks who were Venetian subjects were also very active in the Mediterranean and beyond. Second, Greeks participated in commercial life as
Venetian or as Ottoman subjects, and as such were regulated under different legal and diplomatic arrangements. While being Greek was not
inconsequential, Venetian or Ottoman subjecthood was far more important in the lives of these merchants. This fundamental difference has
tended to get lost in studies that speak of the "Greek community" of this
or that city.[122]

In a recent article published in *Annales*, Maria Fusaro points out that
most members of the Venetian community in London in the sixteenth

century were, in fact, Greek. This is in line with what we would expect, given the economic and social trends outlined above, but here I want to suggest why this rather simple observation (in retrospect) has never been made.

Fusaro writes that these Greek merchants have been taken for Venetians, "which has concealed them to the eyes of the historian; in reality they were 'Venetian subjects.'"[123] But there is another way of looking at it. Rather than suggesting that historians have mistakenly taken them for Venetians, one can argue that in important ways they *were* Venetian. Yes, the Venetian merchants of London were Greek-speaking, they were Christian Orthodox, and their family origins lay in historically Greek lands. But as merchants operating in the international arena they were Venetian, with all the benefits that status conferred. It is interesting to see how very different an individual can look depending on which historiography is describing him.

In her study of Greek sailors and shipowners in sixteenth-century Venice, Kristas Panayiotopoulou makes reference to one Mathios Bernardes, whom she describes as "a rich Greek banker and shipowner of Venice."[124] As luck would have it, Frederic Lane makes reference to the same individual in his study of Venetian bankers. Here his name is rendered as Matteo Bernardo, and he appears in a list of bankers, indistinguishable from his colleagues (significantly, Jewish bankers are described separately because they had a different legal status).[125] Lane describes him as "a great merchant" and as "one of the four leading merchants of Alexandria," but what he never describes him as is Greek.

One Zuanne Nufri, a ship captain, appears in the records of the Greek Fraternity in the mid-1560s. Thirty years later he appears in Venetian notarial records, once again as a ship captain, but with no reference made to his being Greek.[126]

When we think about the Greek community of Venice, even a brief glance at the historical record demonstrates that merchants whom we call Greek operated in vastly different worlds. Let us consider again the Vergis family, who were prominent members of the Greek Fraternity from the early sixteenth century and closely connected to the Venetian elite. The first Matthew Vergis transported the Venetian consul to Damascus in his own ship in 1522. During the Ottoman-Venetian war of 1537–40 he built a large ship for the use of the republic.[127] As mentioned earlier, a subsequent Matthew Vergis was prominent enough that when he was captured by Hugenot pirates on a voyage back from London, Queen Elizabeth herself intervened for his release. At least two members of the Vergis family served as president of the family and were patrons of Greek culture. These were the Greeks who, in the words of one scholar, "occupied a central place in the Venetian state."[128]

And then there are the other Greeks, men of modest means who were not members of the fraternity and for whom Venice was just one stop in a peripatetic routine. These merchants, Christians from the Ottoman Empire, did not know Italian and often relied on brokers for the conduct of their business. For the most part we do not know their names, but it is highly unlikely that their paths ever crossed the path of someone like Matthew Vergis.

It is highly problematic to try to bring these two sharply divergent worlds together with terms like "the Greek community of Venice" or "Greek" commerce and shipping. Our anonymous merchant and Matthew Vergis belonged to two different worlds and two different legal regimes, the former as a subject of the Ottoman sultan and the latter as a subject of Venice.

Let us consider again the Ionian Islands and the persistent complaints of the Ottoman merchants, including Greeks, against the customs officials in Corfu. The Ionian Islands were populated almost exclusively by Greeks who were Venetian subjects (the Jewish community was also important), and they were a crossing point for Ottoman Greeks going to and fro between Venice and the empire. As such, they are a particularly good site for viewing the fracturing of the Greek world into its Venetian and Ottoman spheres.

It is clear from the language of the complaints that the Ottoman Greeks were being taxed as Ottoman subjects. The 1510 report refers to "some merchants of Ioannina and other places under the rule of the Turks."[129] When Ottoman merchants approached the doge directly in 1561 they introduced themselves as "we, levantine merchants and subjects of the Signor, Christians, Jews and Turks" and distinguished themselves from Venetian subjects.[130] They objected to repeated demands that they swear they had not entered into any partnerships with Venetian subjects, given that they had already sworn this in Venice. They also condemned one Arseni Paniperi for presenting himself as consul for "our nation and for all the subjects of the Grand Signor," whereas according to them he was nothing but a fraud.[131] In the final set of complaints, about twenty years later, the petitioners once again identify themselves as "mercanti levantini."[132]

While the Greeks and other Ottoman merchants were enduring the vexations of officials in the Ionian Islands, the Greeks native to the Ionian Islands—Venetian subjects all—were parlaying their advantageous tax status into a commercial asset. In the second half of the sixteenth century, fast on the heels of Venetian decline, English merchants came looking for the opportunity to export the islands' currants directly to England. They were able to strike up a partnership with the Greek commercial class because each side had something the other needed. The English offered the Greeks a lucrative market for their agricultural surplus, as well as specie to pay for it. The Greeks, in turn, had much to offer the English, one of which was their preferential customs status. In an attempt to prevent the English from exporting currants directly to England (rather than to Venice for reexport), the Venetians levied a heavy tax on the English.

In response, their local Greek allies "falsified the customs registers in order to make it appear that it was them, and not the English, who were the exporters, thus allowing them [the English] to escape the heavy taxation."[133] The English were also happy to purchase boats together with their Greek partners; by having a Greek owner, the English could avoid the heavy taxes levied on foreign ships.[134]

We can imagine a humble itinerant merchant from the mountains of northern Greece passing a Matthew Vergis, sumptuously arrayed, in the streets of Venice. Most likely the two would not even have looked at each other. In Corfu both stories converge at the customs house, yet here too the Greeks were probably very differently positioned. In one room the merchants from the East—Muslims, Christians, and Jews—would be arguing with the local customs official while in another room, perhaps, a Corfiot Greek smoothly enters his name as the owner of a shipment of currants, while his English partner waits in the harbor. Reflexive references to "Greek" communities across the Mediterranean not only collapse these differences, they also fail to grasp the world of Ottoman and Venetian subjects that the doge and the sultan created together.

Istanbul

In the large Greek population of the Ottoman capital we can see the mirror image of the Venetian situation. The Greeks of Istanbul break down into Ottoman and Venetian subjects, except in this case it is Ottoman subjecthood that provided the relative advantage.

To students of the Mediterranean, and of the Ottoman Empire, it may at first seem odd to state that there is a symmetry between Venetian and Ottoman subjecthood. The overriding importance of religion as a determinant of personal status is always cited as an essential characteristic of the Muslim polity, in sharp distinction to the situation in medieval and early modern Europe. Once again, it is the Greeks who call this into question.

On June 1, 1453, Fatih Mehmet granted privileges to the Genoese community in Galata. The document, which in the Turkish text was identified as an *ahd-name*, was the founding text that established the new status of the residents of Galata after the fall of Constantinople to the Ottomans.[135] The text has been widely misinterpreted as establishing autonomy for Galata and its population, similar to what they enjoyed under the Byzantines.[136]

Fatih Mehmet did not grant any status to the colony as a whole. Instead he divided Galata's population into two separate groups. The first were those permanent inhabitants who agreed to submit to the sultan, to become *dhimmis*, and to pay the head tax (*cizye*) that was obligatory for all non-Muslim subjects of the sultan. This group included Greek, Jewish, and Armenian, as well as Italian (mostly Genoese), residents. The second were not Ottoman subjects. Frankish merchants (again, mostly Genoese) who were temporarily in the city for business purposes, or who went back and forth on a continous basis, were given the status of *harbi*, literally "of the land of war." More prosaically, in Islamic law this term refers to non-Muslims who have not submitted to the sultan. In effect, Fatih Mehmet made a distinction between residents and nonresidents; no doubt he was willing to grant the option of harbi status to Galata's merchants as a way of enticing them to stay on and contribute to the restoration of the city's prosperity. Although the two groups shared certain privileges, "their legal status was absolutely distinct," and this distinction was recognized by the *Podesta* at the time. In a letter written home in the same month, he spoke of two groups, *mercanti* and *abitanti*.[137]

Most Westerners, however, both then and now, overlooked this distinction between subjects and foreigners. Whether willfull or not, such a lapse is perhaps not surprising, given the essentialism that continues to plague discussions about anything Islamic. Yet the Ottomans did make such a distinction.

In his article on Ottoman Galata, Halil Inalcık concentrates on the status of the Genoese merchants who had traditionally dominated Galata under the Byzantines. This is probably why he implies, in a rather offhand manner, that all the Greeks of Galata fell in the category of dhimmi or Ottoman subject.[138] In fact, just like the Genoese, some Greeks submitted to the Ottomans while others held the status of foreigner.

The Genoese initially dominated Galata, but over time Venice recovered its position and then surged ahead. Over the course of the sixteenth century the "nazion Veneta" became the most important Frankish community. The Venetian resurgence swept many Greeks into the city in its wake. Just as the "Venetian" colony in London was heavily Greek, many of the "Venetians" in Galata were in fact Greek subjects of the republic.[139] As early as the fifteenth century, Greeks, especially Cretans, enjoyed prominent positions in the community, the better to facilitate trade between Constantinople and Crete. Sanudo mentions that it was "Cretans of the Venetian nation" who were in charge of defense in Galata.[140]

Venetian merchants were confronted with the same choices imposed on the Genoese. The treaty of 1502 decreed that Venetians who resided in Constantinople for more than a year had to pay *haraç* (in other words, become Ottoman subjects), while those who went back and forth on a regular basis were freed from such an imposition. Despite the burden of the haraç, the trend among Venetian (and thus Greek) merchants was to become Ottoman subjects. By so doing, they enjoyed a favorable customs rate (4 percent as opposed to 5 percent), as well as greater protection during the frequent wars between the Ottoman Empire and Venice.[141] During the war for Cyprus, for example, many members of the "nazion Veneta," including Greeks, were arrested and shut up in Rumeli Hisari. The bailo was under house arrest for three years.[142]

Dursteler's recent study of the Venetian community in Istanbul has provided more information on the Greek component within the "nazion Veneta." In between the official nation—which was always small, consisting of no more than one hundred or so merchants and diplomats—and Ottoman society there was a gray area of several thousand men and women who worked closely with the nation and who identified themselves to a certain extent with Venice, but who were not officially members of the nation. Dursteler calls them "the unofficial nation." The majority were Greek-Venetian subjects.[143] The Venetian bailo in Istanbul routinely provided these individuals with certification of their status as Venetian subjects, and these certificates conferred economic and juridical rights, as well as responsibilities.[144] The Greek-Venetians, for example, did not have to pay the head tax (haraç), which was the essential mark of submission for Ottoman Christians and Jews. As Venetian subjects, they were able to use the Latin rite hospital in Galata and to turn to the Venetian chancellery in the Ottoman capital to avail themselves of certain services that were provided to members of the *nation*, such as the registering of wills and testaments and the recording of property sales.[145] On the other hand, they were obligated to pay Venetian customs duties, the *cottimi*, when they sailed in and out of the city.[146]

The Ottomans not only recognized Venetian jurisdiction over these Greek individuals, they were willing to help enforce it. As might be expected in a community so heavily oriented toward maritime trade, customs evasion was a serious problem. In 1615, at the request of the bailo, the sultan commanded Ottoman officials at Gallipoli and at the entry to the Dardanelles to ensure that Cretan ships leaving Istanbul for Venetian territories paid their ten-ducat duty to the Venetian consul in Gallipoli.[147] This doesn't mean there were not jurisdictional scuffles. The Ottomans were ever alert to try and levy the haraç tax on Venetian subjects; long-term residence in the city or marriage to a local made the Greeks vulnerable on this account.[148] But the Venetians were just as assiduous in fighting them off, and the fierceness of these battles is a testimony to just how important these legal statuses were.

For our purposes it is especially important to note that Greek merchants who were Venetian subjects operated under Venetian jurisdiction. This involved obligations, such as customs duties, but also the protection of the bailo. When a Cretan merchant died on board an Ottoman ship, the sixty-three barrels of wine he had loaded were confiscated by Ottoman officials. The bailo intervened, just as he would have done for a properly "Venetian" merchant, and was able to take possession of the goods.[149] It is interesting that Venetian jurisdiction over Greek merchants was recognized not just by the Ottomans but by others in the commercial world as well. When an Ottoman Jewish merchant bought wine from Crete that was delivered watered down, he went to the bailo to complain and declared that he was "not desiring to seek any other Justice."[150]

Legally speaking, then, there was no such thing as a Greek commercial community in Istanbul (including Galata). The salient divide was between those who were Ottoman subjects (some of whom were Greek) and those who were subjects of Venice (many of whom were Greek). That is why, in her study of the Greek community of Galata based on the records of the Venetian bailo, Phane Mavroeide acknowledges that she cannot provide any global figure on Greek trade, since "We can't know how much we are missing in terms of Greeks who were not Venetian citizens."[151]

I hasten to add here that, despite the importance of this legal distinction, the social line that divided the two Greek communities was far more blurry than that obtaining either in the Ionian Islands or in Venice. The Greeks (often Cretans) who came from Venetian-held territory were often from humble backgrounds; they might have been fleeing a desperate situation. Once they reached the Ottoman capital they found it easy to mix in with the large, often transient population of sailors, shipbuilders, arsenal workers, and merchants that made up the Greek community in Istanbul. It was not at all unusual for these Greek Venetians to choose to become Ottoman subjects, and one can imagine that it was not always easy to know the legal standing of each and every individual. And whatever their legal status, Greeks of all stripes frequented Orthodox, not Catholic, churches. Mavroeide describes this state of affairs as "an exceptionally irregular and delicate situation."[152] She doesn't go on to lay out the nature of this delicacy, but her meaning is clear. Through the dhimmi system, the Orthodox patriarch was given substantial authority over the Greek Orthodox. But what was the nature of his authority when it came to the Greek Orthodox who were not Ottoman subjects? At this point we don't know. We cannot even say whether the situation was seen as irregular and delicate by all those concerned; perhaps it was unproblematic.

What can be said here is that the fact that this issue has not been raised, let alone explored, by historians suggests the extent to which we have assumed that religion, and religion alone, determined personal status in the Ottoman Empire.

It is more difficult to assess the importance of subjecthood when it comes to the Greek elite. Many of the wealthy Greek families in the Ottoman capital were established in Venice as well; a web of commercial and family ties bound together the elites of the two cities.[153] The members of the Marmaretos were wealthy Greeks, leaders of the Istanbul community, who resided in Galata.[154] By the 1530s, one member of the family, Dimitrios Marmaretos, was established in Venice as part of the family business. He was a member of the Greek Fraternity and was trusted enough by the Venetian state that he was asked to give them a report on Ottoman war plans in 1537, on the eve of yet another Ottoman-Venetian war, which he did.[155]

The Koresse were also residents of Galata.[156] Family members and family property were spread out across the Aegean, the Black Sea, and the Balkans. The Koresse probably had their origin in Chios, but by the sixteenth century they were landowners in Crete; they traded with Italy, France, Moldavia, the ports of the Black Sea, and many points in the East. Their ties to Venice ran deep. The family enjoyed the extraordinary status of *cittadinanza Veneta originaria* for services they had rendered to the republic. These included spying and the management of Venetian debt vis-à-vis the sultan. One Antonios Koresse was established in Venice at mid-century, where he was one of the most active members of the Greek Fraternity. At the same time, he had a close relationship with the famed Ottoman naval commander Hayreddin Pasha.[157]

References to an individual's status are few and far between. The Venetian bailo's identification of Antonios Koresse as "*cittadino nostro venetiano*" is rare.[158]

A court case before the Venetian bailo reveals that elite families were opportunistic when it came to the question of legal jurisdiction. Manoles Kantekouzenos established himself in Venice, where he was a member of the Greek Fraternity, while his brother, Antonios, stayed behind in Istanbul to handle that branch of the family's business. When the bailo ruled against Antonios in a commercial dispute, the latter took advantage of his status as a dhimmi to avoid the judgment.[159]

From these admittedly few examples, it seems likely that the Greeks played a role very similar to that of the sixteenth-century Jewish elite; both groups thrived through mediating the relationship between the Ottoman Empire and Venice.[160] Their wealth, their connections and their ability to serve both masters, the Venetian doge and the Ottoman sultan, would play a greater role in determining their fate than would their status as Venetian or Ottoman subjects. This would help explain why the literature on these prominent families rarely bothers to identify them as one or the other.

Conclusion

The Greek mercantile world was much vaster and more complicated than the literature on any one community, be it Istanbul, Venice, or Crete, can convey. In the sixteenth century the Greeks developed into a truly international community that stretched from Italy in the West to the Black Sea in the East. They would not know such a moment again until the second half of the eighteenth century. And yet, though they were everywhere, the Greeks were also nowhere. They moved throughout the eastern Mediterranean as Venetian or Ottoman subjects, part of a vibrant commercial world that cut across religious difference and rested on a tenuous partnership between the Venetian Republic and the Ottoman Empire. But religion was not in abeyance. It was there, simmering just beneath the surface. The next chapter turns to the Greeks, not as Ottomans, not as Venetians, but as members of the Greek Orthodox community. Once again, in considering the Greeks we will also be able see most clearly how the claims of religion tugged on this fragile regime that the Venetians and the Ottomans had constructed.

CHAPTER 2

The Claims of Religion

● ○ ●

In considering the Greeks as members of the Greek Orthodox community, we plunge back into the world of religion. The claims imposed by the reality of religious allegiance—Catholic, Orthodox, Muslim—were not easily brushed aside. They persisted alongside the world of subjects and sovereigns created by Ottoman and Venetian diplomacy. This chapter considers two aspects of this side of the Mediterranean. First, the most persistent and most articulate opponents of Venetian-Ottoman cooperation were the Knights of St. John, who, early in the sixteenth century, were defeated on Rhodes, but soon reestablished themselves on the island of Malta. Where did the Greeks fit into this world of bitter Christian dispute over the proper place of the Ottoman Empire in the Mediterranean? Second, I shall consider the religious status of the Greeks as Orthodox Christians, in Venice and in Istanbul. In both places, particularly in Venice, the liminality and ambiguity that so often attached themselves to the Greeks were also present in religious matters.

Venice and the Corsairs

It would not be possible, nor would it make for a very coherent discussion, to describe every hostile encounter at sea in the sixteenth-century Mediterranean. Here the focus will be on the tense and difficult relationship between Venice and the Western corsairs—primarily but not exclusively the Knights of St. John on the island of Malta. The corsairs are important because they presented an alternative, admittedly not always well articulated, to the world of subjects and sovereigns that the Ottomans and the Venetians had fashioned together.

The Knights of St. John practiced what was known as the *corso*, derived from the Latin *cursus*, meaning sea voyage. The corso, while specific to the Mediterranean, can be situated within the general context of violence at sea in the early modern period. Historians and jurists have traditionally distinguished between two types of violence at sea. The first is piracy. A pirate is one who operates outside the bounds of all laws and for himself and his band of marauders only.[1] The other type of violence is closely bound up with war waged by the state. With limited fiscal resources, early modern states turned to seafarers, both pirates and others, to fight on their behalf during times of war. For the state, it was warfare on the cheap, and for the recruited individual it was a chance to profit from the proceeds of war. The English term for such individuals was "privateers." The Mediterranean corso, along with its practitioners, the "corsairs," falls somewhere between these two poles. Like piracy, it was perennial rather than limited to periods of declared war. Yet in the minds of its practitioners it was more elevated than mere piracy precisely because there was a kind of permanent war in the Mediterranean between Christianity and Islam, as discussed in chapter one.[2]

Corsairing, along with ordinary piracy, was practiced from one end of the Mediterranean to the other. Because of the overarching frame of religious hostility, it was an option that anyone could exercise at any time.[3] But there were also certain states for which corsairing was a major occupation, to the point that we can speak of "états-corsaires," another distinctly Mediterranean phenomenon.[4] On the Christian side of the divide, the Knights of St. John ran the most formidable état-corsair. Since the Venetians, more than other European power, maintained a dense network of commercial and diplomatic relationships with the Ottoman world, it is not surprising that the knights regarded them with barely concealed hostility. As the leading, and self-proclaimed, protagonists of the eternal crusade against Islam, the Knights of St. John directly challenged Venice's relationship with the Ottoman East.[5]

The following description, from the knight and chronicler of the order, Fr. Bortolomeo dal Pozzo, dates from 1636 but provides a good example of the type of cruise that departed from the Grand Harbor of Valletta, year after year, throughout the seventeenth century:[6]

> The six galleys of the Order departed recently, under the Command of General Nari. After obtaining supplies in Syracuse and Messina, they embarked on the corso in the Levant [*passarono a corseggiar in Levante*] where, in the space of a month and a half they took a galeotta, a polacca and a tartana carrying diverse merchandise and many infidels. They acquired 134 slaves, both Turks and Moors.[7]

Most commonly, the knights challenged Venice by attacking Venetian shipping in the waters of the central and eastern Mediterranean or by putting into Venetian-held ports with Ottoman prizes. Most of the examples I discuss here are from the last quarter of the sixteenth century. Prior to that, the Western corsairing presence in the eastern Mediterranean was much less intrusive; it was only after Lepanto that Western corsairs flooded into the East.

The knights often acted brutally in the course of carrying out their attacks, and the usual emphasis in the literature is on the lawlessness of corsair behavior. Despite this brutality, their challenge was rooted in law and defended, at times, in legal terms, even if the niceties of the law were not always observed. The world described in chapter one, by contrast, was a creation of diplomacy. The challenge represented by the knights was only incipient in the sixteenth century; with the decline of Venetian maritime strength in the seventeenth century, the full implications of this challenge would become apparent.

The picture of trade in the early modern Mediterranean, as sketched in the previous chapter, is one of busy routines, of Ottoman and Venetian merchants criss-crossing the Adriatic and the southern Balkans as they moved between Venice and the Ottoman Empire. Commercial life was not without its hazards, but these merchants could count on a certain amount of solicitude from both the Venetians and the Ottomans when faced with a problem. This solicitude was framed by the agreements, the capitulations, which structured relations between the two states.

To a certain extent this rather orderly picture is a consequence of the sources on which it is based. Ottoman-Venetian correspondence assumed the existence, the normality, and the desirability of trade (except in times of war) across the religious divide. A rather different set of assumptions emerges when we consider the same century through the lens of Venetian correspondence with the Knights of St. John on Malta.

Already by the sixteenth century the Venetians and the knights had a long history of sour relations. The knights' successful conquest of Rhodes in 1306 (in 1234 the Venetians had tried and failed to take the island for themselves) brought them squarely into the commercial world of the eastern Mediterranean. Their raison d'être as a crusading order was fundamentally at odds with Venice's identity as a fiercely independent city of merchants, and this divergence was deep enough to be reflected at the social as well as the political level.[8] The knights drew on aristocrats from all across Europe to serve in the order, but the Venetians were notable by their absence. Most Maltese galleys were actually built outside Malta, in places like Naples, Livorno, and Genoa, but the Maltese never ordered a galley from Venice.[9] The merchant oligarchy of Venice did not mix with the knightly aristocracy of Rhodes, and Venetians were probably forbidden from joining the order. An old law preventing citizens from accepting offices or commands in lands not subject to the Venetian republic was reasserted in 1356.[10]

In the fourteenth century, Venetian antipathy toward the knights was fed by the latter's alliance with the Genoese. Genoa was favored at Rhodes, and the Venetians knew it. The Muslim emirs of the coast of Asia Minor were not yet very strong, particularly in the first half of the fourteenth century. Thus, Genoese-Venetian rivalry explains more about the poor relationship between Venice and the knights than does disagreement over how to face the Muslim threat.[11]

Things were quite different two hundred years later. The knights were no longer on Rhodes. Sultan Süleyman had defeated them in 1522, and they were forced to look for a new home. They found one in 1530, when the Hapsburg emperor Charles V granted them the islands of Malta and Gozo, as well as the fortress of Tripoli on the North African coast.[12] As long as the knights were on Rhodes, their relationship with the Muslim emirates, and then the Ottoman Empire, was necessarily ambiguous. Situated on a small island surrounded by Ottoman territory, the knights found they had to trade, although quietly, with the Anatolian mainland if they were to survive. And they did their best to avoid a direct confrontation with the Ottoman Empire, knowing they would likely lose.[13]

Once on Malta there was little to lose and much to gain by an aggressively hostile stance toward the Ottomans. Grain supplies now came from Sicily, not Anatolia, and the knights knew that attacking Malta, in the central Mediterranean, would be much more difficult than taking Rhodes had been. In addition, Malta was a resoundingly poor place: "Small, stony, sterile, and singularly ill-defended, the windswept central Mediterranean island of Malta in 1530 offered the vagrant Knights Hospitallers no pleasant or reassuring substitute for the luxurious Dodecanese fortress of Rhodes."[14] The inhabitants of the rocky islands of the Mediterranean had traditionally turned to piracy to compensate for the lack of resources at home, and the knights, along with the ordinary Maltese, would prove to be no different. Less than a year after their arrival in Malta the knights struck at Ottoman Modon, in southern Greece, thus making it clear that the crusade against Islam would continue.

The Venetian position, too, was less ambiguous than it had been in the fourteenth century. Back then, Venice had dominated the eastern Mediterranean, and it was not at all clear that the Muslims would be able to prevail. Venice had every reason to fight, and fight hard, against Muslim expansion, even as the city pursued trade agreements during more peaceful times. By the sixteenth century it was clear that the Ottomans had won. Even though the Ottoman-Venetian wars were not yet over, Venice now made protecting its trade in the Levant its highest priority, rather than trying to win back lost territory. This meant appeasing the Ottomans, and the commercial reciprocity outlined in the capitulations negotiated between the republic and the empire is just one example among many of Venetian concessions designed to protect the Levantine trade.

The knights and the Venetians, then, were veering off in opposite directions, which brought them into frequent clashes in the course of the sixteenth century. The Venetians were determined to get along with the Ottomans, while the knights wanted to keep the crusade alive.

There is already a very fine study of this fraught relationship in the early modern period, and it is not my intention to go back over this history.[15] But the often bitter correspondence between the order and the Venetian government is valuable here because it reveals an alternative view of international relations in the eastern Mediterranean, one grounded in the imperatives dictated by a permanent state of war. The correspondence also shows that, contrary to assumptions of Maltese lawlessness, the knights refer to legal principles that had a very long history in the Mediterranean.

Venice was understandably outraged by Maltese attacks on its shipping. A case from the summer of 1575 is particularly interesting for our purposes. In that summer the Maltese sailed home from the eastern Mediterranean with a rich booty of silks, cinnamon, indigo, lacquer, and other goods.[16] These goods had been taken off a Venetian galleon, the *Torniello,* near the Anatolian coast; they belonged to Venetian Jews. In response, Venice focused attention first on the barbarous behavior of the attacker. A letter from the Senate to the provveditore dell'armada spoke of the "great violence" practiced by the knights, claiming that three men on board had been tortured (this was entirely likely, given the knights' record of behavior). The letter continued by saying that the attack was a "manifest outrage" directed at Venetian vessels, as well as a violent interruption of commerce and free trade.

Let us consider the case of the *Torniello* from the point of view of the knights. The chronicler of seventeenth-century Malta, Bartholomeo dal Pozzo, notes that the knights paid the captain for the freight he stood to lose as a result of the seizure.[17] This detail, which is noted in other cases as well, is highly significant. It suggests that, whatever the true motives of the corsairs, they could at least claim to be following maritime custom. Paying the captain for enemy goods seized is straight out of the *Consolato del Mare,* the collection of maritime usages that was first written down in fourteenth-century Catalonia. According to the Consolato del Mare, sovereignty did not extend to the ships of a sovereign power; once at sea an admiral had the right to stop and inspect even ships belonging to a friend, as long as he treated the captain fairly. It remained the source of European, and Mediterranean, prize law right through the seventeenth century.[18] In the chapters devoted to prize law, various scenarios are laid out. The one of interest here discusses the case of an encounter with a friendly merchantman carrying enemy cargo.[19] In such case, the admiral (the commander of the armed vessel) could force the patron of the merchantman to surrender all enemy goods on board. However, the admiral was also under obligation to pay the patron the entire freight the patron would have collected had he delivered the cargo to its original destination. Taken together with other provisions, the rules in the Consolato show great concern to treat the friendly patron fairly. Richard Zouche, English judge of admiralty from 1641 to 1649, was clearly conversant with these rules. He wrote, "by the *Consolato del Mare*, in which the law of the Mediterranean is contained, one who seizes enemy goods in a friendly ship is bound to pay freight for that part of the voyage which the ship has performed."[20]

Another chronicler, the Abbé de Vertot, is probably referring to the same case in his entry for the year 1576. He writes that the affairs of the Jews of Venice came once again upon the carpet and the Senate sequestered the Hospitallers' property and possessions in Venice.[21] In his account, we see the knights making explicit reference to the law. The grand master went to Rome, the Abbé writes, and argued that since those Jews were not subjects of the republic, it was a constant practice—and one, moreover, allowed by all laws whatsoever—to seize an enemy's goods, even though they be found on a friend's ship.[22]

A decade after the attack on the *Torniello* the pope demanded that the knights return a Venetian schirazzo to its owners.[23] The grand master refused on the ground that he had paid for that part of the booty that belonged to Christians "*in accordance with ancient custom and rules of war and in conformity with the dispositione of consulate, that is, the laws, of the sea*" (my emphasis).[24] The puzzle here is that the knights appear to have seized the ship, as well as any enemy cargo they found on board. This was not the usual practice, nor was it in accordance with the *Consolato*, but it was becoming more common in the sixteenth and seventeenth centuries, at least in the Atlantic world. Possibly there was a spillover effect into the Mediterranean, but it is hard to know for sure.[25]

Between War and Peace

For those more familiar with the literature on early modern Europe, it may seem peculiar to write about the Maltese in the context of the Consolato, that is, European prize law. Historians have written extensively on the development of international law, including prize law, at this time. Yet the entire discussion, including reference to the Consolato, assumes the backdrop of the emerging nation-state system. We can see these assumptions at work in Carl J. Kulsrud's classic work on maritime neutrality, published in 1936. He writes about a time, the seventeenth century, when the distinction between war and peace was becoming clearer, thanks to the state's increasingly succcessful efforts to exert control over warfare. For example, states were increasingly disinclined to issue letters of marque, which authorized individuals to retaliate against the nationals of the state that had caused the grievance, during peacetime. More and more, these letters were reserved for general retaliation during times of war.[26] Therefore, in his discussions of various points of maritime law, Kulsrud sees no need to expand on definitions of war and peace. In his chapter on the right of visit and search (which the knights did indeed claim), he explains that this was the right to stop and search the ships of *nations at war* (my emphasis), in order to ascertain whether such vessels were in any way connected with the hostilities.[27]

But this was the rub in the Mediterranean. Did a state of war exist? Certainly there was no declared war in the sense of the Knights of Malta declaring war on the Ottoman Empire on such-and-such a date. It is clear, however, that the knights felt the rules of the *Consolato* concerning behavior during war applied, and this was because there was a permanent war in the Mediterranean, between Christianity and Islam.

Similarly, Kulsrud defines belligerents and neutrals exclusively in national terms: the English, the French, the Swedes, and so forth. But the Maltese defined friends and enemies, neutrals and belligerents, in religious terms. The players were Muslims, Christians, and Jews. Time and time again, throughout the course of the sixteenth, seventeenth, and even eighteenth centuries, they insisted on a world divided into Christians and infidels. One of the fullest expositions of the knights' point of view was given in 1587, in response to a papal bull that extended full protection to Jews and to Jewish merchandise sailing between Christian ports and the Ottoman Empire.[28] The knights were alarmed and outraged by the bull, which they saw as an assault on the order's very existence. The order, they wrote, had been instituted for the universal benefit of the Christian *res publica*, to defend the Catholic faith and to protect the poor. With the steady advance of Muslim power, which ejected the knights first from Jerusalem and then from Rhodes, the Hospitallers could no longer confront the enemy on land. The only way now of "practising its profession of prosecuting the infidels" was to engage the Ottomans at sea. The knights claimed that by so doing they forced the Ottomans to tie up sixty or seventy armed galleys to fend them off.[29]

And yet, beyond the rhetoric of religious enmity, a more extensive review of the knights' position reveals an ambiguity that was entirely characteristic of the early modern Mediterranean. Let us return to the Abbé de Vertot's acccount of the *Torniello* affair. When the grand master went to Rome, he argued that *since those Jews were not subjects of the Republic* (my emphasis), it was a constant practice—which was, moreover, allowed by all laws whatsoever—to seize an enemy's goods, even though they be found on a friend's ship. This argument is a clear acknowledgment that not all Jews were alike; the subjecthood, and not just the religion, of an individual mattered. Two years later, after another bruising battle with the Venetians, the grand master was seeking reconciliation. In the letter patent that he issued to Frà Cuppones before his voyage to the Levant, the instructions were clear:

> We order and command you that throughout the present voyage you will not take any notice of any Venetian vessel unless for obtaining news, you will not stop them to take away from them any sort of contraband and infidel goods and men; you will let them go unmolested on their voyage. We want you, however, to search all vessels of Ragusa and all Turkish vessels, and also those which are loaded for Ancona, provided they are not Venetian, and finding on board Turks, Moors, Jews and other Infidels, you will seize them, together with all their goods; you will, however, pay the Christians their freight charges.[30]

The instructions are a mix of principles: while acknowledging Venetian sovereignty, the detail on the freight charges is from the *Consolato* tradition.[31]

In the Venetian insistence that its ships be free from search and seizure, no matter whose goods they were carrying, it is as if we have an early Mediterranean rehearsal of the "free ships, free goods" debate that embroiled the European maritime powers in the second half of the seventeenth century. In direct contravention of the *Consolato*, some European jurists began to argue that a neutral flag could protect enemy goods, and the clause began to show up in some treaties.[32] In the

Mediterranean case, the neutral power would be Venice and the enemy would be the Jews.

The Maltese were not the only ones who were ambivalent. Although Venice was widely viewed as "the whore of the Turk" for its willingness to trade with the Ottomans, even the relentlessly commercial republic seemed reluctant to directly assert the right of all to trade peacefully in the Mediterranean. In its argument with the knights over the Jews, it did not take issue with the knights' enmity toward the Jews, just the right of Venetian ships to be free of search and seizure. Even when coming to the defense of Ottoman shipping, it never mentioned the capitulations, the diplomatic agreements that it had signed with the Ottoman sultan, which enjoined respect for each other's shipping.

The Ottomans, by contrast, did not hesitate to bring up their agreements with the Venetians. In 1553 a Maltese knight seized various Venetian ships laden with grain in the ports of Crete.[33] The Ottoman sultan took up the case because a number of Ottoman merchants had sustained losses during the attack. He reminded Venice that, because of the capitulations, Ottoman subjects traveling on Venetian ships enjoyed the same protection as all other Venetian subjects; therefore, these merchants had to be compensated for their losses. The sultan had had to intervene precisely because an uproar had ensued when it seemed Venice was going to look after the Venetian merchants but neglect the Ottoman passengers who had been traveling on board. Following the attack, examiners had been dispatched to various cities and islands in the Venetian Levant, among them Famagusta on Cyprus, Canea on Crete, and several places in the Ionian Islands. All claimants had to submit, within fifteen days, authentic evidence of their claims. The uproar developed when it became clear that no effort was being made to include Muslim merchants from the Ottoman Empire in the investigation of the claims, even though they too had sustained losses.[34]

The following year Venice was more responsive to Ottoman concerns. Once again the knights attacked a Venetian ship, the *Donada*, and seized sixteen passengers, all Muslims and Jews, all subjects of the sultan. They also confiscated a large quantity of goods and cash. A *sequestro,* or seizure of assets, was imposed, but this time the Senate instructed the Venetian bailo in Constantinople to inform the sultan of the steps that had been taken and the efforts that were being made. The sultan was told that the sequestro would not be lifted until the grand master set free the Muslims and Jews and restored all their money and goods.[35]

It is interesting that the Senate's decree included a provision for the protection of the foreign merchant precisely to avoid the awkwardness of the year before. The capitulations signed between the Ottoman Empire and Venice should have already settled the matter; Ottoman subjects trading in Venetian domains or traveling in Venetian ships enjoyed the right to state protection, like all other Venetian subjects.[36] Yet the actual record with regard to particular cases suggests that protection of Ottoman subjects was not always forthcoming.

Venice most often came to the defense of Ottoman shipping in the context of the republic's territorial waters. If, while bringing a Muslim prize back to the home port, the knights (or other corsairs) sought refuge in any Venetian port, then the Venetians would demand the return of the prize.[37] In the sixteenth century the Venetians still controlled a number of ports in the eastern Mediterranean—Crete being the most important possession—and thus the issue was a constant source of tension.

In the winter of 1582–3, a distinguished Spaniard and Knight Hospitaller named Don Diego Brochero de la Paz y Añaya embarked on a corsairing cruise to the Levant.[38] He surprised three Turkish ships in the vicinity of Crete; the ships were carrying Ottoman grain to the island.[39] He seized the ships and diverted the grain to Sicily.

Where, exactly, had the ships been seized? This was the issue that the two parties quarreled over. Venice claimed that Diego had seized the ships along the coast of Crete. The Hospitaller version was different and carefully laid out where each of the ships had been seized, one in the Gulf of Thessaloniki (very far from Crete), one near the island of Samos, and the third near Rhodes, more than 150 miles off the coast of Crete. The clear implication behind this line of argument, and one that Venice did not contest, was that at a certain point beyond the Venetian-held coastline, infidel ships could legitimately be seized.[40] By insisting that the Hospitaller ships had, in fact, cruised along the Cretan coastline, the Venetians implied a certain agreement with this point of view. In a letter written to the pope in 1583, the Grand Duke of Tuscany defended the corsairs of Livorno against Venetian complaints precisely on these grounds. He said, "the galleys went to the Levant in the company of those of Malta and took as prize a Turkish boat *outside of their islands and their places*" (my emphasis).[41]

Venetian disputes with the Maltese were not always strictly bilateral affairs. Sometimes their confrontations mobilized a Catholic network that went all the way up to Rome. The pope's influence on Mediterranean commerce extended beyond his role as secular ruler of Ancona. In his capacity as the head of the Catholic Church, he also sometimes functioned as a mediator between Venice and the Catholic corsairs—principally in Malta and Livorno—whose power was on the rise in the second half of the sixteenth century.

In the summer of 1583 the grand master authorized a corsairing cruise in the Levant.[42] The cruise resulted in an immensely rich prize, a large Turkish galleon with a very heavy cargo of timber and the capture of some eighty wealthy merchants. On the way back home, however, the two Maltese galleys had the misfortune of running into the Venetian fleet, which, operating out of Crete, regularly patrolled the Aegean. According to the Maltese, the Venetians acted with great savagery, wounding and pillaging everyone without respect for status and dragging the Hospitaller cross in the most disdainful manner. Venice towed the two galleys, with the Hospitaller captives on board, to Crete, where they remained for forty days. After that they were taken to Corfu, where they remained on board the galleys for another four months. During those months they were, again according to the Maltese, "dying of hunger, cold and fatigue."[43]

We know a great deal about this incident because the order submitted an account of it to a congregation of cardinals in Rome. A certain Frà Don Pedro Gonzales de Mendoza was sent to Rome to persuade the pope, "with the greatest vehemence possible," of the tremendous destruction that the Venetians, acting in cold blood, had caused. Venice eventually bowed to papal pressure, as well as that of the Spanish and French ambassadors in Rome, and returned the two galleys to Malta. It refused, however, to make reparations for financial losses and other damage.[44]

Just a few months later the Venetian Senate voted yet another sequestro following a Maltese attack on a Venetian vessel carrying merchandise belonging to Venetian merchants. Venice usually communicated a sequestro directly to the Receiver of the Order in Venice, but this time relations between the two were so strained that the republic chose to direct it to the Venetian ambassador in Rome instead.[45]

But the pope did not always take the side of the Maltese. There is the incident from 1585 in which the pope ordered the grand master to restore a Venetian schirazzo to its rightful owners.[46] A few years earlier, when a certain Frà Giovanni Bareli captured a Venetian ship in the Levant, the Venetian representative in Rome sought papal mediation. Gregory XIII sent a brief to Grand Master La Cassière. Since La Cassière was in the middle of negotiations with Venice on a matter of much greater import, he moved quickly to arrest Bareli, who was tried, found guilty, excommunicated, and deprived of all Hospitaller privileges.[47] Earlier in the century, in the case of the *Donada*, and even stretching back to the 1530s, the papacy supported various Venetian sequestros.[48]

The Knights of St. Stephen of Livorno also turned to the pope when they had a complaint with Venice. A long letter from the Grand Duke of Tuscany (as head of the order) to the pope in 1583 has been preserved; it conveys a good sense of the pope's mediating role and his direct involvement in the commercial life of the Mediterranean. It begins, "Monsignor Nuntio showed me yesterday the brief of your Holiness, and passed with me that *offitio* that you have laid out to him, concerning navigation in the Levant. If I may be permitted to reply to it at length, I wanted Your Saintliness to hear in what manner the Venetians have treated me."[49] Although the letter does not say what was in the offitio, from the long diatribe against Venice that follows, it must have been an order to stay away from coastline and harbors belonging to Venice:

> Also we stay away from their islands and their other places as much as possible. But being that that is the central route, I cannot promise—in case of necessity or to get water, or in case of emergency—to avoid these places entirely, although I will as much as possible.[50]

The Greeks and the Catholic World

How did the Greeks fit into this world of knights and popes, of Venetian sequestros and petitions to Rome? Let us consider first the Greeks, Venice, and the corsairs. Once again, Venice is the most apposite power on the Catholic side because it ruled over many Greek subjects in the sixteenth century. At the same time, it was the principal opponent (besides the Ottomans) of Maltese adventurers in the central and eastern Mediterranean.

The Greeks and the Corsairs

Here the story is little different from the narrative I gave in the first chapter. The distinction between Greeks who were Venetian subjects and Greek subjects of the Ottoman sultan was an important one. This is rather remarkable, when one considers the crusading rhetoric of the knights. Three aspects of the situation must account for it. First, Venice was willing and able to impose sequestros on the knights to try to bend them to its will. Second, Venice was willing to confront the Maltese over attacks on its Greek subjects, and third, Venice's Greek subjects turned to the republic for help with the Maltese. (The situation was entirely different when it came to Greeks who were subjects of the Ottoman sultan, as will be discussed in subsequent chapters.)

Let us return briefly to the case of the *Torniello*. In their defense, the Hospitallers drew a distinction between Jews who were subjects of the republic and Jews who were not. Since the Jews in question were not Venetian subjects, they held the status of enemies on a friendly (Venetian) ship. The Jews are highly visible in both the history and the historiography of the sixteenth century. Part of the reason for their prominence is the steady stream of pronouncements issued by the papacy and the Italian city-states—Ancona, Venice, and Livorno—as they tried to reconcile historic Christian enmity toward the Jews with their desire to maintain trading links with the East.

The Greeks are much less visible, overshadowed by the more obvious Catholic hostility toward the Jews and the Muslims. Official pronouncements may be lacking, but Greek merchants and seamen did get caught up in the strife between Venice and the Hospitallers, and, as with the Jews, the knights did make a distinction between Venetian Greeks and Ottoman Greeks.

A particularly clear instance of this discrimination comes out in an attack in the fall of 1641.[51] According to the Venetian complaint lodged with the order, the knights boarded a Greek vessel, conducted by Greek subjects of the republic. The ship was sailing in the Ionian Sea, starting out from the island of Modon and heading north; it was attacked, the Venetians said, "not far from the island of Zante" (today's Zakynthos), which was Venetian-held territory. The pirates seized a number of Muslims on board, as well as a quantity of money.

The Maltese did not deny the fact that the attack took place, but they disputed all the particulars of the case. The knights conducted their own inquiry and said that the Greek vessel was in fact proceeding from Tripoli (in North Africa), that there were no Venetian subjects on board, and the vessel was not flying the banner of St. Mark, the Venetian flag. They only agreed with the Venetians in that they had seized a number of Muslims on board. That part, at least, was relatively uncontroversial. The Maltese commissioners concluded their report by saying that the Hospitallers had acted strictly in accordance with their letters of instruction. This was probably true. The instructions issued at the commencement of a corsairing cruise were fairly standard. If we look again at those given to Frà Cuppones, mentioned earlier in the chapter, before his voyage to the Levant in 1577, we see that he was ordered to "not take any notice of any Venetian vessel." But Ragusan and Turkish vessels were fair game, and "Turks, Moors, Jews and other Infidels" could be seized. In other words, a Greek vessel that was not (at least according to the knights) Venetian was by definition Turkish, although this was not stated explicitly. Greek merchants of the Ottoman Empire would take exception to this definition, but for now, this particular dispute shows that both Venice and the knights distinguished between Venetian Greeks and Ottoman Greeks.[52]

It is difficult know whether the Greeks involved in the case were Venetian or Ottoman. The fact remains that Venice was willing to confront the Maltese over attacks on its Greek subjects. An early mention of this dates to the middle of the 1550s. A Maltese galley commanded by one Domenico Gondi actually shelled a chateau along the Cretan coastline, sailed into one of the island's harbors, and seized a Greek ship carrying grain that belonged to one Manoli Paleologo.[53] Venice promptly imposed a sequestro and managed to recover 6,400 ducats. It also obtained an order from the pope to the knights instructing them to leave maritime traffic alone.

Greek merchants themselves seem to have been alert to the ups and downs of the Venetian-Maltese relationship and would have seized the opportunity to have their case heard. In late 1640 Venice was indignant that four galleys of the order had ended up in the port of Oristoli on the Ionian island of Cephalonia.[54] The knights protested that they had been forced by strong winds and bad weather to take shelter there. This one quarrel sparked a series of mutual recriminations, at which point two merchants from Crete revived their claims from several years earlier. Giorgio Gentile harked back to the so-called de Villages case, in which two brothers had preyed on some Cretan merchants. In response, Venice had imposed a sequestro, and the case had been settled on Venice's terms. But now Gentile claimed that he had been left out of the final settlement, and was seeking compensation in the amount of 1,500 reales. Another Cretan, Ambrosio Chrisochiera, had lost merchandise on board a ship that three knights, Beauvisé, Castelli, and Seillons, had seized three years earlier; he had paid an insurance premium of 3,300 ducats on the goods.[55]

The Religious Status of the Greek Orthodox

In commercial matters Venice was quick to come to the aid of its Orthodox subjects; the knights, for their part, recognized the latter as Venetian subjects. The religious status of the Greek Orthodox in Venice was far less clear and far more contentious. Once again, Venice is the most important site from which to consider the Greek Orthodox position in sixteenth-century Italy. This is true for two reasons. First, the community in Venice was by far the most important one on the Italian peninsula (and, in fact, anywhere outside the Ottoman Empire) in terms of population size, cultural production, and any other measure. Greek settlement in Livorno did not predate the middle of the sixteenth century, and Ancona, while important, could in no way rival Venice as a center of Greek life.[56] Second, prior to the Council of Trent, there is simply much less of a story to tell about the Greek Orthodox in Italy (outside of Venice) because the pre-Counter-Reformation Church had not yet targeted them for proselytization.

Although far more is known about the Greeks in Venice and its territories than about Greeks elsewhere in the Italian world, we do know that
the Venetian story is in some ways atypical. First, Venice's treatment of
the Greek community in Venice was never divorced from larger imperial
concerns, particularly the desire to keep its large Greek colonial population content, given the mounting losses vis-à-vis the Ottoman Empire.
Second, Venice's historical determination to keep the papacy at arm's
length meant that the Council of Trent, although not unimportant, was
not the watershed event that it was for other Greek communities in Italy.

In one regard, however, the Greeks in Venice were little different from
their Orthodox brethren elsewhere. The Council of Ferrara-Florence
(1439) had arguably achieved the union of the Eastern Orthodox and
the Roman Catholic churches, with the former recognizing the authority of the pope. Although the results of the council were roundly rejected
by the Orthodox world once the Eastern bishops returned home and
made known what they had done, the agreements reached in Florence
would cast a long shadow over the Mediterranean for many years to
come. The result was to add yet another layer of ambiguity to the religious status of the Greek Orthodox living in Catholic lands.[57]

Let us return to the subject of the Greek Fraternity of Venice and the
Church of St. George built by the fraternity. In the previous chapter I
emphasized what we might call the "Venetianness" of the Fraternity's
members. They were Venetian subjects, and many of them enjoyed close
ties to the elite of the city. Yet if we twist the kaleidoscope and put the
Church of St. George in the center, then the fraternity appears in a rather
different light. The members might have been Venetian subjects; their
religious status was much less clear.[58]

Greek Orthodox attempts to worship in Venice date back to the fifteenth century.[59] After the Council of Ferrara-Florence they were allowed to move out of private houses and to worship in Catholic churches
because now, at least in the eyes of the Catholic Church, they were in
union with Rome. They then asked for permission to build their own
church. A papal bull granted them this right in 1456, but the Venetian
Senate revoked the right soon after, before any building had actually
commenced.[60] No more gains were realized in the fifteenth century.

The Greeks achieved a breakthrough early in the next century. In
1511 they approached the doge and asked for permission to buy a lot on

which to build a church; they also wanted a place to bury their dead. In 1514 permission was granted, subject to papal approval. Two papal bulls issued that same year allowed the project to go forward, but they did more than that. In the words of one scholar, the two bulls represented "an extraordinary shift in the relationship between the Greeks of Venice and the Papacy."[61] They put the Greek community under the direct authority of the pope, thereby freeing it from the control of the local, Latin patriarch, who had traditionally maintained an adversarial position toward the community.[62]

Although another papal bull, this one issued in 1526, allowed the actual construction of the Church of St. George to go forward, this does not mean that the religious status of the Greek Orthodox was any clearer than it had been before. The patriarch of Venice, and the Latin clergy more generally, continued to insist that the Greeks of Venice were "Catholics of the Oriental Rite" and rightly part of the patriarch's flock, and the middle of the sixteenth century saw some reversals for the Greeks.[63]

In 1542 Pope Paul III issued a bull that took up the question of the priests serving in St. George's, a traditional point of friction. He acknowledged the privileges that had been granted to the Greek Orthodox of Venice by his predecessors. However, he said, the Greeks had proved unworthy of these privileges because they had condemned the Latins as heretics, rejected the Council of Florence, and installed priests in St. George's who rejected the Council. He ordered the papal nuncio, Georgios Klouzines, to restore order and reinstate those priests who accepted the Council of Florence. All priests desiring to serve at St. George's had first to declare their acceptance of the union of the two churches in front of either the nuncio or the Latin patriarch of Venice. Any resistance by the Greeks would result in a fine. He concluded by saying that St. George's was under the authority of the nuncio and the patriarch of Venice, both of whom had the right to go to the political authorities if the church was appearing to stray from Catholic dogma.[64] At this point, Venice showed itself willing to go along with the pope, despite the general desire to placate the community. The Council of Ten helped enforce the dictates of the 1542 bull.

The same pope revoked this bull seven years later, but in 1564, under the influence of the Council of Trent, which sought to restrict the religious freedom of the non-Catholic minorities, Pius IV again required examinations for fidelity to the Council of Florence.[65] One year later he issued another bull that denied university degrees to non-Catholics studying at the University of Padua, which had traditionally hosted a significant Greek student population.[66]

But before the full force of the Counter-Reformation could sweep over the Greek community, Venice stepped in. In 1569 it forbade the publication in Venice of a bull that said that no prince could give shelter to non-Catholic persons.[67] Then in 1577 it took the extraordinary step of accepting an Orthodox metropolitan in Venice, ordained by the patriarch in Istanbul, with no ties to the Catholic Church. Prior to this time no cleric above the level of priest had served in the city. Above and beyond the decision itself, the timing of this decision shows just how atypical the Venetian situation was within the larger context of the Greeks in the Catholic world. Just seven years earlier Counter-Reformation reforms had created the Greek College of Rome, which aimed at the conversion of the Greek Orthodox living under Ottoman rule. Only four years prior to that, in 1573, the Congregazione per la riforma dei Greci viventi in Italia was formed. Its goal was the Latinization of the Greek and Albanian communities living in southern Italy.[68]

The date, 1577, is not accidental. The Venetians had lost Cyprus to the Ottomans in 1570. As Ottoman armies continued to advance, Venice attempted to moderate its position toward the Greek Orthodox in the hope it could win their loyalty.[69]

Gabriel Severos was the Orthodox metropolitan appointed in 1577, and the story of his appointment demonstrates an important aspect of the Greek Orthodox community at this time, its internationalism. Despite the legal distinctions I have discussed so far, and despite persistent Venetian unease at contact between her own Greek Orthodox subjects and the Orthodox hierarchy in Istanbul, common membership in the Greek Orthodox community brought together Greeks from across the Ottoman and Venetian worlds. This was particularly true at the level of church elites, and in that way the hierarchy of the Orthodox Church resembled the Greek mercantile elite.

In 1575 the Council of Ten in Venice received a memorandum from one of their Greek subjects, a rich Cretan merchant named Leonino Servo, a longtime resident of Istanbul. It had been sent through the good offices of the bailo.[70] The memo concerned Crete, not Venice. Servo proposed that one Orthodox archbishop and four bishops, all loyal to Venice, be installed on the island. This would satisfy the religious demands of the Cretans and would stop them from coming to Istanbul, where there were many enemies of Venice, for religious counsel. The council was willing to consider the proposal—after the loss of Cyprus it was greatly concerned that Crete was next—and sent it along to Foscarini, the provveditore on the island. Foscarini, a fervent Catholic, rejected it, and the Council of Ten acquiesced in his decision.

In the meantime, Gabriel Severos, a former priest at the Church of St. George in Venice and a rising star in the Orthodox Church, was ordained metropolitan of Philadelphia in Istanbul.[71] It is Stephen Gerlach, the Lutheran scholar from the University of Tübingen, who allows us to make the connection between these two events. Gerlach was present at Severos's ordination and observed that the ordination would not have been possible if Leonino Servo, whom he described as a rich merchant of Galata, had not financed it, with all the necessary gifts given, the meal that followed, and other expenses.[72] He also observed that Severos had no intention of leading the impoverished diocese of Philadelphia; instead he was going to return to Crete (hiding, of course, his new identity as a metropolitan), where he hoped a favorable decision would come through and allow him to become the first Orthodox metropolitan of Crete. Clearly, Severos was Servo's candidate of choice.

Once Crete was out, it seems the Venetians wanted to reach a compromise, in order to please the Cretans (including Servo himself) and the patriarch. Therefore, Severos was allowed to come to Venice and be the head of the church there, although the seat was never formally moved. The experience with Severos proved to be such a positive one— he had prestige with the Orthodox but was a loyal servant of Venice— that the republic acquiesced in future metropolitans. After Severos, it was the fraternity that chose the metropolitans of Philadelphia, a decision the patriarch in Istanbul would then confirm.

Perhaps the most dramatic example of this network in action comes from the seventeenth century. Despite Venice's repeated attempts to block communication between the Greek Orthodox of Crete and the Orthodox hierarchy in the Ottoman Empire (which Servo alludes to in his 1575 memorandum), the most famous patriarch of the century—and perhaps of the entire period of Ottoman rule—was from Venetian Crete.

Kyrillos Loukaris was born in the capital, Candia (today's Herakleion), in 1572. After basic education in Crete, he was able to study in Italy, thanks to the support of his uncle, who was the patriarch of Alexandria, in Ottoman Egypt.[73] He studied in both Venice and Padua, and then, in the early 1590s, went to Alexandria to serve in the patriarchate under his uncle's guidance. His linguistic abilities reflected his cosmopolitan education: he knew Latin, Italian, Turkish, and Arabic, in addition to Greek. He succeeded his uncle as patriarch of Alexandria, and eventually, in 1620, he became the ecumenical patriarch in Istanbul. Loukaris's story shows not only that a Greek born under Venetian rule could become a patriarch who served with the sultan's consent. It also demonstrates that families spread out across Ottoman and Venetian lands maintained close contact with each other.

Despite the presence of an Orthodox metropolitan in Venice from 1577 on, we should not conclude that the religious status of the community was now crystal-clear. Venice's decision to allow Severos and his successors to serve was a political decision made outside the purview of the Catholic Church. The (Catholic) patriarch of the city continued to insist that the Greeks were Catholics of the Oriental rite, and the Latin clergy continued their attempts to interfere in the life of the Greek Orthodox.[74] The papacy continued to assume the continuity of the reunion of the Greek Church achieved at the Council of Ferrara-Florence; Orthodox rejection of the council from 1484 on was treated as if it concerned only these Greeks living under Ottoman rule. This was "something of a legal fiction," but one that Venice chose never to challenge directly.[75] The council remained the platform that regulated the politics of both Venice and the papacy with regard to the Greeks, a stubborn insistence that continued to render somewhat uncertain their status in the Catholic world.

Finally, we must bear in mind that the Greeks themselves were willing to take advantage of this ambiguity.[76] It was not just the Latin clergy that insisted the Greeks were Catholic. In their numerous petitions to the Venetian authorities the Greek community consistently referred to itself as "true and Catholic Christians."[77]

Elsewhere on the Italian peninsula the Greek Orthodox were without the protective Venetian cloak. We do know that the program of Latinization envisioned by the Congregazione per la riforma dei Greci viventi in Italia was largely achieved in the south. A history of the Greeks in Counter-Reformation Ancona has yet to be written, but it seems likely that Ancona became a less welcoming place. Livorno is the most intriguing place to consider in terms of the Greeks and Counter-Reformation Italy. It was one of the fastest-growing ports in the seventeenth-century Mediterranean, and the Medici grand dukes were eager to attract the Greeks, as sailors, rowers, and merchants. Thus, as we shall see, the grand dukes often closed their eyes to the ambivalent status of the Greek Church in an echo of Venetian policy, although for different reasons. According to Rome, and to the archbishop of Pisa who directly oversaw the community church of Santissima Annunziata where the Greeks worshipped, the church was, or should be, a Uniate church. Yet the vast majority of the priests who served in the church were from the Levant and practiced the Oriental rite. The Catholic hierarchy routinely intervened in the affairs of the church, and individual Greeks were not infrequently hauled in front of the Inquisition to answer questions about their practices. But the grand dukes met these issues with a studied silence that mitigated the impact of the Inquisition.[78] That is a story that belongs to the seventeenth century, and it is taken up in the next chapter.

The Ottoman World

The Greek Orthodox in the Ottoman Empire were in a much more secure position than their compatriots in the Latin West. The endless wrangling that we see in the latter over the appointment of priests, over which rite was to be used, and the interrogation of the beliefs of individual parishoners are completely absent. The sultans accepted religious diversity as a matter of course and early on developed fairly stable arrangements for the place of non-Muslims in the Ottoman Empire.

Nor did the Ottomans see the Orthodox Church and its hierarchy as potentially traitorous in the way that Venice did. It was the possibility of a renewed Catholic crusade that worried the sultans, and part of their strategy for facing this was a deliberate favoring of the Greek Orthodox. Thus we see no attempt to control the movement of priests or bishops in and out of the Ottoman domains, no attempt to prevent Greeks from studying, for example, at the University of Padua, as was the tradition.

But the sixteenth-century Orthodox community in the capital, and particularly in Galata, did have its peculiarities. As we know from the previous chapter, many Greeks living in Galata were Venetian subjects. Yet at the same time they were Greek Orthodox in religion, they attended the same churches as their religious compatriots who were Ottoman subjects, and, as Orthodox, they were subject to the authority of the patriarch, who reported to the sultan. On the one hand, the wealthy merchant Leonino Servo was a subject of Venice. On the other hand, it was Servo who arranged for Gabriel Severos to be ordained at the patriarchal court as metropolitan of Philadelphia. Clearly, he enjoyed a close relationship with the patriarch. Once again, the Greeks were in a liminal position. In Venice they were Venetian subjects but not Catholic, in the Ottoman Empire they were Greek Orthodox but not dhimmi, that is, Christians who had submitted to the sultan's rule. This situation does not fit into the enduring and often well-founded assumptions about the important dividing lines in the eastern Mediterranean. From the time of the Crusades, Catholics were the foreign Christians, while the Orthodox Christians were distinguished—in their own eyes and in the eyes of others—by their submission to Muslim rule. Islamic law even makes the distinction between subject Christians and foreign Christians, those who had not submitted. The former were dhimmi, the latter were harbi. In most cases and in most places, the dhimmi-harbi distinction coincided with the Orthdox-Catholic divide, but not in this instance.

One scholar has written that "This reality constituted an exceptionally irregular and delicate situation."[79] Certainly the situation was irregular; but was it delicate? And if so, for whom? In Venice the state was greatly concerned (although it eventually gave up) to bring religious status into alignment with subjecthood. Non-Catholic subjects of Venice were seen as problematic, and it was only after 1577 that the republic gave up its attempts to create a Uniate church for its Greek Orthodox population.

In a multireligious empire, the Ottoman sultans did not share these anxieties about religious status. In that sense the situation was not delicate. But the sultan was always concerned to expand the ranks of those who paid the head tax required of non-Muslims who had submitted to his rule, that is, who were Ottoman subjects.[80] That was the motivation behind some of the measures mentioned in the previous chapter, such as the capitulations granted to the Venetians in 1502, which stipulated that Venetians who resided in Istanbul for more than a year had to pay the head tax or *haraç*.[81] A scuffle from the Ionian Islands toward the end of the fifteenth century illustrates the jurisdictional quarrels that could erupt between the Ottomans and the Venetians. In 1487 several individuals went and lived for several years in (Ottoman) Kefallonia, where they were obliged to pay the head tax. Apparently they returned to Zakynthos, because when the subashi of Kefallonia visited Zakynthos to arrest subjects of the empire who had fled, those individuals were found, and he wanted them turned over to him. The Venetian in charge refused, saying they were Venetian subjects.[82] But this Ottoman concern was not religious in nature, nor was it directed particularly at the Greeks; the authorities were just as interested to see Catholic foreign subjects accept dhimmi status as they were the Orthodox.

The other party that could conceivably have entertained objections to Venetian subjecthood for Orthodox Christians is the Orthodox Church. After all, the church had the right to collect taxes from the Orthodox Christians of the empire, and this right was given to it by the Ottoman sultan. The church could even call on military support in the form of the janissaries if it had difficulty collecting the tax. This raises an interesting question: were those Orthodox Christians who were not dhimmi obligated to pay their church taxes? And if they did not, would they find a defender in the bailo, much as they did in more secular matters? Unfortunately, no information has come to light on this matter. What can be said is that the patriarchate in Istanbul worked very closely and was in nearly constant contact with the Venetian bailo. Church officials appear routinely in the documents generated by the bailo's office; they might serve as translators or as witnesses, and they also went there for their own personal reasons.[83]

It is quite striking that the bailo was called on even in matters one would have thought to be purely internal to the Orthodox Church. In 1590 the Orthodox bishop of Venice, Gabriel Severos, wrote a letter to the Venetian authorities in which he asked them to approach the patriarch *through the bailo* (my emphasis). Severos was seeking permission to celebrate Easter together with the Latins in Venice. He explained that the intervention of the bailo would be "more efficacious."[84] Why the bailo would carry more weight with the patriarch than an Orthodox bishop is not clear, but it does suggest that the Venetians played a mediating role among the scattered communities of Orthodox Christians. Most likely the patriarch, rather than seeking to police the boundary between his parishioners and the Venetian state, actually valued his Venetian connections and those of the Greek community in Istanbul.[85] For its part, Venice was very mindful of the role the patriarch could play in influencing Greek behavior, and also used the bailo to make contact with church officials.[86]

The Pope in the East

The Orthodox Christians had their protector in the person of the Ottoman sultan, and therefore the pope had little or no role to play in the lives of the Orthodox communities in the East prior to 1570 and the founding of various Counter-Reformation institutions designed to bring the Greeks under papal supremacy. There was an exception, however, and that exception was the Monastery of St. John on the eastern Aegean island of Patmos.

The monastery was in a war zone throughout the fourteenth century and into the fifteenth as well. The Knights of St. John were on Rhodes and controlled the Dodecanese islands as whole; just across the water various Turkish emirates faced them along the Anatolian coastline. By the end of the fourteenth century the Ottomans had conquered the most important of these emirates and controlled the coast.[87] There is very little documentation concerning the monastery from the first half of the fifteenth century; the paper trail begins to thicken after mid-century. Evidence indicates that a Patmiot representative went to Edirne in the summer of 1453—that is, right after the conquest of Istanbul—to submit to the sultan.

The Ottomans treated the island well because of the monastery. The tax was low, and they were confirmed in their privileges. Fatih Mehmet declared that the provisions the monastery bought not be taxed, and Bayezit the Second (1481–1512) guaranteed the monastery the right to buy twenty modia of grain per year from Palatia. He also gave them the right to buy wheat and legumes from the provinces of the Aegean.[88]

Perhaps because of this favorable treatment of an important Christian site, various Catholic powers felt obliged to respond with their own offers of protection in what was still a very dangerous area. In 1457 the patriarch of Venice warned that no one was to harm the Patmiots, and threatened with ex-communication anyone who did so. In 1461 the pope sent a similar order to the archbishops in Crete and in Rhodes. He did this, it seems, on the instigation of the monks who had approached him on this matter. In 1508 and 1514 the grand masters of the Order of St. John, still at this point on Rhodes, ordered their own subjects not to harm the islanders, who should be considered *vassalli* of Rhodes.

The Catholics also showed their interest in the island by helping those monks who came asking for contributions. In 1507 a grand master gave two monks letters of introduction to take with them to Rome. And in 1513 the pope gave indulgences of two hundred years to anyone who helped the monastery monetarily.

The year 1522 was a turning point. Süleyman the Magnificent ousted the Knights of St. John from Rhodes, and for the next half century or so Ottoman naval strength and further conquests in and around the Aegean would guarantee the relative tranquility of the eastern Mediterranean. Not surprisingly, then, references to Catholic protection of the monastery die out. They would return at the end of the century, but with a somewhat different emphasis. The late fifteenth-century and early sixteenth-century correspondence between the monks and the Catholic world, during which time there was near constant fighting between the Ottomans and the knights, showed a concern with the basic security of the monks and the monastery. Among the monks there was even some thought of abandoning the island altogether around the year 1500.[89] By the end of the sixteenth century things had much improved, and Patmos was conducting a thriving trade that went as far as Ancona. The correspondence reflects a concern to protect this commerce. By and large, the monks addressed themselves to two centers of Catholic power: the knights, now ensconced on the island of Malta, and Rome. But Patmos was no longer exceptional in the Greek world. In the waning days of the sixteenth century Greek Orthodox merchants turned less and less to Venice or Istanbul for the protection of their trade and more and more to Catholic authorities.

CHAPTER 3

The Age of Piracy

● ○ ●

The seventeenth-century Mediterranean was the age of the pirate, as it was across the globe. When North Americans think of piracy, it is a Caribbean landscape they imagine. From Captain Hook in *Peter Pan* to Johnny Depp's starring role in Disney's recent blockbuster, *Pirates of the Caribbean,* piracy is indelibly linked to a black flag with the skull and crossbones and a pirate ship drawn up in a sandy cove, resting beneath waving palm trees and a blue sky. Many aspects of popular culture bear the stamp of the Caribbean's piratical past, although the historical referent has faded from memory. Such is the case with Captain Morgan's rum, named after the Welsh pirate (or privateer, depending on your point of view) Henry Morgan, who burned down the city of Panama in 1670 and was later granted a title of nobility by the English Crown.[1]

Move the word "pirate" to the Mediterranean, and the historical associations fall away. If anything comes to mind at all, it is likely to be the Barbary pirates, because of the Barbary Wars pursued by the fledgling American republic against the North African states in the early nineteenth century. The line "to the shores of Tripoli" in the Marine Hymn derives from the experience of these two wars (1801–5 and 1815). Yet the Barbary pirates were just one aspect of the much larger phenomenon of Mediterranean piracy. In many ways, Mediterranean pirates were the local expression of a worldwide phenomenon. In other respects they were quite distinct.

Like their Caribbean counterparts, these pirates flourished in the seventeenth century. Both were part of a global upsurge in violence at sea that was triggered by the discovery of the New World and the rise of the new maritime powers of England, Holland, and to a lesser extent France, all seeking to challenge Spanish wealth and Spanish power, both in Europe and overseas. These new conflicts spread across the globe, not just to the New World but to the far reaches of the Indian Ocean as well. It was, after all, the seizure of the Portuguese carack *Santa Catarina* off the coast of Singapore in 1603 by the Dutch admiral Jacob Heemskerck that led eventually to Hugo Grotius's famous commentary *Mare Liberum*, or *The Freedom of the Seas*, which remains one of the classic texts of international law.[2]

Although they share the seventeenth century in common, the trajectory of piracy in each international theater was distinct. Nevertheless, the coincidence of dates between the Caribbean and the Mediterranean is remarkable. In 1564 the French were the first to establish a non-Spanish port in the Caribbean, Fort Caroline, near today's Jacksonville in Florida. It was the first successful incursion into territory that Spain fought desperately but in vain to keep to itself. The French would be followed by the Dutch and the English, all of them after the prize of the great convoys of Spanish silver that sailed through the Caribbean on their way home to Seville. During periods of declared war the attack on Spanish wealth took the form of privateering as part of the formal hostilities; in peacetime pirates operated throughout the theater of the Spanish Main.

In the Mediterranean, the great age of piracy began less than a decade later, in 1571, immediately following the Ottoman defeat at Lepanto (today's Navpaktos, in Greece). European pirates took advantage of Ottoman naval weakness and flooded into the eastern Mediterranean. In the western Mediterranean the three Ottoman provinces of Tripoli, Tunis, and Algiers similarly benefited from declining Ottoman control and began to attack European shipping, both in the Mediterranean and along the Atlantic coastline.

Piracy flourished in the Caribbean throughout the seventeenth century, and even intensified during the period 1660–1720, known across the globe as the golden age of piracy.[3] Yet by the eighteenth century the tide was turning against the pirates. European governments, wealthier and better organized, were less and less inclined to turn to pirates for manpower and maritime expertise during wartime and more able to chase them down during peacetime. After 1720 the numbers dropped sharply; the British Royal Navy, based in Port Royal, Jamaica (the setting of *Pirates of the Caribbean*), was particularly adept at patrolling the seas.[4]

The end of piracy in the Mediterranean was more gradual. The numbers dwindled dramatically throughout the eighteenth century, for reasons that are still the subject of some dispute, but piracy continued. In the end, it would take the Napoleonic invasion of Malta, a great center of piracy, in 1798 and Lord Exmouth's bombardment of Algiers in 1816 to finally defeat Mediterranean piracy.

After the Ottoman defeat at Lepanto in 1571, both the Ottomans and the Hapsburgs turned their attention and their navies away from the Mediterranean, and violent adventurers moved in to fill the power vacuum. Older commercial centers such as Barcelona, Genoa, and Venice stagnated, while the cities that lived off stolen goods—Valletta and Livorno on the Christian side and the North African trio of Tripoli, Algiers, and Tunis on the Muslim side—saw their populations soar. The population clinging to the barren rock of Malta, for example, almost doubled between 1590 and 1670, from 32,000 to 60,000.[5] On the Italian peninsula, the Medici frontier settlement of Livorno almost quadrupled in size, from less than 1,000 in 1591 to 3,700 just ten years later. By 1622 its population had passed the 10,000 mark.[6] Algiers, the capital of Muslim piracy, grew to a spectacular 100,000 in 1650 from around 60,000 at the end of the sixteenth century.[7]

In the western Mediterranean, North African pirates preyed on northern European shipping heading for the Ottoman Empire, as well as raiding the Spanish and Italian coastlines. After hauling their goods back home, merchants from Livorno eagerly waited to buy up the goods stolen from fellow Christians. The combined efforts of the North Africans and the Livornesi made Livorno the contraband capital of the Mediterranean.

Further east, Western pirates, mostly Catholic but English as well, poured into the Aegean and the Levant and rendered conditions at the watery center of the Ottoman Empire far more precarious than they had been in the sixteenth century, when the imperial navy had effectively provided security. One scholar of the seventeenth century speaks of a "wave of crusader-like enthusiasm" on the part of the Knights of St. John, the Knights of St. Stephen, and the Spanish viceroyalty of southern Italy.[8] Small fry set up shop for themselves in the Aegean islands, while the rich Ottoman convoy that sailed between Alexandria and Istanbul was reserved for the well-funded expeditions of the knightly orders.

Piracy is often viewed as the defining feature of the seventeenth-century Mediterranean. Two other broad developments have received less attention, or at least their connection to piracy has not been considered. First, the Catholic Church began to take a far more active role in the eastern Mediterranean, largely as a result of the Counter-Reformation but also because France, fast replacing Venice as the most important Catholic power in the Ottoman Empire, was more willing to work closely with the Church than Venice had been. Second, the strong ties between at least a segment of the Greek mercantile community and the city of Venice began to fray, as Venice lost more territory in the East and lost its attraction as a place of settlement. Taken together, these three altered circumstances—piracy, the new interest of the papacy in the eastern Mediterranean, and the fraying of the tie between Venice and the Greek Orthodox community—all pushed in the same direction, namely, toward the increased importance of religion and religiously based networks as merchants were forced to look for new ways to protect their commercial endeavors. I want to emphasize the experimental aspect of this search. Greek merchants claimed protection based on their identity as Christians (both Orthodox and Catholic), but it was not clear just what this entitled them to, nor was it obvious how one's religious affiliation could be determined. Unlike Ottoman or Venetian subjecthood, which, despite some ambiguities, was a legal status negotiated between two states, it was the merchants themselves who tried to construct some sort of protective Christian blanket for their own benefit. The legitimacy of their endeavor was profoundly contested.

Christian Pirate Cities and the New International Order

The relationship between the Ottoman Empire and the flourishing capitals of Christian piracy, Livorno and Valletta, was distinctly different from that which existed between the Ottomans and the two great centers of sixteenth-century commerce, Venice and Ancona. Let us start with the Medici capital.

The seventeenth century is the century of Livorno. The city emerged as the ideal port of call in the Mediterranean for ships on their way to and from the Levant. In so doing, it surged ahead of the Italian ports that had prospered in the sixteenth century, especially Venice and Ancona. The latter's moment as a crossroads between East and West proved to be a brief one; by the end of the century it had once again sunk into relative insignificance. Its good fortune had been the result of temporary political circumstances rather than of anything intrinsic to Ancona.[9] The history of Venice in the seventeenth century is a much more complex one. Historians no longer take an apocalyptic view of the city's fortunes in that century. But the city's days as the vital link between Europe and the Near East were fast coming to a close, as the Venetians began to invest in agriculture and industry on the mainland and as other ports, most notably Livorno, did a better job at attracting merchants, particularly the English.[10]

To move from Venice and Ancona to Livorno is not just to travel from the Adriatic to the Ligurian Sea. It is also to move from one type of commercial regime to another. Like Ancona and Venice, the Tuscan port was eager to attract merchants from around the Mediterranean and beyond. But fundamental differences distinguished Livorno from its sixteenth-century predecessors. First, its relationship to the Ottoman Empire was distinctly more hostile. Second, it was a city that was deeply implicated in the corsairing economy that developed in the seventeenth-century Mediterranean. It boasted a corsairing order of its own, the Knights of St. Stephen, which routinely cruised the eastern Mediterraean in search of infidels and their goods. It was also a market for the booty the North African corsairs seized from Christian ships. Merchants operating out of Livorno sailed to Tripoli or to Algiers to buy up the stolen goods, then returned to Livorno to sell them for a handsome profit.

Despite this willingness to do business (or perhaps because of it), the city's ideological stance toward the Muslim world was deeply antagonistic. The first thing travelers saw when they sailed into the port was a representation of enslaved Muslims. This large sculpture, dedicated to Ferdinand I, was known popularly as the Monumento dei Quattro Mori, or Monument of the Four Moors.[11] It was built by one Giovanni Bandini in 1595. The bronze figures of the Moors were added by Pietro Tacca between 1623 and 1626 to commemorate Ferdinand's success in routing North African pirates.[12] Merchants of the time often remarked on the

FIGURE 3.1. The Statue of the Four Moors still stands in Livorno today.

statue. The English merchant John Evelyn sailed into Livorno in 1644 and exclaimed,

> Just before the sea is an ample Piazza for the Market, where are erected those incomparable Statues, with the fowre slaves of Copper much exceeding the life for proportion; and in the judgement of most Artists one of the best pieces of modern Worke that was ever don.[13]

Livorno was a city of the seventeenth century in two ways, one concrete and the other metaphorical. It was a fast-growing port that became an essential way station for the English and the Dutch on the way to the Levant. It was also a symbol of a new age of violence, as corsairs both Muslim and Christian filled the vacuum that had been created by the retreat of the Ottoman and the Hapsburg fleets from the Mediterranean.

The Medici Creation

Livorno grew rapidly in the seventeenth century, and its growth attracted attention. In 1622, when its population passed the 10,000 mark, five foreign consulates had been settled in the city for more than a decade.[14] Between 1633 and 1642 the population went up by another 27 percent.[15] Writing around 1630, the English merchant Thomas Mun said, "within these thirty years the trade of Leghorn is much encreased, that of a poor little town (as my self knew it) it is now become a fair and strong City, being one of the most famous places of trade in all Christendom."[16]

The city's spectacular growth was the product of several factors. The Medicis were able to bring political stability to Tuscany early in the sixteenth century after a long period of turbulence. On August 12, 1530, the Spanish imperial army put an end to the independent Republic of Florence. Charles V came to an agreement with Pope Clement VII, the Medici pope, that henceforth the latter's family would rule in Florence.[17] With the Medici assumption of power, Livorno began the long ascent to its position as a major port in the Mediterranean. Prior to this time the city's development had been stymied by the constant wars between the Republic of Florence and its neighbors, particularly Pisa.[18]

The long-ruling Cosimo I (1537–74) set about the business of improving the city's port, a goal that had always eluded the Florentines, and his successors followed suit. A new customs house and a new arsenal were built in the 1540s. New jetties were added in 1569. In 1590 a new fort went up in just five months, along with a deep-water dock for the great sailing ships. Various other engineering projects were taken on to ease the difficult entrance to the Arno river; by the seventeenth century Livorno was the most modern and the best-equipped port in the Mediterranean.[19]

The new city became the center of English commerce in the Levant. English ships began stopping at Livorno as soon as trade with Italy revived, toward the end of the sixteenth century. When war broke out between France and Spain in the mid-1620s, the English preference for Livorno was sealed.[20]

The port was very conveniently positioned for ships coming into the Mediterranean from the north, much more so than Ancona or Venice. It was a city where English ships could take on provisions and carry out necessary maintenance and repair work and where English merchants would find a ready market for their goods. Having sold their goods for Spanish pieces of eight, the merchants could now venture further east, where these coins were much in demand.[21] In 1667 the city was described as "the port or the warehouse of all English commerce in the Levant."[22]

More than anything else, however, the Medicis succeeded in their creation because of the liberality of their regime. They declared a free port, free movement of goods, and extremely low customs duties.[23] It was cheaper to unload goods in Livorno and send them on to Venice than to unload them directly in the latter city.[24] Goods that were intended for reexport could be stored in one of the port's many warehouses free of charge.

The government's enlightened policy was not limited to economic incentives narrowly defined. Livorno's renown, both then and in the historiography, was due more to the very liberal terms of settlement that were offered to all the merchant communities of the Mediterranean. In the words of one historian, "The Medici were tireless in seeking to attract people, ships and capital to Livorno."[25] In 1548 Cosimo I issued a general invitation "to any subject of any country" to settle in Livorno.[26] But it is Ferdinand I (1587–1609) whose name is most associated with the port's embrace of tolerance. His fame is due to the fact that it was Ferdinand who issued the famous privileges, known as *La Livornina*, which granted extraordinarily liberal terms of settlement to foreign, and especially Jewish, merchants. In the competition among the Italian ports to attract the Jewish merchants of the Iberian diaspora, Livorno was by far the most liberal in the terms it was willing to grant.

In two charters dated 1591 and 1593, Ferdinand invited "all you merchants of any nation" to settle in Pisa and in Livorno, where they would enjoy an astonishing array of privileges: freedom of trade, tax exemptions, good housing, storage facilities, and a relative freedom of religion.[27] These privileges, moreover, were to remain in effect for twenty-five years and were subject to automatic renewal for another twenty-five unless notice was given five years in advance.[28]

The liberality of the Livornina is immediately apparent when we compare the treatment of Jews in Livorno to the terms offered to the Jews of Venice. The Venetian charter of 1589, radical as it was for Venice, was good for only ten years. The Jewish merchants of Venice were restricted to wholesale importation and exportation, while the Jews of Livorno were given the same rights as Christian merchant citizens of Florence and Pisa (only the trade in second-hand goods was forbidden to them). Jews in Livorno could purchase real estate, whereas they could not in Venice, and so on.[29] All of these measures made Livorno a very welcoming place for the Jews; the Jewish nation "almost came to see in Ferdinand I the desired Messiah and to see in Livorno another Jerusalem."[30]

Little wonder, then, that the city's history is often told within the framework of increasing religious toleration. Scholars of early modern Jewry consistently emphasize this aspect of the city's history. Bejamin Ravid, for example, has argued that the generous terms granted to the Jews in Livorno anticipated Jewish emancipation later on in Holland, England, and southern France.[31] More general histories of Livorno echo the same theme. A recent study of the city described it in this way:

> The port, which offered both provisioning and ship repair, also boasted a city which, in a climate of religious tolerance, favored the settlement of merchants, including non-Catholic as well as merchants of the Jewish and Armenian diasporas. Thanks to their vast networks, these merchants could ensure connections with both Amsterdam and the Islamic world.[32]

This description, written in 1997, expresses much the same sentiment as the judgment of the economic historian J. M. Kulischer, writing forty years ago. Livorno was "the only place in Italy where Muslims, Jews, English, Dutch and Armenians could settle."[33]

These policies, and the success they created for a new Mediterranean emporium, have accounted for most of the attention the city has received from historians.[34] The story that historians have told is not incorrect. But it is, I think, incomplete in the sense that it considers Livorno exclusively from the point of view of European history. In the savage world of early modern Europe—torn by the Wars of Religion, the Thirty Years' War, and religious persecution in Spain and Portugal—Livorno's achievements were indeed remarkable. And the treatment of the Jews has always been an important benchmark in European history.

Livorno and the Age of Little Wars

If we consider Livorno in its Mediterranean context, then things look rather different. Ferdinand I came to power in 1587. His rule, then, roughly coincided with the beginning of what Braudel has called "the secondary and minor forms" of war.[35] The epic clash between two empires, the Spanish and the Ottoman, that had marked the entire sixteenth century came to an end as the two enemies disengaged after Lepanto. What followed was a more amorphous phase, lasting over a century, in the long struggle between the Christian and Muslim halves of the sea. Lesser actors—corsairs and pirates—swarmed into the newly vacated waters of the Mediterranean, using the language of religion to justify a wide range of hostile acts. The relationship between these individuals and existing states was uncertain, sometimes deliberately so, and the net effect was to undercut the claims of state sovereignty in the organization of commercial life in the Mediterranean. The port of Livorno bore the stamp of this historical moment.

In the medieval period Pisa, not Livorno, had been the port of Tuscany. The Italian city-states—Venice, Genoa, and Pisa—rose to prosperity through their trade with the eastern Mediterranean and the Muslim world, and Pisa was no different. Pisa's 1157 agreement with Tunis is the earliest surviving agreement establishing trade between North Africa and the Italian peninsula. Moving further east, Pisans were active participants in the Crusades—the first patriarch of Jerusalem was a Pisan—and used that opportunity to found a number of merchant colonies in the East. On a more peaceful note, the Byzantine emperor granted them an establishment in Constantinople in 1111 as well as favorable tariffs; at mid-century they signed a treaty with the Fatimid caliphate of Egypt.[36] Under Florentine rule, which commenced in 1406, the city continued its ties to the East. The Florentines signed a new commercial agreement

with the Ottoman Turks in 1455, just two years after the latter had conquered the Byzantine capital.[37] These capitulations were renewed in 1513,
less then twenty years before Spanish troops marched into Florence.

Therefore, while the harbor of Livorno was new (Porto Pisano, Pisa's
port in the medieval period, was now silted up), the whole Medici project was a self-conscious attempt to revive Tuscan seapower. Not surprisingly, the question of Livorno's relationship to the Ottoman Empire soon
raised its head. What is surprising is how little attention this aspect of
the city's history has received. No doubt this is due in part to the fact that
the attempt to establish diplomatic relations was unsuccessful. Livorno's
fame and achievement ultimately lay elsewhere. But the attempt to revive at least part of Tuscany's medieval heritage, and the reasons for its
failure, provide a window onto the changes that separate the early modern Mediterranean from its medieval past.

Spain, with its implacable hostility toward the Ottoman Empire,
brought Tuscany's ancient ties to the East to a temporary halt when Spanish troops marched into Florence in 1530.[38] The end of formal relations
with the East was part of the dramatic realignment of Mediterranean affairs under the pressure of the intense Ottoman-Spanish rivalry. But old
orientations are not so easily dispensed with. In 1574 the new grand duke,
Francis I, moved to renew the capitulations the Florentines had signed
with Mehmet the Conqueror more than a century before. He sent his
emissary, Lodovico Canacci, with instructions to renew the old capitulations. He did request, however, the addition of one new article. He hoped
the sultan would agree that "neither Florentine merchants nor their
things be molested on account of wars of the Grand Duke of Tuscany or
any other Christian Prince. Neither on account of any gallies or other
ships of the Grand Duke or of his Order of the Knights of St. Stephen because such things are relevant to princes and not to merchants."[39]

Canacci's mission seems to have come to naught, and the next we
hear of any contact is a letter sent by an Ottoman dragoman to the grand
duke in 1575, expressing continued interest in an agreement with the
Tuscan state. Beyond that, the contents of the letter are not known, but
the subject of the Knights of St. Stephen must have come up again. In
1574 the grand duke had sought to distinguish between the actions of a
government and the commerce of its private citizens. Now he tried a
different tack. In two letters written in 1577, the grand duke sought to

persuade the sultan that since individuals entered the order as dependents of the pope or of the king of Spain, they should not be considered Tuscan subjects. In reply, the sultan's representative shared his suspicion that the gallies of the order did, in fact, belong to the grand duke. The Tuscan reply, somewhat inconsistent with what had been said before, was an attempt at compromise: the grand duke would not permit the knights to engage in the *corso* against Ottoman merchant ships, but he could not be held responsible for damage caused by the knights when in the service of the pope or the Spanish king.[40] This was also unacceptable to the Ottomans, but negotiations continued nevertheless.

Events conspired, however, to put an end to Ottoman-Tuscan talks in 1578. In October, as talks continued between the sultan and the grand duke, twenty-five ransomed slaves stepped off the boat in the harbor of Pera in Istanbul. Muslims all, they had been seized by the Knights of St. Stephen and ransomed in Ancona. They were vociferously opposed to the negotiations and insisted that the knights' gallies did, in fact, belong to the Grand Duke of Tuscany. The sultan broke off negotiations.

The Tuscans were fuming. They were certain that Venetian gold was behind the protest of the ransomed slaves. It is true that both France and Venice, viewing Tuscany as a potential commercial rival, were happy to see the talks break down. Nevertheless, the Knights of St. Stephen created the situation at the root of the matter when they seized these twenty-five individuals. Who were the knights? And how does their history fit into the history of the free port of Livorno?

The Knights of St. Stephen

The Medici attempt to revive Tuscan seapower was not limited to the creation of the port of Livorno. Cosimo I also sought to develop his own fleet, for both commercial and military purposes. In addition to the very real Ottoman threat to the Italian coastline, he was also aware of the new importance of the Mediterranean in international politics. He wanted Tuscany to have a role in a vast political, diplomatic, and military game of international dimensions.[41]

Cosimo personally drew up a *Memoria* in which he proposed, among other things, the creation of a military-knightly order styled on the

Knights of St. John on Malta. Its raison d'être would be to fight "per la fede di Cristo."[42] The Order of the Knights of St. Stephen was authorized by the papacy in a brief dated October 1, 1561. In a solemn ceremony held at Pisa the following year, Cosimo I became the first grand master of the order.

Given that Cosimo created a naval force in the service of the Tuscan state at the same time (although in practice it was difficult to distinguish between the two), the question arises as to why he established the knightly order as well.[43] First of all, the *corso* was flourishing at this time, and the Medici state certainly did not want to be left on the sidelines. By creating a formally legitimate navy—and both the knights and the navy answered to him—he provided himself with some diplomatic cover should the need arise.[44] Second, the Knights of Santo Stefano were naval power on the cheap. Aspiring knights were expected to make financial contributions and, after a number of years in the order they would be eligible to enter in the nobility."[45]

Finally, it was a jealous age. Cosimo had to be careful about even appearing to challenge Spanish power over Tuscany. We can see this concern to placate Spain during the negotiations between the Ottomans and the Tuscans in 1570s. He neatly rolled trade into security issues. These new capitulations, he wrote, were not so much for the benefit of his own population. Rather, through trade he would be able to secure information on the plans and designs of the enemy, information he would, of course, immediately pass on to His Majesty. Therefore he asked that the ships of the grand duke be allowed to travel freely with all merchandise, as did the ships of Venice, without being stopped by the Spanish navy.

Similarly, an expansion of Tuscan naval power was less likely to alarm Spain if it could be couched in the rhetoric of crusade. Even as the grand duke was corresponding with the sultan and distancing himself from the Knights of St. Stephen he was writing to Spain, saying he had decided to resume trade with the "Turks," but that his new order would be available for any and all needs of Christendom and would not abandon the corso.

Ironically, the grand dukes used the rhetoric of Christian-Muslim enmity to justify both initiatives—trade and the corso—even though they were diametrically opposed in their intentions.

The Knights of St. Stephen soon became famous as avid and violent practitioners of the corso, trailing only the Knights of St. John in their attacks on Mediterranean shipping both east and west. Alberto Tenenti's study of piratical attacks on Venice toward the end of the sixteenth century provides many such examples, and countless others could be presented from a wide variety of sources. Joint ventures with the Maltese were common; in 1577 Francis I actually reached a formal agreement with the grand master to combine their forces in periodic excursions into the Levant.[46]

The expeditions to the eastern Mediterranean and North Africa were known as cruises. One such cruise, an account of which is preserved in a report to the grand duke, left Messina toward the end of April 1597. In the month of May alone they reported the following encounters. Sailing in an area between Cyprus and the southern coast of Anatolia they captured two vessels on May 10. The first, manned by Muslims, was laden with corn; the second was a Greek boat carrying timber. They sank both boats. They seized another boat carrying timber on the 14th. The crew was armed, and in the struggle that ensued three knights were killed, while the other side lost fourteen. More captures came on May 15, 17, and 20; all three ships were heading north, carrying rice from Damietta in Egypt. On May 20 another ship carrying timber was also seized. On the 21st they caught up with two vessels, one quite large and carrying a cargo of flax, rice, and spices. They had to fight to overpower the other ship, and the Tuscans killed fifteen of the enemy. Badly in need of water, they arrived in Crete on May 25 and stayed there for the remainder of the month. In every instance Muslims and Jews were seized as slaves, in addition to the cargo, and by the time they sailed back into the port of Livorno, forty-two days later, the total prize was estimated at 120,000 crowns.[47]

Histories of Livorno do not neglect to mention the crusading Order of the Knights of St. Stephen that operated out of the port. Nor do they ignore the larger theme of piracy—to the contrary. The historiography has clearly established the intimate ties between the North African states, which also practiced corso, and the new port. Goods seized by the North Africans, in operations similar to the one just narrated for the Knights of St. Stephen, were taken back to the markets of Tunis, Algiers, and Tripoli. There European merchants bought them up and sailed directly to Livorno with their cargo, the plundered goods of Christian ships. Everyone was well aware of the doubtful provenance of much of the merchandise for sale in Livorno.[48]

And yet the story of the free port and the story of the port of the knights tend to be told separately. As a result, the full measure of Livorno's contradictions has not yet been taken. Let us return to the negotiations between the grand duke and the sultan in the mid-1570s. The audacity of asking for Tuscan commercial privileges in the Ottoman Empire when Livorno, the port of Tuscany, was the home base of the Knights of St. Stephen is truly breathtaking. The Italian scholar Sergio Camerani, writing more than sixty years ago, remarked rather drily that it was "a curious way to understand international relations."[49] Curious indeed, but it was also entirely characteristic of the age. The Medici grand dukes were not only the rulers of a Spanish vassal state. They were also full participants in a great game of entrepreneurial violence that undercut the power of the state, even though particular individuals within the state drew enormous benefit from their association with the raiding economy.

In the cruise related above, where the knights returned with a prize worth 120,000 crowns, they sailed into port "with a fine volley from their guns and many flags flying from prow to stern, in good order and high spirits."[50] Such an open celebration suggests the extent to which Livorno—like Valletta, Algiers, and Tripoli—was a city of pirates. The same could never be said of the staid gentlemen of Venice who for centuries had ruled the seas from their city on the lagoon.

Livorno and Ottoman Merchants

The absence of diplomatic relations between the Medicis and the Ottoman Empire, combined with the corsairing spirit that animated Livorno, served to render meaningless the term "Ottoman merchant," a category that had enjoyed real legal and diplomatic content, despite some ambiguities, in Ancona and Venice.[51] Instead, it was religious identity—as a Muslim, a Jew, or a Christian—that determined one's experience with both the city and its corsairing order, the Knights of St. Stephen.

The extremely favorable terms of settlement granted to the Jews in Livorno have been the topic of ongoing scholarly interest. However, little attention has been paid to the fact that the privileges Ferdinand I granted decoupled the Jews from Ottoman sovereignty. All Jews, regardless of origin, were invited to settle in Livorno, whereas in Venice the first concessions made were specifically to Levantine Jews, that is, Jews who were Ottoman subjects.[52] In Livorno, then, we see the privileging of religion over subjecthood that would be so characteristic of the seventeenth century.

The welcome mat was not similarly extended to all merchants from the East. Muslim settlement, for all intents and purposes, was nonexistent, for understandable reasons. Ferdinand, the same man who granted the Livornina privileges to the Jews, also had a *bagno* or barracks built outside the city walls in 1605 to house all the Muslim slaves; like the Statue of the Four Moors, it became something of an attraction for tourists passing through.[53] Livorno had the highest percentage of Muslim slaves of any city in Italy, an amazing 20 percent of the population in 1601 and a still very high 10 percent in 1622.[54]

Something of the fraught atmosphere in Livorno is conveyed by an early eighteenth-century account left by a Redemptionist Father returning to the city from a mission in Tunis just as a shipload of captured Muslims was brought in. Among them, he recounts, some Christians in the city who had been enslaved in North Africa recognized their former masters. Some jeered over the Muslims' sudden turn of fortune, but others "were filled with fear at the sight of their old masters. They could not believe that they were free."[55]

Greek Orthodox settlement in Livorno, in this case by its presence rather than its absence, also testifies to the new prominence of religion in the international relations of the Mediterranean. The Greeks came not as Ottoman or Venetian subjects but as Christians, and they came through private networks. Early on, most settlers came from areas of the Greek world that were under Venetian control, but as time went on the majority were Ottoman subjects. There is no evidence that either the grand dukes or the Catholic Church ever remarked on this aspect of the community.[56]

Their arrival was tied to the foundation of the Knights of St. Stephen and the subsequent need for maritime labor of all kinds. In 1564, just three years after the founding of the order, Cosimo I invited Greeks to settle in his new city. The invitation went out through a Basilian monk named Dionisio Paleologo, and sailors, pilots, bombadiers, and caulkers began to stream in.[57]

Recognition "como corpo nazionale" came in 1589 with the nomination of a "protettore della nazione greca," who was none other than the governor of Livorno himself, one Manoli Volterra of (Venetian-held) Zakynthos.[58] In the same year (and before those granted to the Jews) privileges were granted to Greeks currently residing in Livorno, as well as to those who might settle there in the future.[59] Just a few short years later, in 1601, they received permission to build a new church, Santissima Annunziata, which would become the cultural and religious anchor of the Greek community.[60]

Despite the welcoming attitude of a series of grand dukes, the Greek community had to endure a certain amount of harassment from the Catholic authorities, just as they had in Ancona and in Venice. The Inquisition in Pisa investigated Santissima Annunziata on numerous occasions. Officially, the Greek Church was in communion with Rome, but the Inquisition nursed its suspicions that the community was filled with schismatics and heterodoxy. In the 1620s the Inquisition actually lodged a formal accusation against "The Greeks who reside in Livorno, who are not only schismatics but heretics as well. They live as such and thus cause great scandal and damage to the Catholic Italians."[61]

The trial that followed the accusation saw a parade of members of the Greek community—sailors, sea captains, and others—come through the offices of the Inquisition to answer questions about the rite followed in the Church, the books used, and the perennial question of the primacy of Rome.[62] The Inquisition launched another trial in 1653, and a report in 1699 underlined "grave abuses," of this Greek Church and complained about their priests, who were "barely Catholic," and their refusal to convert to the Gregorian calendar.[63] As late as 1757 another document divided the community into Orthodox (those who were in communion with Rome) and Heterodox (those who were not). Throughout, the Catholic Church was uneasy about the Greek community's ties to the East; it did not like the fact that the vast majority of the clergy came from the Levant, nor did it appreciate the community's insistence that its holy oil come from Jerusalem rather than from the archbishop of Pisa, as was required, at least in the eyes of the Roman Church. We shall see, later on, that suspicion hovered over Christian business practices as well, for similar although not identical reasons. Just as the Inquisition in Pisa never managed to satisfy itself that the Greeks were truly obedient to Rome, so too those who were called on to rule in commercial disputes used the Greek location in the eastern Mediterranean to see a Muslim behind every purported "Christian" business transaction.

Malta: Bulwark of Christianity

A recent, and exhaustive, study of Malta in the early modern period states flatly, "From the beginning of the seventeenth century Malta became a veritable corsair-state and was without a doubt the benchmark for Christian corsairing, just as Algiers and Tunis symbolized Barbary corsairing."[64] As such, Malta entered a period of tremendous growth in the seventeenth century, all of it fueled by the tremendous expansion of the *corso*. The population hardly budged throughout the course of the sixteenth century, from 28,500 in 1535 (five years after the knights took up residence on the island) to 29,354 in 1590.[65] A series of calamities— famine and the plague—reduced the population by almost 8,000 souls in the following five years, but after that it began an ascent that would continue through the seventeenth century. By 1670 the population had reached 60,000, although just five years later the plague reduced it by 11,000.[66]

The Malta of the knights was distinguished by the public and official character of the Christian *corso*, as well as by the relative independence of the knights in its pursuit.[67] Unlike the Knights of St. Stephen in Livorno, who were subsumed under the authority of the Medici princes, the knights ran Malta as they saw fit, and did not hesitate to proclaim the island as the new center of the ongoing crusade against Islam, now expressed as maritime raids along the North African coastline and deep into the heart of the Levant "*a danno di infideli.*"[68]

In a structure again unique to Malta, there was both a public and a private corso on the island. The public corso was carried out by ships belonging to the order itself. A squadron of galleys, headed up by a knight or knights, would depart Malta with specific orders as to where it was going and what it was supposed to be doing. All the proceeds of the *caravane*, as these official cruises were known, were to be turned over to the treasury of the order. The reward for those who participated, in other words, was not material in nature but rather was the more eternal gift of honor and glory, not money. In the sixteenth century those who aspired to be a Knight Hospitaller were obliged to go on three caravans, each one lasting no less than six months. The number required went up to four in the following century. Having completed his two years of naval service, the knight was then entitled to appointment as the head of a commanderie.[69]

These cruises enjoyed a high profile in Europe. Pamphlets, sheets, and short reports trumpeted the knights' successes, singling out the booty and the prizes that had been won.[70]

The knights increased the number of their own galleys from five in 1596 to six in 1628 and then to seven in 1651.[71] When we consider that each galley required between 180 and 200 rowers or *galeotti*, we can understand 'the tremendous investment the order was making.[72] Equally impressive is the fact that there were more knights on the small and stony island of Malta than there had been in Rhodes; the numbers went from roughly 300 to 600.[73]

More remarkable than that, however, was the flowering of a parallel private corso, which went from being a peripheral activity to the dominant enterprise in Malta. Basing ourselves on the mandatory patents that were issued every time a ship or ships left to pursue the *corso*, the public *corso* accounted for almost half the departures between 1575 and 1605. That percentage dropped to just 27 percent over the course of the next thirty years.[74] This dramatic change, however, does not mean that the knights retreated from the corso. Knightly participation in the private corso was very significant, as we shall see. What distinguished the public from the private corso was that in the latter case the ships belonged to private owners, not to the order, who sailed under their own names. In addition, they had to turn only over a certain percentage of their gains to the public treasury; this was crusade for profit as well as glory, and it attracted not only the Maltese but Christians from across the Mediterranean world. Between 1605 and 1635 nearly four hundred patents were issued, more than double the number issued in the previous thirty years.[75] The number of ships actually leaving was far higher than four hundred, since one patent could cover any number of ships.[76]

The knights participated in the private corso as backers. Ironically enough, it was a rare knight who was a good sailor; they much preferred to apply for the patent and to provide a well-armed ship, which they would then turn over to others to sail for them.[77] In the Maltese context these investors were known as "armateurs," and it was for their benefit that new efforts to control the private corso were made at the beginning of the seventeenth century.

The number of men pouring into the island to pursue the corso was such that the grand master felt the need to establish a new tribunal, the *Tribunale degli Armamenti* or *Magistrato degli Armamenti*, in 1605 in order to more effectively regulate all the activity.[78] The establishment of such a court is very much in keeping with the public and official character of the *corso* mentioned above. A list of the new tribunal's Statutes and Ordinances (of which much more shortly) was prefaced by an introductory paragraph that makes clear how the new popularity of the corso was threatening order on the island, at least in the eyes of the knights.

The grand master and his council, it began, had gathered to consider the matter of the corso or the armamenti. Their first concern was that the very number of individuals pursuing the corso was endangering the proper provisioning of the island. Not only were they buying up large quantities of provisions and war materiel, they were also doing it "in secret," and thus threatening not only the people of Malta but the Public Treasury.

On the other hand, it continued, to prohibit the corso would be to deprive both ordinary subjects and members of the order of the opportunity to maintain their seafaring skills. This was something the island had always been known for and indeed that had been encouraged by the granting of certain concessions to those who were willing to arm ships for the corso. The aim was to attract as many "bellicose" people to the island as possible to best pursue maritime warfare.

Bearing these things in mind, the introduction continued, the grand master and his council had decided to draw up certain rules that would both encourage war against "the enemies of our Christian name" and at the same time get rid of certain "abuses" and "inconveniences" that have caused harm. These rules also aimed to put an end to the lawsuits that had become so common. The introduction finished on a hopeful note: "With these rules, each person will have what belongs to him, without deception and confusion."[79]

Despite its commitment to corsairing, Livorno had something of a split personality. The Medici dukes eagerly threw themselves into the great game of religiously justified violence at sea, but at the same time they were famously tolerant toward the Jews, and they sheltered the Greek community, more or less, from the power of the Inquisition.

No such ambiguity prevailed at Malta. The knights, of course, never made any attempt to establish diplomatic relations with the Ottoman Empire; that would have been antithetical to their raison d'être. As it was, the island's very name was synonymous with the horrors of slavery for Muslims across the Mediterranean world; Malta had the highest number of Muslim slaves, as a percentage of the population, of any country in Europe.[80] For two long centuries, a huge community of about 10,000 Muslim slaves suffered through slavery in the *bagni* of Malta.[81] When on occasion it was decided to permit Muslim or Jewish merchants to stop on the island—for reasons linked to the public good, such as famine—the Inquisitor had to give his permission, and that only after a pledge that while in Malta they would wear a sign to distinguish themselves from Christians.[82] If they arrived on the island by accident, without prior permission, they were promptly enslaved.[83]

Also unlike Livorno, the burgeoning city of Valletta was not a pole of attraction for Greek merchants and seafarers. A small Greek community had departed Rhodes with the knights in 1530, but their already marginal presence on the island dwindled over the course of the seventeenth century. The number of baptisms conducted in Valletta fell from seventy-one between 1610 and 1625 to twenty-one over the next quarter century to just seven between 1675 and 1690.[84] Actual settlement on the island was not, of course, the only possible point of contact between Malta and the Greeks. The relationship between the knights and the Greek world was a complicated one, and the Greeks appear in the historical record in every possible permutation: as captives but also as merchants ransoming slaves; as victims of the knights but also as participants in corsairing ventures; as allies, as enemies, and as something in between. Nevertheless, their experience was distinct from that of Muslims and Jews, who could expect only unremitting hostility from the knights.

The Shrinking Venetian World

Venice's first serious loss of territory to the Ottomans came in 1470, when Mehmet the Conqueror took Negroponte, the large island just off the Greek mainland. During the next war, at the turn of the century, the Venetians lost nearly all their strongholds on the Greek mainland. The Aegean islands went next (during the 1537–40 war), and then the great loss of Cyprus came in 1570. That left only Crete (outside of the Ionian Islands, much farther west, which never came under Ottoman suzerainty), which hung on until the middle of the seventeenth century.

This history is well known. But a little considered consequence of these progressive losses is the following: over the course of the sixteenth and the seventeenth centuries we have the gradual de-internationalization of the Greek merchant community as the majority of Greeks became Ottoman subjects. The implications of this development are vast, but the most important is the following. As discussed earlier, Greek merchants who were Venetian subjects were in a separate and meaningful category, one that distinguished them from those who were Ottoman subjects. One of the benefits of Venetian subjecthood was that Venice would challenge the Maltese over the latter's seizure of the city's subjects' goods. State-to-state diplomacy was a channel for the resolution of these disputes. But the knights and the Ottomans had no such diplomatic relations. Maltese (and Livornese) corsairing concentrated on the eastern Mediterranean after the Ottoman loss at Lepanto. Venice lost Cyprus in 1570, just before the onslaught of Maltese and other Catholic pirates into the eastern Mediterranean. The result was that most Greeks who suffered through a Maltese raid were now Ottoman subjects and could not look to Venice for the restitution of their goods. They had to look elsewhere (as did Muslims and Jews who hoped to ransom themselves). One of these options was the court on Malta, the Tribunale degli Armamenti. The other option was an appeal to Rome itself. Neither one of these options was open to Ottoman Jews or Ottoman Muslims, a clear indication of the new importance of religion in resolving commercial disputes. This change did not come all at once, and of course the Cretans continued to be Venetian subjects, and to turn to Venice for help with the Maltese throughout the first half of the seventeenth century.[85] But the trend was toward the use of networks whose identity was clearly Christian. Greek petitioners in Rome are the focus of chapter seven. But before we consider those petitioners, the new importance of the papacy in the seventeenth-century Mediterranean must be explained.

The Counter-Reformation in the Eastern Mediterranean

The Catholic Counter-Reformation extended the long arm of the papacy into the eastern Mediterranean. In his recent study of eastern Christians and the Vatican during the period of Catholic reform, Bernard Heyberger points out that the sheer amount of documentation in Vatican archives concerning the eastern Mediterranean shows just how much the papacy was thinking about the Christians of the Near East, at a time when one might think that China or America would have been more of a preoccupation.[86] In fact, he argues, the Church was more concerned about the "heretics" and the "schismatics" among eastern Christians than it was about the conversion of "idolaters."[87] Viewed from Rome, the union of the churches, which was how the Vatican thought about the project, was part of the defense of Catholicism and the suppression of heresy and schism that had already produced Protestantism.[88]

The Catholic Church's ambition to bring the Greek Orthodox back into the fold resulted in the establishment of several Counter-Reformation institutions that were particularly important in the subsequent history of the Greeks. The idea for a Greek College in Rome came out of the Council of Trent; it was founded in 1576 under the name of the College of St. Athanasius of Alexandria.[89] It was meant to unite the Orthodox Church with Rome through the rigorous education of Greek students from the East who, it was hoped, would convert to Catholicism and bring their communities with them.[90] Ideally, pupils would begin their instruction at the age of nine or ten and continue on for ten or even fifteen years, gaining their doctorate in philosophy or theology at the end. Not all completed the course, but between 1576 and 1700, which was the time of its greatest flourishing, nearly seven hundred students passed through the doors of the college.[91] Students were drawn from the upper crust of Greek society, and the college produced many celebrated graduates, the most famous of whom was Leon Allatios (Leone Allacci). Born to an Orthodox father on the island of Chios in1587, he rose to become a professor of Greek at the Vatican and scriptor at the Library.[92]

The creation of the Sacra Congregatio de Propaganda Fide in 1622 was also critical in extending and expanding the papacy's presence in the East. The Propaganda was charged with missionizing across the globe, including the eastern Mediterranean.[93] As a result, Catholic priests went out by the score to the Ottoman Empire, where they engaged in missionary work, founding schools and distributing literature intended both to strengthen the faith of those who were already Catholic and to bring the Orthodox over to the Catholic side. As early as 1576 the Roman catechism had been translated into modern Greek, and 12,000 copies were dispatched to the Levant.[94]

French ascendancy at the Ottoman court was absolutely critical in allowing the Propaganda to be so active in Muslim territory. Toward the end of the sixteenth century France emerged as the Ottoman Empire's most important and steadfast ally, a position it would hold for most of the empire's existence. Drawn together by their mutual antipathy to the Hapsburgs, the Ottoman sultans were willing to grant substantial privileges to the French. France for its part used its strong position to simultaneously strengthen the position of Catholics in the empire and establish French patronage over and protection of Ottoman Catholic communities.[95] In a series of agreements, France steadily expanded its role in the internal affairs of the empire. The capitulations of 1569 granted freedom of worship to the French in the empire, along with permission to employ sufficient clergy to make religious services available to all Catholic merchants and diplomats.[96] Seventeenth-century agreements gave French subjects the right to visit Jerusalem and guaranteed the safety of Latin clergy residing in the Holy City.[97] The French ambassador and the various French consuls throughout the port cities of the empire were granted the right to monitor the behavior of Ottoman officials with regard to these and other agreements that were concluded between the French kings and the Ottoman sultans. Given these arrangements, it is no wonder that the Catholic clergy very quickly began turning to French officials for all sorts of matters, including intercession with Ottoman authorities.

France was not just the new protector of Catholicism in the East, it was a rather different sort of patron. The French kings were willing, even

eager, to work closely with the Catholic Church, whereas Venice had always held the Church at arm's length. Part of Venice's attitude derived
from its fierce defense of the republic's autonomy at home. The other
part grew out of its position in the East. Venice ruled over large numbers
of Greek Orthodox, and as the Ottoman armies advanced it grew more
and more concerned to placate its subjects. This dictated that Venice try
to reign in the more zealous representatives of the Catholic Church in
the East. In 1602 a Venetian official newly returned from Crete warned
that the Latin clergy must not be allowed to use their pulpits to speak
against the Greek faith.[98] The French, of course, had no such concerns
and pursued pro-Catholic policies relentlessly. Time and again they
were willing to be conspicuous supporters of initiatives from Rome.

In 1580 Pope Gregory XIII wanted to send his representative, the
bishop of Nona, to Istanbul to gather information on the state of the
Catholic community there.[99] The bishop had trouble with his travel arrangements. The Venetians refused to issue him a safe-conduct, nor
would they allow him to travel with the bailo. Finally, he secured permission from the sultan through the intervention of the authorities in
Dubrovnik.[100] When he finally arrived, none of the Europeans would
meet with him except the French.[101] When the Jesuits returned to Istanbul in 1609 (an earlier effort had come to naught), only French embassy
officials were there to welcome them; the Venetians and the English
stayed away. It was the French who sponsored the Jesuit community in
Istanbul, and they remained their most steadfast patrons.[102] Soon after,
during the reign of the zealous Louis XIII, they sponsored the Capuchin
advance into the East as well.[103] Throughout the seventeenth century the
French ambassador in Istanbul provided a direct link to Rome and
played an active part in supporting the pro-Catholic factions within the
Orthodox patriarchate. Philippe de Harlay, comte de Césy, the king's
ambassador in Istanbul during the 1620s, was also the formal representative of the Propaganda.[104] It is hard to imagine the Venetian bailo being
a paid agent of Rome.

The Catholic push into the eastern Mediterranean, and French protection of this endeavor, has been written about extensively, but the picture we have thus far is still a very partial one. Activities among the
Arabs, particularly in Syria, have received the lion's share of the attention, to the detriment of other areas.[105]

Scholarly interest in the Arab Christians has been driven by twentieth-century concerns. Historians of Arab nationalism, particularly in the Arab world itself, argued for the leading role of Arab Christians in the development of Arab nationalism in the waning decades of the Ottoman Empire.[106] In addition to this narrative, it is a fact that the Vatican's only solid victory in the Levant was scored in the Arab world when the Melkite patriarch of Antioch openly declared in favor of Rome, thus creating a Catholic Melkite church.[107] Given that these breakaway Melkites were a success story, from Rome's point of view anyway, they have been written about extensively. Finally, Syria and Lebanon became French colonies after World War I. Therefore the temptation to see seventeenth-century developments, when missionaries supported by France created a client Catholic community, as a foreshadowing of what happened three centuries later, has been very strong.[108] Thus, within the general interest in Syrian Christians, there has been what can only be called a fascination with the Catholics in particular. The Greek world was never colonized, by France or anyone else, and thus French influence among non-Arab Christians has compelled less interest.

These preoccupations have obscured the extent to which both papal and French efforts were directed at all Ottoman Christians, Arabs and Greeks, Catholics and Orthodox.[109] We have already mentioned the founding of the Greek College in Rome in 1576. In the Ottoman capital there were extensive and ongoing relations between various papal representatives; the Jesuits were particularly prominent in this regard, and the Orthodox patriarchs. In the Greek islands, where Catholicism had traditionally been strong, missionaries established themselves early in the seventeenth century and began offering instruction in Christian doctrine to all and sundry; they were also more than willing to hear confession irrespective of the penitent's religious allegiance.[110] Capuchin missionaries made inroads into the Aegean littoral both east and west in places such as Athens and Smyrna.[111]

The initiatives, then, were wide-ranging and energetic. Nevertheless, in almost every instance they failed in their goal of creating new Catholic communities even as they succeeded in protecting and strengthening existing ones. This failure, however disappointing to Rome, does not mean there is nothing more to say. That would mean evaluating the significance of the Propaganda solely according to the professed goals of those who worked to further its mission. There is an equally important story to be told, and that is how the eastern Christians who were its object used Rome's interest in them for their own purposes.

This brings us to the second characteristic of the existing historiography, which is its overwhelming emphasis on cultural, religious, and intellectual history.[112] This is understandable, given that the concerns of the Propaganda were focused on these areas, both in Rome with the various colleges that were founded and in the Levant. The effect of Jesuit teaching and Jesuit schools on Orthodox theology, the new educational opportunities available to Ottoman Christians, the translation work that was undertaken in Rome—these sorts of topics have received a good deal of attention, particularly when it comes to the relationship between the Greek world and the Vatican. The scholarship on the Arab Christians in particular has greater range.

But telling the story in exclusively religious or cultural terms severely underestimates the impact of the Counter-Reformation in the East. In fact the renewed interest of the Church in both the Catholics and the Orthodox of the eastern Mediterranean spilled over into every area of life, including and especially commerce. When we consider that various missionary houses, as well as other institutions of the Catholic Church, and French consuls were scattered around the Aegean, all under the protection of the French ambassador, and when we add to that the fervent wish of the Church that eastern Catholics remain steadfast in their faith and that the Orthodox submit to the pope, then we can readily see that an entire communication network was set up at the watery heart of the Ottoman Empire. Although the intention in Rome and at the French ambassador's in Istanbul was certainly to reach down and properly catechize the Eastern Christians, Ottoman Christian merchants sailing in these very same waters (both Catholic and Orthodox) turned it around and petitioned French and Catholic authorities for relief from the Maltese corsairs.

They were helped in this by the nature of the missionary endeavor in the field. The missionaries made very few demands of the Orthodox among whom they worked. Worship in common, *communicatio in sacris*, was routine, and the Orthodox could receive communion and take confession from Latin priests without having to convert.[113] In places such as Chios and Istanbul, where the Catholic community was strong, intermarriage was common, and Catholic and Orthodox served as each other's godparents at baptism. The relationship between the Orthodox and Catholic clergy was cordial as well. A Jesuit report from the period observed that "The Orthodox Metropolitan in Smyrna has given his subjects complete freedom to go to our clergy for confession . . . and to our clergy he has given full power to hear confessions in his church both from Greeks and Latins."[114] Looking at the sum total of all these practices of mutual accommodation, it would have been very hard to recognize the schism between the two churches at the local level.[115] Muddying the picture even further was the phenomenon of crypto-Catholicism. Even when individuals did make a formal act of adherence to Rome, they were usually told by the missionaries to continue outwardly in their previous allegiance, receiving communion as before from Orthodox priests.[116] Crypto-Catholicism reached every level of society; high-ranking officials of the Orthodox Church are now known to have sworn a secret allegiance to Rome.[117]

Historians have offered several explanations for the behavior of the Latin missionaries; they suggest a mix of calculation and uncertainty. Certainly the missionaries, and behind them the Vatican, had the very recent successes in Ukraine in mind. There the strategy of secret conversion had worked just as it was supposed to. With the 1595–96 Union of Brest-Litovsk, the hierarchs of the Kievan Church broke with the patriarch of Constantinople and declared their submission to Rome. The Jesuits, who had worked patiently in Ukraine for years before the formal break, were hopeful that the same feat could be accomplished in Istanbul.[118] But it is also the case that from the very beginning the eastern Christians, sometimes referred to as heretics, at other times as schismatics, occupied an ambiguous place in the mission of the Propaganda Fide. A founding document from 1622 stated two goals: to conserve and guard the faith of *"les fidèles,"* that is, the Catholics, and to propagate the faith among the infidels, meaning, in the case of the Levant, the Muslims. The strategy to be adopted toward the Orthodox was never as clear-cut, and this ambiguity is evident in the hesitant response that the Propaganda in Rome gave to missionaries' questions from the field, often turning to the pope for guidance.[119] When it came to Kyrillos Loukaris, the formidable Orthodox patriarch in Istanbul who held his office off and on throughout the 1620s and the 1630s and who made no secret of his Protestant sympathies, the cardinals of the Propaganda could not decide between wooing him and persecuting him.[120]

Whatever the reasons, what is important for our purposes is that missionary interest was in no way limited to Catholics but was extended to all eastern Christians as *potential* Catholics. In addition, the situation just described meant that the Church was either unwilling or unable—probably both—to create certifiably Catholic individuals. Local Christians turned this situation to their advantage and petitioned Catholic authorities on a wide range of issues. And here we see the divergence between the preoccupations of those intent on delivering the message of the Counter-Reformation and those to whom it was addressed. Heresy and schism may have been on the mind of Propaganda, but the Christians living in and around the shores of the eastern Mediterranean wanted help with more mundane problems: they were having business difficulties. Heyberger's study of correspondence between the Propaganda and Arab Christians reveals that, after claims of persecution, attacks suffered while engaged in maritime trade were the most common reason for recourse to Rome.[121] Although no similarly comprehensive study exists for Greek-speaking Christians, there is enough evidence to make it clear that the Greeks also turned to Rome for help with maritime security.[122]

What we are confronted with, then, is a rather remarkable coincidence. The Catholic Church, backed by French officials, began to take a general interest in Eastern Christians just when Catholic piracy was on the upswing in the eastern Mediterranean.[123]

Greek Orthodox merchants, the most active Christian community by far in Ottoman maritime trade, drew a connection that was not intended but certainly made sense from their point of view. They used Catholic networks to try to gain protection from Catholic depredations.

Finally, we must throw into the mix the rather ambiguous role of the French consuls to fully round out our picture. We have been speaking of French policy, but here we must muddy the waters somewhat. To speak of "the French" in the seventeenth-century Mediterranean is really to speak of numerous actors, all of whom were, as often as not, pulling in different directions. Of particular importance is that consuls were at best haphazard executors of policy emanating from Marseille and Paris.[124] Early in the sixteenth century the position of consul, formerly

the representative of a society of merchants, was turned into a royal office as the crown made a concerted effort to raise more money and to
gain control over a wide array of local and regional institutions. This
control proved to be ephemeral. By the end of the century it had become
common practice to transfer consulates to private persons, who in turn
often farmed them out yet again. In the seventeenth century it was exceptional for a consul to reside at his post, and some did not even both
to get a formal appointment.[125] The principal concern of the person who
had purchased the office was usually to make as much money as possible
from the position as long as he held it.

French consuls figure very prominently in our story, as Greek Orthodox merchants sought redress against Maltese attacks. But the consuls'
motives did not necessarily have anything to do with protecting the
Greeks as Christians. They also provided services for Muslims and Jews
in exchange for a fee. The French consul in Izmir in the mid-seventeenth
century, for example, was heavily involved in the ransoming business.
He retained two partners in Malta precisely for this reason, and in a little
more than three years the partnership had helped twenty-eight Ottoman captives regain their freedom. The business aspect of the consul's
activities is powerfully evoked by the fact that his first documented
transaction took place in 1625, a year before he assumed the consulate.
As a French official one year later, he continued with the business he had
already started.[126] It is characteristic of the incoherence (or perhaps the
cleverness) of French policy at this time that the consul was able to make
money by ransoming Ottoman subjects who had been seized by his own
countrymen.[127]

As we shall see, French assistance to Greek Orthodox merchants was
of a different nature than the assistance given to Muslim captives on
Malta; this difference, I will argue, derived from religion. Nevertheless,
if we consider the French role within the larger framework that I described in the opening chapter—the oscillation in the Mediterranean
between the claims of religion and the reality of state power—then I
think it is most accurate to see the consuls acting as a counterweight to
the religiously defined networks that I have been describing. Relative to
the sixteenth century, the scales had tipped in favor of religion, but a
very characteristically Mediterranean ambiguity persisted.[128]

The Age of the Pirate Reconsidered

The Knights of Malta, and the corsairs of the Mediterranean more generally, are often presented as anachronisms, as the final hurrah in a waning religious struggle that was fast being replaced by a new economic battle sparked by the entry of northern ships into the Mediterranean. Speaking of the difficulties that the Maltese confronted in pursuing the *corso* as the seventeenth century went on, Peter Earle writes that some problems "arose partly from the undoubted abuses which the corsairs themselves had introduced into their business, but also from changing circumstances in the Mediterranean, as commerce between Christian and Muslim increased and as religious intolerance became less marked outside Malta."[129] Mallia-Milanes, another scholar of the Maltese *corso*, observes that the figure of the warrior-crusader no longer seemed relevant or convincing.[130]

Earle's argument assumes that increasing Muslim-Christian interaction would lead naturally to declining intolerance. But the one does not automatically follow from the other. A recent work on Malta argues just the opposite, that a greater social and economic openness was accompanied by religious and mental closure, with ever more vociferous expressions of the Catholic faith on the island.[131] The entry of the northern newcomers into the Mediterranean did not put an end to religious antagonisms. Rather the new competition came to coexist with the old rivalries.[132] Similarly, even if, as Mallia-Milanes argues, the figure of the warrior-crusader came to seem anachronistic, there were still many ways for religion to be deployed.

For Ottoman merchants, sailors, and shipowners, the seventeenth century was the beginning, not the end, of something, namely, the search for security in a maritime world that was far more violent after 1570 than it had been for many decades. For Greek Orthodox merchants in particular (who by now were almost all Ottoman subjects), it is indisputable that they attempted to cope with the prevailing insecurity by asserting their religious identity and by turning to networks based in religion, in striking contrast to their behavior in the sixteenth century, when they moved through the Mediterranean as Ottoman or Venetian subjects. Catholic piracy, Venetian retreat, and the ambitions of the

Counter-Reformation came together to produce a sort of perfect storm, whereby such behavior made sense.

The island of Cyprus provides an excellent example of the confluence of these factors. In 1570 the Ottomans wrested the island from the Venetians; thus another large Greek population center fell under Ottoman sovereignty. One year later, in a direct response to the loss of Cyprus, the Holy League inflicted a major defeat on the Ottomans at the battle of Lepanto. The Ottoman loss was the green light for the onslaught of western corsairs into the eastern Mediterranean; it was also the single most important political consideration for the founding of the Greek College in Rome.[133] The Church's push into, and new interest in, the Greek world coincided with the Maltese push into the eastern Mediterranean, although for very different reasons.

Along with all the other luckless inhabitants of the islands and the littorals of the eastern Mediterranean, the Cypriots were the constant targets of the Knights of St. John, as well as other Western corsairs, throughout the course of the seventeenth century. In the year 1629, for example, the Cypriots lost forty of the forty-five ships they had sent that year to Egypt to attacks by the Maltese.[134] Being Ottoman subjects, they could no longer turn to Venice for justice. Instead, the Cypriots would turn to the representatives of France and of the papacy in the various ports of the Levant for help. In every instance, they took care to present themselves not as Ottoman subjects but as Christians. From their point of view, a Christian identity was the only viable one in the complex negotiations that were thrust upon Greek merchants as they tried to retrieve their goods. Let us now turn to some of these negotiations.

CHAPTER 4

The Ottoman Mediterranean

● ○ ●

In 1633 two Greek merchants, Athanasio di Pancratio of Salonica and Comneno from the island of Mytilene, on behalf of themselves as well as Nikita from Rhodes, petitioned the court in Malta known as the Tribunale degli Armamenti. They were seeking compensation for an attack on their ship by a Maltese vessel captained by one Captain Salio. The petitioners did not come empty-handed. They had with them a document signed by the Venetian vice-consul on Rhodes attesting to the facts of the attack. They also had a paper from the French vice-consul in Chios confirming their identity and their purpose and asking all whom they might encounter to let them go freely and to extend every assistance. Finally, they had a number of witness testimonies produced in the chancery of the court of the bishop of Chios.[1]

These institutions, and the documents they generated, represent an institutional and legal order about which we know almost nothing. There are several reasons why this is so. First, the legal principles that structured international trade in the Mediterranean in the early modern period have not received a good deal of attention. Second, when these principles have been considered, the focus has been on agreements between states, such as the Ottoman capitulations.

The Tribunale where the merchants made their claim was not the court of a state, or at least not the court of an ordinary state. It was a court set up by the Knights of St. John, an international military order directly under the pope. The Tribunale is singular in another way. Given its function, it is fair to call it a prize court. The Knights of St. Stephen in Livorno also had a prize court, but one will look in vain for any mention of these two courts in general studies of the development of prize courts and prize law.[2] The literature on these topics assumes the emerging nation-state system, a clear distinction between wartime and peace time, and general agreement on who is and who is not a belligerent. None of these things holds true when it comes to the Tribunale. It was there to preside over the conduct of combatants in a permanent war whose full scope and extent were necessarily vague. Finally, the Tribunale does not fit easily into existing models because it was a court run by the pirates themselves, essentially. This very peculiar situation, which would be unthinkable in the Atlantic world, is a reflection of its specifically Mediterranean context. The middle ground of the *corso*—somewhere between piracy and privateering—was just legitimate enough that a legal framework to regulate it seemed both logical and possible.

Historians of the knights are not unaware of the Tribunale's existence. They also make reference to the "rules" of the *corso*, but no study of these rules exists. An argument from silence is always hazardous, but the reason for this lack of interest seems to be the assumption of corruption and lawlessness. To many people, then and now, they were simply pirates, plunderers. At one time, perhaps, yes, they were warriors for Christendom, but by the seventeenth century no longer.[3] If the legal principles governing commerce between states have generated little interest, one can imagine that legality is not the first thing that comes to mind when considering the history of a piratical order. Since the knights were going to seize whomever they chose anyway, whenever they could, why bother with the legal details?

"Corrupt," "arbitrary," "lawless": whether or not these epithets are deserved, the statutes and the proceedings of the Tribunale in Malta represent an attempt to create and implement a legal and normative order based on certain norms deeply rooted in a Mediterranean reality that was very different from the regime of sovereignty that organized trade in the sixteenth century. For that reason alone the Tribunale is worthy of our attention. But its interest extends beyond the mere fact of its existence. It is striking that petitioners to the court appear to have been able to draw on previously unknown networks of individuals spread across the eastern Mediterranean. Through the documents presented in court our view is extended far beyond Malta, deep into the Ottoman Mediterranean of the seventeenth century. The proceedings of the Tribunale also give voice to an individual who is usually scarcely visible, the ordinary Ottoman merchant. Studies of piracy and corsairing in the early modern Mediterranean concentrate overwhelmingly on the state perspective, based on the complaints and correspondence of officials charged with responding to attacks on their shipping.[4] At the Tribunale in Malta we see instead the response of Ottoman merchants to pirates, the efforts they made and the strategies they used to try to protect their commerce in a very dangerous sea.

Finally, although historians know that the Tribunale was the court where disputes stemming from the pursuit of the corso were adjudicated, the significance of this has not been sufficiently appreciated. The most fundamental rule of the corso concerned the identity of the enemy. All Muslims and all Jews were fair targets, while Christians were off-limits. Therefore the court and everything about it rested on the basic assumption that clear lines could be drawn between Muslim, Jewish, and Christian commerce. But this proved much harder to do than the rhetoric of the corso would suggest. And it was not just the court that relied on such rhetoric. "Muslim," "Jewish," and "Christian" commerce are still conceptual categories that are alive and well in Mediterranean history. The reflexive adherence to these categories is one reason why historians have charged the Knights of St. John with cynicism when it comes to their conduct in the corso. The assumption seems to be that if they had only wanted to, they could easily have determined who was who and what was what. The brutal and predatory behavior of those flying the flag of St. John cannot be defended; nevertheless, the proceedings of the Tribunale demonstrate that making such a determination was not a straightforward task in the seventeenth-century Mediterranean.

The Tribunale degli Armamenti

The Tribunale, also known as the Magistrato degli Armamenti, was established in 1605 at the behest of the grand master of the Order of Knights of St. John, the long-serving Alofius de Wignacourt.[5] Four knights and one judge presided in the courtroom, all of them appointed by the grand master.[6] The introductory paragraph, which explained the reasons behind its creation, was discussed in chapter three, so here I confine my remarks to a brief review before going on to consider the new tribunal's statutes and ordinances.

The introduction lays out the authorities' dilemma. The grand master and his council were concerned that the large number of individuals pursuing the corso was putting the provisioning of the island at risk. In addition, they were also threatening the Public Treasury, since much of their activity was secret, at least according to the grand master. Yet there was no desire to prohibit the corso, since the attraction of so many skilled seafarers to the island was essential to the knights' ability to pursue maritime warfare. To reconcile these contradictions, certain rules were going to be drawn up, rules that would both encourage war against "the enemies of our Christian name" and at the same time get rid of "abuses" and "inconveniences." The desire to get rid of lawsuits is specifically mentioned. The introduction finishes on a hopeful note: "With these rules, each person will have what belongs to him, without deception and confusion."[7]

Several things are worth remarking on here. First, despite the obvious concern to regulate the flow of goods produced by the corso, the grand master is careful to place his actions squarely within the context of the eternal war against the enemies of Christendom—that is, the Muslims. The desire to attract corsairs to the island is explained in terms of the desire to pursue war rather than in terms of material gain. This framing was essential to retain financial support from across Europe (which is not to say that it was insincere). Second, the large number of people pursuing the corso on Malta is testimony to the huge rise in corsairing activity at this time, in Malta and across the Mediterranean. And third, the large numbers were clearly causing confusion and disputes and upsetting the delicate equilibrium of a barren island that was highly dependent on external sources of supply. The reference to illegal trade and the Public Treasury also shows that the grand master intended to extract some benefit for the order from all this activity. In short, corsairing had slipped out from under the hand of the grand master, and he was determined to regain control.

It makes sense, then, that the majority of statutes and ordinances that were promulgated (and added to over the years) were concerned with regulating the relationship between the order and individuals pursuing

the corso.[8] Anyone wanting to outfit a ship for the corso had first to secure a license from the grand master. He in turn was obligated to refer
the matter to the new Magistrato, which would inform itself about the
quality of the ship and the amount of munitions on board.[9] The insistence on a license also meant, at least in theory, that the grand master
would be able to collect the 10 percent that was due him by custom but
that many had avoided paying. In an attempt to protect the island's supplies, the new rules prohibited the purchase of arms, munitions, or supplies without the express permission of the grand master.

Another group of statutes sought to protect all those who contributed
to the success of a corsairing venture. Upon his return to Malta, a corsair
was to register the quantity and nature of his spoils with the Magistracy
and his prizes were to be shared with the owners of the vessel, his creditors, and his crew. Failure to do so was punishable by service in the gallies, as were many of the offenses. Even so, fraud at the expense of investors was widespread.[10]

Statute number fifteen is the only one of the fifty-nine that addresses
the question of licit and illicit prizes. It states that before a license would
be granted, the *armatori* (those who invested their money in arming a
vessel for the corso) had to pledge they would not cause any injury to
Christians themselves, their goods, or their merchant vessels. Nor would
they attack infidels who could show authentic safe-conducts issued by
either the grand master or other Christian princes. They also had to
swear they would not injure any Christian vessel carrying goods belonging to Christians and to friends.[11]

This one statute, like the court itself, is far from being the product of
an outlaw organization that stands outside the norms and attitudes of
its more law-abiding neighbors. Brief as it is, it reflects the same ten-
sions and ambiguities that were characteristic of the sixteenth-century
Mediterranean. By forbidding attacks on infidels who possessed safe-
conducts from the grand master or other Christian princes, the court
sought precisely to strike that balance between respect for state sovereignty and the recognition of religious difference. But in the seventeenth
century the balance had shifted against the former because the legitimate authority of a Muslim state was not accepted in the Tribunale.
Only Christian powers, and not the Ottoman sultan, could protect infidels and infidel shipping.

The statute also participates in the widespread fiction that the Christian identity of a person, a ship, or cargo was unproblematic and exclusive of other categories. This fiction flowed logically from the raison d'être of the court, which was the corso. But it wasn't only the practitioners of the corso who insisted on a dichotomous world divided into Christians and Muslims. We have seen in earlier chapters that, despite a rather more complicated reality, no one was willing to openly challenge the essential rightness of the eternal war between Christianity and Islam. The primacy of religious identity was a natural corollary of this worldview.

Once again, it is Greek Orthodox merchants who best bring out the nature of this complicated reality. The first reason for this is in part a matter of the historical record that has come down to us. Greeks do appear as petitioners at the Tribunale, whereas Jews and Muslims do not. Given that the court was a direct legal expression of the corso, which existed precisely to fight the infidel, and given the tremendous burden of pursuing a lawsuit even under the best of conditions, the absence of the latter is understandable.

Second, Greek merchants continue to occupy an intermediary position because they were at one and the same time both Christians and Ottoman subjects. They continue to embody, therefore, the tension in the Mediterranean between the claims of religion and the reality of state sovereignty. The challenges they faced in the Tribunale were new. In this court they could not claim protection for their shipping on the basis of their Ottoman subjecthood. Rather, they had to prove, to the court's satisfaction, both their Christian identity and the Christian identity of the trade in which they were engaged. This would prove to be a difficult challenge. This difficulty was not solely a function of Maltese cynicism and corruption. Others also harbored suspicions toward the Greeks. Nabil Matar, the historian of captivity and enslavement in the western Mediterranean in this period, calls the English "undiscriminating" because of their willingness to seize the Greek Orthodox.[12] As late as 1675, Sir John Narbrough asked the English crown what he should do with twenty-four Greeks he had seized (along with "ninety-eight negroes") from a merchant ship of Tripoli along the North African coast: "he desires directions as to their being made slaves (they *pretending themselves Christians*)" (my emphasis). He was told "to resolve, in consideration of the Greeks sailing not as passengers but as of the ship's company, and so in hostility with us, as also of their being dwellers in Tripoli and consequently unlikely to be Christians otherwise than in pretence."[13] Here the particular twist was the status of the Greeks on board the ship and their residence in Tripoli. This was enough, apparently, to bring their Christian identity into doubt. In the Tribunale too, despite the stern admonition against causing injury to Christians, their goods, or their merchant vessels, "Christian" was a highly contested category when it came to the Greeks.

The cases brought before the Tribunale in the seventeenth century generated thousands of pages worth of legal records. Most of the cases concern internal squabbles, arguments among those pursuing the corso over monies owed, agreements broken, and obligations unfulfilled.[14] This makes sense, in that the primary purpose of the court was to regulate and control the practice of the corso to ensure, as the founding document said, that "each person will have what belongs to him, without deception and confusion."

But the records also show that on more than one occasion, Greek Christian merchants from the Ottoman Mediterranean made the long trek to the island and appeared before the court in the hopes of recovering what had been taken from them. They did so even though they must have known that the proceedings would be long and costly. Three Greek petitioners at the Tribunale in 1617 expressed the hope that they could recover their merchandise "without long disputes and lawsuits."[15]

Fourteen court cases, some of them consisting of more than one hundred folios, have come down to us from the first century of the court's operation, a time when corsairing, both Muslim and Christian, was at its height.[16] These cases, which stretch from 1602 to 1687, are a rare opportunity to peer into a world that would otherwise remain obscure. The men who appear before the court are ordinary merchants and captains, people who, except for the misfortune of having encountered the formidable knights and their determination to seek justice, would never have entered the historical record. An attack by the Maltese corsairs was a tremendous misfortune for Greek merchants, but their bad luck is the historian's opportunity. Ordinary as they may be, these victims and the witnesses who supported them left behind records that are sometimes quite poignant in their ability to convey the despair of those who had been attacked. Here is what the clerk recorded of the testimony of the

Athenian Demetrio, son of Petro, who testified on behalf of the sea captain named Nikita whom we met in the opening pages of this chapter:

> A saica arrived, with this Nikita and five sailors on board. The wit-
> ness, as a friend of this Nikita, went up to him and consoled him.
> And the witness asked Nikita if all of the cargo had been taken.
> And Nikita responded, "Come and see," and Nikita showed him
> how all that remained in the ship was sand.[17]

Let us begin with a synopsis of the cases. Having done that, we can
then situate the documents within the context of the Ottoman Mediterranean in the seventeenth century.

The Cases

In almost every instance, the victims were assaulted off the coast of Egypt,
where they were heading to or (more often) departing from either Rosetta or Damietta. This is in keeping with what we know about Maltese
corsairing; the Egyptian coast was one of their principal areas of activity.[18] Rice was the most frequently identified cargo.[19] The merchants were
also carrying coffee, sugar, and textiles. A ship coming from Crete and
heading for Chios or Istanbul was loaded down with olive oil and honey.

The plaintiffs tended to be from the small islands of the eastern
Aegean. A number were from Rhodes; others were from Kalymnos,
Leros, and Mytilene. Athanasio di Pancratio was from Thessaloniki, and
two others were Cretan. Aside from a name and a place, such as "Patron
Nikita di Rhodi" or "Giovanni Mathsopulo di Calimo," little direct in-
formation is given about the individuals involved.[20]

In most of the cases a value is assigned to the cargo, and it is usually
given in Spanish reales.[21] This makes sense, because the Spanish real was
the most commonly used coin in the seventeenth-century Mediterranean (ransom prices were usually stated in reales).[22] Whether we consider the amount or the monetary value of the cargo, it is clear we are
talking about substantial investments.[23] Most of the cases use the measurement known as the *ardeb* or *irdabb*. This was a specifically Egyptian
unit used for measuring grain and other dry products.[24] Throughout the
seventeenth century Egypt was obligated to supply the palace in Istanbul

with 3,000 ardebs of rice per year.[25] The merchants who appeared before the Tribunale were typically carrying at least 250 ardeppi of rice; in two cases they reported having loaded the astonishing amounts of 1,010 and 1,230 ardeppi, that is, roughly one-third of the yearly supply to the capital, in just one shipment. In two cases the merchants were carrying substantial amounts of olive oil and honey from Crete. Theodoro Taulari was heading for Chios or Constantinople with 400 quintali of olive oil and 50 quintali of honey.[26] Given that each quintal was the equivalent of a little over 56 kilos, we are speaking here of roughly 21,000 kilos of olive oil and more than 2,600 kilos of honey. The petitioner in the other case claimed compensation for 240 quintals of olive oil, or 12,663 kilos.[27] Monetary values were high, too. The merchants who appeared before the Tribunale were typically carrying cargo that ranged from 2,000 to 3,500 reales in value.[28]

Happily for our purposes, many goods and services across the Mediterranean at this time were priced in reales, given its ubiquity, and this allows us to make comparisons. A study of nearly thirty years of Cretan shipping in the middle of the century (1635–61) found that the amount invested in a shipping venture ranged from 150 or 200 to 3,500 reales. The average individual investment was 25 to 30 reales.[29] Also in Crete, the construction of the Moresini Fountain in Candia in the 1620s, probably the major public work undertaken in seventeenth-century Venetian Crete, cost 13,000 reales.[30] Across the Mediterranean the price for human cargo, the ransoming business, was usually given in reales and thus provides many opportunities for comparison. In 1628 a Maltese bombardier enslaved in Tunis fetched a ransom price of 200 reales.[31] On average, Ottoman captives paid 442 reales for their freedom in the 1620s.[32] In a high-profile case from 1590, where the release of the Muslim captive on Malta included the intervention of both the governor of the Morea and the *valide sultan*, the price paid was approximately 750 reales.[33] The cargoes lost to the Maltese were, at the very least, more than twice that amount.

Finally, the historian of the fraught relationship between Venice and the knights, Victor Mallia-Milanes, provides us with numerous examples of the reales involved in fights between the two powers. The amounts claimed in front of the Tribunale compare very favorably. In a rather spectacular Maltese attack against two Venetian vessels, "laden with merchandise," in the 1650s, the knights relieved both ships of their cargo. When they were eventually forced to compensate the owners by the Venetian government, the bill came to 3,390 reales.[34] A decade earlier the injured merchant Giorgio Gentile pursued his claim against the Maltese for a number of years: "the damages he had sustained were far from negligible, amounting to some 1,500 reali."[35] In 1645 the Venetians were persuaded to lift a sequestro against the Maltese on payment of 3,200 reali.[36]

The attacks themselves in most cases were vicious. Not only did the merchant lose his goods, the corsairs usually took all the cargo on board and the ship itself, and dumped the luckless travelers in some desolate place from which they were lucky to make it back alive. In one case the French consul in Saida reported that "they put them in a skiff belonging to the saicha, and left them to the mercy of the sea and of the winds which, by the Grace of God, brought them eventually to Saint Jean d'Acre. Once there, they were able to procure some clothes through the charity of others, and this allowed them to present themselves in front of us."[37] In another case the court was told that, after being robbed of everything they owned, Antonio Cantanin and his shipmates were brought to a rock called Gaidronisi and everyone was made to disembark. There they were left "without any sustenance or provisions at all and they remained there for eleven days. It was a miracle of God that they did not die of thirst or hunger."[38] They were saved by the appearance of a small boat on the horizon that took them to Crete. In 1684 "the Greek Giovanni" told the court how he and all the merchants on board his ship had been attacked and detained by the Maltese in the vicinity of the island of Nissero.[39] First the boat and everything in it was towed to the island of Stampa.[40] Then, after about fifty days at sea, Giovanni, all the merchants, and the ship's scribe were forced to disembark on the island of Kas and robbed of everything except the clothes on their backs.[41] In another case the ship was seized and the victims were loaded into a small boat that had been on board. They were put out to sea with no provisions but were given oars to row with. The fact that they had been robbed of all their goods, explained the plaintiffs, is why they had arrived in Malta "almost nude."[42]

There is every reason to believe these accounts of violence. Travelers in the seventeenth-century Mediterranean who were unfortunate enough to meet up with the knights routinely describe scenes of brutality.

We can recall the account of Henry Blunt in the introduction. Now the location of the attack is more meaningful: it was just off the coast of Alexandria, exactly where most of the attacks documented in Malta took place. Blunt recounted how the Greek vessel came up to the ship he was traveling on, hoping for assistance. But when "we appeared as Christians, and from us no help to be had," the captain had to acquiesce in the Maltese attack. He gave up three "Turks," but the fourth bound himself with some rope and then threw himself overboard, committing suicide to avoid being captured by the knights.[43]

Blunt does not mention the theft of cargo. Possibly the Maltese confined themselves to human cargo in this case, but the records from the Tribunale make it clear that theft of merchandise was a distinct possibility. Of course, offloading goods is much less dramatic than watching a wretched passenger fling himself into the sea; perhaps Blunt just didn't think to mention the former. But it is equally likely that outside observers of the Maltese corso, however disapproving of its violent methods, did not think to challenge its ideological fiction of a world divided cleanly into Muslims and Christians, with the former being the enemy and the latter a friend. Thus, Blunt identifies the ship as "Greek," even though the ship could have been co-owned by a Muslim. Similarly, the theft of Christian cargo would not have fit into this worldview and thus would have remained invisible, whether consciously or not. But it is striking that Blunt is quite open about the fact that the Greeks, albeit Christians, could expect no help from other Christians.

In 1716 Giacomo Cappello, the Venetian resident minister in Naples, spent four months on the island and had this to say about the conduct of the corsairs toward the Greeks:

> One cannot but unveil what is most dreadful to learn about the protection enjoyed by corsairs, by the most villainous corsairs. There was one such when I was there, Magrinè by name, from Majorca. Covered by the Maltese flag [i.e., the Hospitaller cross], this corsair was known to have pillaged Greek Christians; to have had them bound in sacks and thrown overboard; to have had the heads of others tied up and squeezed in such a way that the cranium was separated from the brains; and all this to make them confess, or for the sake of money.[44]

The corsairs were as audacious as they were brutal, as we see from an attack that occurred just one year after Cappello's account. Here they took on not the relatively defenseless Greeks but the French. The corsairs appeared in the harbor of Damietta, where two Ottoman boats were being used to load several French merchantmen. Despite a warning from the French merchants not to interfere, the corsairs promptly captured two of the French vessels, threw the French flag overboard, and took the crew prisoner.[45]

Even the knights themselves were not concerned to hide their actions. Alonso de Contreras, whose picaresque account of his cruises with the knights is one of the most famous corsair works, speaks of such things in a matter-of-fact tone. Near the island of Cerfanto, he writes, "I came across a little brigantine, which was careened on one side for cleaning its hull. There were ten Greeks aboard, and I had them come aboard my frigate."[46] He then began pressing them to reveal the presence of Turks on board, and when they denied that there were any, "I started to torture them and not lightly, either. All stood it, even a boy of fifteen whom I had stripped naked and trussed up."[47] Throughout the book Contreras is careful to justify his ill treatment of the Greeks in the context of some misdeed on their part—in this case, supposedly hiding Turks on board. He wants to give the impression that the Maltese would not attack Orthodox Christians without provocation.

The other inside account is that of the Knight Luppé du Garrané. His first cruise was in 1605, and over the course of the next nine years he spent more than five hundred days at sea.[48] His account is more restrained than that of Contreras. His tactic when it comes to the Greeks, I believe, is to be deliberately vague. In the summer of 1605 he and his fellow knights chased their target, which he simply calls a "*vaisseau*," for four hours off the coast of Anatolia. When they finally caught up to it and captured it, he described it as "une djerme qui venait de Damiette et allait a Constantinople charge d'environ cinq cents salines de riz avec 48 turcs."[49] It was decided to take it to Malta. A ship coming from Damietta, headed for Constantinople, loaded with rice; although Luppé-Garrané never mentions it, it is highly likely this was a Greek ship.

Archival sources and travelers' accounts also record violent behavior toward the Greeks, above and beyond the removal of cargo and passengers identified as "Turkish." In 1562 the knights encountered a Greek ship at the entrance to the harbor at Rhodes. They tortured them to learn the location of the Ottoman fleet, despite the Greeks' protest that they were simply sponge divers and knew nothing of the fleet.[50] The records of the Knights of St. Stephen from the year 1597 relate how they came across a small ship with a cargo of wood. Seven Greeks owned the ship and the cargo and they were all on board; the knights forced them onto their own ship and then sank the Greek vessel.[51] The French traveler Monsieur de Monconys sailed in a small boat from Egypt to Syria half a century later; the pilot of the vessel, he wrote, was a "poor" Greek who had had his boat stolen by Maltese pirates.[52]

Even in cases where the corsairs limited their seizures to Muslim passengers or cargo, Greek captains could still, of course, suffer economic injury. A 1602 expedition came across the boat of Dimitris Papayiannopoulos just off the coast of mainland Greece in the central Aegean. The captain was headed for Chios with a load of cheese; he also had some passengers on board, five Turks and six Greeks. Presumably at least some were merchants traveling with their goods. The corsairs took off the cargo belonging to the Turks and let the ship go its way.[53] At the very least, one imagines that the captain Papayiannopoulos was not going to be able to collect the freight due him from his Turkish passengers.

The Ottoman Mediterranean

Like driftwood washing up on shore, these plaintive stories of things gone horribly wrong are fragments of a much larger world that lies unseen. Hundreds of miles to the east of Valletta, Ottoman merchants, sailors, and sea captains were flocking to the Egyptian port cities of Rosetta (Reshid) and Damietta (Dimyat), where the particular circumstances of the seventeenth century were creating new opportunities. The Greek petitioners in Malta were part of that world.

The imperial repercussions of the Ottoman conquest of Egypt in 1516 are well known. The fertile Nile Valley was put into the service of the capital, supplying Istanbul with rice (the essential ingredient in the Janissary diet) and sugar, as well as goods coming from India through the Red Sea.[54] It was the possession of Egypt that allowed Süleyman, who succeeded Selim to the throne in 1520, to extend the empire's reach into the Red Sea, where he tried to stop the Portuguese advance. With the incorporation of Syria and Egypt into the empire, Selim completed his encirclement of the many Latin statelets that remained in the eastern Mediterranean. Süleyman took Rhodes, home of the Knights of St. John since the early fourteenth century, in 1522. A string of Aegean islands fell in 1538, and by the end of the century Cyprus was Ottoman as well. Only Crete remained as a significant Venetian stronghold in the East.

The integration of the eastern Mediterranean under the Ottoman sultans put other things into motion, developments more longlasting than what would turn out to be a rather brief imperial moment. But as is so often the case in the history of the Ottoman Empire, they have received less attention because they were not the result of any sort of official initiative.

Egypt's commercial possibilities created a stream of migration from the Anatolian coastline and the Aegean islands, and the development of the port cities of Damietta and, especially, Rosetta. This did not happen right away. It was a seventeenth-century development, just at the moment, in other words, when naval control was slipping from Istanbul's grasp. The timing was probably not coincidental. Nelly Hanna in her book on the wealthy Egyptian merchant Isma'il Abu Taqiyya (active in Cairo between 1580 and 1625) argues that the crises confronting the state at the end of the sixteenth century did not mean a decline in commercial activity, as is often assumed, or in the Egyptian economy as a whole. Rather, the increasing inability of Istanbul to dominate the country's flourishing trade created opportunities for entrepreneurs such as Abu Taqiyya.[55]

Rosetta became Egypt's major port in the seventeenth century, a position it held for two hundred years. It functioned as both a transfer point for goods between Cairo and Alexandria and as a harbor in and of itself for Mediterranean trade.[56] Coming through in 1517, Leo Africanus observed that it was "plutôt un gros bourg qu'une cité," but toward the end of the sixteenth century it began to grow.[57] In 1585 Rosetta impressed the German captive Michael Heberer as "une importante et riche ville marchande. Elle n'a ni portes ni murailles, et est située tout près du Nil; la arrivent toutes les marchandises du Caire et de toute l'Égypte, ainsi que de l'Arabie et de la mer Rouge."[58] By the seventeenth century travelers were describing it as the second biggest city in Egypt, after Cairo.

FIGURE 4.1. The grand houses in Rosetta testify to the migration of Anatolian merchants to Egypt in the seventeenth and eighteenth centuries.

A French vice-consul was in residence, and twenty-nine French merchants were resident there between 1685 and 1719.[59]

But Rosetta has left behind other reminders of its prosperous past in addition to the accounts of European travelers. Quite unusually, a number of Ottoman houses survive into the present in what is now a small

FIGURE 4.2.

town. These monumental dwellings, twenty-two in number, all date from the seventeenth and eighteenth centuries, and their magnificence suggests the great wealth that the town once enjoyed. Most rise four and even five stories tall, and ornate windows adorn the brick walls of their exteriors. Many of the windows are wooden, carved in the intricate style known as *mashrabiyya*, and jut out over the street. Others boast elegant iron grates. Carved wooden ceilings and wall panels are common in the spacious interiors.

When we consider that inter-Ottoman trade was superior in value to foreign trade right through the eighteenth century, and that an important city like Thessaloniki depended on Rosetta for some of its staples, then the centrality of the city becomes clear.[60] Nevertheless, it is nearly invisible in most accounts of the early modern Mediterranean, overshadowed by Alexandria, which, although it did not surpass Rosetta in size until the nineteenth century, became the favored port of Europeans.[61]

Heberer also took note of Damietta, on the eastern branch of the Nile. The ancients described seven spots where the Nile opened out onto the sea, he wrote, but of those seven, only Damietta and Rosetta remained; both were "full of ships and well-known."[62] Damietta seems to have been the smaller port; no European consuls were there, and it traded mostly with ports along the Levantine coast, the southern coast of Anatolia, and the islands of Crete and Cyprus. Ships heading out of Rosetta were more likely to be going to Smyrna, Istanbul, or Thessaloniki.[63] But Vansleb, visiting the city toward the end of the seventeenth century, thought Damietta surpassed Rosetta: "Next to Cairo it is the greatest, most beautiful, the richest, the most populous, and the fullest of merchants of all Egypt, for the conveniency of trade draws hither a great number of people from all parts of Turkey." Although his claim that five hundred ships laden with rice left the port every year is certainly an exaggeration, it does suggest that he was impressed by the level of activity that he witnessed.[64]

Greek islanders, like those who went to Malta, were active participants in this world. The several studies that exist on Egyptian trade in this period agree that the merchants trading out of the cities of the delta were not Arab Egyptians. Sometimes identified as Muslims and Christians, at other times as Greeks and Turks, in any event they came from elsewhere, namely, southern and southwestern Anatolia and the islands of the southeastern Aegean. Daniel Panzac has studied the contracts drawn up in the French chancery in Alexandria in the eighteenth century between Muslim freighters and French sea captains; fully 40 percent of the Muslims came from the Aegean coastline of Anatolia or the nearby islands of Lesbos, Chios, Samos, Kos, and Rhodes.[65] Throughout the seventeenth and eighteenth centuries about half the shipping between Egypt and the rest of the empire was carried on "navires turcs et grecs."[66]

The extensive trade between Rosetta and Thessaloniki was in the hands of Muslims from the latter city, who maintained partners or family members in Egypt to handle the Egyptian end of the trade. Christians from Thessaloniki also traded between the two cities, although not nearly to the same extent.[67] But the sea captains were Greek, and a mid-eighteenth-century court case from Thessaloniki identifies a sea captain from an island near Rhodes, the same location as so many of the petitioners in Malta in the previous century.[68] Specifically in Rosetta, travelers commented that the city was populated by Turks, and two of the remaining mansions make that connection crystal-clear; they are named Tokatli and Amasyali (from Tokat and Amasya, respectively, in Anatolia). A European in Damietta toward the end of the seventeenth century remarked that the Greeks were "most numerous" and had "a considerable church."[69]

The houses themselves testify to the migration of Anatolian culture to the Egyptian delta through trade. Travelers had always noticed the radical difference between these houses and the house that is much more typical of an Arab city. Most dramatically, the latter opens onto an interior courtyard and presents only blank walls along the street. The Rosetta houses open out to the road and proclaim their grandeur to the passerby.[70] An architectural study done in the 1970s argues forcefully for the Anatolian model behind the structures.[71] The use of alternating rows of brick and wood is reminiscent of façades in southern Anatolian cities such as Antalya and Alanya; taken together, they form a style that is common to the Mediterranean littoral both north and south.[72] Two centuries, then, before the rise of what would become the fabled city of Alexandria, there was a similar ingathering along the Egyptian coastline of people from the larger Mediterranean world.

We know very little about the islands of the southeastern Aegean, where most of the plaintiffs in Malta were from, in the first two centuries after Süleyman the Magnificent wrested Rhodes from the Knights of St. John in 1522. During the preceding several hundred years the Dodecanese, as the islands are collectively known, had been on the front line of the struggle between the Turkish emirates and the various Latin principalities as the former reached the shores the Aegean and attempted to develop their own seapower. Historians have lavished attention on this turbulent period, when the knights ruled Rhodes and the battle between Christianity and Islam seemed to have found its epicenter in the southeastern Aegean. After 1522 and the triumph of Ottoman sovereignty, the islands disappear rather abruptly from our view. It only makes sense, however, that Rhodes, the capital of the Dodecanese, would have continued to be important in internal Ottoman trade. Rhodes and its neighbor Kos were on an itinerary that had remained unchanged since Byzantine times; they connected the northern ports of Thessaloniki and

FIGURE 4.3. The harbor at Rhodes.

Istanbul to Egypt and the Syrian coast. A study of the island in the eighteenth century describes it as a vitally important way station for ships.[73]

Nevertheless, the Dodecanese islands were no longer included on the itinerary of most Western travelers. Here we must acknowledge, however, that active hostility as much as indifference might have kept them away. One of the very few studies of Rhodes in the sixteenth century describes two conspiracies on the part of Catholic powers to bring the knights back to the island, the second one as late as the 1570s. This attempt might have led the Ottomans to view contact with the West with suspicion, as the author of the study notes himself.[74] By the seventeenth century these attempts were over. We shall return to the subject of Catholic interest in Rhodes in greater detail in a later chapter.

Nor have the Dodecanese attracted much attention from historians relative to the western Aegean, particularly the Cyclades. Greek historians have favored the Cyclades, and the eighteenth century, because their commercial revival during this period can more plausibly be presented as the first act in an emerging nationalist drama.[75] Others have been intrigued by the Cycladic islands because of their long history of Latin and Catholic settlement, including the presence of Western missionaries, who produced voluminous reports, beginning in the seventeenth century. Their uncertain status between Latin (primarily Venetian) and Ottoman sovereignty wins them favor in an age that is captivated by liminality.[76] It is still the case that those areas of the empire that were not of great interest to Westerners in their day (or where it was difficult for them to go) have continued to suffer a certain invisibility today, and the Dodecanese are no exception.[77]

We do know quite a bit, however, about the Ottoman convoy between Istanbul and Alexandria, and this is probably our best clue as to the place of the Dodecanese and their inhabitants in the commercial world that I have been describing. The islands' southerly location in and of itself would already have encouraged a connection to Egypt, and the route of the Ottoman convoy must have made Egypt's commercial importance crystal-clear to the mariners and merchants of Rhodes and the smaller islands. As mentioned earlier, Egypt was the most important food supplier to the imperial capital. That is why the only regular Ottoman convoy system that existed was developed for the sea-lane between Alexandria and Istanbul. Every year a convoy of heavily armed galleons, escorted by numerous gallies, left Alexandria for Istanbul. They sailed to the west of Cyprus in the direction of Rhodes. From Rhodes they followed the Aegean coastline, passing Chios, Samos, and Mytilene before entering the Dardanelles.[78] The essential supply route connecting Egypt and Istanbul, in other words, went right through the eastern Aegean, and thus it was people from these islands who jumped at the opportunity to ply these waters as well.

Declining Ottoman naval strength may have created opportunities for the islanders, similar to what Nelly Hanna has suggested for seventeenth-century Egypt. Most accounts of the convoy stress its imperial character, dominated by ships of the Ottoman navy, but one Florentine accounts says something slightly different. Like the Maltese, the Knights of St. Stephen regularly cruised off the coast of Egypt, and one participant observed that, among the ships loaded with rice that left Alexandria early in the fall, there were always some Greek ships from the town of Lindos, on the island of Rhodes. Tellingly, this detail comes from the early

FIGURE 4.4. The town of Lindos today. In the seventeenth century, mariners from Lindos ended up in front of the Tribunale degli Armamenti.

seventeenth century, a time when the Ottoman navy was struggling to control the eastern Mediterranean.[79]

Commerce between Egypt and the ports of the northern Aegean was not, of course, restricted to the demands of the palace. All commerce flowing north and south followed the very long-standing itinerary described above, and this must explain what appears to have been a pronounced orientation toward commerce, and particularly trade with Egypt, among both the Muslims and the Christians of the Dodecanese. The observations all come from the eighteenth century, but they fit well with the picture that emerges from the testimony at the Tribunale, suggesting that the islanders' commercial prowess predates the eighteenth century. The Dutch traveler Cornelis de Bruyn, writing a century after the Florentine source, also mentioned the town of Lindos on Rhodes: "the small fort of Lindos around which are many Greeks, all of them sailors."[80] Just a few years later, in 1739, the French vice-consul in Alexandria observed that the islanders, both Muslim and Christians, controlled all the trade between Rhodes and Alexandria. Throughout the eighteenth century, French officials would complain about their inability to make gains along this important route.[81]

On Rhodes itself another French consul, also writing in the 1730s, said that the Greeks of the island are "to a very great extent, very wealthy traders with ships that they have made here on the island and then command themselves or have some Venetians do it for them."[82] It is particularly interesting for our purposes that the French consuls, as well as more casual observers, all noted the strong presence of Rhodes's Muslim community in the trade with Egypt. Rhodes and Crete seem to have been the two islands where Muslims not only participated in maritime commerce but may even have been dominant.[83] The ordinary sailor and the wealthy shipowner were both likely to be Muslim. A French observer in 1795 counted five hundred Muslims among the island's eight hundred sailors.[84] A few years later Pouqueville said that the largest ships on the island belonged to Muslims and that the governor of the island himself owned the two largest.[85] Popular songs from the island refer to Muslim shipowners, including owners from the political elite.[86] Two cases from the Tribunale make explicit reference to Muslim shipowners or captains, although their origins are not given. Testifying in front of the magistrates in 1686, the Armenian merchant Giovanni Marchara told the court that he loaded his goods onto a frigate belonging to Haji Chasan "Turco," captained by Epiffanio reis and Georgio reis.[87] In 1677, according to testimony from another case in front of the Tribunale, Sig. Andrea Mavranza Choroneo of Chios loaded his goods onto a ship captained by one "Selim Reis."[88]

Merchant Culture

The court cases, then, draw our attention to the islands of the southeastern Aegean and their role as a lynchpin linking the southern and northern shores of the eastern Mediterranean. They also provide glimpses of some of the more elusive aspects of commercial life in the empire.

This was a world of enduring relationships stretching out over many years. And these connections were spread out over the entire eastern Mediterranean, from Thessaloniki in the north to Alexandria in the south. When two merchants from Mytilene, Duca Galeazzo, son of Constantine, and Nicola, son of Micaele, sailed from Mytilene to Alexandria, they stopped on the island of Chios. Upon arrival, they stored two big bags of money in the home of a Chiot named Pantalco Vestarchi, to keep the money secure from the Barbary corsairs. At the time of the attack the two merchants had known Pantalco for about fifteen years.[89]

In 1687 Theodoro Taulari loaded his merchandise onto a boat in Rethymnon (in Crete) together with another merchant named Strati Stranghili. Taulari traced his acquaintance with Strati all the way back to Taulari's place of birth, Mistra, in the Peloponnesos. He knew him then from a place called Zarnata, and the two renewed their ties in Rethymnon, where they had a friendship going back about ten years.[90]

In the spring of 1633 a merchant from Thesaaloniki and a merchant from the island of Mytilene set sail from Damietta in Egypt on board a ship captained by Nikita of Rhodes.[91] We know that the merchant from Thessanloniki, Athanasio, also did business in Volos, on the Greek mainland, and in Chios as well, because one of witnesses, Georgio of Volos, testified that he had done business with Athanasio in both places.[92]

By definition, merchants feature prominently in the court records. We have less information on the sailors who were on board, who might or might not appear as witnesses. But the little information that is available indicates that the crews were not uniformly from one island or another, nor were they necessarily from the same island as the captain. When Andrea Mavranza Choroneo of Chios was attacked while going from Rosetta to Constantinople, he ended up back in Rosetta, giving testimony at the French chancery. One sailor who testified was from Limnos, while another was from Stanchio.[93] All of the sailors (there were four) who testified on behalf of Andrea of Chios had known the merchant for at least two years; one had known him for seven and noted that he had been on numerous trips with him. In another case a sailor from Syros sailed on a ship captained by a Greek from Skopelos.[94] Limited as this information is, it does suggest a very different organization of maritime and commercial life than the much better known example of the central Aegean islands, which rose to prominence in the eighteenth century. In the latter case it was customary for the ship's crew to consist of the relatives of the captain or the owner (and they might well be one and the same person).[95] Maritime enterprise was run as a sort of communal endeavor of this or that island, with Hydra being the most famous case.[96] In the seventeenth century in the eastern Aegean, something like a wider labor market for sailors and captains seems to have been in operation.

Merchants often worked with people whom they had known for a long time. At the same time, there seems to have been nothing compulsory about these relationships, and market conditions were taken into account in the course of making business decisions. The two merchants from Mytilene—the ones who had stored two bags of money in a friend's house on Chios—sailed from Mytilene to Alexandria on the saica of a fellow islander. But coming back, they chose a captain from Lindos, on Rhodes. Initially, they approached a shipowner from Mytilene, Giovanni, son of Manolachi, but the negotiations came to nothing because they could not agree on a freight price.[97] Georgi, a ship captain from the Peloponnesos, helped the Armenian merchant Giovanni Marchara find another ship when his own was full. He testified that he put the merchants' goods in his "*barca*," sailed over from the customs post to a ship owned by the Turk, Haji Chasan, and introduced him to the two Greek captains. Giovanni's goods were promptly loaded.[98]

The stories told in court also illuminate one of the most elusive aspects of the Ottoman commercial world—of any commercial world, actually, in the premodern period. This is the problem of information: what did merchants know, and how did they know it? The question of information flow, commercial or otherwise, in the Ottoman Empire is still a great unknown.[99] The little work that has been done on commerce argues for a strong link between ethnic or religious identity and access to information. Benjamin Braude, who has worked extensively on Ottoman Jews, writes, "each trading network provided . . . its own distinct system of market intelligence."[100]

Contrary to Braude's model, the documents paint a world where information flowed freely through informal, oral channels that cut across religious lines and that were not restricted to particular communities. The phrases "I heard" or "he told me" or "I saw" appear constantly throughout the depositions that merchants and sailors give. The very informality of information exchange suggests that there would be little or no trace of this phenomenon in official documentation; it is only through the accident of a corsairing attack that we have access to it at all.

As they set sail, Ottoman merchants in the eastern Mediterranean clearly felt confident they would be able to discover the best market for their goods. Setting out from Crete in 1687, Theodoro Taulari did not have a specific destination. He loaded olive oil and honey onto the ship of Captain Agostino Plati and explained that he planned to "take it to Chios, to Constantinople or somewhere else in order to realize its full value."[101] The mention of Chios was not by chance; the island seems to have functioned as something of an information clearinghouse, even though, by the seventeenth century, the new port of Izmir was taking away a good deal of business from Chios.[102] Another merchant on that same voyage said that they had left Crete, then gone to Stantia and then "to Chios to get the necessary information" as to where the demand for olive oil would be the greatest.[103]

Merchants could also learn a lot simply by being on the scene. A certain Giovani from Gallipoli ended up testifying on behalf of three merchants because he was in Rhodes when the victims limped into port. The Venetian vice-consul on the island wrote down Giovani's testimony:

> The witness had been in Rhodes for ten days when the skiff which belonged to the saica of captain Nikita of Rhodes arrived. In it were twenty three sailors from the crew, among whom was the ship's clerk, as well as the merchants Athanasio and Comneno. From these sailors and these merchants he heard that the saica had been taken by a Maltese ship at Cape Chilidoni. After three days had passed the Maltese captain sent away these merchants as well as the twenty three members of the crew. He kept only the captain of the ship Nikita and five sailors.[104]

As was customary procedure, the witness was asked how he knew this (*como lo sa*), and the vice-consul recorded his reply: "He was in Rhodes at this time, and he saw these men, stripped and nude, come in with the skiff, and from them he heard the following." Giovani, along with others, no doubt, must have hung around for a while because he finished his testimony by saying that, about two hours after the skiff had arrived, the saica with Captain Nikita and the other five sailors arrived as well, at which point he heard the details of the attack again, this time "from the mouth of the captain."

Information on prices also circulated through word of mouth. One of the points at issue in the case of the attack on Captain Nikita was the value of the cargo of rice he was carrying. The Venetian authorities in Rhodes relied on the "latest news" coming from Smyrna to set the price of rice (the expression used is *li ultimi avisi da Smirne*).[105] A witness named Lascari was called on to confirm the price of rice. When he did, he was asked how he knew this, and the notary recorded the following: "[He knows this because] yesterday some merchants arrived in port from Smyrna, and they had a cargo of rice with them. They had left Smyrna four days ago and they heard that that was the price it was selling at."[106]

The extensive paperwork generated by the attack on the ship coming from Crete makes it clear that information passed across the religious boundary. This incident involved multiple ships, on one of which were eighteen Turkish passengers who were seized by the Maltese. Three of them ransomed themselves while on the island of Spinalonga, just off the coast of Crete, and then returned to Rethymnon, where they had started their journey. Back in Rethymnon, they met up with Strati Stranghili, one of the Greek merchants who had been attacked, and told him the whole story.[107] This was how their fate made it into the deposition that Strati gave to the French consul in Rethymnon. No doubt Strati shared his own story—he had a series of adventures before eventually making it back to Rethymnon—with the Turkish merchants as well.

Braude's model of networks of information has a strong spatial dimension. The reliance on one's own community, he writes, made it logical that communal spaces were also physical sites for information exchange: "Time spent in public worship, in communal celebration, at the coffee-house, or by the fountain in a mosque-courtyard, could help make a contact or confirm a deal. Such gatherings were venues for the informal negotiations the preceded and accompanied most business transactions. Customers were more quickly found in one's own group."[108]

The testimony from Malta puts another physical space front and center, and that is the port. It is striking how little we know about Ottoman ports, particularly the smaller ones such as would have been found in the Aegean islands. From these documents it is clear that the port was a vital area for information exchange and deal-making. Lascari, one of the witnesses in the case of Captain Nikita, learned the price of rice in Smyrna from some merchants, recently departed from that city, who arrived in the port of Rhodes.[109] Two captains from Lindos recounted to the court how they were in the port of Alexandria when they were approached by two Turkish merchants who wanted to hire their ship to go to Constantinople.[110] They agreed on a price, loaded the ship, and were off.

And it was at the port of Rosetta that the Armenian merchant Giovanni Marchara was assisted by the Greek captain whose ship was too full to take on more cargo. We recall that the captain rowed the merchant and his goods over to another ship, one owned by a Muslim but captained by two Greeks, whereupon his goods were promptly loaded. It is impossible to know whether such solicitude was the norm or not. Of note is that several of these transactions crossed religious lines; the port seems to have been a neutral space where anyone connected to the world of trade could participate on the basis of that connection alone.

Finally, let us recall the witness Giovani from Gallipoli, who became a witness simply because he saw the victims stagger in from the sea. It is true that Giovani does not specifically locate himself at the port, but everything about the description suggests that is where he was: "The witness had been in Rhodes for ten days when the skiff which belonged to the saica of captain Nikita of Rhodes arrived" and "he saw these men, stripped and nude, come in with the skiff." Then, "two hours after the skiff arrived in Rhodes, the empty saica itself arrived, and this witness heard [the testimony that he has relayed] from the mouth of the captain and the sailors who were with him."[111] The captain, no doubt both traumatized and relieved, would have lingered long enough at the port to tell Giovani the story of the attack.

The documents convey a sense of spontaneous association that is not confined to the port. The Cretan merchant who went to Chios to find out the best place to sell olive oil then continued south to the island of Kos, where he and his fellow travelers came upon (*ci trovavamo*) five other ships, and they all began to sail together "*in caravana*."[112] Two of the six then split off, but the others were all sailing together when they were attacked in the vicinity of Santorini. Later on in the account we learn that these four ships were captained by a mix of Christians and Muslims: Psilachi of Santorini, Çavuş Turco, Deli Ali Turco, and Manoli reis. Clearly, despite the religious mix, the five ships were able to communicate with one another and derived a sense of security from sailing together.

When we combine the testimony of the Greek victims of the Maltese with the (admittedly) limited information we have about the Dodecanese islands in the seventeenth century, it is clear that this was a maritime world populated by both Muslims and Christians. And yet no Muslim sailor, merchant, or captain from Rhodes or the surrounding islands made the long journey to Valletta to stand in front of the Magistrato degli Armamenti. This suggests they were well aware of the stark reality succinctly described by a Venetian visitor to the island in 1716: "Any Turk who sets foot on the island is immediately enslaved."[113]

It is certain that Muslims from the Dodecanese and the adjacent Anatolian coastline were in Malta, but in a very different capacity; they would have been among the large Muslim slave community that suffered there throughout the seventeenth and eighteenth centuries.[114] Documents from the French consulate in Izmir show that over a period of three and a half years in the 1620s the consul assisted twenty-eight Muslim captives to gain their freedom in Malta. The majority were from western and southwestern Anatolia, followed by Rhodes and Kos.[115] A petitioner of the court or a miserable slave: the very different positions in Malta of Muslims and Christians who were from a common Ottoman world underscore the diverging fortunes of the two communities in the seventeenth century. For various reasons, all historical attention has been directed at Muslim slaves in Malta. His fellow Ottoman, the Christian merchant or sailor or captain who was on the island in the hopes of retrieving his goods, has been overlooked. Let us turn now to that petitioner.

CHAPTER 5

The Pursuit of Justice

● ○ ●

The Paper Trail

Robbed of their goods, and having decided to make the long journey to Malta, how did these Greek merchants set about fashioning their claim? Here we should note the lopsided state of our knowledge. A good deal of research has been done on the ransoming of captives, both Muslim and Christian, yet we know virtually nothing about how ships and cargo were retrieved.

The first thing that must be said is that the Greek merchants did not set out for the central Mediterranean immediately. Instead, in the majority of the cases the victims endeavored to produce a paper trail, a series of affidavits or depositions mostly, to bring with them.[1] These, they must have felt, would increase their chance of success. In every case but one, the pursuit of documentation led straight to the door of either one of the French consuls stationed in the various ports of the Mediterranean littoral or to the court of the Catholic bishop in Chios.[2] Often they went to both.

Let us follow in the footsteps of one of the petitioners to get a sense of how the paperwork was generated. On May 26, 1616, a shipowner and captain named Haji Pietro de Georgio, from the town of Lindos on the island of Rhodes, was present in the chancery of the French consul in Saida, a coastal city in what is today's southern Lebanon.[3] According to his testimony, on May 8 he was in Damietta, loading his saica with a cargo of rice, linen, silk, and coffee. He then set sail, and when his ship was fifty or sixty miles outside the city it was attacked by "*corsale di Malta*," who relieved the sailors not only of their goods and even their shirts but of the ship as well.[4] The corsairs then loaded the hapless captain and all the passengers onto a skiff (*schifo*) belonging to the saica, where they left them "at the mercy of the seas and of the winds."[5] Eventually the skiff reached Acre, a coastal city in today's northern Israel, whence the captain and passengers were able to present themselves to the French consul in Saida.[6]

A number of people were present in the chancery besides Haji Pietro. On the French side there were Francesco Fante, the French vice-consul in Saida, and Gilles Pantris, a lawyer attached, apparently, to the consulate.[7] A dragoman, or translator, a Jewish resident of Saida named Benjamin, was also there. The description of his position implies that he too was a consular employee, but it also seems to be the case that Haji Pietro sought out the dragoman on his own and brought him to the chancery.[8] Therefore it is not clear whether the French vice-consulate routinely provided a dragoman or whether it was up to the individual involved to seek out a dragoman on his own. What is clear is that, once in the chancery, the dragoman spoke for the various witnesses, and it was the dragoman's words that were taken down. For example, the first witness on Haji Pietro's behalf, a certain Manoli, "stated through the mouth of the said Negrin dragoman."[9] Later on the dragoman read Haji Pietro's testimony to a group of sailors, and they affirmed that everything he had said was true.[10]

On the Greek side numerous witnesses accompanied the petitioner, including the majority of the sailors who were on board, as well as fellow islanders from Rhodes. One by one they came forward, most of them on May 26 but a few two days later, on May 28, and gave their testimony. The content of their testimony is discussed in a subsequent chapter. For now let us continue with an overview of the procedure followed by the victims.

The following day, May 29, when all the testimony had been given, the vice-consul Francesco Fante and the lawyer Gilles Pantris, here described as "consegliero" or adviser, gave the documents, ten folios in all, to Haji Pietro after affirming that the testimony had been given and that the royal seal of the Most Christian King of France and Navarre had been affixed.[11] He was to take these documents and present them to the Illustrious Monsignor, the grand master of Malta.[12] The records of the Tribunale establish that this is exactly what he did do, since the folios from the French vice-consulate in Saida are preserved as part of case number 1/11 in the archives.

A very similar scenario played out twenty years later. This time recourse was had to the French consul in Cairo. Gioannes Cugia, a merchant from Monemvasia in southern Greece, was also attacked off the Egyptian coast, about sixty miles outside the city of Rosseta, which was the ship's destination.[13] In this case the attackers did not take the ship but confined themselves to robbing Gioannes Cugia of the 2,000 Spanish reales he was carrying on board. Although he doesn't give an account of how he made his way to Cairo, as Haji Pietro did when he appeared before the French vice-consul in Saida, it is safe to assume that since the ship was heading to Rosseta anyway, he chose to continue on to Cairo in order to make his case there.

In addition to the victimized merchant himself, two other witnesses testified in Cairo. The first was the ship's captain, one Diaco di Lero, who testified he had seen one Captain Granier take the money and that the money belonged to Signor Cugia and not to any Turks.[14]

The other witness was a fellow merchant, Gioanni di Mercurio, also from Monemvasia, who had been a passenger on board the ship and who testified to the same thing. At the end of the testimony the chancery official affixed the royal seal and explained that he had done so to give the document "greater validity."[15] This comment is worth considering. In the seventeenth century the French monarchy was still struggling to bring the consular service in the Mediterranean under royal control. If Gioannes Cugia had appealed to the French in Egypt around 1500 he would have encountered a consul who was still the representative of a society of merchants rather than of a state. At that time, one Philippe de Paretes represented not just French interests but Naples and Catalonia as well. An important change came in 1523, when Paretes' successor was appointed under royal seal.[16] This control turned out to be only temporary, however, as consulates across the Mediterranean were transferred to private persons in exchange for payment. In the seventeenth century it was exceptional for the consul to be in residence, and those who were farming the office sometimes did not even take the trouble to obtain a formal appointment. As a result, the person holding the office could be someone of rather humble origins, and in the Ottoman case at least, this hurt the authority of the French government.[17] The note on the document issued to Gioannes Cugia indicates a similar anxiety on the part of French officials, in this case toward the authorities in Malta. For Greek

merchants victimized by the Maltese, the shaky status of French authority was just one part of the larger issue of finding protection for their
shipping. But let us consider several more cases before taking up this
question of protection more systematically.

In some cases the litigants went to several venues prior to making the
long journey to Malta. Four years before Gioannes Cugia was robbed of
his money off the coast of Egypt, three Greek merchants were attacked
in a similar spot.[18] In April 1632, Athanasio di Pancratio of Thessaloniki,
Comneno from the island of Mytilene, and the captain of the ship, Patron Nikita of Rhodes, were sailing from Damietta to Smyrna, loaded
with a cargo of rice. They had the bad luck of meeting up with the Maltese captain fra Marcantonio Sciagliu, who took them to the deserted
coast of southern Crete and seized their entire cargo.[19]

The production of documentation began that same month. Two days
after he arrived in the port of Rhodes (on April 27), the captain, Nikita,
went to the Venetian vice-consul in the city. There he recorded his testimony as to what had happened and obtained a document, a *patente*,
saying that the cargo on board belonged to him, as well as to Athanasio
and Comneno. In this case the choice of consul seems to have been more
deliberate and less dictated by the vagaries of the voyage. For reasons
that are not entirely clear, the corsairs detained the entire ship and the
crew for three days, then forced Athanasio and Comneno, along with
twenty-three others, into a small boat (*barca*) that belonged to the saica.
They arrived in Rhodes by chance, as their emotional testimony makes
clear.[20] While their comrades were adrift on the sea, Captain Nikita and
the remaining five members of the crew were taken to Crete, and there
all the cargo was taken from them. They were left with the saica, however, and Nikita must have then decided to set sail for Rhodes, where he
arrived two days after the others.[21] Perhaps he sensed they would end up
there. More certainly, it makes sense to return home to begin the whole
business of trying to get restitution. Being from Rhodes, Nikita would
have been familiar with the officials and the procedures there. The value
of familiarity is also suggested by the fact that Nikita did not travel on to
Chios with Athanasio and Comneno but rather was content to let them
represent him in Chios.

In Chios, now in the month of May, the two merchants went to the
court of the Catholic bishop, described in the documents as the Corte

Vescovale.[22] A Catholic court was a relative rarity in the Ottoman Empire.[23] The one on Chios reflects the fact that a substantial Catholic population remained on the island after the Ottoman conquest in 1566. In accordance with their usual practice, the Ottomans ousted the temporal rulers of the island but left the religious leadership, a Catholic bishop, in this case, as representative of the community. Thus, throughout the seventeenth and eighteenth centuries there were three courts in operation on this one island, the bishop's, the *kadı*'s, and that of the Greek Orthodox metropolitan.[24] The bishop of Chios, like other Roman Catholic clergy in the Ottoman Empire, was nominated by a papal brief, which was then ratified with a berat from the sultan. He was usually a native of the island.[25]

In the bishop's court, Athanasio and Comneno once again ran through the narrative of the attack. Then they produced a string of witnesses, much as Haji Pietro did in the French chancery in Saida. Nine different witnesses came forward on behalf of one, two, or all three of the plaintiffs. In addition to the bishop, referred to as Monsignor Vesvoco di Scio, Nicolaus de Portu, the notary and clerk (*canciliere*), took down what was said. At the end of the testimony, the bishop, one fra Marco Iustiniano, certified that Nicolaus de Portu was in fact the notary and had made this copy, which was faithful to the copy retained in the chancery.[26] The date was May 17, 1632.[27]

Finally, in mid-July the two litigants turned to the French vice-consul on Chios, a man named Jean Dupuy. This document is rather different from the other two. It appears to be a straightforward passport. Mr. Dupuy wrote "to all whom it concerns" that these two Christians of the Greek rite were leaving Smyrna to go and recover, with God's help, some goods. The goods they intended to recover belonged to them, as attested by documents from Chios signed by the bishop. To this effect, then, Mr. Dupuy wrote, we ask all to let them go freely and to give them every assistance. The passport was signed with the royal seal and dated July 14, 1632.[28]

The three litigants in this case were unusually assiduous in calling upon two consular officers as well as the bishop of Chios. But recourse to more than one authority was not unusual. What is uncommon in the case that follows is that one of the authorities was a Greek Orthodox prelate.

In July 1634, just a little more than two years after Athanasio and Comneno testified in the bishop's court, two other Greek merchants made their way to Chios for the same purpose.[29] Duca Galeazzo, son of Constantine, and Nicola, son of Micaele, both from Mytilene, recounted their voyage to the bishop (the same Marco Iustiniano). In March of that year they had left Mytilene with the saica of Gregorio, son of Dimitri of Mytilene, heading for Alexandria. Once there they bought rice and linen, which they then loaded onto the saica of Iani Zagarachi of Lindos.[30] They departed from Alexandria in early May.

On their way north, they stopped at the island of Karpathos, which sits midway between Crete and Rhodes, to take on water and fix the sails. While there, three Christian vessels appeared, one Maltese, one of Livorno, and one of Sardinia.[31] All three corsairing captains boarded Zagarachi's ship, whereupon an argument ensued between them as to whether or not to rob them, considering that they were all Christian, as was the merchandise.[32] This was according to the testimony of the two victims in the bishop's court in Chios. In the end the Maltese captain acted alone, seizing the saica and sailing a little way away, at which point he unloaded all the goods from the saica and put them on his own vessel, leaving the captain with only "a little wet rice."[33] Apparently, then, the captain and all those on board were free to leave; the ship was not taken.

Various aspects of this account, plus other information such as the verification of prices, are repeated by ten different witnesses, all of whom appear in the bishop's court.[34] The witness accounts are followed by a letter, written in Greek. The contents of the letter make clear the reason for its composition.

The author is Ierotheos, the archbishop of Karpathos. The seal of his office is prominently displayed next to his signature. Nine individuals, all of them clergy of one sort or another, witness the document, as does the entire population of the island. The archbishop begins by addressing himself to the Grand Master of Malta at the behest, he says, "of the Christians":

With tears running down my face, as well as those of all my clergy I have ventured to write every truth to you, with the fear of God in my heart. On the (?) of May a saica with the captain Iani was at anchor in the harbor of Pygathoulia on the island of Karpathos. Carrying rice and linen, it wanted to take on water.[35]

The archbishop goes on to describe how three ships appeared and entered the harbor, and what happened next:

> The Knight of Malta sent out a boat and took the ship with the merchants on board as well as the captain.[36] Some of the group fled out of fear.[37] The ship having been taken, the merchants and the crew came to take me to talk to [them], to give back to them the ship and the goods. So I went down to the shore with my monks and my priests, but when the captain, the Knight of Malta, learned of this he up and fled, taking the ship, the ship's captain and some of the crew with him.

Clearly, the sight of a group of black-robed Orthodox clerics sweeping down across the beach had unnerved the Maltese corsair, who decided to finish the job somewhat farther afield. But if the archbishop was not able to stop the robbery, he could at least write a letter:

> The wretched merchants came to me and asked me for a letter and for witness from me. [Thus] I write and I witness, with the fear of God in mind and with the faith of Orthodox Christianity that the truth is that the ship and the cargo are Christian and everyone [on board] is Christian and there were never any Turks and the wretched merchants come crying to you and begging for justice as a just (?) [and we ask that you not] deal unjustly with and rob Christians, which would be a great shame and an injustice.

The merchants themselves must have carried this letter with them, first to Chios, where they appeared in the court of the Catholic bishop, and then all the way to Malta, where it remains part of the archival record today.

The only other documented involvement of an Orthodox authority occurs in the case with which this chapter began, that of Haji Pietro de Georgio, who took his complaint to the French consul in Saida in 1616.[38] The consular documentation was produced at the end of May. One month later Haji Pietro was in Cairo, where he managed to amass an impressive amount of paperwork, thanks to the intervention of several highly placed Orthodox clerics.

First Lavrentius, the archbishop of St. Catherine's Monastery in Sinai, provided a document on Haji Pietro's behalf.[39] The document briefly related how Haji Pietro and his companions had loaded Haji Pietro's ship with rice in Damietta, with the intent to sail to Saida, where they would sell it. He then said that there was no merchandise on the ship belonging to Turks, Jews, or even other Christians, but only the goods belonging to Haji Pietro and his companions, as they had testified. The document continues on with an account of the attack, similar to what was relayed in the chancery in Saida.

Lavrentius then declares, together with his "congregation of *ieromonachi* and monks," that the ship belongs to Haji di Pietro di Georgi and to no one else, and that the merchandise is in conformity with everything that has been previously stated.[40] He asks that the ship and the merchandise be returned.

The next document is remarkable not so much for its content as for its author. The words "Cyrillus Patriarch a Alexandrie" run across the top of the document as a kind of heading. An extravagant and highly stylized signature takes up the bottom of the page. This is certainly Kyrillos Loukaris, the man who went on to serve in Istanbul as the most renowned patriarch of the Ottoman period. He is an important part of our story, and we will learn much more about him in the final chapter. For now, we see him already confronting the damage done by Catholic corsairs, four years before ascending the patriarchal throne in Istanbul and becoming one of the fiercest opponents of the papacy and its policies in the East.[41]

Loukaris begins by affirming Haji Pietro's ownership of the ship. In addition to the familiar refrain of no Turks and no Jews, he adds that Haji Pietro has the sole share in the ship.[42] Although captains in the Aegean could be sole owners of their ship, shares in a vessel were probably even more common.[43] Loukaris would have felt the need, then, to preclude that possibility. Like the previous document, he then recounts the details of the attack and asks that justice be rendered.

Finally, Haji Pietro brought with him a document signed by the French consul in Cairo, Gabriele Firnosi.[44] The consul certified and attested to the fact that, at the request of Haji Pietro, the patriarch of Alexandria had given the following sworn testimony. The details of the attack were then given again.[45] He then writes that the testimony was given "because this said patron Pietro intends to depart and to go to Christendom in order to recover his ship and the rice carried in it."[46] The consul finishes by requesting and urging all the rulers and governors of the places in Christendom where this ship may go to look with Christian charity and piety upon the just cause of Patron Pietro, given that he is Christian and that the merchandise on board was Christian.[47] In these final lines the consular document seems intended to function as a kind of passport across the Christian Mediterranean world.

Outside of these lawsuits which have survived in Malta, there is other evidence of Orthodox involvement in assisting Greek merchants and captains who suffered Maltese attacks. One of the anecdotes that opened this book is such a case. In that instance the metropolitan on the eastern Aegean island of Mytilene wrote a letter to the grand master in the year 1627. He complained that two Maltese galleons had attacked a vessel captained by one Iacomes reis while it was returning from the port of Rosetta, also on the Egyptian coast. The Maltese beat them, tortured them, stole all their goods, stripped them of their clothing, and took the ship as well, even though it belonged to Christians. The vessel was co-owned, the cleric continued, with half belonging to this Iacomes and a certain Kyritze Avvagiano, also of Mytilene, owning the other half. The stolen goods belonged to a merchant named Xatzitriandafylo and consisted of sixteen sacks of linen, six hundred okkas of legumes, some textiles, belts, and spices. The Maltese also made off with the merchant's personal goods.[48] We can see now how much this case conforms to the ones we have been discussing: the trip from Egypt, the accounts of ill treatment, and the seizure of both goods and ship.

Abbots from the famed Monastery of St. John on the island of Patmos also wrote to the grand master. In 1587 Ionas recounted to the grand master how a Maltese pirate named Alessandro had attacked the scribe and the captain of a ship belonging to the monastery. After tying them to the mast with explosives on their feet, he threatened to kill them with a knife unless they confessed that they were Jewish and that the cargo was as well. Ionas wrote to Malta asking for compensation. A few years later, in 1604, Abbot Nikiforos wrote a letter in which he described the sinking of a ship belonging to one Georgio Moschona by a pirate from Naples. Those who managed to escape the shipwreck made

FIGURE 5.1. The Leimonos Monastery on Mytilene (Lesvos).

their way, drenched and naked, to Rhodes, where the bey of Rhodes promptly threw them into jail, assuming that they were working with the pirate.[49]

There is no way to assess how systematically Orthodox authorities intervened on behalf of Greek victims of Maltese piracy. The information available comes from the odd letter or two that have surfaced in one of the many monastic libraries, largely unexplored, scattered across the Aegean. It is certain that Catholic intervention was far more common, even routine, as the record from Malta shows and from other studies that have been done. But even the limited role of the Orthodox clergy shows there was a generalized recourse to religious authority in the search for protection in the seventeenth century.

The earliest case in the records of the Tribunale is dated 1602.[50] It is an exceptional case in that it is the only one in which the primary recourse is to Venetian authorities in Venetian-controlled territory rather than to institutions in the Ottoman Empire. The reason seems to be the fact the victims happened to wash up on the island of Crete, which was still Venetian in 1602.[51]

Antonio Cantanin and his father-in-law departed from Alexandria in their ship in early April 1602.[52] Although the documents never say where the two men were from, the name of the ship makes it highly likely that they were from Rhodes. Their destination was Istanbul, but on April 2 they were attacked by a ship in the vicinity of the island of Cacavo.[53] After taking their goods, the pirates dumped all of them on the small island of Gaidronisi, which lies just off the southern coast of Crete.[54] There they remained, according to Antonio's testimony, for eleven days, at which point a passing vessel picked them up and took them to Crete. He does not linger there; he moves on immediately to say that they were transferred to Zante, where they testified in front of the Supreme Council and produced documentation to take to Malta.[55]

The authority of Venice is repeatedly referenced in the testimony given in Malta. In a document drawn up on Antonio's behalf, for example, it is stated that "the stamp which is on the above referenced document and papers is the stamp of the Tribunal of Zante, which is [under the] the government, administration and jurisdiction of the *Signoria* of Venice."[56] And this stamp, "embossed on whatever documentation, and presented in whatever tribunale . . . and particularly in [the tribunals of] this island of Malta, with regard to any matter at all and particularly in cases of verification with regard to this particular subject matter, is customary and habitual. It should be given the faith that is owed and is habitually given to another seal."[57] The Venetian stamp, and willingness to hear the testimony more generally, appear to serve the purpose of verifying the facts of the case, as recounted by Antonio and others: "The legitimate and lawful evidence of the above stated three *capitoli* is authentically proven and signed by the Supreme Tribunal in Zante."[58]

In only one instance do we come across any documentation issued beforehand, that is, as a preventive measure. In April 1686 a captain named Agostino Plati reis departed from Rethymnon on the island of Crete. According to the testimony of several merchants who had loaded goods onto his ship and subsequently lost them in the attack, the captain had with him a *patente* issued by the French ambassador in Istanbul. The *patente* is clearly some sort of passport that was meant to place the captain and his ship under the protection of French authorities.[59] As one of the merchants explained to the court, Agostino and his scribe told him that on previous voyages they had sailed with a "passaporto, due to which they were not molested by Captain Bavian nor by the Barbary pirates nor the Christian corsairs."[60] They also paid a higher freight charge, an astonishing 40 percent higher, precisely because of the passport.[61] All to no avail, as it turned out. When the corsair captain came on board, Plati showed him the document but he simply tore it out of his hands and, presumably, destroyed it.[62]

Local Institutions and the Search for Protection

By now the picture should be clear. Greek merchants, sailors, and sea captains, sailing for the most part between Egypt and various ports in the eastern Aegean, were attacked by Maltese corsairs (or at any rate people whom it seemed best to pursue in Malta). Often left abandoned in small boats or on one of the many rocky islands scattered across the sea, they eventually made their way to several different courts and chanceries to record their testimony of what happened. Sometimes documentation was produced on the spot, as when the archbishop of Karpathos was prevailed upon to write a letter by merchants who had lost their goods to the Knight of Malta who sailed into the port and attacked them.

Where did these practices come from? And how did they work to constitute the Mediterranean as a legal space?

The first thing that can be said is that they were improvised, and the creation of the petitioners themselves. Alert to every possibility in their search for protection, petitioners took advantage of institutions that existed primarily for other purposes. Let us look first at the most important of these, the French consulates in the Ottoman Empire.[63]

As with the other consulates in the Levant, the French consul had two fundamental tasks. The first was to represent his country before local Ottoman officials. Second, he had authority (not uncontested) over the French nation in his particular *échelle* in his capacity as the agent of the national trade body, in the French case the Marseilles Chamber of Commerce.[64] The greatest part of the literature on European consuls in the Ottoman Empire considers consuls in one or both of these capacities. This makes sense, in that these were consuls' major responsibilities. But the consuls enjoyed authority in another area, one that has received little

attention from historians but is vital to our story. They had notarial powers, which allowed them to register contracts and witness statements,
bills of lading, wills, and similar kinds of documents. Maurits H. van
den Boogert in a recent study of the capitulations in the Ottoman Empire points out that this consular function was particularly important
for merchants, factors, and captains—those connected, in other words,
to maritime and commercial life. He further notes that these documents
had the same legal validity as documents drawn up in France, Great
Britain, or the Dutch Republic.[65]

It stands to reason that the notarial services of each European consul
were intended to facilitate the business of his fellow nationals. Nevertheless, this did not prevent our Greek merchants from turning to the consuls as well for the production of documents. Insofar as these documents bore the stamps and seals of the consular officials, as well as the
fact that they were presented to the Tribunale in Malta, we are justified
in viewing them as public, legal documents. Therefore, recourse to and
use of these documents can be seen as an attempt to extend a European
legal regime into the eastern Mediterranean. The Maltese contested this
attempt.

The willingness of the French consul to hear cases and to issue documents should not be confused with the well-known practice of the extension of consular protection to small numbers of Ottoman Jews and
Christians. This was an eighteenth-century development pertaining to
an individual's status in the Ottoman Empire. Here the consul's intent,
and certainly the intent of the petitioners, was to facilitate movement
across the Mediterranean. We can recall the document written by the
French vice-consul on Chios in 1632.[66] He wrote "to all whom it concerns" that the petitioners, two Christians of the Greek rite, were going
to recover goods that belonged to them. He asked that they be allowed
to go freely and be given every assistance. This emphasis on maritime
space is supported by references—infrequent, admittedly, but present—
to the rules of the *Consolato del Mare*. In court in Malta in the 1630s, one
Papa Iani, another victim of a Maltese attack, complained that what had
been done was against "le legi del Consolato del Mare."[67] In the case of
Antonio Cantanin, he asks for restitution on the basis of "consuetudine
maritime."[68] Although references to actual laws or norms are rare, the

testimony presented in Malta is overwhelmingly in accordance with the maritime usages contained in the *Consolato del Mare*. I return to this point in chapter six.

The issuance of passports in the western Mediterranean is well known in the literature, and thus a comparison can be made. The North African corsairs carried two different types of passports, both of them issued by the French consul in the various port cities. The first, known to the French as "un certificate de nationalité," certified that the ship in question, captained by the captain named, belonged to the Regency of Algiers. All officers in charge of ships belonging to the French king are asked to lend every assistance. The other document, commonly issued together with the first, was known as a "passavant" and was designed to discourage the taking of French prizes. The passavants had a special shape—they had scalloped indentures—and the top half of these documents were provided to consuls in southern Europe. The Algerians were instructed to "allow all vessels producing passes that fitted these tops to pass unmolested."[69] The use of both of these documents was problematic, and they were widely abused, but that is not important here. What interests us is the comparison, and when we compare we find important differences.

First, in the western Mediterranean these documents were issued in advance and on a routine basis. This was not the case in the eastern Mediterranean. As mentioned earlier, the issuance of a passport in advance comes up in only one incident of piracy, namely, the two related cases of the merchants who loaded up with goods in Crete in 1687, only to be attacked near the island of Santorini.[70] This exception must be explained by the War of the Holy League (1684–99) that engulfed the Aegean at this time and would have made sailing particularly hazardous. Except during periods of declared war, it seems that such passports were not routinely carried, and this probably reflects the rather different status of the eastern and western Mediterranean in the seventeenth century. No sooner did the North Africans sail out of their ports than they entered international waters, given the proximity of southern Europe. The Maltese, on the other hand, were sailing into an Ottoman lake. Sailing entirely within the confines of the Ottoman Empire, Ottoman captains likely would not have thought to secure these documents on a

routine basis. (And, of course, they were not corsairs.) Rather, they went
to the consular authorities only after an attack.

Second, they were a product of official policy. Blank copies of the passavants were sent to consuls in southern Europe, where they were sold
to ships departing from ports in southern Europe.[71] There is no indication that the French consuls in the eastern Mediterranean had been instructed to protect Greek merchants and captains against the Maltese or
any other Catholic corsairs. Instead, it is most likely that they assisted
them because they could charge a fee. Repeated warnings from Paris
against charging illegitimate fees and engaging in private trade paint
a picture of officials who were constantly on the hunt for additional
sources of revenue.[72] Consular willingness to provide services for a fee
allowed the Greeks to draw them into their efforts to obtain justice in
Malta.

The specificity of the Greek case also emerges in a comparison with
Ottoman Muslims operating in the eastern Mediterranean. The lack of a
specific desire to protect Greeks as Christians is shown by the fact that
French consuls also assisted Muslims who came to them. Jean Dupuy,
the French consul in Izmir during the 1620s, was in the business of ransoming slaves. He had two partners in Malta, and all three had full powers to act as each other's legal representative. The ransom money being
advanced, the two partners on Malta would hand it over to the slaves in
the presence of a kadı (himself a captive) and witnesses. The amount advanced was understood to be a loan, which the captives agreed to pay in
its entirety to the French consul once they reached Izmir. The kadı issued a legal certificate, a *temessük* or *hüccet*; these certificates eventually
ended up in the possession of Dupuy.[73] It is this same Dupuy who shows
up in the Tribunale degli Armamenti archives, this time as vice-consul
in Chios. Earlier we saw him providing travel documents for two Greek
victims of the Maltese.

Agostino Plati reis, the captain who sailed from Rethymnon with a
French passport, must have received it from Guilhaume Fabre, the French
vice-consul in Rethymnon at the time.[74] The Ottoman archives reveal
another side to the vice-consul's activities. Over the course of roughly
ten years beginning in 1685, just one year before he wrote on behalf of
Agostino Plati, he appears eight times in the documents. Several of the
cases concern his own commercial dealings, but the rest show him

standing as guarantor for the shipment of goods by Ottoman officials. In 1685 he appeared in court to guarantee a shipment of wheat belonging to the defterdar of Crete, Halil Efendi. The wheat was being sent along the northern coast of Crete, from Candia to Chania, and Fabre guaranteed the wheat in the event the ship was attacked by pirates. Just a week later the same shipment is referenced again. The ship is about to depart, and Fabre guarantees that the captain, Jon Salmo, will not go "toward the enemy." It seems, then, that the French guaranteed both the security of the shipment as well as the conduct of the captain.[75] Subsequently he stood as guarantor for a shipment of butter belonging to an Aga, for the safe passage of the kadi of Crete embarking on a trip to Kos, and again for a shipment of wheat going from Candia to Chania.[76]

French merchants were also willing to sell protection (or at least, the promise of protection). For a fee, they would lend their name to Muslim and Jewish merchants so that the latter could benefit from the protection afforded to Frenchmen.[77] The French role as mediator between Ottoman Muslims and Catholic pirates is perhaps most graphically illustrated by the ransoming of ships at sea. A case recorded in the Ottoman court registers of Thessaloniki describes how a Muslim captain under attack had managed, together with twenty-five of his passengers, to escape from the captured ship in a small boat.[78] After a short while a French ship happened to pass by. The Muslim approached the French captain and asked him to convey the ransom money to the pirates. In this way his ship was restored to him on the spot. But the fifteen Muslims on board who had not managed to escape were not so lucky; they were taken off to Malta and presumably enslaved.

Although it was equally sought after, French consular (and other) assistance to Ottoman Muslims and to Ottoman Christians was not the same. Partly this was a function of the different problems the two groups faced: Christians were much less likely to be enslaved (although it did happen). But there is a more fundamental difference, a difference that derives directly from the distinction the Catholic corsairs made between Muslims and Christians.

The negotiations and exchanges between the French consuls and Muslim victims of the Maltese were in the nature of private contracts between contracting parties, as opposed to public legal documents. Eyal Ginio's description of ransoming in the eighteenth century applies equally well to the seventeenth; we need only add the French consuls to those who could organize the ransoming of captives:

> It appears that one of the clearest features of redemption during the eighteenth century was the part played in it by private initiative, the captives themselves or their relatives or acquaintances organizing the ransom. The state . . . was evidently absent from the liberation of Ottoman captives.[79]

The documents generated for the Christian merchants who appeared before the Tribunale are of a different nature. As I said earlier, they should be viewed as public and legal documents. The fact that the Greeks attempted this, and that the documents were accepted (with some debate), suggests a legal order at work in the Tribunale, whether implicitly or explicitly. An extended discussion of this legal order follows in the next chapter; here let us just note that Ottoman Christians turned to the French consuls as notaries who could produce and certify documents that were meant to have legal validity across the Mediterranean. Ottoman Muslims also turned to the French, but their interaction was in the nature of private contracts. The guarantees that Fabre undertook in Crete, for example, were not intended to bind the Maltese in any way. Rather, they were agreements that Fabre would make good the damage to these Ottoman officials in the event they sustained an attack. Without further research, it is difficult to know if French consuls routinely undertook such guarantees or whether Fabre's activities were sought after because of the war (1684–99). Behind this disparity in the treatment of Muslims and Christians was a view of the Mediterranean that denied the very possibility of peaceful coexistence with the former, hence the impossibility of including them in any sort of Mediterranean-wide legal framework. Although disputed in practice, Ottoman Christians, as Christians, theoretically had the right to move throughout the Mediterranean world.

The fact that French consular assistance to the Greeks was not religiously motivated does not mean that the Greek pursuit of justice lacked a religious dimension. Here it is instructive once again to compare the situation in the East to the better-known world of the western Mediterranean. Let us recall that in the West, the French issued a document known as "un certificat de nationalité" to the North African corsairs. The said document certified that the ship in question, captained by the captain named, belonged to the Regency of Algiers (or Tunis or another city, as the case may be). The emphasis is entirely different in the testimony taken down in the various French (and Venetian) consulates across the Mediterranean and later presented in Malta. Over and over, the victims and the witnesses assert not their territorial but their religious identity. They are Christian, they say, as is the cargo, the ship, and anything else that may come up in the testimony. The assertion that the ship belonging to Antonio Cantanin and his father "is a Christian ship, the co-owners and the sailors are baptized and they profess the Christian faith. They were born, they live and have been schooled in [this faith]" is entirely typical in this regard.[80] In the eastern Mediterranean, then, the French could be said to be issuing certificates of Christianity.

The Greeks then turned to representatives of the French state in order to bolster their claims against a Catholic order that (theoretically anyway) answered to the pope. This suggests that, for the Greeks and other Ottoman subjects in the seventeenth century, there was no clear distinction between the French consuls as representatives of France and the French consuls as representatives (and protectors) of Catholicism. In his study of Arab Christian complaints to Rome, Bernard Heyberger notes they had to bring letters of introduction signed by *either* the Latin missionaries *or* the French consuls; French and Catholic authorities were thus interchangeable.[81] This makes sense. As discussed in an earlier chapter, France's emergence as the Ottoman Empire's most steadfast and important ally went hand-in-hand with its development as an aggressive and unapologetic defender of Catholics and the Catholic faith in the Levant. Even though the particular French officials involved were not acting to advance a Catholic agenda, it seems likely that the Greeks hoped their intervention in Malta would be effective precisely because of France's identity as a Catholic power.[82]

This possibility is strengthened by the fact that the other authorities to whom the Greeks appealed, namely, the Catholic bishop in Chios and the several Orthodox clergymen, were unambiguously religious. The assistance rendered by the bishop in Chios was little different from that asked of the consuls; in Chios, witnesses appeared, testimony was taken down, and then the court's officials certified the documentation produced. Instead of the consul (or vice-consul) and his notary, we have the bishop and his notary.[83]

Orthodox assistance came in the form of personal interventions rather than in the mobilization of some kind of institutional structure. The archbishop of Karpathos wrote his letter on the spot at the behest of some of the victims. In the case of Haji Pietro in 1616, he did not go to any sort of Orthodox court in Cairo. Rather, he went to the French consulate, where several Orthodox clergy testified on his behalf regarding the ownership of both the cargo and the ship involved in the attack. Admittedly, these were quite illustrious witnesses—the archbishop of St. Catherine's and Kyrillos Loukaris—but they were witnesses all the same, and the content of their testimony is little different from that provided by merchants, captains, and sailors in other cases. It is also noteworthy that, although the victims turned to the Catholic bishop in Chios in three of the fourteen cases brought before the Tribunale, they never once approached the court of the Orthodox metropolitan, which was there as well.[84] This lacuna could reflect the fact that the Orthodox Church, as far as is known, did not develop any mechanism for the ransoming of Orthodox Christians, whether in North Africa or in Malta.[85] But it also raises a general interpretative question, one that returns us to the constitution of the Mediterranean as a legal space. How should we understand the peregrinations of our victims prior to their arrival in Malta? Were they appealing to Christian authorities as Christians? Or are we talking about a narrower Catholic protectorate, which might, however, be extended to Orthodox Christians as well as they sought to move around the Mediterranean?

Catholics and Orthodox

The relationship between Rome and the Christians of the Near East has been mostly the preserve of cultural, religious, and intellectual historians.[86] Just a few have expanded out to the commercial aspects of the story, and when they have, it is the Roman Catholics who have been considered. Bernard Heyberger has plumbed the depths of the archives of the Propaganda Fide in Rome to uncover the intimate links between the Vatican's ambitions and the commercial difficulties of the Arab Catholics.[87] Most of his discussion concerns petitions that went all the way to Rome, and these cases are examined in the final chapter, when we consider the Greek Orthodox turn to Rome. At that point the two groups can be compared.[88] For now let us say only that, given Heyberger's exclusive focus on the Roman Catholics and the lack of other studies, one could reasonably conclude it was only they who could or would approach Catholic authorities, whether in the *échelles* of the eastern Mediterranean or in Rome itself. This is certainly the assumption made by van den Boogert in his study of the options open to Ottoman subjects whose cargo was seized by European corsairs. He writes, "If the corsair belonged to a non-capitulatory nation, it was nearly impossible to obtain redress. Ottoman Roman Catholic Christians could try applying to Rome for redress."[89]

If we expand our lens to include the Greek world, we see that that Catholic assistance (including France acting as a Catholic power) was not limited to Ottoman Catholics. Let us consider the religious identity of those who approached the French and Venetian consuls, the Catholic bishop in Chios, and the odd Orthodox cleric, as the situation warranted.

Most of the petitioners at the Tribunale are Orthodox Christians. Christian religious identity is presented in several ways in the documentation. Most often Christian individuals are simply "Greco," "di nation Greca," "Christiana della religione," or sometimes a combination of the two, such as is "di natione greca et Christiano."[90] In three cases an individual is identified as a "christtiano di ritto Greco," that is, a Christian of the Greek rite.[91] This phrase is clearly invoked out of a concern to distinguish a Christian of the Greek rite from Catholic Christians because the latter is used only in the three cases that the plaintiffs are "catholici di ritto Greco," or Catholics of the Greek rite. The term "Greek rite," although a misnomer, was widely used at that time and is still invoked by historians today.[92] It is misleading because it implies that the Greek rite (or any rite) is identified by the language it uses, whereas the Greek rite is used by many different languages. A rite, properly understood, should be described by its place of origin, by the patriarchate where it originated; when the term Greek rite is used what is actually meant is the rite of Constantinople. The most widely used liturgy in the East, it was employed by both Catholics and othe Orthodox since the Catholic Church, by and large, did not insist on substitution of the Latin rite as long as papal supremacy was acknowledged.[93] Indeed, the guidelines for witness testimony in one of the court cases explicitly draw a distinction between religion and rite. Those who will testify on behalf of Andrea Choroneo are told to identify their rite *and* their religion.[94]

In the Maltese documentation, then, Catholics are specifically flagged as such, whereas the Orthodox are simply "Greek" or "Christian."[95] It is the default category. It is unlikely that this linguistic convention comes from a desire to privilege the Orthodox; the notaries and other officials who are drawing up the documents are Catholic. Rather it must come from the recognition, however implicit, that in the Aegean world at this time most of the Christians were Orthodox. The Catholics were the exception to the rule. This is borne out by the fact that most of the petitioners, as well as the witnesses who testify on their behalf, are Orthodox Christians. Clearly it was not only Roman Catholics who turned to Catholic authorities for help with the very Catholic Knights of Malta. Orthodox victims did the same.

Orthodoxy as the norm is also suggested by the fact that it is only the Catholic minority (the minority of the petitioners) who are asked to prove their Catholic identity. Two cases involve Catholic victims at the bishop's court in Chios, and it is there that we see the greatest scrutiny. Both are from the 1630s and were discussed earlier in this chapter.[96] Let us return to them, this time with the Catholic identity of the petitioners in mind.

To quickly recapitulate, in the first case, from 1632, Athanasio di Pancratio of Thessaloniki, Comneno of Mytilene, and the captain of the ship, Patron Nikita of Rhodes, were attacked by the Maltese while sailing from Damietta to Smyrna. Among other authorities, the two merchants, Athanasio and Comneno, went to the bishop's court in Chios to record their testimony.[97] There they declared their intention to prove the following points, the first of which was that "they and (?) Nichita were and are Catholic Christians of the Greek rite, born of Christian parents [and are] persons of good reputation and known to be such by all."[98] Two years later the second case produced almost the same language.[99] The merchants Duca Galeazzo son of Constantine and Nicola son of Micaele, both from Mytilene, were attacked by the Maltese while in the harbor at Karpathos. Eventually they made their way to Chios, where they testified. They intended to prove that "Duca and Nicola were and are Catholic Christians of the Greek rite, respectable persons of honor, born of Christian parents [and are] persons of good reputation and known to be such by all."[100] Not content to let it go at that, some (but not all) of the witnesses who testified on behalf of the merchants in these two cases affirmed their Catholic identity, at which point they were asked how they knew the petitioners were Catholic.[101]

All of them derived their authority to pronounce on this matter from long acquaintance with the plaintiffs, usually as neighbors or as fellow merchants. This acquaintance gave them knowledge of their family and their behavior, and it was these two, apparently, that established Catholic identity. Georgio del q. Paulo dal Castello di Metelino, from the same island as Comneno, said that he knew Comneno and Nikita but not Athanasio. Both, he said, were Catholics of the Greek rite. Comneno was his neighbor (*vicino*), and Georgio knew his father, now deceased, as well as his mother and his brothers and sisters. Georgio also knew Nikita's parents, both of whom were dead. Georgio did not identify Nikita as a neighbor, and given that the latter was from Rhodes, it is not clear how he acquired his knowledge of the family. Possibly Nikita was born in Mytilene but was then living in Rhodes. In any event, Georgio asserted that he had seen Comneno and Nikita, as well as the former's parents, go to confession and to communion many times.[102] Other witnesses give the same information about knowing the family and seeing them go to confession and to communion, and sometimes add additional details concerning the religious habits of one, two, or all three individuals. Giovani Apostoli, also from Mytilene, had seen Comneno attend Mass and other divine offices and in general to "live in a Christian manner."[103] Antonio Romano di Giovani of Rhodes knew all three, and during the most recent Lent (Quaresima) he saw them confessing and taking communion in Damietta.[104] The last witness, Caludi Andronico del q. Lambino of Mytilene, said they all confessed and took communication "at the festivals and at Easter and undertook all the actions which are usual for a good and true Catholic Christian."[105]

In the second case, the two merchants from Mytilene, Duca Galeazzo, son of Constantine, and Nicola, son of Micaele, also produced a string of witnesses who averred they were Catholics of the Greek rite. Merchants from Chios or from Mytilene for the most part, they supported this claim with evidence very similar to that provided for Comneno, Athanasio, and Nikita in the first case.[106]

This extensive testimony, designed to establish individual Catholic identity—testimony that we do not see when it comes to Orthodox individuals—suggests that Orthodoxy was the norm, but it points to something else as well. The distinction between Catholics and Orthodox was not obvious but was rather one that had to be drawn with considerable effort. The exception that proves the rule concerns an Armenian Catholic who was attacked by the Maltese in 1683.[107] Witnesses describe him simply as a "*xpriano cattolico*," with no further commentary (nor are they asked to provide any). The merchant's outsider status (he came from Iran and needed translators at the bishop's court, since he could speak neither Italian nor Greek) rendered his identity unproblematic, at least to those involved in his defense.[108]

Here we must confront a central difficulty concerning the "Catholics of the Greek rite" who appear in the Maltese documentation. The Catholic plaintiffs, as well as those witnesses who identify themselves as Catholic, are by and large from the islands of the eastern Aegean: Mytilene, Rhodes, Limnos, and Kos, as well as the mainland city of Thessaloniki. A few are from Chios, which is unproblematic. But for the rest, there is at present no historical evidence whatsoever for Catholic communities on any of these islands. The comprehensive report on the state of Roman Catholicism worldwide written by Monsignor Cerri for Pope Innocent XI at the end of the seventeenth century makes no mention of these islands or of Thessaloniki. He discusses only the islands of the central Aegean, plus Chios and Crete, thereby following the well-known contours of Catholicism in the Greek world. He explains his selection criteria: "The Archipelago contains many islands but I will mention only those where there are Catholics, Latin Bishops and Missionaries."[109] Scholarship on Catholic communities in the Ottoman Empire supports Cerri's description; Latin bishoprics were established in Naxos, Syros, Mykonos, Tinos, and Santorini.[110] Except for Chios, the eastern Aegean is absent from this story.

What are we to make, then, of Catholics from Rhodes, or Mytilene? One possibility is that these are Orthodox in Catholic clothing. Given the Catholic identity of the Knights of Malta, they may have been fabricating an identity for strategic purposes. We know from Bernard Heyberger's work that false claims of Catholic identity were within the realm of possibility. Indeed, they seem well nigh inevitable, given the family and factional quarrels that got mixed into the missionizing effort in Syria. In 1723, for example, al-Usta Mansur, brother of the Catholic archbishop of Saida, Aftimyus Sayfi, wrote to the Propaganda in Rome to say that Ilyas Fakhr, nephew of the Catholic archbishop of Tripoli (in northern Syria) and seemingly a zealous convert to the faith, was "n'est catholique qu'en paroles, pas dans les faits, et qu'il est peut-être même hostile à la foi."[111] The fact that Mansur saw fit to hurl this charge suggests that the establishment of religious identity was not always an easy matter. Just one year earlier the grand master in Malta had accused the Greeks of the same thing. Writing to Rome in 1722, he said that schismatic Greeks posed as Roman Catholics.[112]

Among the many possibilities, I limit myself here to a 1641 *Istruzione* or Instruction sent to Malta from Rome at the request of the papal inquisitor on the island. The inquisitor was frustrated by the problem of captured Muslim slaves who were brought to the island on the knights' galleys. No sooner did they arrive than they would approach the papal inquisitor and claim that, since they had been born Christian and had been forced to convert to Islam, their enslavement was unlawful.[113] Uncertain as to how to go about ascertaining the truth of falsehood of their claim, he asked for guidance from Rome. The opening paragraph lays out the problem and the proper approach for establishing whether the Muslim individual had ever been a Christian. It is worth quoting from at some length to convey the sense of uncertainty on the part of officials confronted with these desperate individuals, as well as for comparative purposes.[114]

The corsairing ships return from raids in the Levant, and particularly the Archipelago, and people seized in those raids approach the Inquisitor and declare themselves to be Christian, without, however, being in possession of any "authentic document" [*autentico documento*]. Nor can we ascertain the truth of where they are from, or the claim of depredation, since with regard to these populations Christians live promiscuously amongst the Muslims and commit the abuse of marrying each other. This Supreme Court has ordained that the present Instruction be sent to the Mons. Inquisitor in Malta so that it may be implemented when these cases, or ones similar to them, present themselves. If it happens, then, that

the victimized person [makes] the request to be admitted, as a
Christian, to the Holy Sacraments, without any documentation of
their Christiantiy, then . . . they must provide the Tribunale with
authentic proof of their Christianity.

This authentic proof would consist of a deposition in which the individual would be asked the following questions:

1. The quality, conditions, and customs of the parents.
2. Their place of birth, whether there was any Christian church,
   the name of the parish priest.
3. If their parents have been baptized and if they had baptized
   their children.
4. Whether the abuse of apostasy from the Christian religion to
   the Turkish sect happens in the place where they are from.
5. If there are any Christian persons in their country who can certify that they are born of Christian parents.
6. If they have received Christian instruction from their parish
   priest.

The problem being addressed in the 1641 *Istruzione* concerns the difficulty of determining whether an individual was Muslim or Christian.
If this seemingly basic question was so opaque, one can imagine that
certainty within Christianity—is this person standing before me Orthodox or Catholic?—was even more problematic.

We do not know if Rome ever developed a set of questions, similar to
the *Istruzione* in the case of Muslims, with the intent of establishing the
identity of a convert from Orthodoxy. What we do have in the cases before the Tribunale is some evidence, admittedly very limited, as to what
constituted relevant information in terms of proving Catholicism. Given
how little we know about the workings of the Corte Vescovale in Chios,
it is difficult to know whether this was information offered up by the petitioners or whether they were responding to guidelines set down by the
court.

What can be said is the following: it is hard to see how the testimony
given could have been particularly persuasive. Its content fell into two
categories: assertions that the family was Catholic and observations
about behavior. With regard to the first, nothing was offered as proof

beyond the assertion itself. Witness statements about behavior are particularly interesting to consider. All of them state that the plaintiffs went to confession and to communion, the implication being that this settles the matter of their identity. But if we remind ourselves of the situation in the eastern Aegean islands in the seventeenth century, it is clear that the testimony settled nothing at all. The missionaries took a very lenient attitude toward the Orthodox Christian among whom they worked. The Orthodox could receive communion from and onfess to Latin priests without having to convert. A seventeenth-century Jesuit report from the Levant notes, "The Orthodox Metropolitan in Smyrna has given his subjects complete freedom to go to our clergy for confession . . . and to our clergy he has given full power to hear confessions in his church both from Greeks and Latins."[115] In his review of Catholic-Orthodox relations in the Greek world in this period, Timothy Ware writes that schism was "quietly ignored" at the local level.[116] To say, then, that someone went to confession and to communion was really to say nothing at all about where they belonged, whether Orthodox or Catholic.

It is possible that Nikita from Rhodes, Nicola from Mytilene, and all the other plaintiffs—as well as all their witnesses—were lying. Despite everything I have said that could cast suspicion on their testimony, I do not believe they were. If things were so simple, then we would expect that everyone, Orthodox and Catholic alike, would go to the bishop's court and claim to be Catholic? These are the only cases in which they do.[117]

In the end, it is impossible to know how the plaintiffs viewed themselves or to uncover their motivations. And it seems to me that this is not the most important point anyway. What is more significant is, first, the fact that the proof offered in the Corte Vescovale was weak, given what we know about the historical context. Second, the bishop did not noticeably exert himself to find out more. Unlike the inquisitor on Malta in 1641, who was vitally interested in knowing whether or not these Muslims should be received back into the Church, the most senior Catholic representative on the island of Chios did not seem particularly bothered. This rather relaxed attitude suggests that the bishop of Chios, like the Catholic missionaries at work in the Greek world, was not going to put a lot of effort into sorting out Catholics from Orthodox.[118]

We can return now to the more general problem of how to interpret the assumptions underlying the generation of this paper trail. Was this a

Christian or a Catholic protective blanket that was being woven under the insistent pressure of those victimized by the Knights of Malta? It seems to me the answer is both. Or rather, the color of the blanket shifted depending on the identity of the individual petitioner. Greek Catholics (assuming they were Catholic) evidently thought it was worthwhile to get that extra stamp of approval; above and beyond their Christianity, they were Catholic to boot. But those (the majority) who were not did not waste time explaining why they were not, nor did they choose to identify themselves as Orthodox. Rather, they were simply Christian or Greek, and the French consular authorities whom they approached also seemed willing to let it go at that. A broader Christian identity was clearly very viable.

The flexibility of the French consuls is further suggested by the case of Andrea Mavranza Choroneo, a Greek Catholic attacked in 1677 near Karpathos while coming from Rosetta. Choroneo's is the only instance we have of a Greek Catholic who did not make the trip to the bishop's court but rather confined himself to testimony in the French chancery in Rosetta. It is difficult to know the reason for this, but it is worth noting that he did not go to Malta either. One of the things he did in Rosetta was give power of attorney to a Maltese named D. Carlo Bonici, so that the latter could pursue his case in Malta. Possibly Choroneo was unwell and thus unable to travel. In any event, the testimony in the French chancery is different from what is produced on behalf of Orthodox individuals. The document begins with the words "In Nomine xpri Amen," and a cross appears after the name of each person who comes forward. Furthermore, the French official writes that each witness will be interrogated as to his name, surname, country, age, rite, and religion.[119] None of this appears in the documents produced for the Orthodox. The (four) witnesses then duly identify themselves as Catholics of the Greek rite and assert that Andrea is as well. The testimony with regard to religious identity is much more cursory than what is presented at the Corte Vescovale in Chios, but the contrast with the Orthodox is still there. Nevertheless, it is very clear that both Greek Orthodox and Greek Catholics felt they could turn to the French consuls for assistance, the one for a Christian stamp, the other for a Catholic one.

This easy slide between the Mediterranean as at once a Catholic and a Christian space is further suggested by several other details from the court cases. Catholics could appeal to the Orthodox for help. It was Duca Galeazzo, son of Constantine, and Nicola, son of Micaele, both Catholics, who brought the letter from the Orthodox archbishop of Karpathos to Malta. Although the extensive witness testimony from Chios refers to both of them repeatedly as "xpriani catholici di ritto Greco," the archbishop speaks only of Christianity. He writes to the grand master at the behest, he says, "of the Christians" and swears that "the ship and the cargo are Christian and everyone [on board] is Christian," and reminds him that it is a shame and an injustice to "deal unjustly with and rob Christians."[120]

Perhaps more surprisingly, the French and the Venetian authorities who write on behalf of Nikita, Athanasio, and Comneno, petitioners who explicitly presented themselves to the bishop as Catholic, do not themselves seem concerned to underline the Catholic faith of these three individuals. The Venetian vice-consul whom Nikita approached in Rhodes said that "this cargo of rice belongs to this person as well as two other Christians [*duo altri Cristiani*] named Athanasio of Salonica and Comneno of the city of Mytilene."[121] It is particularly striking that the French vice-consul in Chios, who wrote out a passport for Athanasio and Comneno prior to their departure for Malta, referred to them as "Christians of the Greek rite."[122] It is hard to know how to interpret what seems to be an inconsistency. One possible explanation is that the European officials drawing up these documents simply did not consider it vitally important to make the distinction between Greek Orthodox and Greek Catholics.

Taken together, these details are telling and support the argument made in chapter three. Counter-Reformation ambitions in the Levant encompassed all Christians as potential Catholics, and French consuls were evidently willing factotums to all and sundry who approached them. Christians, both Catholic and Orthodox, were alert to these possibilities for protection and acted accordingly. Therefore, to speak of assistance rendered to Ottoman Roman Catholics by European Catholic powers is to paint an overly rigid picture of seventeenth-century realities. It assumes—wrongly, I think—that determining who was Orthodox and who was Catholic was a straightforward matter. Although much more work needs to be done, the limited evidence available from the records of the Tribunale suggests that even if such a determination could be made, it was not necessarily considered vitally important to do so.

The differences between the Orthodox and the Catholic seem particularly small when we compare either of them to Ottoman Muslims. There were limits to what the entrepreneurial and obliging French consuls would or could do. Whether Catholic or Orthodox, the French consuls were certifying Christianity. Although it is not stated explicitly, the use to which these documents were put makes the underlying assumption clear: being Christian gave one the right to move freely throughout the Mediterranean and to contest one's victimization in court. Obviously, none of this was true for Ottoman Muslims, and the French consuls acted accordingly. Like the Venetians before them, the French combined formal diplomatic relations with the Ottoman Empire with an unwillingness to question the essential rightness of eternal Muslim-Christian enmity along the ancient sailing routes of the Mediterranean.

CHAPTER 6

At the Tribunale

● ○ ●

We arrive, at long last, in Malta, along with our petitioners. What do we know about the circumstances of their arrival and how they went about pursuing their claims? Unfortunately, very little. It seems certain to have been a daunting experience. Having suffered through an attack and then undertaken the ordeal of a voyage to Malta, petitioners were now faced with initiating and sustaining a lawsuit.

In entering the city of Valletta, these Ottoman subjects were venturing into a newly built city stuffed with the baroque symbols of Catholic power. Construction began in 1566 at the behest of the Grand Master Jean Parisot de La Valette, who had just guided the knights to their victory over the besieging Ottoman navy (1565). Unlike the medieval city of Mdina in the interior of the island, with its crooked streets and irregular shape, Valletta was a planned city with a grid of broad streets laid out at right angles to each other. The plans were drawn up by Francesco Laperelli, student of Michaelangelo, who also served as architect to Cosmo Medici and Pope Pius IV.[1]

Over the course of the next two hundred years this small city, perched on top of a rocky hill, would see the construction of twenty-eight churches, twenty or so palaces and grand residences, and around ten civic buildings, all of them in the baroque style. Unlike in Rhodes, where the knights had their own confined quarter, the buildings of the order— the Palace of the Grand Master, the Cathedral of St. John, the Auberges of the different Langues, and the sprawling Sacred Infirmary—were spread out across Valletta.[2]

The Tribunale itself was probably on Merchant Street in the heart of Valletta.[3] Merchant Street is a main thoroughfare running northeast-southwest from the Fort of St. Elmo to the Grand Harbor. The building

FIGURE 6.1. Fort St. Angelo.

known then as Castellania, or the law courts, where the Tribunale was housed is still in existence today.[4] The imposing baroque façade, with the statues of Justice and Truth prominently displayed, is not the one that would have confronted our petitioners, as the building was substantially rebuilt in the mid-eighteenth century.[5] Nevertheless, the previous structure would have been grand as well, considering the neighborhood it was in. The streets of Valletta descend from the heights in the southwest and slope down toward St. Elmo, which sits at the end of the promontory. Beginning at the top of the hill, the entrance to Merchant Street was graced by the Auberge d'Italie (built in 1574) on one side and by the Auberge de Castile et León on the other.

Continuing downhill, the pedestrian would have passed the Church of St. James, built for the Knights of Castile and Léon in 1612. Then the Castellania and, further along, the Monte di Pietà, followed by the Church of St. Paul Shipwrecked, which became the church of the Jesuits in 1639. Work to rebuild it to a grander scale went on for forty years. Jesuit power was also on display just around the corner, on St. Paul Street, where the Jesuits in 1592 established Malta's first college, the Collegium Melitensia Societatis Jesu.

There are few hints in the documentation of the situation in which the plaintiffs found themselves in Valletta. Occasionally, however, their

FIGURE 6.2. Auberge de Castile, at the entrance to Merchant Street.

frustration seeps through. Gioannes Cugia, our merchant from Monemvasia who was discussed in the previous chapter, made it all the way to the Tribunale but could not find legal representation. Thus he addressed the court:

> he has not found a lawyer or a solicitor who will take his case. Thus he appeals to you to agree to order a Doctor and a solicitor to take up his case. He asks that they be able to speak both Greek and Italian so that he can understand them and they him. He also asks that they be people practiced and experienced in lawsuits and that they be God-fearing.[6]

When Haji Pietro from the town on Lindos, whom we also met in chapter five, stood in front of the Tribunale with two others, also from Lindos, the clerk explained that

> they have come to sit at Your Illustrious feet with the Consular documentation granted to them . . . and ask that the King grant them justice in obtaining their goods without long disputes and lawsuits.[7]

Antonio Cantanin's advocate used stronger language on behalf of his client, who was assaulted as he sailed from Alexandria for Istanbul. It was the attackers, not Antonio, who should provide security money in advance of the trial, since the latter "are wealthy people and they are poor, miserable foreigners, already hurt by the assault committed by these wealthy people."[8]

These excerpts convey the vulnerability of outsiders, far from home and up against an alien legal system. Giacomo Cappello, the Venetian who spent four months on the island in 1716, strongly endorses this view, and adds a corrupt legal system to Greek woes:

> The poor, despoiled Christians proceed to Malta; they bring the action to court, but lose everything, either because of the invulnerability corsairs enjoy on the island or else because they are judged by the same shareholders. Thereupon they appeal to Rome from whence judgments emanate against the corsairs, but having squandered so much on the proceedings, they nonetheless spend the rest of their lives in misery.[9]

It would be foolish to argue against the difficulty and expense involved in bringing a lawsuit. But leaving aside for the moment this obvious point, the sources suggest that we should not be too quick to assume that the Greeks wandered the streets of Valletta as bewildered strangers.

First of all, Greek merchants were a common sight in the city. Early in the seventeenth century Malta emerges as an important market in the ransoming and repatriation of slaves and begins to attract outside shipping as a result. Port records for the period 1616–35 show that ninety-three foreign commercial ships entered the harbor. Of these, the vast majority, sixty-seven, were from Marseilles, but the most numerous after that hailed from the Greek world. Twenty such ships passed through the Grand Harbor in these years. Most came from Venetian-held Zakynthos; they came to Malta to ransom (Muslim or Jewish) slaves, whom they then brought back to the Levant. Others came from the Ottoman world and were sailing to North Africa. They stopped at Malta and, like the Greeks from Zakynthos, were in the ransoming business. Maltese authorities issued a safe-conduct pass to Captain Paolo Paterno from Chios in 1627, authorizing him "to sail from here [Malta] to Constantinople and other places in the Levant and back, and to deal both in Islam and

Christendom in the ransom of slaves, Christians as well as Muslims."[10] In 1633 another Chiot merchant named Stefano Gara sailed into port to drop off some ransomed Christian slaves whom he had brought with him from the Ottoman Empire. He then picked up a number of freed Muslims and Jews and took them to Tripoli; from there he sailed back to Malta with North African merchandise to sell on the island.[11] Chiots were particularly well represented in the exchange of slaves, but merchants from Rhodes were also present.[12] This intermediary role was an enduring one; in the eighteenth century captives on Malta were still relying on Ottoman Christians, among others, to organize redemption.[13]

The Maltese themselves evidently recognized the growing number of Greek visitors to the island. In1623 they appointed the first consul "pro natione Graeca," a man named Joseph Moniglia.[14] Little is known about this individual, but he must have been familiar enough with the Greek language to be able to communicate with the Greeks. This would suggest he was either a descendant of the Greek community that left Rhodes with the knights in 1522 or a naturalized Maltese.[15] Like other consuls on the island, Moniglia was entitled to a 2 percent fee every time he assisted a Greek merchant, but we cannot assume that he actually provided much help. In a departure from standard practice in Europe, all consuls on the island were appointed by the grand master. France, England, and Venice all complained that their respective consuls were inept and apathetic.[16] Helpful or not, the Greeks did have a level of institutional representation not dissimilar to that accorded to the French, the English, or the Venetians. This is rather remarkable when one considers that the Greeks represented only themselves, and obviously had no state behind them.[17]

Moniglia actually appears in the one of the cases we have been discussing. He appears in court with the plaintiff Papa Iani, on behalf of those who were victimized but could not make it to Malta. He is identified as "the legal representative and consul of the nation."[18]

It seem very likely, then, that our petitioners would have found fellow Greeks (including those from Venetian-held territory) to assist them in Malta throughout the seventeenth century. Evidence from the Tribunale points to these connections. A late seventeenth-century case provides the most information on the relationships that could come into play in mounting a defense. It also affords us a glimpse into Valletta's demimonde, a place where Christians and Muslims, the freeborn and the slave, mixed freely.

The case stemming from an attack in 1682 revolved around the question of who owned the ship that had been assaulted. Hana, the plaintiff and a Christian, was the captain, and said the ship was his. The corsairs claimed he was not the real owner.[19] A Muslim slave named Haj Mehmet, son of Ali reis, testified on behalf of the plaintiffs, that is, the Maltese corsairs.[20] Let us leave aside for the moment what Haj Mehmet said and the role of Muslim slaves in the court cases. Instead, we will move on to the defendant, Hana reis, and note that he was able to counter with two witnesses of his own. Demetrius Frangulli of Chios went first. He told the court:

> About forty days ago I was in my bottega here in the city of Valletta when the Turk and slave Haj Mehmet passed by. I called out to him because I wanted to talk to him about something. He told me to leave him alone because he was feeling desperate. I asked him the cause of his despair and he told me that he had made a [false] testimony against Chana Reis and Domengo Reis at the request of Antonio, who has a coffee shop across from the Church of the Jesuits. He [Antonio] took him to a taverna before his deposition and they ate together and he got him drunk and got him to testify. And he also promised him some money.[21]

Frangulli was not a witness by chance. The relationship he had with Hana reis originated in the Ottoman Empire and was subsequently reactivated in Malta. Questioned as to how he knew the plaintiff, he said that Hana reis and his father had been friends and that he, Frangulli, had known the plaintiff since he was young.[22] Presumably he had spent his youth in Chios, since that was where he was from, but now he was settled in Valletta, where he had a bottega, another example of Greek connections to Malta.

Hana reis's second witness, Panaiotti Manolachi, was a Greek from the Morea who also knew Haj Mehmet. Four or five months earlier, he related, he was in the shop (bottega) of the "consule Ianii de Constantinopoli" when a slave whom he hadn't met before, Hagmet di Modon (so also from the Morea), came in.[23] He was in the company of one Demetrio from Athens, and together the two of them, the Muslim and the

Christian from the Morea, asked Panaiotti to write a letter for them in Greek. In this way, he continued, he had made the acquaintance of Haj Mehmet, and when, subsequent to this, they saw each other in the street, they would sometimes talk. One day when they happened to meet, Panaiotti asked him if he had received a reply yet to the letter that he (Panaiotti) had written for him. Haj Mehmet responded that he had not. Then, just as he had with Demetrius, the slave poured out his heart to Panaiotti. Once again, saying that he was feeling desperate, he went into the story of Antonio and the false deposition. In this version of the story Antonio was not acting alone; another slave was present, and the two of them got him drunk and so on and so forth prior to concocting the deposition. In this account Haj Mehmet said he had no knowledge of the case and was told that what he was doing would not harm anyone.[24] This suggests a practice in Malta of simply paying people to sign cooked-up documents, people with no connection to the case at all. Later on in his testimony, Panaiotti said that Hana reis came to Malta and that "as a Greek I made his acquaintance."[25]

The case of Hana reis makes it clear that Greeks who came to the island, even from as far away as Damascus, were able to find a community of fellow Greeks, compatriots who could assist them with tasks such as writing a letter in Greek. These Greeks in turn knew others outside their community in Malta, such as the Muslim slave Haj Mehmet, and were willing to use these contacts to assist those in need at the Tribunale. Connections to Malta could apparently be activated even from the eastern Mediterranean. Andrea Mauranza Choroneo, attacked near Karpathos while going from Rosetta to Constantinople, was unable to go to Malta himself to pursue his claim. Instead he went to the French chancery in Rosetta and assigned power of attorney to one Sig. D. Carlo Bonici of Malta.[26]

The Maltese, too, had their connections in the East. These connections could be used both for and against the Greeks. As we see in this case, they were willing to use a Muslim slave as a witness in a case, despite prohibitions against doing so, as a source of information on the plaintiffs. The Catholic missionary effort in the eastern Mediterranean also came in handy in this regard. Writing to Rome in 1726, the Grand Master Vilhena cited a Latin priest, a missionary in Constantinople and Patras, who reported hearing a Greek boast at Patmos that he had made a profit of 100 percent on claims against Maltese corsairs settled in

Rome.[27] Just a few years earlier, Grand Master Zondadari had claimed that the Greeks came to Malta and spied on the goods being unloaded, therefore identifying prize cargoes that were being brought in. They would then send that information to their associates back in Ottoman territory, who would subsequently come to Malta and lodge a claim on goods that were not theirs. Generally, he said, the Greeks did not operate in good faith.[28] The grand masters' complaints were entirely consistent with a larger discourse about Greek deception, one that comes up repeatedly in this chapter and the next.

At the same time, the Greeks were able at times to use Maltese experience in the Ottoman Empire to their benefit. Gioannes Cugia, the merchant from Monemvasia who had two witnesses testify on his behalf in Cairo, produced more testimony in Malta. Petrus Taliana, a Maltese, resident in the neighborhood of Vittoriosa, said that the royal seal and imprint were indeed the ones used by the French consul in Cairo.[29] He knew this because he had been in Cairo and he saw the consul using the seal and imprint.[30]

What is evident here is nothing less than dueling information regimes. The Greek petitioners who came to Malta strived to create official information that would certify them as Christians and as victims. The Maltese sought to counter this tactic by relying on other sorts of information, all of which was designed to undercut the Greeks' self-presentation. Both sides' tactics make it clear that, despite the absence of official relations between the Ottoman Empire and Malta, personal relationships linked the two places. Yet the reality of contact in no way caused either side to jettison the durable ideological construct of a world split irredeemably into Muslim and Christian camps. From the point of view of the knights, the geographic expression of that hostility was an insistence on seeing the Ottoman Empire as a remote, distant, and sinister place, linked to Malta only by war. This was the ideological spear they hurled against the attempts of the Greeks to document their claims.

At the Tribunale

In the previous chapter we focused on the institutional support that the plaintiffs pursued in the eastern Mediterranean, prior to their voyage to

Malta. Now it is time to turn to the substance of the arguments they made, both in the documents they brought with them and in the statements they made once in Malta.

Before moving on to the content of the lawsuits, we must pause to consider the Tribunale itself. In previous chapters I have described the motivations behind the founding of the Tribunale, as well as the new court's statutes and ordinances, including rules about the presiding judges. This much has come down to us from the documentary record. In addition, scattered references to the court can be found in the writings of contemporaries. We have mentioned Alonso de Contreras's exploits and the report of the Venetian envoy, Giacomo Cappello, in this regard. But there is as yet no proper historical study of the Tribunale, although it certainly deserves one. This lack seems to be reflective of a larger lacuna in the historiography of the early modern Mediterranean. During this period there was a burst of institution building, as many European states created new tribunals. These added a new level of regulation to mercantile life, on top of the customary practices that had traditionally sustained merchant communities. Yet studies of these institutions are few and far between.[31]

Whatever the reasons, we must bear in mind that we are proceeding ahead with a consideration of the testimony given by both sides at the Tribunale in Malta without a thorough understanding of all the mechanisms that produced the documentary record. This problem can only be rectified by a study that takes the Tribunale as its main object of investigation. While it is true that the Tribunale is central to the story being told here, it is the Greek victims themselves—their problems and their strategies—who are the real object of concern.

What we can say at this point is the following. The lawsuits before the Tribunale produced an additional layer of documentation, in addition to the consular and other papers the plaintiffs brought with them from the eastern Mediterranean. There was usually a fairly lengthy narrative of the attack, directed at the magistrates and presented not by the plaintiff himself but by his representative.[32] In addition, both sides were often interrogated, and these sessions, too, produced further testimony. What cannot be determined at this point is where these procedures came from. Perhaps more critically, in the absence of studies of other early modern tribunals in the Mediterranean, it is difficult to assess the testimony as critically as one would like. For instance, Greek merchants often emphasized that they were merchants and only merchants and had never pursued any other profession beside that of merchant. Was this insistence a reflection of their particular situation as merchants coming from the land of the enemy, that is, the Ottoman Empire? Or was this the sort of thing that merchants would typically say in court? In the absence of any sort of larger context, it is difficult to say.

With these caveats in mind, let us turn to our Greek petitioners and see what they had to say to the magistrates in Malta. First and foremost, all of the petitioners emphasized their Christian identity. We have seen the efforts they made to try to establish their identity as Christian persons. But this was not enough. They had to do the same for their cargo, their ships, and even the money they used in their commercial transactions. How did they go about doing this?

A key indicator is the almost complete absence of references to flags. The question of flags and Ottoman shipping in the early modern period is an elusive one. An older, nationally minded Greek historiography posited the existence of a Greek flag, without, however, providing satisfactory evidence. More recent work has made it clear that no such flag existed.[33]

In respect to the cases that came before the Tribunale, the exception proves the rule. In only two instances did a Greek plaintiff refer to the flag that he was flying at the time of the attack. Giovanni Mathsopulo, originally from Kalymnos but at the time of his complaint a resident on the island of Patmos, said that he was flying the flag of St. John of Patmos when he was attacked by a vessel bearing the flag of the Maltese knights in 1606.[34] In one other instance a petitioner does refer to a "ship of Patmos." Although no flag is mentioned, this must be what is meant.[35]

The flag of Patmos is a flag we know something about. In 1610, Grand Master Wignacourt, the founder of the Tribunale five years earlier, wrote a letter in response to a request made by Athanasio Carrara, a priest of the Monastery of St. John on Patmos. In that letter he noted that the Patmiots had retained some ships "which bear the flag and symbol [*l'insegna e bandiera*] of our Religion, like our ships of old." They had done so, he continued, to be able to supply the monastery with the provisions it needed. Even so, the monks complained of being oppressed and tormented by corsairing ships. Therefore, Wignacourt, after consulting with the magistrates of the Tribunale, took the further step of issuing patents and safe-conducts "to all in general and everyone in particular of these ships of the said monastery of St. John of Patmos, [these ships which] carry our flag and insignia."[36] The case in front of the Tribunale predates Wignacourt's letter by four years, and it is very likely that the special relationship between the knights and the monastery extended back many years. Corsairs flying the flag of Malta routinely violated agreements that the order itself had made, and thus it was common to issue prohibitions over and over again.[37] It is possible that the monks turned anew to the knights for protection as early as the 1570s, in the wake of the Ottoman defeat at Lepanto. This would mean that the early sixteenth-century arrangement, discussed in chapter two, was resurrected not fifty years after the knights' departure from Rhodes.[38] Writing at just about the time that Giovanni Mathsopulo came to Malta, the corsair Alonso de Contreras wrote that "The people of Patmos were very rich and their ships wore the same flag as the ships of the knights of Malta."[39]

The other case, first discussed in chapter five, concerns the French flag. Captain Agostino Plati reis departed Rethymnon, in Crete, in April 1686, holding a French passport. He was also carrying a French flag, a "bandiera."[40] As I said in the previous chapter, this is the only case in the records where French protection was sought in advance. The explanation is probably the War of Holy League (1684–99), which was ongoing at the time of the attack on Agostino Plati.

No other petitioner references either a French or a Patmiot flag (or any other sort of flag, for that matter). Given the privileged status (at least theoretically) of these flags, especially the French one, it seems certain that, had they been flying them, they would have said so. This suggests that they were flying some sort of Ottoman flag or no flag at all. The latter option may seem surprising, but we must bear in mind that the attacks took place wholly within Ottoman waters. In the last chapter I argued that the disparity in the use of passports between the eastern and western Mediterranean could be due to the fact that the latter was much more of an international sea in the seventeenth century. The same could hold true for the use (or non-use) of flags. The remarks of Henry Blunt, the English traveler who witnessed a Maltese attack on a Greek vessel in 1634, are instructive in this regard: "the Greeks laded with Turkish goods, made up to us, *who carry no Flag* [my emphasis], he judged Turkes."[41] On the other hand, Contreras bragged that, on his return to Malta, the Tribunale allowed him to incorporate an orange-and-white flag that he had captured into his own heraldic blazon.[42] Just one page later he recounts how he and his crew hoisted the "Turkish flag" in order to approach the North African shore. To sum up, then, there was no systematic flag regime in the eastern Mediterranean at this time. Our petitioners might have sailed with no flag, with some sort of Ottoman flag, or with several flags.[43] Whatever their practice was, they must have concluded it would not meet with sympathy in Malta since, with the notable exception of Patmos, they did not raise the issue of a flag.

The Greeks seized on other objects instead: the cargo, the ship, and even the money they traded with. Their testimony is striking for its insistence on going into great detail about matters that seem, on the face of it, to be unimportant and for repeating certain points over and over again.

Duca Galeazzo, son of Constantine, and Nicola, son of Micaele, for example, described how the cargo that they lost had been packaged: "the rice was packed loose onto the saica of Captain Iani Zagarachi of Lindos and the linen was divided into six *cachi*, both large and small, and two *casani*, marked on the outside."[44] In further testimony, several witnesses confirmed this description of the cargo; one witness was actually shown the signs, although it is not clear what this entailed.[45] Antonio Stravelli, who was an eyewitness to the attack, said that when the corsair captains boarded the ship, they saw "the crosses and signs on the goods."[46] Specifically Christian markings are mentioned in another case as well. A witness testified that the captain of the ship had two sacks full of money and both were marked with his stamp, which was the Madonna with Jesus.[47]

The earliest case on record from this series, dating from 1602, provides us with a rare glimpse of what things looked like in this maritime world. It also shows how shipbuilders and shipowners attempted to impart a religious identity to a material object, in this case a ship. Overall, we know very little about the material culture of our protagonists, owing to the almost complete absence of any sort of archaeological record with regard to Ottoman seafaring. Only a few shipwrecks have been exacavated. We have little sense of the objects—from sacks of money to entire ships—being fought over in Malta, even as the plaintiffs sought to establish their identity in the legal record.

This was precisely the point of the description of Antonio Cantanin's ship in the presentation made to the Tribunale:

> The Holy Cross is carved into the stern of the aforesaid ship, along with Greek letters and characters. In no way could anyone suspect or affirm or believe that the aforesaid ship, or even part of it, belongs to infidels. They would never allow that their goods bear the name of Jesus or the image of His Holy Cross, images which are so odious to them.[48]

Through such descriptions, which appear over and over again, the Greeks were attempting to accomplish two things. First, by providing the court with great detail, they sought to convince the court of the cargo's existence and of their ownership of it. Second, when they could, they pointed to physical markings which, they hoped, would establish the object's Christian identity. By their logic, this should have made it off-limits to the corsairs. However, such obviously Christian signs are cited in only a minority of cases. This suggests that cargo and ships were not easily identifiable along religious lines, apart from the assertion of Christian ownership.

Money and the ownership of money receive a great deal of attention in the court cases. To continue with the example of Antonio Cantanin, "the 300 *artepidi* of salt that was loaded in the ship for ballast was bought in Alexandria, Egypt, with money belonging solely to Antonio Cantanin, without the participation of anyone else."[49]

Standing in the bishop's court in Chios in 1633, the witnesses for Athanasio di Pancratio of Salonica, Comneno of Mytilene, and Patron Nikita di Rodi insisted that the men were trading with their own money. Comneno was trading with money that "he got from both his parents and his own work."[50] Nikita and Athanasio also did business with their own money, said another witness, and he knew this because "I have been with both of them in Alexandria and I have seen them invest their money for commercial purposes."[51] Other witnesses veered off into more general statements about the plaintiffs' financial dealings. Georgio from Volos testified that Athanasio was accustomed to travel and trade with his own capital, and that the previous year he had been in Chios, buying and selling grain. He knew this because the year before he had been with him in Chios, and he had asked him about this, as a friend, and Athanasio showed him the money he had realized from the sale of the grain.[52]

The most insistent emphasis on the origins and ownership of business capital comes in the case of the Armenian merchant Giovanni Marchara, who sailed from Rosetta and was attacked by Maltese corsairs in the Gulf of Antalya in 1683.[53] Once again in Chios, Georgi son of Theodori, the captain who had helped Giovanni load his goods in Rosetta, was asked if he knew if the cargo he loaded was the property of this Armenian, bought with his own money. He responded that he didn't know. Yes, it was he who had loaded the goods, but he couldn't speak to the ownership of the goods since, in his words, he had not had a conversation with him.[54]

But an Armenian merchant named Gasparo del q. Asssarsa (or Afsarsa), from the same town as the victim, knew more. He explained that the two of them lived together in the same khan in Rosetta, that they ate together every day, and that, as members of the same nation, they did business together. Many times Giovanni had counted his money in Gasparo's presence, and he (Giovanni) had packed his goods in his presence, and together they had loaded his goods.[55] Therefore, when he was asked if the capital was entirely Giovanni's or if others participated, he could say "for sure that the money is all his." He also added that Giovanni worked with large amounts of capital because his father was a prominent merchant.[56]

A second witness, also an Armenian, gave similar testimony about living with Giovanni and helping him pack his goods, and he too was asked specifically whether Giovanni worked only with his own money. He said yes, because Giovanni was not an ordinary merchant. He was also asked to give his opinion about Giovanni's general financial status, and said he was a merchant who worked with roughly 1,500 to 2,000 piasters per trip.[57]

Why so much detail? Why bother to say you watched someone pack up his goods or that you had seen the coins themselves that had been earned from the sale of grain a year prior to your testimony? Although we know very little about this Tribunale, and even less about the Ottoman Greek subjects who made their way there, we are not entirely lacking the larger seventeenth-century context. Two aspects of the Mediterranean world at this time are highly relevant to understanding the testimony that has been preserved in the records of the Tribunale.

Let us return first to Heyberger's work on the relationship between Arab Catholics and Rome in the seventeenth and eighteenth centuries. His research into the records of the Propaganda Fide has shown that, after claims of persecution by the Ottoman authorities, maritime commerce and its problems were the most common subject in terms of recourse to Rome.[58] The correspondence reveals a triangle of suspicion that linked Rome, the Arab Catholics, and the Ottomans. When the Propaganda wrote to the Duke of Etrurie in 1712, for example, asking that Tuscan ships not seize merchandise belonging to Catholic Syrians, the duke responded that "the Turks" obliged the Melkite bishop of Tyre and Sidon to sign as the owners of merchandise that was really "Turkish."[59]

When we also take into account the facts that charges of false documentation were widespread across the Mediterrranean at this time and that Catholic corsairs, including the Maltese, were as fervently suspicious as anybody else, we can safely conclude that the Greeks were well aware of this mistrust and sought to pre-empt it through this detailed testimony.[60] Although most of the charges of misrepresentation of ownership, both at the time and in the secondary literature, relate to cargo, the example of the Greeks in Malta shows that suspicion could extend beyond the cargo itself to the money used in commerce. This must be way the Greeks took up the even more daunting task of proving the Christian identity of something as fungible as money. We do know that Ottoman Christians entered into partnerships known as *mudaraba* with Ottoman Muslims. Most often, at least in the Arab lands, the Muslim partner supplied the capital while the Christian did the traveling.[61] We do not have direct evidence that Catholic authorities were aware of such arrangements, whether in Malta, Rome, or elsewhere, but the insistent questioning that we have seen in the Tribunale cases—was so-and-so trading with his own money, were others participating—suggests they were. Heyberger's work does show that Arab Catholics complained to the Propaganda about loans gone bad that had been extended to them by Ottoman Muslims, and the fine line between a loan and a partnership must not have seemed very crucial.[62]

The other problem confronting the Greeks can be described superficially as a lack of adequate documentation. We do not know very much at all about what sort of paperwork was on board the typical Ottoman ship in the seventeenth century. The evidence from the Tribunale suggests there wasn't much. We already know that passports were the exception rather than the rule. Only cargo books, described as the "libro del scrivano," seem to have been routine. Several cases make reference to such a book, and in one case it is included in the record of the case.[63]

Daniel Panzac's work on French trade in the Ottoman Mediterranean also suggests a commercial culture that was largely oral, at least in the seventeenth century, even across the religious divide. It was only in 1732 that French shippers began insisting on written contracts and bills of lading in their dealings with Muslim merchants.[64]

On several occasions, clearly under pressure from the Maltese, the plaintiffs felt obliged to directly address the question of why they could not produce this or that document. These instances provide valuable insight into the balance between written and oral culture in the Ottoman merchant community; they also show the difficulty the Greeks faced, as they were at pains to explain what the Maltese were certainly framing as inadequacies on the part of the plaintiffs.

In 1683 the Greek captain of a ship that had been seized (along with all of its cargo) by the Maltese on its way to Istanbul from Rhodes had to submit to an interrogation by Captain Franceso Real, who stood accused of the attack. Real asked the captain, Hana reis, if there was a written freight agreement and, if not, to give him a detailed description of the verbal agreement, including who was present, the price charged to each, the place where the agreement was concluded, and so forth.[65] Hana reis explained that "There was no written freight agreement, because the departure took place in front of a wide group of people, and the scribe noted it down in his book." [66] He continued on, saying that the cargo had been loaded in the winter, while the attack had not taken place until May. Although the merchants had loaded their goods in front of "a diverse group, both Turks and Christians," he could not remember their names, nor could he remember details about the merchandise that was loaded since the merchandise that had been taken was not his. He was able, however, to give the exact charges for the freight, which makes sense. As the captain or owner of the ship, freight charges would have been of vital interest to him.[67]

Several years later the merchants who had shipped their goods from Crete on Agostino Plati reis's ship were similarly obliged to explain documentary practices to the Tribunale. Strati Stranghili told the magistrates that "it is not customary for us to get a bill of lading for our merchandise from the customs official; simply the official notes [*everything down*] on a strip of wood . . . for this reason we have not drawn up a bill of lading listing our merchandise but our ship's scribe noted down the cargo in his book. This book was taken by Captain Paolo."[68] The reference to a strip of wood is obscure and difficult to understand. Theodoro Taulari, who filed a separate lawsuit concerning the same attack, described the same practice and said that "the scribe of the ship and the customs official were in the shop with a piece of wood."[69] Most likely the plaintiffs are describing a system of proof of customs payment whereby notations were made on strips of wood, which were then divided between the merchant and the customs official. The merchant's strip, functioning as a receipt, would then be shown at a subsequent Ottoman port as proof of payment.[70]

The somewhat casual nature of this procedure is suggested by the fact that it took place not in any sort of customs building but rather in the shop, the "*magazeno*," owned by the various participants in this lawsuit. The customs official, it seems, came to them rather than the other way around. In any event, through their explanations the plaintiffs seem to have been well aware that the practice did not match the level of formality that had by now become customary in the European Mediterranean. By this time bills of lading were generally issued in triplicate.[71]

Now, the distinction between a cargo book and a bill of lading might seem like an arcane point, particularly since, as the testimony makes clear, the corsairs tore up whatever documents they found on board. But the comments of A. Roberts, an English traveler who was marooned near Chios in the last decade of the seventeenth century and forced to serve on a corsairing ship, make clear the importance of the distinction. His experience also supports the impression gained from the Tribunale, namely, that Ottoman ships carried little paperwork on board other than the cargo book. Roberts observed that the corsairs occupied themselves "not in taking Turkish vessels, but Geek saicks or any small ships that came in our way."[72] He continued:

I shall now proceed to shew how they use the poor Greeks they take in the Saicks: First they threaten the Master severely, especially of a Wood-laden Saick, to make him confess what money

there is and then if they find him fearful and pliable, as they generally are, they give him 10 Dollars and send him packing. But if he
be morose and sullen, then they plague him for 3 or 4 months and
are not afraid of his going to Leghorn to make his Complaint, or
that he can give any intelligence to their Owner, how much Goods
he had on Board, as not knowing what a Bill of Lading is: Only he
has an old doting Scrivener with him, who has only a Manifesto in
general, which they immediately get from him.[73]

Roberts clearly saw a bill of lading as more of a threat to the corsairs
than a feeble manifesto. Although he does not spell it out, the implication is that a bill of lading could have been presented in Livorno (Leghorn). This was presumably because, owing to multiple copies held by
various parties, the victim could have gone back to the point of departure and picked up another copy. It seems that the (potential) power of
the bill of lading was not so much that it could reveal an illegitimate attack on fellow Christians; rather, it was because the Greeks would then
be able to document how the corsairs were cheating their backers, those
who funded the venture and were due a certain share of the goods and
people seized. Fraud at sea, with the corsairs underreporting their tak-
ings, was widespread but difficult to document, as it is today.[74] Inadequate
as it may have been, the fact that the corsairs routinely took the manifesto shows that, unlike the well-established procedures that were in
place for ransoming Ottoman Muslims, attacks on Ottoman Christians
were dubious enough that they had to be kept as invisible as possible.

But the difficulties that the Greeks faced in Malta were connected to
something more fundamental than an inability to find documentation
that would stand up in court. Through their efforts to retrieve their
goods and ships, they raised the question of the status of the Ottoman
Mediterranean within the larger Mediterranean world. As Ottoman subjects and as Christians, they were uniquely positioned to bring Ottoman
maritime life into a European court. One is tempted to say that they
shone a spotlight on this shadowy world, but that is to assume the van-
tage point of the West peering into the mysterious East. Here we must
remember that the Greeks who were victimized were engaged in routine
commerce within an entirely Ottoman sphere. It was Maltese attacks
that turned their commercial problems into international disputes.

Contemporary Western sources form a fascinating counterpoint to the testimony in the Tribunale. In his recent article on Ottoman shipping in the eighteenth century, Edhem Eldem had this to say about a French report on a particular ship: "The absence of any reference to the name of the captain and to the nationality of the ship—*never omitted in the case of a French ship*—suggests that this was also a local boat that had been chartered by French traders to transport their wool to Istanbul."[75] As mentioned earlier in this chapter, Henry Blunt sees a flagless ship as a "Turkish" ship: "the Greeks, laded with Turkish goods, made up to us, *who carry no Flag*, he judged Turkes."[76] Already by the seventeenth century, then, Europeans were identifying Ottoman shipping with shipping that was local and undocumented, as opposed to European shipping, which possessed flags and proper national identity.

Difference, of course, is usually inflected with power, and the emergent category of "local" was no different. In the long and increasingly unequal encounter between the Ottoman Empire and Europe, "local" became an ever more vulnerable category. In his study of foreignness and localness in late nineteenth-century Alexandria, Will Hanley argues that "foreigners were whole, possessing a broad range of rights and privileges. It was the local that was pathologized improper and impure."[77] A similar attitude of suspicion hovers around Ottoman or, in European eyes, "local" shipping. A recent study has observed that many historians assume "that there were no rules and regulations, that the Ottomans vessels owned either by Christians or Muslims were under no jurisdiction and that they were synonomous with piracy and fraud."[78] The authors cite the very recent comments of a British historian writing about Ottoman shipping during the Napoleonic era:

> What indeed was an Ottoman ship? Few local mariners knew any rules of the sea, their papers were often incomprehensible, their crews resisted investigation with spirit. . . . The only true test was to see his cargo and his ship's papers. So unless a pirate were actually caught at his trade, naval captains risked a diplomatic row every time they sent a boarding party to search a suspect vessel.[79]

Already in the seventeenth century the Greek petitioners in Malta seem aware of how the the local and the undocumented (at least according to European standards) could be turned into an object of suspicion, even though it was the knights who were intruding into Ottoman waters. From this follows their attempts to explain why something had not been written down or why a document that was common farther west, such as a bill of lading, was not in use in Ottoman ports.

The knights, of course, were highly motivated to cast suspicion on these troublesome Ottoman subjects who came all the way to Valletta, with their fistfuls of documents and their sad stories, to try to recover their goods. Before moving on to the knights' response, we should acknowledge here the problem of corruption and the interpretation of sources coming out of the Tribunale. It is very true that the court was a corrupt institution in the sense that a conflict of interest lay at the very heart of it. The magistrates hearing the cases, after all, received 3 percent of the captured booty.[80] More generally, the entire island lived off the corso. Nor are we lacking in explicit condemnations of the court, such as Cappello's earlier in this chapter. But this does not mean that the magistrates and all those who were interested in defending the corsairs operated without constraints. As Benton shows again and again in her study of the Indian and Atlantic Ocean world, pirates tried to justify their actions, no matter how heinous, in terms of prevailing legal norms. The Mediterranean was no different. Like the Greeks, the Maltese attempted to justify their actions, and in so doing they revealed what was considered justifiable at the time

The Limits of the Consolato del Mare

A good example of the Maltese attempt to fit into prevailing norms is the following: contemporary witnesses and historians today often remark on the fact that the Maltese tortured Christian captains and merchants to say that the cargo they carried, although marked as Christian, really belonged to Turks and Jews, but they rarely say why they did this. They did it precisely because, according to their interpretation of the Consolato del Mare tradition, they had the right to seize Turkish- and Jewish-owned cargo as enemy cargo aboard a friendly ship.[81]

At the Tribunale the Greeks appealed to the same reasoning as well. These Greek victims tried to prove the Christian identity of their cargo and their ships, and even their persons, because Christians were friends, or supposed to be. Although they rarely made their reasoning explicit, on two occasions they did mention the rules that they thought should apply. Papa Iani, appearing on behalf of his brother Captain George in the 1630s, complained that Captain Jacinto had attacked George's ship and forced George, his scribe, and ten sailors into a little skiff, where they were left to the elements. In doing this, Jacinto "does not observe the rules of the Consolato del Mare, since he knows that they are all Christian."[82] Captain Antonio Cantanin asked for restitution on the basis of "*consuetudine maritime*" and then, happily for us, went on to explain his understanding of what they were.

In his opening statement to the court he said that he was in Alexandria, in Egypt, where he was approached by several Turkish merchants, who asked if they could hire his boat. They agreed on a price, and off they went.[83] During the course of the attack, he and his sailors were forced off the ship onto a small deserted island.[84] Now, in Malta, he was demanding the return of the ship and all its accoutrements, salt that had been carried as ballast, the freight charges he was due from the Muslim passengers, and a long list of goods and personal effects belonging to the captain or to the crew. He said, "Since the ship belongs to Christians, and the shipowners and the sailors are all baptized Christians, it is not just that they be defrauded of their goods simply because they hired out their ship to infidel merchants."[85] We should note here that Cantanin did not ask for the return of the cargo belonging to the "infidel merchants," only that he be compensated for lost freight charges. A more perfect understanding of the rules of the Consolato del Mare would be difficult to find. Let us remember the comments of Richard Zouche, the English admiralty judge writing in the middle of the seventeenth century: "by the Consolato del Mare, in which the law of the Mediterranean is contained, one who seizes enemy goods in a friendly ship is bound to pay freight for that part of the voyage which the ship has performed."[86]

When outlining the arguments from the other side we must note an imbalance in the legal record. The voice of the corsair is less in evidence in the court documents than that of his victim. This is not an entirely unhappy situation given that generally, both in the historical record itself and in the historiography, the corsairs' victims (like victims everywhere) have not received as much attention as have the perpetrators of the attacks. Nevertheless, their relative absence does mean that their response to the legal challenge mounted by the Greeks often has to be inferred. The reason for the imbalance is not entirely clear. Most likely, however, the absence of corsair testimony reflects the absence of the corsairs themselves. Sometimes the record explicitly states that the corsair named by the plaintiff could not be located and brought to court.[87] Even when this is not said explicitly, we know that in the early modern legal system the most common way for a defendant to delay a case was to simply refuse to appear.[88] And in those instances where the case was thrown out because of lack of jurisdiction, the defendant would not have to present himself either.

Despite these limitations, the records of the Tribunale, along with other sources, have preserved enough to at least suggest the general outlines of the Maltese response. Even when the corsairs are absent, Greek arguments can function as a sort of negative snapshot of what the corsairs would have said; it makes sense that the plaintiffs would try to anticipate the accusations of the other side. Sometimes, fortunately, we can see that counterattack quite directly in the form of questions that are put to the Greek plaintiffs.

At times, the accused respond within the logic of the Consolato del Mare tradition but with the opposite intent: they try to disprove the Christian identity that is being claimed. Just as frequently, however, they sidestep the issue of religious identity altogether and turn the focus elsewhere. First, they hold up Greek behavior, as opposed to identity, for scrutiny. Second, they try to wrap the Greeks in a cloud of suspicion because they come from enemy territory. In other words, despite their professed adherence to a world defined exclusively in terms of religious identity, the knights show the same kind of inconsistency that we laid out in chapter two, even here in their own court. The circumstances are somewhat different, admittedly. In chapter two it was Venetian hostility that forced the knights to acknowledge the distinction between Jews who were Venetian subjects and those who were not. In the Tribunale it was the knights themselves who downplayed the religious identity of the petitioners and emphasized their Ottoman connections. Cynical ploy or not, the two poles of identity, religious or territorial, remain the same and suggest that the knights, often viewed as an anachronistic relic, were not so far out of the mainstream after all.

The various corsairing attempts to undercut Greek assertions about Christian ownership are too numerous to be reproduced in their entirety here. Several examples should suffice, however, to convey the Maltese line of attack in the Tribunale.

Let us recall the case discussed at the beginning of the chapter. Hana reis, a captain from Damascus, came to Malta in an attempt to retrieve his ship, which the corsairs had taken from him in an attack in May 1682.[89] Two of his witnesses accused Haj Mehmet, son of Ali reis, witness for the defense, of giving false testimony. What was this testimony that he gave? He told the court that he had been sailing "the seas of Alexandria" for twenty years and that this was his second sojourn on Malta, having been enslaved twice.[90] He knew Hana reis "very well," and he also knew his ship, having seen it many times. The ship, he said, did not belong to the Christian captain. Its ownership was split between two "Turkish" merchants, one resident in Cairo, the other in Damietta, and he gave the names of both.[91]

The intent of the testimony is clear and straightforward enough; it is to show that the ship was Muslim-owned and thus legitimate prize. But the larger context is quite remarkable. Here are corsairs, whose justification for the corso is the pursuit of the Muslim enemy in defense of the Christian world, asking that the word of a Muslim slave be taken over that of a Christian victim and his Christian witnesses. In addition, his testimony reveals a willingness to claim, and to use, deep familiarity with the Ottoman world. Just as the Maltese Petrus Taliana, cited earlier in this chapter, knew the seal and the imprint used by the French consul in Cairo, so Haj Mehmet could tell the court who did business with whom in the shipping coming out of Egypt. Muslims, and the Muslim world, hovered in every corner of the courtroom and, as often as not, they were invited in by the corsairs themselves. Yet these transgressive ties did nothing to dislodge the ideological foundation of the Tribunale and the corso, namely, the eternal opposition between Christianity and Islam.

Along the same lines, we can return to the case of Haji Pietro, the captain from Rhodes who was attacked off the coast of Egypt in 1616.[92] As his case dragged on in Malta, a lawyer for the opposing side drew up questions that seem to have been meant for Haji Pietro's witnesses.[93] The intent of the questions is clear. Do they (the witnesses) know whether the rice belonged to Haji Pietro, or was some of it owned by Turkish merchants? Do they know who the reis paid for the rice, and how much it cost? Hadn't they previously said that the ship belonged to the reis while the rice belonged to the Turks? Did they know that the Greeks were accustomed to navigate with Turkish ships and merchandise which they claim is theirs?

The Greeks had only the Christian card to play, and they played it over and over again. The usual Maltese response to this was to ignore the Greeks' protestations of a common Christian identity and instead to put the focus elsewhere. Their first gambit was to try to charge the Greeks with hostile intent. The tenor of the testimony makes it clear that the latter understood this line of attack.

Sometimes the record shows explicit claims of peaceful behavior. Strati Stranghili was a merchant on board Agostino Plati reis's ship, assaulted in April 1686 as it was coming from Crete.[94] Under questioning in Malta, he gave a vivid account of the attack. After a chase of two or three hours, the corsairing vessel drew near, and they saw that the ship was flying the flag of Malta. He said, "We immediately raised the white flag and threw the caicco into the sea in order to render obedience to the captain of the (corsair) vessel."[95] A caicco is a small light boat; during an attack it was very common for those on board to flee to land in such a craft. By saying that they threw it into the sea, he must have been trying to demonstrate that they had no intention of fleeing.

More often, however, Maltese suspicion, and Greek attempts to confront that suspicion, run as undercurrents through the testimony and help explain certain emphases that otherwise seem puzzling. Just as the plaintiffs went into great detail about the packaging of their goods in order to demonstrate (Christian) ownership, so too they also asserted their identity as merchants.

When Duca Galeazzo, son of Constantine, and Nicola, son of Micaele, went to the bishop's court in Chios in 1634, they were concerned not only to show they were Catholics of the Greek rite. They also said they intended to prove that "for many years now they have been accustomed to travel for purposes of trade."[96] Their witnesses testified to this effect and, when they were asked how they knew this, said they had seen them coming and going many times.[97]

Similarly, Francesco Fante, the French vice-consul in Saida, verified that Haji Pietro, the captain from Rhodes, and his sailors were "Greek

Christians and good merchants, never having pursued any other profession than that of commerce."[98] A fellow Christian from Rhodes gave testimony to back this up. The language is particularly interesting, as he seems almost to conflate the two identities, the Christian and the commercial: "He says he knows him to be a good merchant; the witness has never seen the said Hagi pursue any other profession other than that of a good Christian and a merchant, sailing the seas and conducting business in many places with ships and boats."[99]

The testimony to establish a merchant's identity as a merchant often shades imperceptibly into testimony about that person's behavior, as we can see in what the Rhodiot says about Hagi Pietro. In that sense it merges with the testimony given to establish ownership. Witnesses knew that the rice, for example, belonged to the victimized merchant because they had seen him buy it. All of this was intended to convince the court that the plaintiff was a good Christian and a peaceful merchant who had legitimately come by the merchandise that had been stolen from him.

Cynical or not, the Maltese could construct a plausible case for Greek hostility quite easily, and the plaintiffs must have known this; hence the insistence on their peaceful pursuit of commerce. In the early modern Mediterranean commercial voyages could dabble in a bit of piracy on the side, making it hard to draw the line between a mechant and a pirate.[100]

But the corsairs could also levy a more specific charge against the Greeks. Yes, they were Christians, but they were also vassals of the Turks. Although the Tribunale statutes forbade attacks on Christians, things were not always so straightforward in practice.[101] In the long wrangling over the case of Hana reis and his attempts to retrieve his ship, the court observed that in order to rule on the justice or injustice of the attack, it would be necessary to look at the letters patent the corsairs had been carrying with them. Had the attackers been given license and permission to attack "not only the common enemy the Turks but also the Christians who are their subjects and vassals?"[102] The court then took it even further, saying that it was not necessary to distinguish whether the subjects were "Turkish" or "Christian," since "in war it is not religion that is considered but rather vassalage, that is to say, it is not a question as to whether the victims are Christian, but rather if they are recognized as subjects."[103]

Considering that the ideological basis for the corso was an insistence on a world divided by religion, this is an astonishing statement to make. Yet in its logic it is the same reasoning that the Maltese used in their frequent wranglings with the Venetians, when they distinguished between Jews who were Venetian subjects, whom they could not attack, and Jews who were not. The latter, at least according to the Maltese, were fair game.[104]

The Maltese were adept at laying out gradations of guilt that, in their view, made the Greeks legitimate prize. In the case discussed above, the court continued that even if the letters patent did not authorize attacking the Greeks as vassals of the Turks, one must take into account the situation at the time of the attack. Perhaps the Greeks were fighting in defense of the common enemy at that moment, and this would be sufficient to justify an attack.[105] As we shall see in the next chapter, the Maltese made similar arguments to the papacy. During the Ottoman-Venetian war of 1714–18, the knights were quick to send off an emissary to the pope with the argument that all Greek vessels serving the Turkish fleet in any way should be good prizes.[106]

Another tactic was not so much an assault on the Greeks per se; rather, they tried to arouse suspicion about them since they came from the land of the enemy. Although the Maltese corsairs and Ottoman subjects were linked by a web of daily interactions in the eastern Mediterranean, in the courtroom the corsairs were able to turn the Ottoman world into a distant realm of brutality and injustice.[107]

I have already referred to the case of the shipowner Antonio Cantanin on several occasions. Cantanin played the Christian card in court. He told the Tribunale that the Holy Cross was carved into the stern of his ship, and he asked for the return of what had belonged to him and to his crew, all of whom, he asserted, were baptized Christians. He also asked for the freight charges due to him from his Muslim passengers, but not the return of the Muslim-owned cargo.

The accused brushed aside these protestations in the defense they presented to the court. They said that the Greeks purported to say which goods belonged to Christians, which to infidels, "but no person who lives under the tyranny of Mohammed should be allowed to testify, since they have been forced through beating to say what they [the Turk] want."[108] The Greeks hit back, saying that while it was true that they were vassals of the Turk, the ship belonged entirely to Christians. In addition, the evidence they brought from Zante had been drawn up in the land, territory, and jurisdiction of Christians. Nor could they have possibly have had the time to consult the Turks between the attack and their arrival in Zante.[109] Antonio Cantanin himself addressed the court directly on this issue, sounding particularly aggrieved. He said he had been notified of a petition entered by Captain Oratio and other parties to the lawsuit, arguing that the judges should not give any credit to the plaintiffs' claims because the latter were pushed and forced into their testimony by the Turks. And what will happen, he asked, when similar persons come to the court asking for the restitution of their goods and their ships? He continued:

> The *Religione* professes to help Christians, and especially those who are oppressed in their country by the Muslim tyranny. The witnesses can't be Frenchmen, or Italians, or Spaniards but rather those who were on the boat with him, the co-navigators.[110]

Gioannes Cugia, the merchant from Monemvasia who was robbed of 2,000 Spanish reales off the Egyptian coast, was confronted with a similar line of questioning during the course of his lawsuit. His opponents had the following, rather loaded questions (among others) put to him and his witnesses:

1. Say what country they are from.
2. Say if they are Levantine Greeks or dependent upon them.
3. Say if they know that many times the consuls who are resident in the regions of the Turk are forced to attest [things which are] contary to the truth, because the Turks make them.
4. Say if they know that the Turks command whatever they want, without regard for the law or for justice.[111]

Here even European consular attestation was included in the broad swath of evidence that could not be admitted from the eastern Mediterranean, as a result of the supposed consequences of Turkish tyranny. One witness, a Greek from Mytilene, gave a stout defense of Ottoman justice in response: "The Turks conduct themselves with justice, and don't force anyone."[112] The reference to the Levantine Greeks and their dependents (*Greci Levantini o da loro dependeno*) is a singular one in the records of the Tribunale and thus it is difficult to fully understand its connotation.[113] But its intent to draw a distinction between Greeks who were Ottoman subjects and those who were not is clear.[114] Once again, the Ottomans loom large in the Tribunale.

Beyond the Tribunale

The story of Greek merchants and captains and their difficulties with Catholic piracy extends far beyond the cases from the Tribunale I have been discussing. First and foremost, both Greek and Arab Christians approached the Vatican when they had problems with Maltese and other Catholic pirates. But other tribunals saw Greek petitioners as well. In Malta itself, we know that some cases were heard not in the Tribunale degli Armamenti but in the Grand Court of the Castellania. Although the practice dwindled during the course of the seventeenth century, ships flying the flag of the grand master as a lay ruler were quite common at the end of the sixteenth century. In those cases it was the Castellania that had jurisdiction and victims had to go there. In correspondence from 1704 the grand master specifically mentioned that "the suits of Greeks arising out of these . . . have always been heard in the Grand Court of the Castellania."[115] Outside Malta, the Greeks also tried their luck in Florence and in Spain; the history of these attempts is completely unknown.[116] But we do know something about at least one instance in which the search for justice took a Greek merchant all the way to distant Turin, the capital of the Duchy of Savoy. This case is valuable not only because it shows just how far beyond the Mediterranean our story extends but also because of the remarkably detailed and wide-ranging arguments that are preserved in the papers from this long-forgotten litigation.[117]

On the May 6, 1678, two ships sailing the flag of Savoy attacked the ship *Agios Georgios* near the island of Symi, which lies about twenty-five kilometers northwest of Rhodes. The Savoyards took over the ship and sailed it west to the island of Amorgos. There they released Mellos and made off with the ship and the cargo.[118] Eventually, Mellos made his way back to Chios. The story of his journey to Turin, and the help he received along the way, is an important one, and I return to in the final chapter.

For now we shall confine ourselves to the arguments made at the duchess's court and ask how they compare to those made in Malta.[119]

Mellos began his defense with the diploma issued by the Duchy of Savoy. He underlined its importance—without it the Savoyards were simple pirates—and then laid out its language for the court. The diploma gave permission "andare in Corso contro li Pirati Turchi et altri Infedeli all'Impero Ottomano."[120] The attack violated the terms of the diploma, he argued, for the following four reasons. First, the Greeks, who belonged to the Christian faith, should not be considered Turkish subjects because they were forced to bear Turkish rule.[121] Second, the Greeks were neither infidels nor schismatics. The Greeks followed the Catholic faith but used the Greek rite. Therefore, as a "Catholic," Mellos should not have been attacked by Christian pirates.[122] Third, it was not an excuse to say that the attack took place in "enemy territory" because what mattered was not the place but the people who were attacked.[123] Finally, Mellos said, he was not flying the Turkish flag, but even if he were, that would not have been reason enough because he was a Christian. He pointed out that even the Catholics had been known the fly the Turkish flag, either to fool the Turks or to save themselves.[124]

The response to Mellos was handed down on the July 20, 1679, or a little more than a year after the attack.[125] The duchess's advisers denied his claim and responded to the defense he had mounted. First, as Mellos acknowledged, the boat in question had loaded its cargo at Rosetta, a port that was under Turkish control. Second, the seizure took place in territory that also belonged to the Turkish state. Third, the boat was flying a Turkish flag and was headed for Constantinople, not Messina.

This last argument, about the destination of the boat, generated extensive documentation and was a sharply contested point. Although Mellos did not refer to it when he was laying out his defense, it is clear that he knew the ship's itinerary would be an issue when he reached Turin. As part of preparing his case he took care to get papers from French authorities in Rosetta and in Sicily; the intent being to show that the boat was going from Rosetta to Messina.[126] Once in Turin, he presented his ship's voyage as a mission of mercy; he was serving the king of France by going to Messina, where there was hunger.

The other side went on the offense. Five witnesses from the *Perla*, one of the two ships that attacked the *Agios Georgios*, were brought in to assert that, at the time of attack, Mellos had said that the ship's destination was Smyrna, not Messina. The Savoyard side continued with the point. The boat was captured between Rhodes and the Anatolian coastline, which is the route to Constantinople, used to bring rice and linen to the capital city. In addition, two Turkish çavuşes were on board, and this would be unlikely, they argued, if Sicily were the intended destination.[127] Even market conditions were brought into the argument. The linen that was on board is not in demand in Sicily, where it is abundant. It would make far more sense for Mellos to sell it for a healthy profit in Smryna, rather than to undertake the dangerous trip to Sicily. Finally, the Spanish took Messina on March 15, 1678, two months before the attack, so the French authorities in Sicily could not have been the intended recipients.

Because of all this, the Savoyard authorities concluded that the goods belonged not to Mellos but to Turks. And if the goods did indeed belong to the Greek, he had falsely put down Messina as the destination in order to avoid the punishment, dictated by law, for Christians who transported goods in lands belonging to the Turks.[128]

This final point, concerning Christians who transported goods in lands belonging to the Turks, is a line of reasoning that does not appear in the Tribunale records. As such, it represents yet another imagining of the Mediterranean as a maritime space. Something very similar is articulated in the instructions given to a cruise departing from Livorno in 1607.[129] The knights were told not to attack the French when they were carrying goods, even Turkish goods, between France and the Ottoman Empire. But if they were carrying goods from port to port *within* the Ottoman Empire, the so-called *caravane* trade, then they were fair game. The same applied to the Greeks.[130] And in correspondence between the Knights of Malta and the French king in the 1670s, the knights, who were under great pressure at this particular juncture, asked that at least French ships not carry "Turkish" goods between "Turkish" ports.[131]

Although the principle behind this distinction was not articulated by either the Savoyards or the Tuscans, we do not have to look too far to discover their reference point. In the context of the ongoing struggle to define neutral shipping, early modern admiralty law distinguished between international voyages and cabotage or coastal trade, more exactly, trade between two ports belonging to the same sovereign. The British used this distinction, for example, between 1793 and 1801 to seize American ships trading in the French Caribbean while Britain was at war with France.[132] For various reasons, the British permitted neutral shipping between French colonial ports in the West Indies, but American ships trading between the West Indies and Europe could be seized.[133] The arguments that confronted Mellos, and the instructions given to the Knights of St. Stephen, seem to have been a Mediterranean twist on this distinction in admiralty law. Trade between the Ottoman Empire and Christian Europe was legitimate, but internal Ottoman trade, trade between ports lying within the sultan's realm, was not. The reasoning behind this thinking might well have drawn on certain seventeenth-century realities. Given increasing European commercial interest in goods coming from the Ottoman Empire—witness the growth of the port of Smyrna during this century—Tuscan and Savoyard authorities might have felt compelled to signal their acceptance of European-Ottoman trade. But trade between Ottoman ports could more persuasively be depicted as illegitimate because (it could be argued) it redounded to the benefit of the sultan and his subjects. Therefore, the cargo on board the *Agios Georgios* was legitimate prize because it was benefiting the Ottoman Empire.

The distinction between international and the cabotage trade aside, this case is very similar to what we have seen in Malta. Like the petitioners in front of the Tribunale, Mellos attempted to turn the dispute into a question of the religious identity of the victims, in this case himself and other Greek merchants who had had cargo on board the *Agios Georgios*. All four of his points of defense rested on his status as a Christian. Point three stated this explicitly: it was not an excuse to say that the attack took place in "enemy territory" because what mattered was not the place but the people who were attacked. But his insistence that the Greeks were really Catholic—that they were Catholics who follow the Greek rite—is not something that we see in Malta. The reason for this may be the following. The statutes of the Tribunale in Malta prohibited attacks on all Christians and did not distinguish between Orthodox and Catholic. But in Tuscany the distinction was drawn; corsairs (and here we are speaking principally of the Knights of St. Stephen) were required in their oath only to desist from attacking Roman Catholics.[134] Possibly it was the same in neighboring Savoy, and hence Mellos's argument, which we don't see in Malta, that the Orthodox could be considered Catholic.

Mellos's claim in this regard, by the way, was quite reasonable. As noted in chapter two, this was the position of the patriarch of Venice, who insisted that the Greeks of Venice were "Catholics of the Oriental Rite," and many other Latin clerics held this view as well.[135]

Like the corsairs and their defenders in Malta, the Savoyards' response to this line of reasoning was characteristically ambiguous. Mostly they ignored Mellos's defense of his Christian identity and focused exclusively on the territorial distinction. A similar attitude is found in the 1607 instructions, which treat the Greeks and the French in an identical manner. What is intended is clearly a broad attack on the legitimacy of the caravane trade, regardless of who is engaging in it. But a certain hesitancy crops up in their final summation. They accuse Mellos of lying and say that goods belonged not to him but to Turks. Thus, for a brief moment, they take up the question of the ownership of the cargo. But then they abruptly shift gears again. *Even if the goods* (my emphasis) did indeed belong to Mellos, they could still be seized, since he was transporting goods in lands belonging to the Turks (given that they did not believe his destination was Messina).

The Mediterranean context of the Savoyard ruling is apparent in another way. All European debates about neutral shipping—and the distinction between cabotage and international trade was part of these debates—were predicated on the presence or absence of war. It was the onset of war between Britain and France in 1793 that precipitated the British justification of its seizure of American shipping. To do so, it resurrected the Rule of 1756, which was itself the product of the Seven Years' War (1756–63).[136]

There was no declared war between the Duchy of Savoy and the Ottoman Empire in 1678. There was, however, the permanent war between Christianity and Islam, whose manifestation was the corso. What the Savoyards (and the Tuscans and the Maltese) did was to apply the evolving debates about neutral shipping—debates that depended critically on the presence or absence of war—to a world that lived in a gray zone between war and peace. The Greek Orthodox added another layer of ambiguity to this already uncertain situation. Even if there was a permanent war, should the Greeks be exempted due to their Christian identity? Should they constitute, as it were, floating islands of neutrality in an Ottoman sea? Mostly the Savoyards ignored this question. By doing so they implicitly said no. But by declining to tackle the question head on, they sustained the ideological framework of a world divided into Christians and Muslims.

Even declared war in the Mediterranean displayed this characteristic hesitancy between a territorial definition of neutral shipping and one that focused more on the identity of those engaged in maritime endeavors. In 1715, at the beginning of yet another Ottoman-Venetian war (which would prove to be the last), the Venetians saw fit to publish legislation on the law of seizures during war. Part of this legislation took up the question of when Greek Ottoman subjects were *buona preda*. They were legitimate prize when: they traveled together with Turks who had been seized, when they behaved in a hostile manner toward Venetians, and when Greek merchants, flying the flag of Patmos of the *Agios Georgios*, carried goods destined for Turkish ports or when Turks were members of the crew.[137]

When we put the cases from the Tribunale next to the lawsuit in Turin and the Venetian legislation of 1715, it becomes difficult to sustain the argument that the knights were somehow outliers or outlaws. In all three cases the special protection that the Greeks supposedly enjoyed as fellow Christians was surrounded by restrictions. This protection that turned out to be not much protection after all reflected the fundamental ambiguity of the early modern Mediterranean. The ideological commitment on both sides to a world divided between Christianity and Islam was still there, but when the Greeks threw down the gauntlet and asked for restitution as Christians who had been victimized by other Christians, it turned out that the world was a good deal messier than the rhetoric implied. Just as interestingly, the evidence suggests that the Greeks were well aware of the different strands that made up this delicate balancing act. They knew about the Consolato del Mare tradition and, more generally, about the special status their Christian identity supposedly gave them. At the same time they knew, for example, that their behavior at sea could be held against them; hence Agostino Plati Rayes' statement to the court that he raised the white flag and threw the auxiliary ship overboard as soon as the Maltese approached. George Mellos was aware that the itinerary of the *Agios Georgios* might be an issue in Turin, which is why he got papers from the French authorities in Rosetta and in Sicily to show that the ship's destination was Messina. There was a shared knowledge about legitimate and illegitimate violence, in other words, that spanned the Ottoman-European divide; it was pan-Mediterranean.

Frustrated by the secular princes of Catholic Europe, the Greeks were not, however, without other resources. The historical record shows that these anonymous merchants and captains were willing and able to go all the way to the top of the Catholic hierarchy, to Rome itself. In European history the seventeenth century is associated with the irrevocable establishment of the sovereign state at the expense of the Catholic Church. But in the Mediterranean, the Counter-Reformation and the ferocity of Catholic piracy combined to give Rome a new lease on life.

CHAPTER 7

The Turn toward Rome

● ○ ●

Over the course of the last three chapters I have sought to bring an unknown world to the surface. But the fact that this world is obscure to us does not mean that it was so for contemporaries. In this chapter we shall see that the anonymous victims of the Maltese corsairs connect up to one of the most important religious and political battles of the seventeenth century, namely the Counter-Reformation attempt to woo the Orthodox Greeks, with the ultimate goal of bringing them into the Catholic fold. The victims were connected in two ways: first, the Greeks themselves turned to the institutions and the people of the Counter-Reformation to try to gain relief from Catholic corsairing. From the Vatican to Istanbul, the Counter-Reformation created new centers of Catholic power that professed an interest in the Greeks of the Ottoman Empire. Corsairing victims were quick to identify and approach these new additions to the landscape, much as they had already learned to do with the French consulates. Second, the Vatican did not hesitate to tie its response to the Christian victims of Catholic corsairing to its greater political and religious goals in the region. I have argued that the Greek encounter with the Knights of Malta in the Tribunale degli Armamenti is a way of viewing the Mediterranean as an international legal space. In this chapter we see the political side of that encounter: Catholic corsairing was not only not outside the law, it was not outside politics. Commercial and political history intersect in the confrontation between Greek commerce and Catholic piracy. As the story unfolds we will spend more time in centers of power—places like Istanbul and Rome—than we have in previous chapters. But Counter-Reformation politics reached into even seemingly out-of-the-way places like Rhodes, where it intersected with the concerns of Greek victims, many of whom were from the Dodecanese.

The cargo of rice that Greek merchants sought compensation for is as much part of the religious and political history of the Mediterranean as it is part of the commercial history of the inland sea.

In his article on the corso and its decline, Roderic Cavaliero presents Greek recourse to the Vatican as an eighteenth-century development, a tactic Greek victims of corsairing took up only after repeatedly failing to prevail in Malta.[1] In fact, this is not a sequential story. From the evidence it is clear that Greeks were petitioning Rome as early as the 1630s. Even earlier than that, in the 1620s, the cardinals in Rome were making the link between Greek merchants and Catholic corsairing. This suggests that this story follows the same timeline as that of the Greek confrontation with Catholic corsairing. It was the changed circumstances in the eastern Mediterranean after 1570 that produced the link between the religious and political program of the Roman Catholic Church, on the one hand, and the problems created by Catholic corsairing on the other. The influx of Catholic corsairs into Ottoman waters after the empire's defeat at Lepanto in 1571 coincided with the creation of a web of institutions as a result of the Counter-Reformation. Certain dates stand out in this latter story: 1576, the founding of the Greek College in Rome, and 1622, when the Sacra Congregatio de Propaganda Fide, known conventionally as the Propaganda, was established. But the story of the Counter-Reformation effort among the Greeks is a continuous one. These dates are part of an ongoing engagement in the East through missionaries, special embassies, and representatives of the European powers, particularly France, in the Ottoman Empire. Nor did the Greeks wait until the eighteenth century to complain to Catholic officials about attacks on their commerce. Rather, they pursued this tactic throughout the 1600s, alongside the direct recourse to the knights described in previous chapters.

What follows is not a systematic or comprehensive history of the relationship between the Greek Orthodox and the Vatican in the seventeenth century. Even if we restrict ourselves to the more limited area of commercial history, I cannot claim to have presented every communication between a Greek victim of the Knights of Malta and the Vatican or its representatives. Extensive research, primarily in the records of the Sacra Congregatio de Propaganda Fide, would be necessary to accomplish that.[2] In this chapter I present several encounters between the Counter-Reformation Church and Greek commerce. These encounters

FIGURE 7.1. Kyrillos Loukaris, patriarch of Constantinople and the determined protector of Greek Orthodoxy.

span the seventeenth century. Taken together, they are of sufficient scope and variety to show that the conflict between Catholic corsairs and Greek merchants and shipowners is also part of the story of the Counter-Reformation in the Levant.

Loukaris, the Vatican, and Greek Commerce

Let us begin our story in Istanbul. By its very nature, the Vatican's effort in the East was bound to be fraught with difficulties, since its ultimate goal was the unification of the two churches. This was something that was bound to incite the resistance, even the hatred, of the Greek Orthodox. But a whole new layer of anxiety was folded in when Kyrillos Loukaris ascended the patriarchal throne in Istanbul in 1620.

Loukaris is a notorious figure about whom much has been written; certainly he has received more attention than any other Orthodox patriarch of the Ottoman period.[3] The Catholics found him deeply alarming. In Loukaris they were confronted with a highly educated man who was both politically active and seemed to have some sympathy for both

Calvinism and Anglicanism.[4] Philippe de Harlay, Comte de Césy, the French ambassador whose long tenure in Istanbul overlapped with Loukaris's time in office, wrote, "This Patriarch was a most dangerous heretic, whose one aim was to weaken and ruin the Roman Church and to establish Calvinism in Greece and in all parts of the east."[5] Although Loukaris's true feelings about Calvinism are debatable, there is no debate over his strong feelings of animosity toward the Catholic Church. Long before he became ptriarch he was deeply involved in the Orthodox attempt to counteract the unionist aims of the Counter-Reformation Church. In 1596 he was sent to Poland to spearhead the Orthodox opposition to the Union of Brest-Litovsk, when the Orthodox hierarchs in Kiev broke with the patriarch in Constantinople and declared submission to Rome.[6] He would certainly have recognized similar tactics at work in the Ottoman Empire. On a less exalted note, but just as important for our purposes, we know that Loukaris was aware of the difficulties that Maltese corsairing was causing for Greek shipping and commerce, and this could only have added to his anti-Catholic animus. Let us remember that it was Loukaris himself who signed a document in 1616 that Haji Pietro brought with him to Malta.[7]

It is no surprise, then, that trouble began soon after Loukaris ascended to the throne. Césy managed to have the sultan banish the patriarch in 1623, but the latter, equally adroit at Ottoman politics, was back after several months. In revenge, Loukaris moved to have the Jesuits banned, but the French ambassador blocked him.[8]

The Vatican equivocated and was initially unwilling to come out with guns blazing against Loukaris.[9] But in 1627 it decided to take action. On November 13 of that year the cardinals of the Propaganda gathered in the palazzo of Cardinal Bandini and formulated an eight-point declaration that was an all-out attack on the patriarch. Loukaris was to be publicly denounced as a Calvinist and his theories refuted with learned treaties. Seven of the eight points were directed at the well-known players in this high-stakes game playing itself out in the Ottoman capital as well as in other European centers. The French ambassador in Istanbul, for example, was directed to endeavor to remove the patriarch through bribery, but he was not to reveal the Vatican's hand in this. The Ottomans were to be pressured to close down the patriarchal printing press, and an emissary was to be sent to the king of France notifying him that the spread of "heresy" in the East, and the potential joining together of the Orthodox with the English, the Dutch, and other "heretical" states in northern Europe, constituted a danger both for religion and for the Catholic states, particularly France. And so on and so forth. It is these dramatic developments that have received the lion's share of the attention, as high politics often do. But what interests us is point 7, the only one of its kind and one that has gone unremarked. It reads:

> The Greek merchants, those who trade in Christian cities, should be warned that they should work towards casting out Cyril, patriarch of the heretics, from the patriarchal see and that they should take care that another, who abhors the western heresies be substituted. Otherwise, their ships and goods will be destroyed by Christian soldiers. Until now, they were safe, but they will become their prize.[10]

It would be hard to find a clearer indication of the Vatican's willingness to draw Greek merchants into religious and political quarrels of the very highest order.

A few months later, in July 1628, the cardinals met again to formulate a plan of action, a plan that depended on a sustained and deep engagement with the Orthodox hierarchy across the Ottoman world. Catholic clergy, for instance, were charged with approaching the patriarchs of Alexandria, Antioch, and Jerusalem to speak with them and convince them that Loukaris's ideas were heretical. Opponents of Loukaris across the board were to be encouraged and supported. They even envisioned having the Orthodox Church put Loukaris on trial, with a representative from Rome present at the proceedings.[11]

Given this ambitious plan, it is not surprising that struggles between the Orthodox Church and Catholic representatives of the Counter-Reformation were in no way confined to the Ottoman capital. Historians such as Frazee and Ware have provided ample evidence of conflicts between the two in the islands and along the Aegean littoral where the Catholics concentrated their energies. The most famous example, of course, is the Holy Land, where Orthodox-Catholic animosity reached a new level of intensity in the seventeenth century. In 1634 Murat IV, backed by the Greek elite in Istanbul, expelled the Franciscans completely from their churches in Palestine.[12] Toward the end of the century the Catholics were still fuming. Writing a report for the Propaganda Fide, Mosignor Urbano Cerri complained about Panayiotis Nikousios, the Ottoman grand dragoman: "Panionotto, a Schismatical Bishop (and heretofore the Grand Vizier's Interpreter), who was educated in our Greek College, has proved to be the greatest persecutor of the Catholicks, and contrived false writings to deprive them of the Holy Sepulchre."[13]

For our purposes, what is most interesting is an arena that might seem something of a sideshow. Once again we return to the island of Rhodes. As mentioned earlier, Rhodes drops out of sight, historiographically speaking, once the knights depart and the Ottomans arrive in 1522. Nor does it figure in the surveys of the Catholic presence in the empire in the seventeenth and eighteenth centuries.[14] As we know, however, the island figures very prominently in our story. Although little recognized, the Dodecanese islanders, and the Rhodiots in particular, enjoyed a prominent position in the maritime time of the empire. As such, they were more likely than others to end up in the clutches of the Maltese. It turns out that Orthodox-Catholic quarrels also echoed in Rhodes, and these echoes created opportunities for those seeking help against the Maltese corsairs.

The battles that roiled the capital came to Rhodes because the sultan selected the island as a place of exile for Greek clerics, including deposed patriarchs.[15] Exiling enemies to Rhodes was not an Ottoman invention; it was a tradition that stretched all the way back to Roman times.[16] In addition, even the limited amount of information that we have on Ottoman Rhodes shows that the Orthodox metropolitans on the island were themselves deeply implicated in the struggles over the direction of the Orthodox Church in the seventeenth century. How the two related to each other—the metropolitans and the exiles from the capital—remains to be explored.

Several seventeenth-century metropolitans enjoyed connections with the Catholic world and with the institutions of the Counter-Reformation. Eremia, who served briefly at the very beginning of the century, was in Rome in Janury 1628, where he managed to enroll his godson in the Greek College. Pachomios served as the metropolitan of the island from 1625 until 1637. He was a graduate of the Jesuit College in Istanbul and known to the French; the ambassador in Istanbul wrote that he was a friend of the Roman Catholics. At some point he must have formally declared his Catholicism because he ended up in the leadership of the Greek Uniate community in Livorno.[17]

Turning to the exiles, Loukaris himself spent almost a year on the island, from May 1635 to June 1636.[18] Pachomios accompanied him, purportedly as a friend but actually to spy on him for the French. In this overheated atmosphere, it is not surprising that even the pashas of the island had reputations as pro- or anti-Latin.[19]

It is with the next exile that we are fortunate enough to have direct evidence of a link to the problems of Greek merchants and captains. Just one month after Loukaris's departure, Kontaris the Second took his place as the exile of note on the island. Predictably, given the revolving-door pattern at the patriarchate where pro- and anti-Latin factions battled it out, Kontaris was a friend of the Catholics.

From there, in July 1636, he wrote a letter of introduction to the Jesuit Denis Guillier in Constantinople, introducing him to the bearer of the letter, one Alexandros of Galata. Kontaris began by lamenting the fact that, once again, "Calvinism" (that is, Loukaris) had taken over the long-suffering patriarchate of Constantinople.[20] He expressed his hope that Loukaris would be deposed and that he himself would ascend to the patriarchal throne.

Then he moved on to the matter at hand. He asked Guillier to help Alexandros with "words and letters" when the latter presented himself to the Jesuit. He had lost his goods in an attack "by the galleys," although it was not clear whether these galleys belonged to Saint John or to the grand duke—that is, to the Knights of St. John or to the Knights of St. Stephen.[21] He added that Alexandros knew the Jesuit, having studied at his school when he was a child. Clearly, Kontaris and the victim were hoping that a Jesuit education would pay off.

This example from Rhodes suggests that Catholic officials, and Orthodox clergy sympathetic to them, were seen by the Greek Orthodox as people who could be approached with regard to commercial problems. Orthodox clerics, for their part, were willing to help and to mix petitions for aid with church politics at the highest level. To complete the circle, we have seen from the 1627 document that the Vatican itself connected commerce and politics. None of these three levels can be understood outside the context of the heated battles of the Counter-Reformation in the eastern Mediterranean. Despite barely concealed antipathies on both

sides, the Greeks and the Vatican continued to circle each other, the former because of the Maltese invasion of Ottoman waters and the latter in
the hope that the Greek Church could be brought back (as the Vatican-
saw it) into the Catholic fold.

By a rather remarkable coincidence, Rhodes in the seventeenth century was both the place where prominent Orthodox Christian clerics
from the hothouse of Istanbul whiled away their time in exile and home
to many of the seafaring Ottoman Christian subjects who were the
prime targets of Maltese attacks. One would like to know more about
the nature of the encounters between the clerics and the victims of
the knights, as the passions of church politics and the consequences of
Catholic corsairing washed onto the shores of this small Aegean island.
We do know that Loukaris also spent time in exile on the island of Chios
and that while he was there he argued with the local theologians.[22] We
also know that some of the petitioners who appeared before the Tribunale in Malta had gone to the court of the Catholic bishop on Chios to
record their depositions. Loukaris was certainly aware of the knights'
assaults in Ottoman waters, and even some of the mechanisms involved
in attempts at redress. We may recall the document he signed in 1616 on
behalf of Pietro, when Loukaris was patriarch of Alexandria, affirming
that Pietro was indeed the owner of his ship.[23] Was he on the island
when victims of the Maltese came ashore? Were they swept up into the
competition between the Orthodox and the Catholics as they set about
documenting their claims, or were they left alone to handle matters as
they saw fit?

So far, these questions cannot be answered. But if we could, we would
have a better sense of the extent to which clerics on both sides of the divide actively sought out the petitioners, thereby gaining clients and
drawing them to their side, or whether it was the merchants and the
captains who approached those who seemed powerful.

Malta, Rome and Greek Merchants

By a stroke of good fortune, the case of Alexandros of Galata shows up
again six months later, this time in Rome. Through him we can move to
the central Mediterranean and to two other offices that were important

points of entry into the Catholic network for the Greek victims of Maltese corsairing.

On December 20, 1636, Cardinal Francesco Barberini, cardinal-nephew of Pope Urban VIII, wrote a letter to Fabio Chigi, who was serving as the papal inquisitor and apostolic delegate on Malta.[24] In that letter Barberini recommended the restitution of some merchandise belonging to one Alexandros of Galata. Clearly, some investigating had been done in the previous six months, because now the blame was placed squarely on the knights. The merchandise, he said, had been on a ship that had been plundered by the order's galleys near Rhodes. Three months later, the grand master wrote to both the cardinal and the father general of the Jesuits on this matter.[25]

Thanks to the fact that he went on to become Pope Alexander VII (1655–67), Fabio Chigi's correspondence from his tenure in Malta (1634–39) has been published, and therefore we know much more about his activities than we do those of any other inquisitor and apostolic delegate on the island in the seventeenth century. His correspondence with the cardinal-nephew was extensive; the two exchanged more than 350 letters during this five-year period. This epistolary trail, along with several other sources, reveals that both offices are an important part of our story.

Francesco Barberini was a key player in the Counter-Reformation's drive to bring the Greek Orthodox back from schism, as the Vatican saw it. His name appears everywhere we turn in the 1620s and 1630s. His uncle, Pope Urban VIII, made him a cardinal in 1623, when he was only twenty-six, and just four years later his name appears on the 1627 declaration against Loukaris.[26] In 1631 he set up the Accademia Basiliana, whose goal was to reconcile the two churches.[27] He was also a cardinal protector (*Collegii Protectores*) of the Greek College in Rome, which meant that whenever the College needed to approach the Vatican, it would go through him or one of the other three such protectors. By definition, then, he was deeply involved in the affairs of St. Athanasios, since the cardinal protectors decided everything, from the content of the curriculum to who would be admitted.[28]

He was also the patron of Leo Allatius, a Chiot who was the most prominent Greek Catholic intellectual of the seventeenth century. Born an Orthodox Christian, Allatius studied at the Greek College in Rome

between 1600 and 1610, and it was around this time that he made a formal profession of Roman Catholicism.[29] In his career, which included
thirty years as a Greek scriptor in the Vatican, Allatius had to negotiate
his way through the treacherous waters of Church politics. Nevertheless
he formed an enduring relationship with Francesco Barberini. He had
acted on the latter's behalf in scholarly matters as early as the 1620s, and
in 1638 he entered Barberini's services formally. By the time he died, in
1669, he had known the cardinal for almost half a century, and left him
a number of books in his will.[30]

Francesco Barberini was a man of immense personal importance in
Rome during this time; all business with the pope had to pass through
him.[31] His deep involvement with the Greek world, including Greek
problems with knights, suggests that the Christian Orthodox and their
voluble patriarch loomed large at the Vatican.

Two offices were created in Malta late in the sixteenth century as the
Counter-Reformation gained steam. The inquisitor's main duty was to
preserve the Catholic faith and doctrine from any kind of heretical con-
tamination. He enjoyed broad powers of jurisdiction, including over the
knights, at least theoretically. The office of apostolic delegate was also
created at this time. He was the official representative of the Holy See on
the island and was obliged to deal with matters sent down to him from
Rome. The two positions were held by the same person. It appears that
early on the two offices merged and were exercised by one and the same
individual.[32]

Relations between the knights and the inquisitor were often extremely
poor, to the point of physical attacks on the inquisitor's palace, in Vittoriosa, and an accusation in Rome that the inquisitor was planning to
murder the grand master. In one of the more colorful incidents preserved in the historical record, the inquisitor serving in the early 1630s
was on the point of being thrown headlong into the sea from the bas-
tions of Valletta for having arrested a knight who, he claimed, had in-
sulted one of the inquisitor's officers.[33] Despite these assaults, the inquisitor had good reason to try to get along with the knights, and this must
have undercut his authority even further. The office was viewed as a
stepping stone to something better, and a letter of recommendation
from the grand master was highly prized. The inquisitor, then, was keen
to avoid a clash if at all possible.[34]

That said, it is also true that the inquisitor was the only official on the island who was not appointed by the grand master; as late as the eighteenth century a Venetian representative on the island puzzled over the odd system whereby even consuls representing foreign communities were appointed by the grand master.[35] This must have given him a certain authority, at least relatively speaking, which can explain why he was one of those points on the Catholic map to which the Greek Orthodox turned for support.

Leaving aside for a moment the correspondence between Chigi and Barberini, the special relationship between the inquisitor and the Greek Orthodox on Malta is evident in other arenas. When ships came back from the corso in the Levant, the inquisitor was often waiting at the harbor and would insist on boarding to make sure that no Christians—Copts, Greeks, Armenians, and others—were being held against their will. The complicated relationship between Maltese corsairing and the eastern Christians is evident in these cases; the latter would sometimes volunteer to work on board—the corso thus provided opportunities for them—but when they tried to leave they were forcibly detained.[36]

This duty was important enough that Chigi left instructions for his successor on the matter. He wrote,

> The poor Greek Christians who are seized by the ships armed in Malta will be recommended to you with the intent of releasing them from the power of their adversaries, and making the Grand Master be their advocate and representative. Otherwise they often do not dare [presumably, approach the inquisitor] out of fear of the Knights. In representing them he [the grand master] must ensure that they receive justice at the Armamento.[37]

It was also to the inquisitor that Muslim slaves arriving on the island would turn with pleas for liberation, claiming they had been born Christian and had been forcibly converted to Islam. We saw in chapter five that the inquisitor requested assistance with this matter from Rome in 1641, in response to which the latter sent down an *Istruzione*.[38] A number of such instructions have survived and make it clear that the inquisitors had to deal with these sorts of problems throughout the seventeenth century.[39]

All of these issues generated extensive correspondence between the Vatican and the inquisitor in Malta. The letters exchanged between

FIGURE 7.2. Fabio Chigi, the papal inquisitor in Malta (and future Pope Alexander VII).

Chigi and Barberini, then, were part of a larger context in which Rome interested itself in the affairs of the corso, with a particular eye to the fate of Christians (or people claiming to be Christian), through the office of the inquisitor on the island. In 1638, Ottoman-Venetian relations were put under a severe strain by the so-called Valona incident. Venice went into the harbor of Valona (in present-day Albania) and seized all sixteen galleys belonging to the Algerians and the Tunisians. It claimed it had the right to do so according to agreements it had with the empire, in which no port or harbor (of the sultan's) would give shelter to pirates. Nevertheless, war threatened. In Rome, Francesco Barberini picked up his pen and wrote to Chigi in Malta. He urged the inquisitor to restrain

FIGURE 7.3. Francesco Barberini.

the Maltese from going on corsairing raids at this critical moment in the name of the "public good."[40] It is difficult to assess what the Greeks knew about this relationship, but we do know they did not hesitate to go all the way to the top in their pursuit of justice against the knights.

According to the published correspondence, Barberini first wrote to Chigi on behalf of an individual Greek on July 8, 1634. In the letter he recommended Angelo Mangiaco from Thessaloniki, who complained that Maltese vessels had stolen his merchandise.[41] Barberini wanted Chigi to intervene with the grand master in order to recover the property. Although we don't know how this case ended, we do know that the grand master felt compelled to respond quickly. In September of that year he wrote to Cardinal Barberini assuring him that he would do everything to expedite the case.[42] During that same month of July Barberini wrote another letter, this time for two Greeks, Lascario di Franco and Giovanni Mercurio, who also said that Maltese vessels had stolen their goods.[43]

Although letters continued to flow between Chigi and Barberini on all sorts of matters related to the corso, almost a year passed before the affairs of the Greeks came up again. Between June and November 1635 a number of letters went back and forth in the matter of the Micheli brothers, Luca, Costantino, and Nicolo. In June 1635 Barberini wrote to Chigi, explaining that a certain Knight fra Valanze had taken goods from these three merchants and that he (Chigi) should raise the issue with the grand master.[44] It is in this case that we see, once again, Rome's willingness to raise the question of Church politics when considering Greek petitioners. Barberini told Chigi that he should ensure the return of their goods, since the new patriarch seemed to hold the Catholic Church in great esteem.[45] If we return these goods, he continued, the patriarch would be with them, "and not with the English and Dutch heretics, as was his predecessor Cirillo, now sent into exile on the island of Rhodes by the Turks." Chigi wrote back several months later saying he would make every effort at restitution in order to assure the patriarch of Constantinople.

The next letter, which Chigi wrote to Barberini in October, provides a rare revealing glimpse of the political forces operating on the Tribunale. Chigi wrote that the papal brief that the Micheli brothers had brought with them had caused a great stir on the island: "The breve of the Greek merchants, the Michelis, has set off many rumors. The fear [which it has caused] the Religion is not such a bad thing, as it makes it more likely that they will get justice in the Armamento."[46]

The final letter, from Barberini to Chigi, conveys the distinct impression that the Micheli brothers would have preferred to have had their case directly settled by Rome rather than going through the Tribunale. He said he approved of Chigi's handling of the papal brief and that the Greeks had no reason to worry, since they could always launch an appeal if necessary. No doubt the Greeks knew very well the low esteem in which they were held by the knights, to put it mildly. Speaking for the order, the grand master wrote to Barberini, and others, in tones that were always politic. But his tone was very different when he wrote to the order's agent in Rome on the Micheli case:

> Certain crafty Greeks, claim to have been harmed in the Levant by the Knight Valense, while he was engaged in the corso against the Turks (which is completely false). Instead of appearing in our Tribunale de gli Armamenti to ask for justice, as is the custom, they have come to Rome.[47]

Eventually, the Micheli brothers lost their case, and their appeal, in Malta. The appeal stated that the rice and the flax belonged to Turks, and therefore the Greeks had no rights at all.[48]

Just a few months later the grand master complained again to his agent in Rome, this time about Alexandros of Galata, whose case we have already discussed. He said it deserved mentioning that "very often these Greeks come here, fraudulently claiming merchandise which belongs to Turks but which was loaded under their name. Perhaps they feel sure that they can benefit from the pity that many [feel for them]."[49] Clearly the grand master felt that this pity was misguided and misplaced.

Correspondence from the summer and fall of 1637 is of particular interest because it is the only case we have in which the merchant in question also appears in the records of the Tribunale. As mentioned earlier, Gioannes Cugia was attacked off the Egyptian coast in the late summer of 1636. In November of that year the victim appeared before the French consul in Cairo, and testimony was taken that would later be presented in Malta. By the following summer he had made his way to Malta, where his case was heard before the Tribunale.[50]

Now it appears that Gioannes Cugia went to even greater lengths than that in his attempt to retrieve the money that had been stolen from him. In August 1637 Cardinal Barberini wrote a letter to Chigi asking him to protect a Greek merchant by the name of Giovanni Cuia, whose lawsuit was pending in Malta.[51] Since Cugia (or Cuia, as Barberini renders it) was actually on the island during this period, he must have gone to Rome earlier in the year, prior to even starting the lawsuit at the Tribunale, to ask for Barberini's help. Cugia presented himself rather plaintively in court; he told the judges he had not been able to find a lawyer to take his case, and he asked that whoever ended up representing him know both Greek and Italian. This implies that he did not know Italian.[52] Nevertheless, this was clearly a man who knew how to approach powerful people—from the French authorities in Cairo to the cardinal nephew himself in Rome—and did not hesitate to do so.

Nevertheless, the difficulty of prevailing against the knights is apparent from two letters that Chigi subsequently wrote to Barberini. On October 17 he said that he had received the cardinal's August letter regarding Giovanni Cuia. He explained that Garnier, the knight in question, was away from Malta and that he would begin a lawsuit against him once he returned.[53] More than a month later he still had not been able to track Garnier down.[54]

Chigi's service in Malta concluded in 1639, and he was dealing with the problems of Greek merchants all the way up until the end. Barberini wrote to him on the first day of that year, seeking the restitution of merchandise and a ship stolen from one Antonio Bumbaca of Santa Maura (Levkada) in the Ionian Sea.[55] Bumbaca said that he was on his way to Civitavecchia (the port of Rome) with merchandise from the East when a ship flying the order's flag overcame him and forced him land on the wild Mani Peninsula in southern Greece. Both his vessel and his cargo were taken from him.

Toward the end of February Chigi replied; he told Barberini that he had intervened with the grand master on behalf of Bumbaca and had urged him to see to it that there be a swift and just resolution.[56]

In addition to these cases of individual merchants, there is one exchange of letters concerning the monks of St. John on Patmos. Barberini wrote to Chigi in June 1637 and said that the monks must be compensated for money that was taken from them by "a subject of the Religion." He describes himself as their protector (*protettore*), which suggests that the Catholic ties to the island, evidence for which dies out in the sixteenth century when the Ottomans were at their zenith, had been revived.[57] The wording of Barberini's letter strongly implies that the monks had actually traveled to Rome to petition for justice in person. Several months later, Chigi wrote back to Barberini. He said that the monks' case was being heard in the order's tribunals and that he would intervene to ensure good results.[58]

Fabio Chigi's correspondence has been published because he went on to become pope. Without further research we cannot know how often Vatican officials approached inquisitors after Chigi on behalf of Greek petitioners to Rome. But it is clear that Orthodox Christians continued to see both the pope and the inquisitor as people whom they might approach even into the eighteenth century. Correspondence between the grand master in Malta and various officials in Rome, including the pope, demonstrates the persistence of seventeenth-century patterns. In 1705 the pontiff insisted that a case lodged by a Greek against the knight Giuseppe Preziosi be transferred from Malta to Rome.[59] Toward the end of the seventeenth century we also see the inquisitor move to protect the general right of the Greeks to appeal cases to Rome when the grand master moved to close off that possibility.

From its inception, the Tribunale always included the right of appeal to Rome.[60] The cases I have discussed thus far went the other way around: Greek petitioners went directly to Vatican officials, who then asked the inquisitor to intervene in Malta, but it could, and did, also work in reverse. In 1697 Grand Master Perellos moved to establish a new court, the Consolato del Mare, which precluded the right of appeal to Rome since it was a lay court. The inquisitor objected to the court on precisely these grounds and in 1706 appointed an official to receive Greek cases against corsairs.[61] We have at least one case showing that the victims of the corso shared the inquisitor's antipathy toward the Consolato: in 1719 a Maronite merchant named Abraham Massard, whose case was being heard in the Consolato, asked that it be transferred to the Magistrato. From there, he said, it could be appealed directly to Rome if he should lose.[62]

Perellos's establishment of the Consolato is perhaps the clearest indication of an aspect of the Maltese corso that is often overlooked by those who emphasize its lawlessness: the Vatican mattered to the knights. In petitions from the seventeenth and eighteenth centuries grand masters repeatedly asked that the Greeks be declared legitimate prize. In 1635 Cardinal Antonio Barberini approached the knights over the problem of Greek Orthodox gains in Palestine vis-à-vis the Catholics: "The pope desires the grand master and council, as better acquainted with the disposition of the Ottoman court, to take measures for restoring the Latin friars to the guardianship of the holy places." The grand master, Antoine de Paul, was swift in his response, saying, "The grand master and his council are of the opinion that they should try what force could do, and not spare the schismatical Greeks whenever they fell into the hands of the Catholic princes."[63]

In his response to Cardinal Barberini, de Paul noted that some Vatican officials thought that an all-out war was the solution to the problem. The order was against this approach and preferred a "war of reprisal" against "the schismatic Greeks of the Levant."[64] He argued the case in some detail: "His Holiness [la Santita] can readily concede that most of the cargo and goods that the Greeks have been carrying for many years now on their ships belong in fact to Turks. They mark the bales fraudulently with Christian markings, and with the sign of the Holy Cross."[65] If the pope would grant such authorization, he confidently predicted that the Greeks would have to give way and return the holy places to Catholic control in short order. In fact, he argued, reprisals against the Greeks would be a blow against the Turks themselves, since Constantinople, this "vast city," depended on Greek maritime transport to sustain itself.

As if that were not enough, the grand master threw in for good measure a recent example of what he called the "impiety of the Greeks of the Levant."[66] A certain French captain had been sailing in the Aegean, pursuing the corso against the Turks. He came across four Greek ships and sent one of his soldiers in a small boat to see what news he could obtain from them. The Greeks responded, he said, with an attack on this poor individual, tying his legs and arms to their four separate skiffs and then, by rowing hard in opposite directions, tearing him apart. Whether or not such a truly vicious assault took place, it is clear that de Paul wanted to persuade the Vatican that the Greeks were odious. He concluded with "This is the kind of barbaric cruelty that the schismatic Greeks of the Levant consistently show toward the Latin Catholics."[67]

In 1638 Chigi wrote to Francesco Barberini, raising once again the issue of the status of the Greeks. He said that, given the Greek "seizure" of the holy places of Jerusalem, many on the island were insisting that the grand master obtain from the pope due authorization to consider the Greeks enemies.[68]

The grand master must have been disappointed by the Vatican's response, which was, essentially, to stall. Barberini wrote back to Chigi several months later. He said that Rome had already been informed concerning developments in Jerusalem and that the Propaganda Fide was studying what could be done. At present, it had been decided to leave aside any hostile action, lest the Turks be provoked.[69]

In 1716 the grand master seized on the opportunity of another Ottoman-Venetian war (1714–18) to send an emissary to Rome to argue that all Greek vessels should be good prizes if they were taken while provisioning the Turkish fleet.[70] The order continued to press its case into the early 1720s, long after the conclusion of the war. Grand Master Zondadari wrote to his ambassador in Rome, saying that it was time for the pope to do what the Tuscans had done, namely, issue the decision that for a vessel to be immune from attack, its captain and half the crew had to be Roman Catholic.[71]

All of the Greeks who petitioned Rome in the cases discussed so far were anonymous individuals. Although it is clear that the Counter-Reformation church was actively interested in the Greek Orthodox of the eastern Mediterranean, and that Greek merchants (and others) turned to church officials for help with various issues, we still know very little about the specifics of individual cases, such as how individuals went about soliciting the aid and assistance of the Vatican. How did these seemingly ordinary people manage to obtain a breve from someone as powerful as Francesco Barberini? Clearly there is a story here that is yet to be written about Eastern Christians and their access to Rome in the wake of the Council of Trent. What we can offer here is only one story, but it is a particularly valuable one because it shows how one of these anonymous individuals went about approaching the Vatican.

George Mellos Goes to Rome

Let us return to the late seventeenth-century case of George Mellos that was introduced in the previous chapter. Mellos was on board the ship *Agios Georgios*, northwest of the island of Rhodes, when it was attacked in 1678 by corsairs flying the flag of the Duchy of Savoy. Chapter six examined Mellos's experience in Turin as he argued his case at the duchess's court. Now we will backtrack and follow Mellos in his journey from Chios to Turin. The documents of the lawsuit are uniquely valuable in the information they provide on how Greek merchants used Counter-Reformation networks to pursue their claims against Catholic corsairs.

The goods that had been stolen belonged to four merchants: Mellos himself, a partner named Theodoros Cui or Chui, who was not on board, and two merchants from Chios, who were.[72] By the time Mellos arrived back in Chios, all of the victims of the attack had gathered, and it was decided that Mellos would pursue the case. Together with the owner of the ship, George Klironomos of Chios, they all appeared in front of a notary named Michael De Porto and recorded their testimony of the attack. Further documents also gave him power of attorney with regard to all the interested parties.

Mellos then set out for Turin, but he did not go there directly. Instead, he stopped first in Rome to meet with Ioannes Benaldes and his son, Argeros.[73] The son would eventually become a scholar of some repute, but no doubt Mellos approached him for other reasons. First, both were from Athens, and thus the merchant could prevail on him because of their shared origin. Second, in 1679 Argeros was twenty years old and a student at the Greek College in Rome. This was vital. Using their connections, the father-and-son team was able to procure letters of introduction from the pope himself, as well as other Vatican officials.[74] They also translated certain Greek documents into Italian. The son, for his part, penned a particularly fascinating document in which he advises Mellos on how to conduct himself in his journey farther west. Written in a colloquial style, the document has the feel of a set of instructions written for someone who was venturing into uncertain territory, as Mellos undoubtedly was:

> This is what you must first do. As soon as you arrive in Livorno, find a certain Gaspare, who will help you with regard to money. Do your very best to dress unobtrusively in the "Frankish" style. Around your neck wear one of those things the Franks call "cravat" and an ordinary wig for your head. But if you can't find Gaspare, and time doesn't permit, then it is all right to go as you are.[75]

We have already seen in chapter six that Mellos made the (not unreasonable) argument that he was Catholic, a Catholic of the Greek rite. Here we see that being a Frank, and therefore Catholic, presupposed a certain appearance, and that looking the part was considered an important aspect of inhabiting that identity. The possible significance of the wig is suggested in an anecdote from Heyberger's study of Eastern Christians.

FIGURE 7.4. The Greek College in Rome and the Church of Saint Athanasios as they appeared in 1935.

One Antonio Callimeri was a Cypriot graduate of the Greek College who was posted to Alexandretta in 1679, where he was supposed to serve the church and to send regular written reports back to the Propaganda. Evidently he was a disappointment to the cardinals, because they accused him of neglecting his duties. Callimeri defended himself, perhaps not in the most intelligent way, by saying he had been busying himself with commerce. Perhaps this was why, when he asked to become a "Frank" and to adopt the Latin rite, he was refused.[76] Nearly thirty years later we see him still having difficulty with the authorities and still in an ambiguous situation. He had lodged a complaint at the French chancellery in Tripoli and told the officials there that he was a graduate of Saint Athanasios and a good Catholic. It seems that this incensed the official, who responded that Callimeri was a schismatic, and forced him to remove his hat *and his wig* (my emphasis) before proceeding any further.[77] The wig and the hat, then, were not simply personal sartorial choices but rather a declaration of Catholic identity.[78] This must have been what Mellos was after.

Benaldes then instructed Mellos as to the order in which he should present the letters of recommendation—the letter from the pope should come first—to the papal nuncio in Turin. He is clearly anxious that Mellos position himself as a humble petitioner. He tells him to kiss the nuncio's feet and beg him to ask the duchess to save him. The nuncio should explain to her that Mellos is a foreigner and has neither the time nor the money to sit through a trial.[79]

Benaldes's solicitude for Mellos is evident throughout. He urges him to write as soon as he arrives in Turin to let him know that he is well, and to write to him as a brother. He also asks to be updated concerning developments in the case and even writes out for him, in Italian, how he should address the letter so that it will be sure to reach him in Rome.

Despite all of these efforts, Mellos obtained no satisfaction at the court of the duchess. From Turin he left for Spain to pursue the case further, but again he was disappointed.[80] At some point he wrote to Benaldes, whose optimism and energy were evidently still running high. In a letter dated March 23, 1680, Benaldes urged him to return to Rome. He said that in Rome things could be resolved quite easily, as other Greeks had received justice there. In Malta and other places, he continued, the Greeks were told that their goods were Turkish, and do not receive justice. Sometimes they were even seized and forced to serve as galley slaves. Benaldes told Mellos he had actually spoken to the pope personally regarding this matter, even though others had said the case could not be heard in Rome since Turin had jurisdiction. But the pope was willing to hear it; since a knight was involved, he could do so. Benaldes had also found lawyers who were willing to take the case for little or no money.[81]

Against Benaldes's urgings, Mellos did not return to Rome, and the case petered out without resolution. He eventually settled in Venice, where he died in 1732.[82]

The case of George Mellos is the most explicit we have to date on the relationship between Counter-Reformation institutions and the Greek merchants who were seeking to prevail against corsairs coming from Catholic Europe. Unfortunately, we cannot know how Mellos knew that his fellow Athenian, Argeros Benaldes, was a student at the Greek College in Rome. But he clearly did know, and he deemed it worthwhile to stop in Rome to solicit Benaldes's assistance. Although he did not win the lawsuit in Turin, he was not disappointed in his compatriot. Benaldes (and his father Ioannes) went straight to the highest circles at the Vatican to procure documentation for Mellos. Later on Benaldes spoke directly to the pope himself, who agreed to hear the case should Mellos be willing to return to Rome.

Mellos made his trip in 1679. This was more then forty years after the cluster of cases we discussed above, when Fabio Chigi was serving in Malta and the Barberinis ruled Rome. In addition, there are numerous references to other cases being tried in Rome as well, even if the cases themselves remain to be discovered.[83] Clearly, then, Greek recourse to Catholic authorities spanned the entire seventeenth century and continued on into the following one.

Conclusion

● ○ ●

There are many ways of traveling across the Mediterranean Sea in the early twenty-first century. It is obvious, but still worth pointing out, that Western tourists on a cruise ship will have a very different experience, both at sea and as they come into port, than refugees setting sail for Spain from a deserted North African beach in a small craft crowded with people. So too in the early modern period there were distinctive maritime experiences. This book has chosen to trace the footsteps, whenever possible, of one group of maritime travelers, those people who are known, perhaps conventionally but still usefully, as the Greeks. Beginning with the Ottoman-Venetian modus vivendi that was established in the sixteenth century, we follow the Greeks into the seventeenth century, when the inability of any one state to police the inland sea meant high levels of insecurity as they tried to make a living through maritime trade. Throughout the book I have argued that the Greeks are uniquely valuable for the project which has been at the heart of this book, namely, describing and explaining the early modern Mediterranean as an international maritime order. Before concluding with a definition of that order, let us take this opportunity to expand our view beyond the particular experience of the Greeks and consider several other cases of conflict at sea in this period. These cases support a central argument of this book, namely, that it is wrong to dismiss corsairing in the seventeenth century as some sort of anachronistic curiosity. Rather, the Knights of Malta were simply the most vicious and vocal practitioners of a set of practices and assumptions that structured a wide range of maritime encounters in the early modern Mediterranean.

● ○ ●

In 1607 a Frenchman from Normandy named Jacques Pierre set out on a corsairing cruise to the East under license from the Medicis in Livorno.[1] He was captain of a galleon named *St. John the Evangelist.* While he was in the harbor of Haifa selling goods from a raid, the French consul of Sidon informed him there was an English ship in the harbor at Sidon with cargo worth more than 100,000 scudi.[2] Tuscany was not at war with England—after all, the Medicis welcomed English pirates who wanted to operate out of Livorno—but in the blurry world that was the early modern Mediterranean, an English ship was considered a legitimate target. This was because, in addition to Livorno, English adventurers were also to be found in all the harbors of North Africa. They were working with the Muslim enemy and attacking Tuscan shipping, to boot. This was enough, apparently, to justify hostile intent against an English ship in Sidon, at least in Pierre's eyes.[3] By the time he got back to Livorno, however, the situation had shifted a bit. Prior to the seizure Pierre had heard rumors about the cargo that was on board. It was said that the ship, named *The Triumph,* was carrying rubies and gold coins, among other treasures, all carefully hidden under a cargo of honey in the hope of avoiding detection.

Pierre seized the ship on August 29. The ship with its cargo was taken back to Livorno, where it arrived on December 15. In this case it seems there was to be an orderly reckoning of the prize, although it is clear that things were not always handled in this way. Just a month prior to the seizure of the English ship, Pierre had taken a "Turkish" caramousal and then sold off the goods in Haifa, which is how he heard about the English ship in Sidon in the first place. Although it is difficult to know for sure, it seems likely that the *Triumph* was handled differently, both because the English were involved and because of the high value of the cargo on board; it would have been difficult to keep news of the latter from trickling back to Livorno.

In any event, a court hearing was convened that commenced in Pisa in March of 1608. The point of the hearing was to determine which part of the cargo was legitimate prize and which not. The criterion for this decision was which goods belonged to the English and which to "Turks." It seems, then, that the seizure of the *Triumph* must have caused enough of an uproar in England that the Medicis had decided to return at least some of the goods to English ownership. In the course of the hearing, the judges came to the conclusion that it was very common to disguise the ownership of Muslim cargo by shipping the cargo under Christian names in an attempt to prevent seizure by Christian pirates.[4]

This knowledge was probably widespread—we hear the same sort of thing in Malta, after all—but in this particular case the judges were helped along by what must have been the rather remarkable appearance in Pisa of one of the Muslim merchants who had shipped his goods on the *Triumph*. "Aga Maomet" traveled all the way to Pisa to give the following testimony. He told the court that he had shipped from India to Mecca and thence to Damascus 180 bundles of indigo dye, 69 bundles of turbans, 12 bundles with an assortment of textiles, 12 more with various dies, and, finally, 29 bundles of silk. He had spent more than a year in Damascus, he said, arranging for their transport to Sidon so they could be shipped to North Africa.

What he had done was to come to an agreement with the English consul in Sidon, identified as Gugl. Patt, who had happened to be in Damascus at the time. In exchange for a freight of 540 scudi, the consul would take on the shipment of his goods. Aga Maomet's servant had to go back and forth from Damascus to Sidon five times in order to bring everything. The goods were loaded under the name of Gugl. Patt.

It is not clear what Aga Maomet hoped to accomplish by coming to Pisa and making such a declaration. Perhaps he truly thought that justice would be served and he might be able to reclaim his goods. In any event, this was simply more ammunition for the judges. With the help of an English merchant who had been on board the *Triumph*, along with several others who knew Patt, the judges identified certain documents as being in Patt's handwriting. They compared these with the documents that accompanied the shipment of goods whose ownership was in question and came to the (not surprising) conclusion that all of the goods in question belonged to Aga Maomet.

In the end, the court concluded that only the cotton, the currants, and the rice belonged to English merchants. These, along with the ship itself, were returned. The rest, the judges ruled, belonged to Turks, enemies of the faith, and thus was the legitimate prize of Captain Jacques Pierre.

Unlike the seizure of the Portuguese carack *Santa Catarina* off the coast of Singapore in 1603, the attack on the *Triumph*, which happened just four years later, has been forgotten, along with the subsequent hearing in Pisa. The case, after all, did not produce one of the classics of international law, namely, Hugo Grotius's *Freedom of the Seas*. But it is important nevertheless. The case of the *Triumph,* when combined with George Mellos's suit in Turin, strongly suggests that the legal regime we have described for the Tribunale in Malta was Mediterranean-wide, at least when it came to collisions with Catholic power. Moreover, it was not just the Greeks who found themselves in the position of having to go along with distinctions rooted in religion but the English as well. If we believe Aga Maomet's account, and there is no reason not to, English consuls too were familiar with the practice of mislabeling cargo in an attempt to ensure that their clients' goods reached their destination. The reality of the seventeenth-century Mediterranean is that, even when there was no formal war, the eternal war between Christianity and Islam influenced the way people moved across this maritime space.

Evidence also suggests that this legal regime had a longer life than is generally recognized. The Consolato del Mare, set up in 1697, has been presented as part of the normalization of trade that took place in Malta and throughout the Mediterranean in the eighteenth century.[5] And it is true that the court was originally intended to serve the island's maritime trade. However, it soon grew into something else, a second prize court for the corsairs, operating under the magistral flag.[6] In chapter seven we saw that the Inquisitor and, in at least one case, a Maronite victim of the corso viewed the court with trepidation on precisely these grounds.

Evidence suggests that Eastern Christians and the papacy continued to connect religious goals and commercial matters well into the eighteenth century. In 1713 a cleric named Giovanni Giuseppe Mazet, returning from a trip to the Levant, stopped in Livorno and wrote to the Propaganda Fide about the case of Giuseppe Francesco, who was a close relative of the Maronite patriarch.[7] He said that Francesco had come to Livorno in an attempt to recover goods taken from him by a corsair named Franceschini. He had brought with him, he said, authentic documents "plus claires que le soleil à midi," and yet had found himself threatened with jail and a beating in the Medici port. Francesco could not return home because of his debts, nor could he afford to stay indefinitely in Livorno. Therefore, he had gone to Algiers and "turned Turk."

He said that while he was in the Levant, people had come to him to complain

> que les Francs sont des chiens, qu'ils ne cherchent des catholiques
> au Levant que pour les manger, et les tenir comme esclaves de leur
> jurisdiction, sans leur porter aucun soulagement dans le dur escla-
> vage dans lequel ils se trouvent.[8]

We cannot know, of course, if Giuseppe Francesco really did go to Algiers and convert to Islam; this could well have been a rhetorical strategy designed to goad the Vatican into stronger action. But the bitterness of the Eastern Christians was certainly real, as was Mazet's linking of commercial and religious matters.

As late as 1757, or more than one hundred years after the cardinals of the Propaganda warned Greek merchants not to support Loukaris, the Arab historian Mikha'il Burayk wrote of events that happened toward the end of that year. The news reached them, he said, that the pope had excommunicated the patriarch in Constantinople, and this was announced in all the "Frankish Kingdoms." Further, permission had been given to the corsairs to capture the Greeks wherever they found them on the sea.[9] This was certainly a Syrian echo of the battle raging in Istanbul, where Cyril V, a fervently anti-Latin patriarch, had caused an uproar by declaring that Latin baptism was invalid.[10]

We may recall from chapter seven that, writing to Rome in the early 1720s, Grand Master Zondadari had said that generally speaking, the Greeks were people of *mal fede*. It was also at the beginning of the eighteenth century that Eastern Christians told Giovanni Giuseppe Mazet that Franks were dogs. It is remarkable to witness the loathing coming from both quarters—dogs on one side, people of bad faith on the other—and yet neither was willing to relinquish its insistence that, really, Christians should be united as one against the Muslim world.

Returning to the theme of ambiguity with which I began this study, it is important to underline that there were other ways of resolving disputes over attacks at sea in the seventeenth century and on into the eighteenth. In other words, we see that same mix of a Mediterranean world regulated (however ineffectively) through state diplomacy and a Mediterranean where individuals tried to maneuver based on an assertion of religious identity. As an example of the workings of diplomacy in this period we can turn to the valuable study of Maurits H. van den Boogert, which considers attacks on Ottoman commerce in the context of Dutch-French hostility during the War of the Spanish Succession.[11] The cases involved the Dutch and, since the Dutch had signed capitulations with the Ottomans, could be handled through diplomacy. Van den Boogert lays out the procedures that were generally followed. When an Ottoman victim complained to the Porte, certain juridical and political procedures were triggered.[12] After a complaint was filed it went to the Divan-i Hümayun, which functioned as both the Imperial Council and also as the highest court of the land. By the terms of the capitulations, cases against foreign consuls and ambassadors had to be tried there, although redress was demanded against the relevant government rather than the ambassador personally. In exceptional cases, van den Boogert tells us, an Ottoman representative, or çavuş, would actually be sent to Europe.

These mechanisms are clearly distinct from the way in which Greek merchants pursued their claims against the knights and other Catholic corsairs, and they remind us that state-to-state diplomacy continued. But when we consider what actually happened at sea, the events that brought about the complaints, the practices of those who were sworn enemies of the Ottomans (like the knights) and those (like the Dutch) who had diplomatic relations with the Ottomans do not look that different.

Supposedly the Dutch were at war with the French during this period, not the Ottomans, but this did not stop Dutch privateers from remarkably brutal attacks on Ottoman shipping.[13] In 1709 they captured an Ottoman vessel near Crete and took the ship, its cargo, and all on board to Livorno, where they remained in captivity. In an attempt to keep it legal, the captives reportedly had been tortured to deny being Ottoman subjects.[14] A recurring pretext for imprisoning Ottoman subjects was the claim that they were of North African, not Ottoman, origin. Since the Dutch cycled so quickly through war and peace with the various North African states, a Dutch privateer could always defend himself by saying that he thought a state of war existed at the time of the attack. Legal fictions aside, the fact remains that that Dutch were willing to seize Muslims and take them as captives to Catholic Livorno, much as the knights did.[15]

In another case from the same period a ship captain, a reis named Abdurrahman "el Borgi," was seized, along with his ship, his crew, his passengers, and 4,500 *guruş* worth of barley, wheat, and honey sailing from Crete to Benghazi in North Africa. Captain Jacob van der Heijden took his prize first to Zakynthos (one wonders how the Venetians reacted) and then to Livorno. Once again, those on board had been tortured to say they were from North Africa. The Ottoman captain, Abdurrahman, was eventually released through the efforts of the Dutch consul in Livorno, but only after spending a year in captivity.[16] Van den Boogert lays out several other cases whose general outlines are the same—capture at sea by the Dutch, followed by imprisonment in Livorno. Eventually these cases came to the attention of the Ottoman and Dutch governments, but out on the open waters of the Mediterranean the Christian-Muslim divide clearly still mattered.

The line between legitimate trade and something closer to piracy continued to be a vague one. We already know that French consuls were widely suspected of collusion with Catholic corsairs. The Dutch case was not dissimilar. In Dutch Zeeland, where privateering was especially important for the local economy, it was usually merchants who owned the ships engaged in privateering. Commissioners abroad, who were responsible for all prizes brought within their jurisdiction, were sometimes the Dutch consuls themselves, although this was formally forbidden. In Livorno, in fact, this was the usual practice: the privateers' commissioner and the consul was one and the same person, even though the privateers' goals often conflicted with the directors of Levant Trade. The latter wanted to preserve good relations with the Ottoman Empire and to that end "had explicitly forbidden the Western powers to commit hostilities against one another in its waters."[17]

In his study, van den Boogert notes that the Divan-i Hümayn, which handled these cases, has received little attention as the supreme court for the Ottoman Empire.[18] The Tribunale degli Armamenti has been similarly neglected. Taken together, they reflect the neglect of the early modern Mediterranean as an evolving legal maritime order, much like the Indian Ocean or the Atlantic world. A comparison of the proceedings of the two courts would be very valuable in terms of seeing how they understood the norms and rules that should govern conduct at sea. This would help us understand just how different or alike were the two visions that have always competed for primacy in the Mediterranean, the one rooted in religion and the other drawing on the long tradition

of treaty-making in the inland sea. But that will have to remain for
another day.

● ○ ●

In the great Age of Exploration the Mediterranean is the sea that has
been left behind. When it has been considered as an international space,
it has been confined by its own supposed peculiarities—such as the
"anachronism" of the Knights of Malta—or by overly schematic and te-
leological statements about the decline of religion and the rise of a world
of normalized trade.

This book has taken a different view of the early modern Mediterranean. By focusing on individuals and asking how they moved, or tried
to moved, across the sea in the sixteenth and seventeenth centuries, I
have uncovered some of the norms and customs, the reference points
that people drew on when disputes arose over conduct at sea. In short, I
have tried to describe the Mediterranean as an international maritime
order, not a sui generis sea but rather a space comparable to both the Indian and the Atlantic Oceans. Two broad conclusions can be derived
from this investigation. First, individuals moved not exclusively as subjects of a sovereign or, on the other hand, as Muslims, Christians, and
Jews but as an uncertain mix of both state subject and religious subject.
Only the relative mix shifted over the course of the two centuries; it was
not the case that religion was left behind in an increasingly normalized
international order.

Second, the disputes echo those found in other parts of the globe,
demonstrating that individuals drew on a common stock of maritime
tradition, even if there was a peculiarly Mediterranean twist, most
prominently the eternal war between Christianity and Islam. The long-
simmering battle between the Venetians and the knights was a version
of the struggle over the possibility of neutral shipping, the "free ships,
free goods" debate that has been explored for other parts of the globe
but not the Mediterranean.[19] When the Greek petitioners at the Tribunale degli Armamenti spoke of the "legi del Consolato del Mare," they
were referring to rules that would have been familiar to any admiralty
judge in Europe. In the argument between George Mellos and the authorities in Turin over the captured ship's ultimate destination—inside

or outside the Ottoman realms—we can discern the distinction in admiralty law between international voyages and coastal trade, even if the participants did not articulate it that way.

Indeed, I have argued that, in the Mediterranean, much of what was at stake was left unspoken. This too was peculiar to the inland sea. It was the reflection of an enduring Mediterranean dynamic in which Muslims and Christians had traded, negotiated, and signed agreements with each other for centuries and yet never let go of the conviction that the other was eternally, and rightfully, the enemy.

Notes

● ○ ●

Introduction

1. Blunt, *Voyage into the Levant*, 59–60.

2. "*Reis*" is an Arabic word for captain, particularly sea captain. It was adopted as a word by the Greeks during the Ottoman period. Its spelling was not standardized at the time, and in the documents it sometimes appears as *rais* or *raies*. For simplicity's sake, only *reis* will be used here.

3. Krantonelle, Ιστορία της Πειρατείας στους μεσους χρονους της Τουρκοκρατίας 1538–1699, 115–16. A copy of the letter survives in the archives of the Leimonos Monastery on the island.

4. Ibid., 37.

5. Ibid.

6. Matar, *Turks, Moors and Englishmen,* 5–6, 58.

7. For Venice, which early in the seventeenth century still had significant possessions in the eastern Mediterranean, English pirates were the greatest threat. See the classic study by Alberto Tenenti, *Piracy and the Decline of Venice.*

8. The Gulf of Macri is on the coast of southwestern Anatolia.

9. Luttrell, "The Earliest Documents on the Hospitaller *Corso* on Rhodes."

10. For now I will continue to call them pirates.

11. Fodor, "Piracy, Ransom Slavery and Trade," 119–20.

12. Jews were treated like Muslims and enslaved. Although not the focus of this book, the Jewish position vis-à-vis Catholic piracy is discussed from time to time.

13. This sixteenth-century moment has been written about extensively. See Hess, "The Evolution of the Ottoman Seaborne Empire in the Age of the Oceanic Discoveries," and his book, *The Forgotten Frontier*, for an introduction.

14. In the North African case it is true that adventurers from the eastern Mediterranean, operating independently of the Ottoman Empire, were instrumental in drawing the Ottomans into the western Mediterranean. But once Ottoman rule was established in places such as Algiers and Tripoli, they were quickly absorbed into the Ottoman navy. See Hess, *The Forgotten Frontier.*

15. Historians have argued as to whether they were motivated by religious zeal or by poverty. This, it seems to me, is a knot that cannot be untangled, and at any rate the two impulses probably coexisted quite easily in the minds of the pirates. Most historians come down on the side of poverty. See Braudel, *The Mediterranean and the Mediterranean World in the Age of Philip II*, 2:890, and Earle, *Corsairs of Malta and Barbary*, 3. Earle writes that by the seventeenth century, "cynicism and greed had replaced religious enthusiasm."

16. Braudel, *The Mediterranean and the Mediterranean World in the Age of Philip II*, 2:890.

17. From Negroponte in the early sixteenth century to Cyprus in 1570 and all the way to Crete in 1669, among other places.

18. See my article "Beyond the Northern Invasion."

19. The phrase is Dominic Cutajar and Carmel Cassar's in "Malta's Role in Mediterranean Affairs: 1530–1699," 67. Robert Paris, the historian of Marseilles, also uses the term "interregnum" in his description of the seventeenth century, although typically he omits any mention of Christian piracy in the Mediterranean: "Between the decline of the Portuguese and Spanish navies and the rise of the maritime powers of Holland, France and England, there was an interregnum which profited those who lived off plunder. In the Antilles, it is the golden age of the buccaneers and the filibusters while in the Mediterranean it is that of the Barbary chiefs." Rambert, *Histoire du commerce de Marseille*, 5:182.

20. Luttrell, "Venice and the Knights Hospitallers of Rhodes in the Fourteenth Century." Speaking of the late medieval period, Luttrell notes that "the merchant oligarchy of Venice did not mix with the knightly aristocracy of Rhodes" (196).

21. See Benton, "Legal Spaces of Empire," 702: "Europeans did not invent a new maritime politics for the Indian Ocean but sought to continue older practices from the Mediterranean and, later, from the West Indies."

22. Sebastian Vella's statement nicely encapsulates this widespread vision of the early modern Mediterranean: "The international developments whereby European states began to come to terms with the Ottoman Empire and individual North African beys was to signal the decline of corsairing. The corso flourished only as long as Muslims were feared, but once normal trading relations were established it became a nuisance to trade ... the Order's crusading ideal was becoming more anachronistic." Vella, "The *Consolato del Mare* of Malta," 12.

23. I am taking my inspiration here from the work of Lauren Benton, both her article "Legal Spaces of Empire" and her book, *Law and Colonial Cultures*.

24. In using the word "secular" I mean to distinguish a system of international relations based on the rights of states and on natural law from one limited by, on the Christian side, the common corps of Christendom, and on the Muslim side, a division of the world into *Dar ul-Islam* and *Dar ul-Harb*. For an example of this use of the term, see Baumer, "England, the Turk and the Common Corps of Christendom."

25. The vast majority of conferences on the Mediterranean revolve around the interactions of Christians, Muslims, and Jews.

26. Goitein, *A Mediterranean Society*, 42–43.

27. Here and elsewhere I am following the text. It was a European convention to refer to Muslims in the Ottoman Empire as Turks. This was not a term that would have been used by Ottoman Muslims themselves.

28. Contreras, *The Adventures of Captain Alonso de Contreras*, 20.

29. Ibid., 24.

30. Lauren Benton speaks about the "flawed narrative" that sees piracy "as a phenomenon of political opposition or lawlessness." "Legal Spaces of Empire," 701.

31. Ibid., 707–8. When William Kidd was put on trial for piracy in London in 1701, one of the charges against him was that he had seized two ships at the mouth of the Red Sea. One of them was leased by a high official of the Mughal court. Given that Kidd's commission only permitted him to capture pirates and French merchant ships, both seizures were illegal. But Kidd defended himself vigorously, citing his possession of French

passes seized from the ships. In fact, it was common for ships to carry multiple flags and passes, and clearly Kidd had gone to some effort to get the ships to present their French passes, with a view, no doubt, to constructing a plausible defense for himself.

32. Dokos, "Μια Υπόθεσις Πειρατείας κατα τον 17ον Αιώνα," and van den Boogert, "Redress for Ottoman Victims of European Privateering."

Chapter 1
Subjects and Sovereigns

1. Born René d'Auber de Vertot in 1655, he was named an academician by Louis XIV. After the publication of his multivolume history of the knights he was given the additional title of Commander and Official Historiographer of the Order of the Knights of Malta. Vertot, *The History of the Knights Hospitallers of St. John of Jerusalem*, 5:159. Téméricourt was a Knight of St. John. See Slot, *Archipelagus Turbatus*, 201.

2. For Andrew Hess, this is the defining characteristic of Mediterranean frontiers. See his *The Forgotten Frontier*.

3. This was when Tunis concluded a commercial treaty with Pisa. Alexandrowicz, *The European-African Confrontation*, 18.

4. For more on the term corsairing and the related term *corso*, see chapter two.

5. Between 1384 and 1797, the Ottomans sent more than 550 diplomatic missions to Venice to communicate the will of the sultan. Pia Pendani, *In nome del Gran Signore*, 10.

6. See, e.g., Mallia-Milanes, *Venice and Hospitaller Malta*, xix: "The international developments whereby European states began to come to terms with the Ottoman Empire and individual North African beys, was to signal the decline of corsairing. The corso flourished only as long as Muslims were feared, but once normal trading relations were established it became a nuisance to trade. . . . [T]he Order's crusading ideal was becoming more anachronistic."

7. "Malta was a strange anachronism in a Europe increasingly dominated by nation states." Earle, *The Pirate Wars*, 47.

8. Although he is describing the western Mediterranean, Fisher's description in *Barbary Legend* works for the eastern Mediterranean as well: "A system, under which the comity of nations and the sovereign rights of civilized countries were subordinated to the pretences or convictions of religious organizations, cut at the roots of international law and the sanctity of treaties" (29).

9. The exception is the Sephardi Jewish diaspora created by the expulsion from Iberia, which has received a great deal of attention. See, among others, Ravid, "A Tale of Three Cities."

10. Earle, *Corsairs of Malta and Barbary*, 145–46, quoting a Maltese galley captain.

11. Although references to "Greek shipping" and "Greek commerce" in the more general literature on the Mediterranean are common.

12. Vlassopoulos, Ιόνιοι Έμποροι και Καραβοκύρηδες στη Μεσόγειο, 16ος–18ος Αιώνας, 9.

13. Pangratis acknowledges this as a methodological problem. "Researchers of the history of Greek shipping face certain methodological problems. First, the identification

of Greeks is difficult since they were blurred with other Venetian or Ottoman subjects." Pangratis, "Sources for the Maritime History of Greece," 146.

14. As Traian Stoianovich put it nearly half a century ago in an article that is still authoritative: "The victory of the Ottoman Empire symbolized, in the sphere of economics, a victory of Greeks, Turks, renegade Christians, Armenians, Ragusans and Jews over the two-century-old commercial hegemony of Venice and Genoa." The Italians had long enjoyed virtually unlimited access to the markets of the eastern Mediterranean, but now they suffered various disabilities, such as paying higher customs duties than the locals. Stoianovich, "The Conquering Balkan Orthodox Merchant," 6.

15. Ibid.

16. Inalcık, "The Policy of Mehmed II Toward the Greek Population of Istanbul," 247. In the city proper there were 8,951 Muslim households and 3,151 Orthodox Greek households.

17. The 20 percent estimate is O. L. Barkan's, "Essai sur les données statistiques," 28.

18. Mavroeide, Ο Ελληνισμός στο Γαλατά, 90.

19. Ibid., 41.

20. In 1477 the population of Galata was 535 Muslim households and 592 Orthodox Greek households. Inalcık, "The Policy of Mehmed II toward the Greek population of Istanbul," 247.

21. So much so that Greek sources of the time spoke of the "archontes of the City and of Galata." Mavroeide, Ο Ελληνισμός στο Γαλατά, 70.

22. Slavs began to settle in Ancona in the second half of the fourteenth century. Stoianovich, "The Conquering Balkan Orthodox Merchant," 2.

23. Earle, *Corsairs of Malta and Barbary*, 40.

24. For a discussion of this stereotype and its effects on the scholarship, see Kafadar, "A Death in Venice," 191–92.

25. Between 1550 and 1590 the cost of constructing a ship at Venice quadrupled and the strength of the merchant marine fell by half. See Greene, *A Shared World*, 141.

26. Albèri, *Relazioni degli ambasciatori veneti al Senato*, ser. 3, I (Florence, 1840), 275, quoted in Cooperman, "Venetian Policy Towards Levantine Jews," 67.

27. For a description of these developments, see Earle, "The Commercial Development of Ancona 1479–1551," 34.

28. Florence boasted a population of 90,000 in the 1480s. By the 1540s that number had dropped to just a little over 50,000. Cochrane, *Florence in the Forgotten Centuries 1527–1800*, 54.

29. See Ravid, "A Tale of Three Cities."

30. Kafadar, "A Death in Venice," 192.

31. Ravid, "A Tale of Three Cities," 140–41. The famous Venetian historian and diarist Marino Sanudo (1466–1536) refers to "li subditi nostri da parte da mar, et li subditi del Signor turcho." Everyone else was a *forestiero*, and the *forestieri* were explicitly barred from these privileges. Sanudo, *I diarii*, 36:240.

32. For more on the Muslim presence in Venice in the sixteenth century, see Kafadar, "A Death in Venice."

33. For more on the religious situation of the Greeks in Venice, see chapter two.

34. Panayiotopoulos, "Έλληνες Ναυτικοί και Πλοιοκτήτες από τα παλαιότερα Οικονομικά Βιβλία της ελληνικής Αδελφότητας Βενετίας," 286.

35. Mavroeide, Συμβολή στην Ιστορία της ελληνικής Αδελφότητας Βενετίας στο ΙΣΤ Αιώνα, 65.

36. Greeks from a much wider area of the Ottoman Empire, including the entire western coast of mainland Greece, and some Aegean islands as well, traded with the Venetian-held Ionian Islands. More research is needed, but it seems there was a division of labor whereby Ottoman Greeks would go as far as places such as Zakynthos and Corfu, and then the Ionian islanders, subjects of Venice, would go to Venice itself. For information on Ottoman Greeks trading in the Ionian Islands, see Oikonomou, "Όψεις της Ελληνικής Ναυτιλίας κατά το 17ο αιώνα," 363–438.

37. "Sono za piu et piu zorni in questa cita nostra alcuni mercadanti de la Janina et altri luochi subditi del Signor Turco," Sathas, Μνημεία της Ελληνικής Ιστορίας, 5:248. The trade routes came down out of the mountains to the harbor of Sangiada. From there the traders went in little boats to Corfu, a major center of transit trade, as was Zakynthos after the fall of Coron and Modon. Pangrates, "Γιαννιώτες Εμποροι στη Βενετία στα μέσα του 16ου Αιώνα," 139.

38. Pangrates, "Γιαννιώτες Εμποροι στη Βενετία στα μέσα του 16ου Αιώνα," 166.

39. Apparently a new tax had been levied in 1559 to help pay for the construction of a bridge at Spilea. Levels of distrust were so high that the merchants charged officials with going over at night and removing the boulders that had been placed during the day, so as to delay the project and keep levying the tax. Ibid., 166.

40. "De qui noi zuramo non haver da far con venitiani," ibid., 166. Here they are referring to a 1492 decree by the Venetian Senate that forbade Venetian subjects from entering into certain transactions with "Christians, Turks and others of the Ottoman Empire." Mavroeide, Ο Ελληνισμός στο Γαλατά, 109. This legislation itself is a demonstration of the categories of subjecthood created by Ottoman-Venetian agreements.

41. Ploumides, Αιτήματα και πραγματικότητες των Ελλήνων της Βενετοκρατίας, 83.

42. Pangratis, "Γιαννιώτες Εμποροι στη Βενετία στα μέσα του 16ου Αιώνα," 134.

43. Kafadar, "A Death in Venice," 196. A slightly different and less detailed version of these events is in Ravid, "A Tale of Three Cities," 141.

44. Natalucci, Ancona attraverso i secoli, 134. George Leon dates the community even earlier: "It seems that Ancona was one of the first commercial centers outside the Balkan Peninsula which attracted a considerable number of Greeks as early as the last two decades of the fifteenth century." Leon, "The Greek Merchant Marine," 15.

45. Saracini, Notitie historiche della citta' d'Ancona, 337–38.

46. Ravid, "A Tale of Three Cities," 141.

47. Kafadar, "A Death in Venice," 197.

48. Natalucci, Ancona attraverso i secoli, 135.

49. Ravid, "A Tale of Three Cities," 145.

50. Ibid.

51. Ibid., 158.

52. Only Kafadar has pointed this out. "How these developments affected non-Jewish Ottoman merchants remains to be studied." "A Death in Venice," 197–98.

53. Ibid, 198.

54. Ibid.

55. Fedalto, Ricerche storiche, 92.

56. Ravid, "A Tale of Two Cities," 145–46. When war broke out between the Venetians and the Ottomans in 1570, both Ottoman Muslim and Jewish merchants were seized. Kafadar, "A Death in Venice," 200.

57. Not only were previously excluded Greeks able to penetrate the Venetian market, one study has shown that as early as the beginning of the sixteenth century they were able to bypass Venice's staple laws altogether and buy woolen cloths directly in Verona. Most of these merchants were from Corfu. Mueller, "Greeks in Venice and 'Venetians' in Greece," 178. Mueller cites the work of Edoardo Demo for this information on Verona.

58. Thiriet, "La vie des hommes de les rapports des collectivités," 280.

59. Mavroeide, Ο Ελληνισμός στο Γαλατά, 109.

60. The consequences for Venice's colonies have not received much attention, but see Greene, A Shared World, esp. chaps. 4 and 5, for a preliminary discussion. See also Fusaro, "Coping with Transition, 95–123. Fusaro points out that the decline of the Venetian fleet in the closing decades of the sixteenth century opened up opportunities for private merchants, among them many Greeks. The range and scope of their commercial enterprise at this time, she argues, have been underestimated (95–96).

61. Frederic Lane discusses this in his Venice. See especially the section "The Peak and Passing of the Merchant Galleys."

62. Fusaro, "Un reseau de cooperation," 610. Lane, Venice, 349.

63. In the late fifteenth century the republic levied a tax on foreigners loading wine in Crete for shipment to England. Lane, Venice, 380.

64. Ibid., 379.

65. With very few exceptions, most notably Fusaro, "Un reseau de cooperation."

66. Fusaro, Uva passa, 14: "Nel 1545 veniva segnalato a Zante un notevole aumento del traffico di transito in mano a 'forestieri,' che si svolgeva quindi non su navi di veneziani o di sudditi della Repubblica." The Senate made this distinction over and over again. A petition submitted to the authorities in 1578 defined foreigners simply as "mercanti non sudditi di Vostra Serenita"(merchants who are not subjects of Your Serenity) without bothering to distinguish between Venetians and subjects of Venice. Fusaro, "Coping with Transition," 29.

67. But see Fusaro, "Coping with Transition," 101. Maltezou refers very briefly, and rather enigmatically, to the fact that "the local population was emancipated economically." Maltezou, "The Historical and Social Context," 92. The fact that the Venetians never formally struck down the laws prohibiting the participation of their subjects in international trade may be one reason why this phenomenon has been so widely overlooked. Thiriet, La romaine vénitienne, 420, writes that the Venetians chose to close their eyes instead. See Oikonomou, "Οψεις της Ελληνικής Ναυτιλίας κατά το 17ο αιωνα," 401, for a brief discussion of how the inability of Venice to enforce her commercial monopoly benefited Greek merchants, in this case Ottoman Greeks bringing grain to Venetian Crete.

68. Crete shared many characteristics with the Ionian Islands but also had its own peculiarities. For that reason it is discussed in a separate section.

69. The Seguro name in Greek is Σίγουρος.

70. Archivio di Stato di Venezia, Capi del Consiglio dei Dieci, Lettere di Rettori e altre cariche, quoted in Fusaro, "Un reseau de cooperation," 614.

71. Vlassopoulos, Ιόνιοι Εμποροι και Καραβοκύρηδες στη Μεσόγειο, 16ος–18ος Αιώνας, 44. Perhaps this contact with the East explains why Agesilao Seguro was appointed

consul for the "merchants subjects to the Turks" in 1618. Fusaro, "Coping with Transition," 105.

72. The Sumacchi name in Greek is Σουμάκης.

73. Such as the aristocratic Corner family and the merchant brothers Ragazzoni, who hired ships from the Sumacchi family for the transport of currants from the Morea and the Ionian Islands to Venice.

74. Fusaro, "Un reseau de cooperation," 616.

75. Vlassopoulos, Ιόνιοι Εμποροι και Καραβοκύρηδες στη Μεσόγειο 16ος-18ος Αιώνας, 45.

76. Fusaro, "Un reseau de cooperation," 610.

77. Vlassopoulos, Ιόνιοι Εμποροι και Καραβοκύρηδες στη Μεσόγειο 16ος-18ος Αιωνας, 15.

78. The second city of Crete, Chania, would overtake Candia later on in terms of commercial importance. In the sixteenth century, however, it was still insignificant.

79. In 1589 an official commented, "Among the population of the cities there are a number of master workers who are used to occupy themselves with the construction of galleons and other ships." Spanakes, "Relazione del Nobil Huomo Zuanne Mocenigo," 23. See Greene, A Shared World, 147–53, for more on the Cretan shipbuilding industry.

80. In 1604 a Venetian official in Crete observed: "I believe, and I think others will concur, that to have fortresses and territories and coastlines in places thousands of miles away, in front of the open mouth of the enemy, without the ability to supply the population and the militia there with food, it is as if one doesn't, in fact, possess that place at all to say the least. Your Highness, your islands and fortresses in the East—and particularly the island of Crete—are in such a situation. Spanakes, "Η Εκθεση του Δούκα της Κρήτης," 521–22.

81. Epeteris Hetaireia Kretikon Spoudon 3 (1940): 241–96.

82. ". . . molti ne vanno in Costantinopoli et nel mar maggiore, et assai in Alessandria dove non si consumano altri vini che di Candia." Pashley, Travels in Crete, 2:56. Pashley is quoting from from Foscarini's 1576 relazione.

83. Spanakes, "Relazione del Nobil Huomo Zuanne Mocenigo," 23. The office of provveditore generale for Crete was created in the second half of the sixteenth century. It was an attempt to reassert central control over the island, with a view to implementing reforms.

84. "Li arti vagliono bene, et il danaro corre largamente." Ibid., 171 The "brain drain" of Greeks from the Venetokrateia to Constantinople, where they served the enemy, was a constant theme in the writings of the Venetian bailos in Constantinople. Mavroeide, Ο Ελληνισμός στο Γαλατά, 53.

85. Mavroeide, Ο Ελληνισμός στο Γαλατά, 39.

86. Ibid., 114.

87. See Greene, A Shared World, chap. 4.

88. Struys, Voiages, 2:102.

89. See Manousakas, Επισκόπηση της ιστορίας της Ελληνικής Ορθόδοξης Αδελφότητας της Βενετίας, 243–64, for a general review of the fraternity.

90. Mavroeide, Συμβολή στην Ιστορία της ελληνικής Αδελφότητας Βενετίας στο ΙΣΤ Αιώνα, 120.

91. This tax was lifted after ten years (ibid., 120). Once again, the merchant community stepped in and provided funds.

92. Ibid., 64–65. Cypriots were also prominent. They too were Venetian subjects.

93. In 1479, followed by a period of instability. Ottoman rule was not solidified until 1503. Ibid., 65.

94. In the middle of the sixteenth century Venice's Greek Orthodox population numbered around 4,000. Ibid., 251, and Ploumides, "Considerazioni sulla popolazione greca a Venezia," 221. In the 1560s about 20 percent of Venice's subjects, across all its possessions, were Greek Orthodox. Benjamin Arbel puts that number at 480,000. Arbel, "Roman Catholics and Greek Orthodox in the Early Modern Venetian State," 73. Arbel's article also suggests rapid growth in the Greek population in the capital city. He puts it at around 15,000 in the 1580s (73).

95. Pangrates, "Γιαννιώτες Εμποροι στη Βενετία στα μέσα του 16ου Αιώνα," 136.

96. Ibid.

97. As the most prominent Greek community outside the Ottoman Empire in the early modern period, known not only for its wealth but also for its scholarship and cultural achievements, the Greeks of Venice have long attracted the attention of scholars.

98. Mavroeide, Συμβολή στην Ιστορία της ελληνικής Αδελφότητας Βενετίας στο ΙΣΤ Αιώνα, 119.

99. Kaklamanes, "Μάρκος Δεφαράνας," 219.

100. Mavroeide, Συμβολή στην Ιστορία της ελληνικής Αδελφότητας Βενετίας στο ΙΣΤ Αιώνα, 124–45, and Vlassopoulos, Ιονιοι Εμποροι και Καραβοκύρηδες στη Μεσόγειο, 16ος–18ος Αιώνας, 43.

101. Or between 560 and 720 tons. The *botte* (plural *botti*) was the wine cask used at Venice in estimating the size of ships. Lane, "Tonnages, Medieval and Modern," 229, and Tucci, "Un problem di metrológia navale," 201–46. In a census taken by the Venetian authorities just one year earlier, the ships in the Venetian merchant navy ranged from 500 to 1,200 botti. Pangrates, "Sources for the Maritime History of Greece," 128.

102. Vlassopoulos, Ιόνιοι Εμποροι και Καραβοκύρηδες στη Μεσόγειο, 16ος–18ος Αιώνας, 35–37. This Matthew was probably the grandson of the first Matthew Vergis. Also see Mavroeide, Συμβολή στην Ιστορία της ελληνικης Αδελφότητας Βενετίας στο ΙΣΤ Αιώνα, 139, for more information on M. Vergis.

103. Ottoman diplomacy in Europe is still a relatively underexplored subject. Some agreements were the result of high-level negotiations between the sultan's representatives and those of European monarchs. Others seem to have had their origin in initiatives taken by Ottoman subjects. The relationship between these two levels of diplomacy is unclear.

104. Celumeau, "Un ponte fra Oriente e Occidente," 32.

105. Ibid.

106. "Il mercanti Levantini subditti del Turcho," Makuscev, *Monumenta Historica Slavorum Meridionalium*, 1:180. But see Oikonomou, "Οψεις της Ελληνικής Ναυτιλίας κατά το 17ο αιωνα," 436. In this context. *Levantini* does seem to refer only to Greeks. E. Natalie Rothman's recent dissertation makes it clear that "levantini" does not have a stable referent. Rothman, "Between Venice and Istanbul," esp. the section "Who's a Levantine?," 405–32.

107. The Venetians worried about this competition. In 1524 the *Cinque Savii alla Mercanzia* wrote of "the fairs of Lanciano and Recanati where the vigor of Greeks, Turks, Persians and others of the Levant concurs with the goods of those lands." Quoted in Kafadar, "A Death in Venice," 196.

108. Ibid., 197.

109. Celumeau, "Un ponte fra Oriente e Occidente," 45.

110. Such a matter-of-fact tone could only come from a contemporary or someone outside Ottoman history. For the weighty legacy of sultans as indifferent to commerce and opposed to travel to Christian lands, see Kafadar, "A Death in Venice."

111. Theunissen, "Ottoman-Venetian Diplomatics," 224, speaks of "the bilateral character of the Ottoman-Venetian treaties."

112. Ibid., 196.

113. Pia Pedani, *In nome del Gran Signore*, 19.

114. Arbel, *Trading Nations,* 78. Ashkenazi was born at Udine and completed his medical studies at the University of Padua.

115. Pia Pedani, *In nome del Gran Signore*, 175.

116. Ibid.

117. Kafadar, "A Death in Venice," 199.

118. Ibid.

119. Turan, "Venedik'te Türk Ticaret Merkezi," 276.

120. Not always without controversy. Often there was a dispute as to whether or not something required the intervention of the authorities. Arbel's study of the bankruptcy of Hayyim Saruq in Venice shows the particular factors that could turn an ordinary business matter into an affair of state between Venice and the Ottoman Empire. See his *Trading Nations*, chap. 6

121. In 1582 Bosnian merchants demanded brokers who spoke Slavic languages; although brokers for Ottoman merchants already existed, they were evidently Turkish-speaking. Kafadar, "A Death in Venice," 203.

122. Mavroeide's study, Ο Ελληνισμός στο Γαλατά (Hellenism in Galata), is a good example of this. Despite its title, in the opening pages she explains that hers is actually a study of the Greek subjects of Venice who resided in Galata (13).

123. Fusaro, "Un reseau de cooperation," 610.

124. Panayiotopoulos, "Έλληνες Ναυτικοί και Πλοιοκτήτες από τα παλαιότερα Οικονομικά Βιβλία της ελληνικής Αδελφότητας Βενετίας," 332.

125. Lane, "Venetian Bankers," 71.

126. Tenenti, *Naufrages, corsaires et assurances maritimes à Venise*, 164. The word in both cases is "patron."

127. Vlassopoulos, Ιόνιοι Εμποροι και Καραβοκύρηδες στη Μεσόγειο: 16ος–18ος Αιώνας, 36.

128. Fusaro, "Un reseau de cooperation," 605.

129. Sathas, Μνημεία της Ελληνικής Ιστορίας, 248.

130. "Noi, mercanti levantini et sudditi del Signor, cosi Christiani come Zudei et Turchi." Pangrates, "Γιαννιώτες Εμποροι στη Βενετία στα μεσα του 16ου Αιώνα," 166.

131. "Della nation nostra et de tutti li sudditi del Signor." Pangrates, "Γιαννιώτες Εμποροι στη Βενετία στα μέσα του 16ου Αιώνα," 167. The use of the terms "nation" is noteworthy, insofar as the petition was submitted by Christians, Muslims, and Jews.

132. Ploumides, Αιτήματα και πραγματικότητες των Ελλήνων της Βενετοκρατίας, 83.

133. Fusaro, "Un reseau de cooperation," 619: "ils allerent jusqu'a falsifier les registres de douane pour faire croire que c'etait eux, et non les Anglais, qui etaient les exporta-teurs, ce qui leur permettait d'echapper a la lourde taxation."

134. Ibid., 621.

135. My account draws heavily on Inalcık, "Ottoman Galata." He points out that Western scholarship has mistakenly considered this document to be a treaty, which is a bilateral and negotiated instrument. An ahd-name is a unilateral grant (21).

136. "Merchants immediately surrendered the colony to the Turks and obtained a treaty granting all the rights and privileges formerly enjoyed under the Paleologi." Mitler, "The Genoese in Galata," 74.

137. Inalcık, "Ottoman Galata," 26.

138. Ibid.

139. Mavroeide, Ο Ελληνισμός στο Γαλατά, 24.

140. Ibid., 85n202.

141. Ibid., 82–85.

142. Ibid., 86.

143. This description is taken from Eric Dursteler's book on Ottoman-Venetian relations in the early modern period. He calls these people "the unofficial nation." See Dursteler, *Venetians in Constantinople*, chap. 3.

144. Ibid., 174.

145. Ibid, 172–73.

146. Ibid., 165. Many if not most of these Greek Venetians were from Crete, and they managed a brisk trade in Cretan products between Istanbul and Crete.

147. Ibid., 168.

148. Ibid., 174.

149. Ibid., 176.

150. Ibid., 175.

151. Mavroeide, Ο Ελληνισμός στο Γαλατά, 130. Despite this disclaimer, the title of her book implies that she is speaking about the Greek community as a whole. This is a good example of how a Greek community is assumed rather than demonstrated, despite important dividing lines such as legal status.

152. Ibid., 82.

153. They also played an important role in mediating the relationship between the Orthodox patriarchate in Istanbul and the Greek Orthodox community in Venice. This is discussed in chapter two.

154. Mavroeide, Ο Ελληνισμός στο Γαλατά, 69, 70.

155. Mavroeide, Συμβολή στην Ιστορία της ελληνικής Αδελφότητας Βενετίας στο ΙΣΤ Αιώνα, 130. This must have potentially exposed the Galata branch of the family to great danger, but Mavroeide does not comment on this.

156. Mavroeide, Ο Ελληνισμός στο Γαλατά, 69, 70.

157. Mavroeide, *Venice*, 131. Venice had a tradition of granting "original citizenship" (as opposed to naturalized citizenship) to individuals who had rendered extraordinary service to the republic. In 1490 original citizenship was given to five brothers, all residents of Constantinople, because of the role they had played in secret negotiations with the sultan. Mueller, "Greeks in Venice and 'Venetians' in Greece," 171. Naturalized citizens were "cittadini de intus" or "de intus et de extra." Rothman, "Between Venice and Istanbul," 20.

158. Mavroeide, Ο Ελληνισμός στο Γαλατά, 137.

159. Ibid., 136.

160. The Jewish role in this has been explored at great length. There is no similar study for the Greeks.

Chapter 2
The Claims of Religion

1. Fontenay and Tenenti, "Course et piraterie Méditerranée," 78.

2. The term is a pan-Mediterranean one. The *corso* in the West is the Greek κουρσον, and Ottoman قورصآن, in the East. The term derives from the Latin *cursus*, meaning sea voyage. Not surprisingly, the term first came into use in the twelfth century, when the antagonism between Christianity and Islam had been given new life by the First Crusade. Kahane and Tietze, *The Lingua Franca in the Levant*, 193. See also Ahrweiler, "Course et piraterie dans la Méditerranée orientale," 1.9–11. In the context of the sixteenth and seventeenth centuries, the *corso* refers to Christian raiding of Muslim shipping, justified within the larger context of an ongoing crusade against Islam. See Earle, *Corsairs of Malta and Barbary*.

3. In the words of Fontenay and Tenenti, "Pratique un peu partout, un peu par tous." "Course et piraterie Méditerranée," 79.

4. Ibid.

5. The structure of corsairing in Malta is discussed in greater detail in the following chapter. Here I am interested only in highlighting its opposition to the Ottoman-Venetian treaty regime.

6. Ventures for the purpose of corsairing were known as cruises. Fontenay, "Corsaires de la foi," 366.

7. *Fabio Chigi*, 224.

8. The knights' traditional alliance with Genoa also did not help matters.

9. Muscat, *The Maltese Galley*, 6.

10. Luttrell, "Venice and the Knights Hospitallers."

11. During the course of the century the Venetians and the knights alternated (as did many others) between fighting and trading with the Ottomans.

12. Mallia-Milanes, *Venice and Hospitaller Malta*, xvii.

13. See ibid., 15–16, for conciliatory measures taken toward the end of the fifteenth century, and Vatin, *L'ordre de Saint-Jean-de Jérusalem*, 26–27, for trade.

14. Mallia-Milanes, *Venice and Hospitaller Malta*, 1.

15. Ibid.

16. Ibid., 47.

17. Dal Pozzo, *Historia della sacra religione militare di S. Giovanni Gerosolimitano*, 1:47. This is just what one would expect to happen if one were following the rules of the *Consolato del Mare*. See Kulsrud, *Maritime Neutrality to 1780*, 109.

18. See Kulsrud, *Maritime Neutrality to 1780*, 15. He notes that, despite attempts to make changes in the second half of the seventeenth century, "the majority of commercial agreements and prize court decisions of the 18th century coincided with the principles of the *Consolato del Mare.*"

19. Kulsrud uses the term "enemy" and "neutral." See ibid., 111–13.

20. Ibid., 122. For example, if the admiral has a place to store the booty nearby, the patron shall deliver it there. The admiral shall pay him for so doing, by mutual agreement "or in default of any special agreement, the merchant vessel shall receive for that service the ordinary freight that any other vessel would have earned for such a voyage." The admiral was often a corsair who had been appointed to the post. Tai, "Restitution

and the Definition of a Pirate," 36. Lauren Benton writes, "In the Mediterranean ships were viewed as extensions of land based power." Benton, "Legal Spaces of Empire," 703. In fact, that was only one view, and it was a contested one.

21. The sequestration, called a *sequestro*, was a common Venetian tactic in the sixteenth century. Venice put pressure on the knights to return prizes by seizing the order's assets, which were considerable, in Venice. See Mallia-Milanes, *Venice and Hospitaller Malta*, 147–48, 56–57, for just two of many examples of sequestro that he writes about.

22. Vertot, *The History of the Knights Hospitallers of St. John of Jerusalem*, 5:83. There is disagreement, then, as to whether or not these Jews were subjects of Venice. No doubt this was another area of ambiguity.

23. Mallia-Milanes, *Venice and Hospitaller Malta*, 88.

24. Archives of the Order of St. John (henceforth AOM), 443, *Liber Bullarum* f.249v–250r: "secondo l'antico uso et usitata Guerra et conforme all dispositione del consolato o sia legge del mare." I consulted these archives at the Malta Study Center at St. John's University in Collegeville, Minnesota.

25. Kulsrud, *Maritime Neutrality to 1780*, 120. Gentili's writings, from the second half of the sixteenth century, fall in line with this harsher regime. He wrote that the ship of a friend did not become a prize because it was carrying goods belonging to the enemy unless the enemy cargo had been taken on board with the consent of the owner of the ship.

26. Ibid., 38. By the end of the seventeenth century letters of marque were no longer issued during peacetime.

27. Kulsrud, *Maritime Neutrality to 1780*, 158.

28. Mallia-Milanes, *Venice and Hospitaller Malta*, 90.

29. For an extended discussion of this brief, see ibid., 92–94.

30. Ibid., 62.

31. Here I would have to disagree with the Ottoman historian Palmira Brummett, who writes as if these were settled matters, without any ambiguity: "In this regard, the ships were like envoys or travelers; they embodied their 'nations' even when they moved through contested terrain or established themselves temporarily in the lands of sovereigns not their own." Brummett, "Imagining the Early Modern Ottoman Space," 48.

32. Kulsrud, *Maritime Neutrality to 1780*, 109–10.

33. Mallia-Milanes, *Venice and Hospitaller Malta*, 19–20.

34. Ibid.

35. Setton, *The Papacy and the Levant*, 4:608. A *sequestro* refers to the Venetian seizure of Maltese assets located within Venice's jurisdiction. The first sequestro imposed after the knights' move to Malta came in 1536, in Venetian territory. This was a common Venetian response to more serious Maltese attacks.

36. Mallia-Milanes, *Venice and Hospitaller Malta*, 20.

37. Ibid., 34. There were of course good reasons for this approach. Venice knew it would be called on the carpet by the Ottomans for allowing Western corsairs to operate in and around Venetian-held territory. This is indeed how the Ottoman war with Venice for control of Crete began in 1645.

38. Among his many accomplishments, he had been an admiral of the Spanish armada. Mallia-Milanes, *Venice and Hospitaller Malta*, 73. At some point after this particular incident the Venetian authorities were able to capture Brochero, and he was held in a fortress in Crete. He was subsequently released on the intervention of the Spanish representative at Venice. Tenenti, *Piracy and the Decline of Venice*, 164.

39. The urgent need for Ottoman grain in Venetian-held Crete was another reason for Venetian anxiety concerning corsairing activity in the Levant. See Greene, *A Shared World*, chap. 2.

40. Whether there was an agreed-upon distance is not clear. At least in theory, the doctrine of Bartole de Sassoferrato was accepted in Italy—the state bordering the sea had authority over the neighboring sea, and this neighborhood was compared to two days' sailing, about 150 kilometers or 93 miles. Ganshof, *The Middle Ages*, 310.

41. Theiner, *Annales Ecclesiastici*, 3:754–55.

42. See Mallia-Milanes, *Venice and Hospitaller Malta*, 80–85, for an account of this incident

43. Ibid., 83.

44. Bartolomeo dal Pozzo talks about this incident as well. Dal Pozzo, *Historia della sacra religione militare di S. Giovanni Gerosolimitano*, 1:249.

45. Mallia-Milanes, *Venice and Hospitaller Malta*, 86.

46. Although in this case the pope was unable to prevail. The grand master refused to return it.

47. Mallia-Milanes, *Venice and Hospitaller Malta*, 60–61.

48. Setton, *The Papacy and the Levant*, 4:608. There are many other cases. See Tenenti, *Piracy and the Decline of Venice*, 38–39, where the Venetians asked the pope to look into yet another Maltese seizure. The pope turned it over to a commission of cardinals.

49. Theiner, *Annales Ecclesiastici*, 3:754–55. I thank Pietro Frassica for help in translating this document.

50. Ibid.

51. Mallia-Milanes, *Venice and Hospitaller Malta*, 154. Despite the date, I would argue that this incident is more typical of the sixteenth century, when larger numbers of Greeks were under Venetian rule. These numbers dwindled as the Ottomans advanced and fewer and fewer Greeks could turn to Venice for protection.

52. The only detail missing is any mention of compensation to the Greeks for what was seized, for the instructions did say that the Christians would be paid their freight charges.

53. Tenenti, *Cristoforo Da Canal*, 154.

54. Mallia-Milanes, *Venice and Hospitaller Malta*, 150–51.

55. He was eventually reimbursed 2,700 ducats by the order. Ibid., 152.

56. See chapter one, for the Greek population of Ancona at the beginning of the sixteenth century.

57. The Council of Ferrara-Florence (1438–39) has received voluminous attention from Byzantine historians. For recent discussions, see Nicol, *The Last Centuries of Byzantium*, 351 59, and Necipoğlu, "Byzantium between the Ottomans and the Latins," 360–71.

58. The religious status of the Greek community of Venice has received a great deal of attention from historians, most of them writing in Greek. See Manousakas, Επισκόπηση της ιστορίας της Ελληνικής Ορθόδοξης Αδελφότητας της Βενετίας, 243–64; idem, "Η εν Βενετία Ελληνική Κοινοτης και οι Μητροπολίται Φιλαδελφείας"; Fedalto, *Ricerche storiche*; Mavroeide, Συμβολή στην Ιστορία της ελληνικής Αδελφότητας Βενετίας στο ΙΣΤ Αιώνα; and Ploumides, Αι Βούλλαι των Παπών περί των Ελλήνων Ορθοδόξων της Βενετίας, 228–66.

59. The following account draws heavily on Manousakas, Επισκόπηση της ιστορίας της Ελληνικής Ορθόδοξης Αδελφότητας της Βενετίας.

60. Ersie Burke notes that the reasons for the failure of the 1456 attempt remain obscure. "'Your Humble and Devoted Servants,'" 15.

61. Fedalto, *Ricerche storiche*, 45.

62. In the words of this same scholar, the bulls gave the Greeks a *"peculiarita giurisdizionale rispetto ai cattolici di rito latinno."* Ibid. For Latin harassment of the Greeks in Venice, see Manousakas, Επισκόπηση της ιστορίας της Ελληνικής Ορθόδοξης Αδελφότητας της Βενετίας, and Mavroeide, Συμβολή στην Ιστορία της ελληνικής Αδελφότητας Βενετίας στο ΙΣΤ Αιώνα. The extraordinary concessions of the papal bulls of 1514 seem to have been motivated by the hellenophilic sentiments of Pope Leo X. Fedalto, *Ricerche storiche*, 45, and Manousakas, Επισκόπηση της ιστορίας της Ελληνικής Ορθόδοξης Αδελφότητας της Βενετίας, 247.

63. Mavroeide, Συμβολή στην Ιστορία της ελληνικής Αδελφότητας Βενετίας στο ΙΣΤ Αιώνα, 12.

64. Ploumides, "Papal Bulls," 245.

65. Ibid., 234.

66. Fedalto, *Ricerce storiche*, 89.

67. Ibid., 92.

68. Pangrates, *Chiesa Latina e missionari Francescani*, 3.

69. And not just in Venice; this was the policy across all its possessions, adjusted for local differences. It consented to the presence of an Orthodox elite in the Ionian Islands, despite the objections of the Latin clergy. Manousakas, "Η εν Βενετια Ελληνικη Κοινοτης και οι Μητροπολιται Φιλαδελφειας," 184. It continued to bar the Orthodox hierarchy from Crete but sought other ways to placate the island's Greek population. By the beginning of the seventeenth century there were more than one hundred Orthodox churches in the island's capital, Candia, and state officials were encouraged to attend them. These same officials worked hard to prevent provocative behavior on the part of the Catholic Church. See Greene, *A Shared World*, 176.

70. Manousakas, "Η εν Βενετία Ελληνική Κοινότης και οι Μητροπολίται Φιλαδελφείας," 193. The following account draws heavily on the Manousakas article. Eric Dursteler provides us with more information on Servo. Venetian officials in Constantinople thought of Servo as arrogant and something of a troublemaker. But he was permitted to participate in the workings of the nation, voted in meetings of the Council of Ten, and traded as a Venetian. Dursteler, *The Venetians in Constantinople*, 53–54.

71. Severos was born in Monemvasia in the late 1530s. When the Ottomans took the city, the family fled to Crete. Manousakas, "Η εν Βενετία Ελληνική Κοινότης και οι Μητροπολίται Φιλαδελφείας," 193.

72. Ibid., 198.

73. Herring, Οικουμενικό Πατριαρχείο και Ευρωπαϊκή Πολιτική, 1620–1638, 31. My account of Loukaris draws on this book.

74. Mavroeide, Συμβολή στην Ιστορία της ελληνικής Αδελφότητας Βενετίας στο ΙΣΤ Αιώνα, 17. There was a dramatic development towards the end of the seventeenth century when the metropolitan Tipaldos (1685–1713) suddenly declared his allegiance to Rome. Venice then demanded that all the Greek priests serving under Tipaldos do the same. Many Greeks left Venice as a result of this. Manousakas, Επισκόπηση της ιστορίας της Ελληνικής Ορθόδοξης Αδελφότητας της Βενετίας, 258.

75. Wright, *The Early Modern Papacy*, 148.

76. This aspect of the history has not received sufficient attention. In the literature the focus tends to be on the attitude of the authorities, while the identity of the community is rarely problematized. But see the following note.

77. Burke, "'Your Humble and Devoted Servants,'" 15.

78. Frattarelli Fischer, "Alle radici di una identita composita," 52 et passim, for details on some of the Inquisition proceedings.

79. Mavroeide, Ο Ελληνισμός στο Γαλατά, 85.

80. The essence of dhimmi status in Islamic law is that the person submits to the sultan, and in return the sultan extends his protection.

81. Mavroeide, Ο Ελληνισμός στο Γαλατά, 82–83. She notes, too, that movement into the category of haraç payer was an "everyday occurrence."

82. Ibid., 79.

83. Ibid., 79–80, for some examples.

84. Fedalto, *Ricerche storiche*, 105.

85. For example, Antoine Cantekouzenos, of the famous Cantekouzenos family, was a powerful member of the Othodox laity, identified by Iorga as an *archon*. In 1565 he selected the next patriarch. His brother Manuel lived in Venice. Iorga, *Byzance après Byzance*, 113–14.

86. Mavroeide, Ο Ελληνισμός στο Γαλατά, 79.

87. Zachariadou, "Συμβολή στην Ιστορία του Νοτιοανατολικού Αιγαίου," 184–229. The account that follows draws heavily on this article.

88. Zachariadou notes that it is not clear if these privileges were only for the residents of the monastery or for all the inhabitants of the island. Ibid., 198–99.

89. Ibid., 199.

Chapter 3
The Age of Piracy

1. The Web site specialtydrinks.com, which sells Captain Morgan's rum, gets around the problem of what to call him by dubbing him a "swashbuckler."

2. When a Dutch prize court ruled that the seizure of the *Santa Catarina* was legal, and thus the proceeds could go to the shareholders of the Dutch East India Company, the decision proved so controversial that Hugo Grotius was retained to write a brief defending the decision. Out of this brief came his *Mare Liberum*, or *The Freedom of the Seas*, which was part of a larger commentary. *Mare Liberum* was published in 1609 at the behest of the East India Company. Grotius, *De jure praedae commentarius*, 1:xiv.

3. The golden age of piracy commonly refers to the second half of the seventeenth century and the first two decades of the eighteenth century. Periodization differs somewhat, however, for the Caribbean and the Indian Ocean. See Rediker, *Villains of All Nations*.

4. Rediker, *Between the Devil and the Deep Blue Sea*, 58. Many of these pirates then went on to greener pastures in the Indian and Pacific Oceans.

5. Fodor, "Piracy, Ransom Slavery and Trade," 122; Brogini, *Malte*, 621.

6. Engels, *Merchants, Interlopers, Seamen and Corsairs*, 42. The city's population reached its highest point of the century around 1670, when it boasted around 17,000

residents, before dropping back down to 12,000 by the end of the 1600s. Pagano de Divitiis, *Mercanti Inglesi*, 132.

7. Julien, *History of North Africa*, 306. Algiers, unlike Malta or Livorno, began growing early in the sixteenth century as a result of incorporation into the Ottoman Empire. The city's population stood at around 20,000 in 1500. Hess, *The Forgotten Frontier*, 165.

8. "Spirito guerresco di stampo crociato." Pagano de Divitiis, *Mercanti Inglesi*, 65.

9. For instance, the location of the English staple at Antwerp. When this moved to Hamburg later on in the century, Venice once again came into favor with English merchants. And Venice made strenuous efforts in the second half of the sixteenth century to regain some of the business it had lost. See Earle, "The Commercial Development of Ancona 1479–1551," 43.

10. See Pullan, *Crisis and Change*, for reassessments of seventeenth-century Venice. See Pagano de Divitiis, *Mercanti Inglesi*, for Livorno as the preferred port of the English.

11. In Piazza Micheli.

12. Trivellato, *The Familiarity of Strangers*, 306.

13. Evelyn, *Diary*, 2:183. Robert Bargrave, Levant merchant, had this to say about the monument. Livorno had "divers stately Statues, of which the cheife are of :3 or :4 Slaves in Brass, without the walls." Bargrave, *Travel Diary*, 65. The statue still stands today.

14. Engels, *Merchants, Interlopers, Seamen and Corsairs*, 42. Cochrane, *Florence in the Forgotten Centuries 1527–1800*, 173. The city's population reached its highest point of the century around 1670, when the city had around 17,000 residents, before dropping back down to 12,000 by the end of the 1600s. Pagano de Divitiis, *Mercanti Inglesi*, 132.

15. Pagano de Divitiis, *Mercanti Inglesi*, 132.

16. Ibid., 133. Mun amassed his fortune in the Mediterranean trade. He is best known as the author of *England's Treasure by Foreign Trade*, written around 1630.

17. Engels, *Merchants, Interlopers, Seamen and Corsairs*, 21. The Medicis ruled Tuscany until 1737.

18. The following account draws heavily on Vlame, Το Φιορίνι, το σιτάρι και η οδός του Κήπου. The long struggle between Pisa and Florence lasted from 1494 to 1509 and ended in the loss of Pisa's independence. After the war, Pisa sank into insignificance as a port. Earle, "The Commercial Development of Ancona, 1471–1551," 42.

19. Pagano de Divitiis, *Mercanti Inglesi*, 136.

20. Ibid., 131.

21. Ibid, 140.

22. Ibid.

23. Baruchello cautions that the term "free port" did not have the meaning at the time that it does today. It was not the case that no taxes were levied at all. The term was a relative one: in comparison to other ports, Livorno offered a number of benefits and exemptions. Baruchello, *Livorno e il suo porto*, 267.

24. Pagano de Divitiis, *Mercanti Inglesi*, 133.

25. Ibid., 137.

26. Vlame, Το Φιορίνι, το σιτάρι και η οδός του Κήπου, 55.

27. Engels, *Merchants, Interlopers, Seamen and Corsairs*, 30.

28. Ravid, "A Tale of Three Cities," 56.

29. See ibid. for a more systematic comparison.

30. Ibid., 156. Paolo Castignoli calls the *Livornina* the Magna Carta of the Jews of Livorno. Castignoli, "La tolleranza enunciazione," 78.

31. Ravid, "A Tale of Three Cities," 139.

32. Fratterelli Fischer, "Merci e mercanti nella Livorno seicentesca," 66. Further on he quotes a contemporary source who described the port as "always free and secure for all." In an even more recent study, Michale D'Angelo and M. Elisabetta Tonizzi write, "Leghorn was typical of the free ports in which trade thrived throughout the entire modern age because of the policies (neutrality, religious tolerance etc.) of the Grand-Duchy of Tuscany wich attracted foreign ships and merchants." "Recent Maritime Historiography on Italy," 60.

33. Kulischer, *Storia economica*, 2:353. Paolo Castignoli is one of the very few to point out that the tolerance extended to the Jews was not similarly extended, at least initially, to other heterodox nations. Castignoli, "La tolleranza enunciazione," 79. See also Baruchello, *Livorno e il suo porto*, 347 where he writes that the port's religious freedom has been exaggerated. A very recent study also points out the limits of toleration for the Jews. Trivellato, *The Familiarity of Strangers*, 71.

34. There is also a large body of empirical work, almost all of it in Italian, on the city's origins, the growth of the population, and the development of the harbor. There is still no general monograph in English on Livorno.

35. Braudel, *The Mediterranean and the Mediterranean World in the Age of Philip II*, 2:890.

36. Postan and Habakkuk, *Cambridge Economic History of Europe*, 2:99; Ganshof, *The Middle Ages*, 141.

37. Camerani, "Contributo alla storia dei trattati commerciali," 85.

38. Ibid., 86.

39. "Per esser cose spectanti a'principi e non a'mercanti": ibid, 88. In modern Italian, *spectanti* is *spettanti*.

40. He promised that the gallies of St. Stephen "non andassiono in corso a'vasselli di mercantia." Ibid., 90.

41. See Angiolini, *I cavalierie e il principe*, for the ambitions of the Tuscan rulers. See also my "The Mediterranean Basin" for the place of the Mediterranean in European politics in the sixteenth century.

42. Angiolini, *I cavalieri e il principe*, 17.

43. "The Order was furnished with some galleys which were technically separate from those of the Tuscan navy, but this was more in form than in fact." Camerani, "Contributo alla storia dei trattati commerciali," 84.

44. Again, Camerani notes that this was done precisely for diplomatic reasons. Ibid.

45. Kirk, "Genoa and Livorno."

46. Mallia-Milanes, *Venice and Hospitaller Malta*, 57.

47. Tenenti, *Piracy and the Decline of Venice*, 43. A crown was worth eight to nine silver lire.

48. As a Venetian envoy to North Africa wrote back to the doge in 1630, "Algiers and Tunis are full of merchants of all nationalities—Livornese, Corsican, Genoese, French, Flemish, English, Jewish, Venetian and others. These merchants buy the plundered goods and send them to the free port of Livorno where they are distributed throughout the whole of Italy." Pagano de Divitiis, *Mercanti Inglesi*, 139. The English translation is

from Stephen Parkin's English translation of the book, *English Merchants in Seventeenth Century Italy* (Cambridge: Cambridge University Press, 1997), 120.

49. Camerani, "Contributo alla storia dei trattati commerciali," 92.

50. Tenenti, *Piracy and the Decline of Venice*, 43.

51. And continued to enjoy in Venice, where trade with the Ottoman Empire continued strong right up to the eve of the Cretan war in 1644.

52. Ravid, "A Tale of Three Cities," 156, distinguishes only between "Jews and judaizing New Christians" when discussing the intended beneficiaries of Ferdinand's reforms. By contrast, he notes that it was Venetian concessions toward Ottoman subjects as early as the first quarter of the sixteenth century that allowed Jews, but only Ottoman Jews, their first real access to the capital city. Ibid., 141.

53. Ralph Davis calls it "a monument to an aggressive slave-taking culture that, like the larger than life bronzes of four Moors situated at the harbor, soon became something of an attraction for passing Grand Tourists." Davis, "The Geography of Slaving," 65.

54. Bono, *Schiavi Musulmani*, 30. Bono calculates a relatively stable number of Muslim slaves, about a thousand, during this period.

55. Clissold, *The Barbary Slaves*, 52. Clissold is quoting from the account of Melchor Garcia Navarro, who traveled to North Africa between 1723 and 1725.

56. Frattarelli Fischer, "Alle radici di una identita composita," 49, and 58 for the changing origins of the Greek community.

57. Ibid., 49. Individual Greeks served in Livorno as early as the 1540s, but their numbers grew substantially only with Cosimo's invitation.

58. Ibid.

59. "Alli greci li quali habitano di presente in Livorno familiarmente et a quelli che verrano per l'avvenire ad habitarvi." Ibid.

60. Ibid., 51–52.

61. Ibid., 52.

62. Ibid., 53.

63. All of these events support Paolo Castignoli's contention that "Analgomente Greci e Armeni sono oggetto di intense pressioni della Congregazione di Propaganda Fide." Castignoli, "La tolleranza enunciazione," 79.

64. Brogini, *Malte*, 253.

65. Ibid., 619.

66. Of that number, 9,000 of the victims were in the vicinity of the port. Ibid., 621.

67. The most serious check on the knights' power came from the papacy. This is discussed at length in a later chapter.

68. This expression appears very frequently in the archival documentation. See Fontenay, "Corsaires de la foi," 361–84, and Braudel, *The Mediterranean and the Mediterranean World in the Age of Philip II*, 2:877–80, for the decisive turn to the eastern Mediterranean after 1574. Braudel writes, "From about 1574 onwards however, the Levant was invaded by pirates from the West."

69. Brogini, *Malte*, 88.

70. Freller, "Adversus Infideles," 423.

71. Fontenay, "Corsaires de la foi," 65. By contrast, the Knights of St. Stephen had four galleys. These galleys were integrated into the Medici navy. Brogini, *Malte*, 254.

72. Davis, "The Geography of Slaving," 62.

73. Brogini, *Malte*, 88.

74. Ibid., 257.

75. Ibid., 256. And Fontenay speaks of 350 patents for the first thirty-five years of the century. "Corsaires de la foi," 367.

76. Brogini, *Malte*, 260. One patent could often serve for an entire squadron of galleys.

77. In the half century between 1585 and 1635, a knight was the patent holder in more than half of the private *corso* ventures. Ibid., 258. Most often these "others" were native Maltese or Frenchmen from Provence. Ibid., 324.

78. On the founding of the Tribunale, see Earle, *Corsairs of Malta and Barbary*, 107–8, and Brogini, *Malte*, 268.

79. Archives of the Cathedral of Malta (hereafter ACM), Misc. 125. *Statuti et Ordinationi dell'Eminetissimio Signor Gran Maestro Fra Alofio da Wignacort e suo venerando conseglio sopra l'armamenti.*

80. Bono, *Schiavi Musulmani*, 12.

81. Davis, "The Geography of Slaving," 65.

82. Bonnici, *Medieval and Roman Inquisition in Malta*, 134.

83. Ginio, "Piracy and Redemption in the Aegean Sea," 145.

84. Brogini, *Malte*, 327.

85. After 1570 Venice held only the three Ionian islands of Zakynthos, Corfu, and Kephallonia, the Aegean islands of Kythera and Tinos, and, most important, Crete. They would lose Crete in 1669, thus adding another large Greek population to the Ottoman mix.

86. Heyberger, "Sécurité et insécurité," 148.

87. Heyberger, *Les chrétiens du Proche-Orient*, 6.

88. Ibid., 232.

89. Herring, Οικουμενικό Πατριαρχείο και Ευρωπαϊκή Πολιτική, 27. A Maronite college was founded in 1584 and the Illyrian college, in Loretto, in 1581. Heyberger, *Les chrétiens du Proche-Orient*, 233.

90. Greek Catholic ecclesiastics, that is, Greeks who were in communion with Rome, were also educated at the college. Pastor, *The History of the Popes*, 19:247.

91. Tsirpanles, Το Ελληνικό Κολλέγιο της Ρώμης, 18.

92. Frazee, *Catholics and Sultans*, 90–91.

93. Wright, *The Early Modern Papacy*, 111.

94. Pastor, *The History of the Popes*, 20:486.

95. The definitive account of these developments remains Frazee, *Catholics and Sultans*, esp. "Part II: The Golden Age of the Missions." My account draws heavily on Frazee. Interestingly, Heyberger argues that French solicitude for Ottoman Catholics was motivated in part by the desire to compensate for the controversial fact of a "more or less permanent" French alliance with the sultan against the Christian Hapsburgs. Heyberger, *Les chrétiens du Proche-Orient*, 241.

96. Frazee, *Catholics and Sultans*, 68.

97. Heyberger, *Les chrétiens du Proche-Orient*, 243.

98. Spanakes, "Relatione dell Sr. Benetto Moro," 4:103.

99. Nona is today's Nin, in Croatia.

100. In Italian, Ragusa.

101. Pastor, *The History of the Popes*, 20:487.

102. Frazee, *Catholics and Sultans*, 81.

103. Ibid., 85.

104. Rambert, *Histoire du commerce de Marseille*, 5:84.

105. Among others, Haddad, *Syrian Christians in Muslim Society*; Masters, "Trading Diasporas and 'Nations'"; and Heyberger, *Les chrétiens du Proche-Orient*. The only book-length study we have of these efforts outside the Arab world is Slot, *Archipelagus Turbatus*.

106. The most influential and polemical statement of this point of view was certainly George Antonius's *The Arab Awakening: The Story of the Arab National Movement*, first published in 1939.

107. This is a long and complicated story, but an important date is 1724, when the split between the Romanist party and those who wished to remain faithful to the Orthodox patriarch in Constantinople became public. See Ware, *Eustratios Argenti*, 28, 30, and Heyberger, "Sécurité et insécurité."

108. Heyberger traces a straight line from Francis I through to the French Mandate. "On pourrait retracer l'histoire de cette 'protection' de Francois Ier jusqu'au delà du Mandat sur la Syrie et le Liban, tant elle est une permanence de la politique française." Heyberger, *Les chrétiens du Proche-Orient*, 242.

109. And Bulgarians and Albanians and others. See Frazee, *Catholics and Sultans*, esp. chap. 7, "The Balkans and Greece." The uncertainty in the literature about the place of the Greek Orthodox within the missionary effort is nicely illustrated by M. Joshua Brewer's comments in his 2002 dissertation. He notes that Louis XIV's instructions to his ambassador, Nointel, who began his term in the late 1660s, recorded "le premier soin que ledit ambassador doit avoir sera de protéger et assister les chrétians et les catholiques de Levant." Brewer comments that no doubt Louis did not mean by this to extend protection to the Protestants. Rather, the king wanted to protect the Maronites and *perhaps* (my emphasis) various branches of Orthodox Christianity. Brewer, "Gold, Frankincense and Myrrh," 92.

110. Frazee, *Catholics and Sultans*, 115.

111. Ibid., chaps. 7 and 8.

112. As recently as 1980, Tsirpanles, the scholar of papal relations with the Greek East in this period, wrote, "the relationship between the Vatican and the Orthodox East was confined to the religious sphere and to humanistic pursuits." Tsirpanles, Το Ελληνικό Κολλέγιο της Ρώμης, 12.

113. See Ware, *Eustratios Argenti*, 18.

114. Ibid., 20.

115. Ibid., 23.

116. Ibid., 22.

117. Ibid., 26. Several patriarchs at Constantinople were won over to the Roman cause. They did not broadcast this, of course. One of the friendliest was a metropolitan of Chios (this is 1640) who went on to become Patriarch Parthenios II. What these declarations actually meant, however, is not at all clear.

118. Ibid., 24. Both Ware and Frazee are in agreement that officials in Rome advocated for a much harsher position vis-à-vis the Orthodox, but for the most part they were unable to prevail.

119. Heyberger, *Les chrétiens du Proche-Orient*, 228–29.

120. Herring, Οικουμενικό Πατριαρχείο και Ευρωπαϊκή Πολιτική, esp. Part III. I return to the subject of Loukaris in the final chapter.

121. "Les échanges maritimes sont le principal sujet des recours à Rome." Heyberger, "Sécurité et insécurité," 151.

122. If the corsair belonged to a non-capitulatory nation, it was nearly impossible to obtain redress. Ottoman Roman Catholic Christians could try applying to Rome for redress. Van den Boogert, "Redress for Ottoman Victims of European Privateering," 91–118.

123. It is not a coincidence, of course, in the sense that both of these initiatives were related to Ottoman weakness. But they were certainly not joint initiatives and they sometimes worked at cross-purposes, as we shall see.

124. See my "Beyond the Northern Invasion," 40–72, and Steensgaard, "Consuls and Nations in the Levant."

125. Collins, *The State in Early Modern France*, 17, 46.

126. Fodor, "Piracy, Ransom Slavery and Trade," 26. The ambiguity of French policy is evoked by Fodor; he says that the consul's "primary" motive was to make money, but that "possibly he was driven by national, political and commercial motives as well."

127. Ibid., 131.

128. Along the same lines, Ottoman victims of European piracy could (and did) still have recourse to state authority when the offender's country maintained diplomatic relations with the Ottoman Empire. Van den Boogert, "Redress for Ottoman Victims of European Privateering."

129. Earle, *Corsairs of Malta and Barbary*, 109.

130. Mallia-Milanes, *Venice and Hospitaller Malta*, xix.

131. Brogini, *Malte,* chap. 5.

132. Brogini, *Malte*, 232. For Malta in particular she persuasively makes the very interesting argument that ever closer relationships between Malta and the Muslim world led to ever more vociferous expressions of Catholic faith. See 233 et passim.

133. Tsirpanles, Το Ελληνικό Κολλέγιο της Ρώμης, 30.

134. Oikonomou, "Όψεις της Ελληνικής Ναυτιλίας κατά το 17ο αιώνα," 372. Chryssa Maltezou, in her article on the ships of the Monastery of St. John on Patmos during the sixteenth and seventeenth centuries, notes that piracy, and especially Maltese piracy, was the greatest threat they faced. Maltezou, "Τα Πλοία της μονής Πάτμου," 123.

Chapter 4
The Ottoman Mediterranean

1. Tribunale degli Armamenti 2/2. (Hereafter cited as T.A.) The cases brought before the Tribunale degli Armamenti (also known as the Tribunal Armamentor) in the seventeenth century generated thousands of pages worth of legal records. These records, which are almost entirely unexplored, are stored today in the Banca Giuratale in Mdina on the island of Malta. The Banca Giuratale, or Municipal Palace, was built in 1726. Its purpose at that time was to house the offices of the civil administration of the Maltese islands. Today it houses, among other things, the records of the various courts and tribunals of the period of the Order of St. John. For a brief description of this archive, see www.libraries-archives.gov.mt/nam/ser_law_courts.htm. The spelling of Greek names especially in the court records is inconsistent even within the same case. For clarity's

sake, I use only one version of the name in the text. In addition, I have used modern conventions in the spelling of names, such as capitalization, again for purposes of clarity. In the notes the name is given as it appears in the document. In this case the merchant from Mytilene is referred to both as Comneno del quondam (deceased) Georgio and as Giorgachi of Mytilene. Comneno is used more frequently, and thus I have favored it as well.

2. Or at least according to H.J.A. Sire. In *The Knights of Malta*, Sire refers to "the prize court of Leghorn" (90–91), without, however, providing any evidence for this claim. The adjudication of cases of maritime theft was handled in many different types of venues, not limited to prize courts. See Tai, "Restitution and the Definition of a Pirate," 34–70, for a discussion of the various venues that ruled on these matters.

3. The opinion of Peter Earle is representative. In the opening lines of his study he writes, "cynicism and greed had replaced religious enthusiasm as the basis of much of their antagonism." Earle, *Corsairs of Malta and Barbary*, 3.

4. Such as the classic work by Alberto Tenenti, *Piracy and the Decline of Venice 1580–1615*.

5. He served from 1601 until 1622.

6. Giacamo Cappello, a Venetian official who traveled to the island in 1716 and wrote an account of his stay there, included a description of the officials presiding over the court: "vi presiedono 4 Cavallieri, et un Giudice Letterato, tutti eletti dal Gran Maestro." Cappello, *Descrittione di Malta*, 70. Dal Pozzo, the chronicler of the order, also says there are five officials and gives further details on the knights. Three must be *Signori della Gran Croce* and the fourth a *Commendatore Antiano*, all from different leagues. Dal Pozzo, *Historia della sacra religione*, 1:493–94.

7. ACM, Misc. 125. *Statuti et Ordinationi dell'Eminetissimio Signor Gran Maestro Fra Alofio da Wignacort e suo venerando conseglio sopra l'armamenti.*

8. Cavaliero, "The Decline of the Maltese Corso," 225. The colorful Alonso de Contreras, whose account is one of the best-known works on corsairing in the seventeenth century, mentions the Tribunale in his book. In the course of robbing a Turkish caramousal, he says, two Frenchmen approached and shouted, "Divide three ways!" An argument ensued, and they took the dispute back to the captain of Contreras's ship. The captain declared that the spoils belonged to Contreras. But the French protested so violently that the captain "revoked his decision and had the case put to the Señores del Tribunal del Armamento in Malta for arbitration." Contreras, *The Adventures of Captain Alonso de Contreras*, 20. A few pages later he gives us the decision of the Tribunal.

9. See dal Pozzo, *Historia della sacra religione*, 493–94, for a summary of the main provisions. Others who discuss the Magistrato are Fontenay, "Corsaires de la foi"; Earle, *Corsairs of Malta and Barbary*; Cassar, "The Maltese Corsairs and the Order of St. John of Jerusalem"; Cavaliero, "The Decline of the Maltese Corso"; and *Dritto Municipale di Malta*. This last book is an 1843 compilation of the municipal law of Malta promulgated in 1784 under Grand Master De Rohan.

10. From Fontenay, "Corsaires de la foi," 377.

11. ACM, Misc. 125. *Statuti et Ordinationi dell'Eminetissimio Signor Gran Maestro Fra Alofio da Wignacort e suo venerando conseglio sopra l'armamenti*: "non offendere Vasselli mercantie, beni persone di Christiani ne d'altre ancorche d'Infedeli che mostreranno autentico salvo condotto dell'Illustrissimo signor Gran Maestro o d'altri Prencipi Christiani . . . di non commettere ne fare danno detentione, ne ingiuria ad alcun Vassello

Christiano carico di robbe apppartenenti a Christiani, et amici," 311 (page number assigned by the Malta Study Center).

12. Matar, *Piracy, Slavery and Redemption*, 7.

13. Matar, *Britain and Barbary 1589–1689*, 284. I thank Nabil Matar for drawing my attention to this reference.

14. Based on my personal review of the archive. No study of the Tribunale has been made.

15. T.A. 1/11, 1617, 1r: "ad ottenere la robba loro senza lunga disputa o lite."

16. One of the cases has two separate plaintiffs, which is unusual. One of the plaintiffs is Greek, the other is an Armenian Catholic. T.A. 13/4, 1686.

17. T.A. 2/2, 1633, 10r.

18. Brogini, *Malte*, 296.

19. In six of the fourteen cases. In two cases (1/1 and 12/4) the reference is simply to "merchandise" or "diverse goods." These too probably included rice. Case 13/1 revolves around the ownership of the boat; a cargo is never mentioned.

20. T.A. 2/2 and T.A.1/2. When the individual is also the captain of the boat, this information is usually given as well; hence the Patron Nikita in 2/2.

21. Pamuk, "Money in the Ottoman Empire," 965. The Spanish *reales de a ocho*, or "pieces of eight," were known as *riyal guruş* in the Ottoman Empire.

22. Ibid. And Fernand Braudel speaks of reales being "shipped by the chestful" to the empire. Braudel, *The Mediterranean and the Mediterranean World in the Age of Philip II*, 495. See the same page for ransom prices.

23. Sometimes both are given, sometimes just one or the other.

24. Inalcık and Quataert, *An Economic and Social History*, 989, use the more unusual spelling of *irdabb*, while Shaw, in *The Financial and Administrative Organization and Development of Ottoman Egypt*, refers to *ardebs* throughout the book. I use the latter, as it in accord with the spelling used in the documents from the Magistrato. The use of ardebs as a dry measure of capacity in Egypt goes back to the Ptolemies and the Bzyantines. Khalilieh, *Admiralty and Maritime Laws in the Mediterranean Sea*, 33.

25. Shaw, *The Financial and Administrative Organization and Development of Ottoman Egypt*, 274. The documents seem to be in rough agreement with Shaw as to the value of the ardeb. According to Shaw, each ardeb is worth 12 kilos of Istanbul. T.A. 2/5, from 1637, notes explicitly that each "ardeppo piccolo" is worth 14 kilos of Istanbul. 5v. There are also "ardeppi grandi," where each ardeb is worth 200 kilos of Istanbul. T.A. 2/2, 1633, 1r. But this case seems to be the only where the larger ardep is used as a standard of measurement. The default ardep, as it were, is the "ardeppo piccolo." (And if we assume the "ardeppi grandi," then the quantity of the rice being shipped is even higher.)

26. T.A. 13/9, 1687, 1r.

27. Martini, *Manuale di metrologia*, 134. A quintal of Candia, in Crete, was the equivalent of 52.766 kilos. A comparison of the 13/10 and 13/9 documents reveals that the two cases stem from the same attack, but the victims filed two different lawsuits.

28. The real is described most commonly as either *reali da otto* or *piastri reali* (sometimes spelled *riali* in documents; spelling not standardized). I thank Şevket Pamuk for his assistance on the monetary history of the Mediterranean. Values are given in ten of the fourteen cases.

29. Panopoulou, "Συντροφιές και Ναυλώσεις Πλοίων στο Χάνδακα (1635–1661)," 2:422.

30. Greene, *A Shared World*, 145. In 1666 the average wage of a common soldier was three or four reales a month. Ibid.

31. Brogini, *Malte*, 396.

32. Fodor, "Piracy, Ransom Slavery and Trade," 127.

33. Ibid., 126. In this case the price quoted was actually 500 guldens. Based on the exchange rate, this amounts to 750 reales.

34. Mallia-Milanes, *Venice and Hospitaller Malta*, 165.

35. Ibid., 152. In one of the court cases under consideration here, a witness was asked how much money the plaintiffs had had with them upon departure from Mytilene. The witness answered that he hadn't counted it and thus couldn't say exactly the amount, but "from looking at it, it appeared to be a major amount, 1500 reales." T.A., 2/5, 11r: "ben vero dall'ochio mostrando esser mag. quantita di reali mille cinq cento da otto."

36. Mallia-Milanes, *Venice and Hospitaller Malta*, 162.

37. T.A. 1/11, 1617, 17v.

38. T.A. 1/1, 1602, 3v.

39. Northwest of Rhodes, just off the Anatolian coastline.

40. In modern Greek it is Astypalaia or, alternatively, Stampalia. It is directly west of Nissiros.

41. T.A. 13/1, 1684, 120r.

42. "Quasi nudi." T.A. 2/4. 2r. This case does not include a date. However, Joseph Moniglia, the first consul for the Greeks on Malta, makes an appearance. Since he was first appointed in 1623, the case cannot be earlier than that date. From its placement in the records it probably dates from the 1630s. See Mallia-Milanes, *Venice and Hospitaller Malta*, 226, for the appointment of the first consul for the Greeks.

43. This incident was discussed in the introduction.

44. Cappello, *Descrittone di Malta*, 95. The translation of this particular passage is by Victor Mallia-Milanes.

45. Cavaliero, "The Decline of the Maltese Corso," 229. The French consul identified the local ships as "Turkish."

46. Contreras, *The Adventures of Captain Alonso de Contreras*, 37.

47. Ibid.

48. Fontenay, "Corsaires de la foi," 373. Received into the order in 1597, he arrived in Malta in 1604. Luppé du Garrané, *Mémoires*.

49. Luppé du Garrané, *Mémoires*, 65.

50. Krantonelle, Ιστορία της Πειρατείας στους μεσους χρονους της Τουρκοκρατίας, 2:139.

51. Ibid., 147.

52. Ibid., 118.

53. Ibid., 154.

54. Nelly Hanna discusses the Ottoman interest in rice and sugar. Rice from Egypt was so important to the Ottomans that some of the lands around Damietta were set aside to provide rice for the sultan and his court; as late as the last quarter of the eighteenth century its export to Europe was prohibited, although smuggling was widespread. In the case of sugar a certain amount had to be sold first for the needs of the palace; once that was accomplished, there was no restriction on its sale. Hanna, *Making Big Money in 1600*, 74, 96. See Shaw, *The Financial and Administrative Organization and Development of Ottoman Egypt*, 125, for the lands set aside for the sultan's rice supply.

See Crecelius and Badr, "French Ships and Their Cargoes," 258, for the ban on exports to Europe.

55. Ibid., 70, 7 et passim.

56. Lézine and Tawab, "Introduction à l'étude des maisons," 152. E. Ginio notes that most goods imported into eighteenth-century Thessaloniki from Egypt came through the port of Rosetta. Ginio, "When Coffee Brought About Wealth and Prestige," 95.

57. The quotation of Leo Africanus is from Lézine and Tawab, "Introduction à l'étude des maisons," 152.

58. Heberer, *Voyages en Égypte*, 39.

59. Lézine and Tawab, "Introduction à l'étude des maisons," 153.

60. Ginio, "When Coffee Brought About Wealth," 96. Egypt provided Thessaloniki with rice, coffee, indigo, cotton, henna, and spices. The principal market located in Thessaloniki's port area was called *Mısır çarşısı*, or the Egyptian market. See Crecelius, "French Ships and Their Cargoes," 271, for the continuing dominance of trade in the Ottoman Empire toward the end of the eighteenth century.

61. Lézine and Tawab, "Introduction à l'étude des maisons," 153. At the beginning of the nineteenth century Rosetta had 35,000 inhabitants, while Alexandria had somewhere between 10,000 and 15,000. Inalcık and Quataert, *An Economic and Social History*, 654. For the seventeenth and eighteenth centuries, Smyrna has attracted far more scholarly attention, certainly because it was a destination point for European merchants.

62. Heberer, *Voyages en Égypte*, 116: "sont pleines de navires et sont bien connues."

63. Crecelius, "French Ships and Their Cargoes," 256–57. The absence of Europeans does not mean a lack of European interest. Evidence suggests that European merchants were held at arm's length in Damietta. The complaint of some French captains toward the end of the century that they were not allowed ashore except in cases involving their cargoes, and that they frequently had to depart before their full cargoes were loaded, is typical.

64. Vansleb, *The Present State of Egypt*, 67. Vansleb, a German scholar and member of the Dominican Order, was sent by Colbert to Egypt in 1671 on a fact-finding mission. He was also charged with collecting manuscripts. He stayed in Egypt for two years, from 1671 to 1673. *Penny Cyclopaedia of the Society for the Diffusion of Useful Knowledge* (London, 1843), 27:55.

65. Panzac, *La caravane maritime*, 146. Panzac studied contracts from the following cities: Algiers, Tunis, Tripoli (in North Africa), Alexandria, Larnaca (in Cyprus), Chanea (in Crete), and Istanbul.

66. Raymond, *Artisans et commerçants*, 168.

67. Ginio, "When Coffee Brought About Wealth," 95, 100–101.

68. Ibid., 99.

69. Vansleb, *The Present State of Egypt*, 68.

70. Lézine and Tawab, "Introduction à l'étude des maisons," 158

71. Ibid., 190. In terms of their façade, the mode of construction, and certain aspects of the interior plan.

72. Ibid., 191.

73. Efthymiou-Hadzilacou, *Rhodes et sa région élargie*, 33, 44. The connection between Rhodes and Egypt continued right through the twentieth century. Christian islanders went to Egypt in the nineteenth century to work on the Suez Canal, and once

Egypt became a British possession, they took advantage of new imperial connections to migrate to Australia. I thank Gelina Harlaftis for this information.

74. Tsirpanles, Στη Ρόδο του 16ου–17ου Αιώνα, chap. 1. In 1529, in response to the first conspiracy, the Ottomans ordered all foreigners on the island to appear before an envoy sent by the Sultan. Forty-nine individuals were killed by impaling as a result of this command. Vatin, L'ordre de Saint-Jean-de Jérusalem, 371.

75. The merchant marines of Hydra, Spetses, and Psara—the storied trio—played a vital and heroic role in the Greek revolution that broke out in 1821.

76. See the very thorough study by Slot, Archipelagus Turbatus.

77. Efthymiou writes. "En effet, après la conquête de Rhodes par les Turcs, l'île a commencé à perdre son importance dans le commerce des nations européennes telles que la France et les villes d'Italie." Efthymiou-Hadzilacou, Rhodes et sa région élargie, 58.

78. Panzac, La caravane maritime, 20. Bernard Randolph, the seventeenth-century traveler, emphasized the connection between Kos and the route to Egypt: "All ships that go from Constantinople and those parts bound to Egypt or that come from Egypt and bound upwards, usually call in here." Randolph, The Present State of the Islands, 26.

79. Krantonelle, Ιστορία της Πειρατείας στους μεσους χρόνους της Τουρκοκρατίας, 157. This observation dates from the early seventeenth century. Panzac, La caravane maritime, 23, writes that the big, heavy Ottoman convoy between Alexandria and Istanbul disappeared in the eighteenth century, to be replaced in part by an assortment of more modest Ottoman boats, manned for the most part by Greeks. The comment of the Knight of St. Stephen, along with the argument I am putting forward, suggests that Greek participation in the convoy, and the convoy's overall transformation, began in the seventeenth century. A ferman addressed to a group of Muslim merchants and shipowners based in Egypt (1719) should probably also be understood as part of an ongoing effort to keep the convoy going through private initiative. Winter, "A Statute for the Mercantile Fleet," 118–22.

80. De Bruyn, Voyage au Levant, 173–74.

81. Efthymiou-Hadzilacou, Rhodes et sa région élargie, 282. In 1776 French consular sources show that 64 percent of the ships leaving Alexandria in the direction of Rhodes and southern Anatolia were "Turkish" or "Greek." This percentage would continue to grow as the century wore on. Ibid., 283.

82. Ibid., 291. Missionaries in the seventeenth century routinely remarked on the fact that the Rhodiots were mariners, most of whom had their own boats. Tsirpanles, Στη Ρόδο του 16ου–17ου Αιώνα, 89–90.

83. For Muslim shipowners in Crete in the eighteenth century, see Kremmydas, "Καταγραφή των εμπορικών πλοίν του Ηρακλείου," 12–17.

84. Efthymiou-Hadzilacou, Rhodes et sa région élargie, 290.

85. Ibid., 155.

86. Ibid.

87. T.A. 13/4, 1686, 1r. In Crete, too, we see Muslim shipowners and Christian captains. See Kremmydas, "Καταγραφή των εμπορικών πλοίν του Ηρακλείου," 12–17. Reis is an Arabic word for captain, particularly sea captain. It was adopted as a word by the Greeks during the Ottoman period.

88. T.A. 11/19, 1679, 1v. In the document "Selim Rayes."

89. T.A. 2/5, 1637, 11r: "due borse grande di danari."

90. T.A. 13/9, 1687, 7r. Stranghili is also rendered as "Sanghila" and "Stranghila" in the documents. And see T.A. 13/4 for another case of a friendship between merchants (in this case Armenians) going back ten years.

91. T.A. 2/2, 1633.

92. One of the witnesses comes from Gallipoli.

93. T.A. 11/19, 1679, 5v and 5r. Stanchio is the island known today as Kos. Other sailors appear as witnesses, but their place of origin is not given.

94. T.A. 13/4, 1686. See 3r for information on the sailor, and 13v for the origin of the captain.

95. "In those days a ship's crew usually consisted of relatives of the master and the owner. Family and ship bound them all together, gave them a common cause and bred community of effort." Tzamtizis, "Ships, Ports and Sailors," 56.

96. Speaking of the island of Spetses, one of those central Aegean islands that became very active in the eighteenth century, Vryonis writes, "The regulation of maritime enterprise lies clearly in the hands of the community's legal, fiscal and judicial organs. It is almost in the nature of a joint stock enterprise." "Local Institutions in the Greek Islands," 105.

97. T.A. 2/5, 8r.

98. T.A. 13/4, 1686, 3r. In the text the Turk's name is written as *Chazzi Chalsan.*

99. But see Aksan's discussion of what Ottoman diplomats knew in *An Ottoman Statesman in War and Peace*, esp. chap. 3.

100. Braude, "Venture and Faith," 528.

101. "Per condurli ó in Scio, ó pure in Constantinopoli ó altrove affin di ritrarre La valuta." T.A. 13/9, 1687, 1r.

102. Goffman, *Izmir and the Levantine World*, 59–64.

103. And then he specified: "per pigliare l'informationi in qual paese sia la piu vendita dell'oglio." T.A. 13/10, 1687, 8r.

104. T.A. 2/2, 1633, 9r: "testando dice, che sono giorni dieci, che ritrovandosi esso testo(o) à Rhodi capito li la barca della sudetta saica patrone Nichita di Rhodi, ch'era à Damiati et in essa 23 marinari della Gente d'essa saica tra quail lo scrivano, e detti mercanti Athanasio e Comneno, dalli quail marinari, e da detti mercanti intese che detta saica fu presa da un vasselo maltese sop(a) Cavo Chilidoni, e che doppo pas(t) giorni tre mando via per forza lo Cap. d'esso vas(lo) essi mercanti spogliati con altri vinti tre persone della Gente d'essa saica con la barca d'essa, retenuto solo detto patro Nichita e cinq marinari."

105. T.A. 2/2, 1633, 8v.

106. T.A. 2/2, 1633, 11r.

107. T.A. 13/10, 1687, 9v: "Questo io l'ha sentito dire a Rethimo dal li sudetti tre schiavi."

108. Braude, "Venture and Faith," 532.

109. T.A. 2/2, 1633, 11r: "perche hieri a porto capitorono da detto luoco di smirne alcune mercanti."

110. T.A. 1/1, 1602, 3v.

111. T.A. 2/2, 1633, 10v: "che doppo pas(ti) circa due hore da chi capito a Rhodi detta barca capito e detta saica voda, et esso test(o) per buoca del pron d'essa, e di detti marinari , che venero con lui intese quanto sopra ha testato."

112. T.A. 13/10, 1687, 8r. There were at least two forms of spontaneous association at sea. The first, "*in caravana*," referred to ships sailing together for purposes of trade. The second, "*in conserva*," was a group of ships engaged in corsairing. I thank Frank Theuma for providing this explanation of these two terms.

113. Cappello, *Descrittione di Malta*, 78: "un Turco se tocca terra è subbito fatto schiavo."

114. See chapter three for the numbers.

115. Fodor, "Piracy, Ransom Slavery and Trade," 126.

Chapter 5
The Pursuit of Justice

1. In his study of French consuls in the Levant in the seventeenth century, Joshua Brewer notes that consuls did not hear or decide criminal or civil cases. What they did do was to conduct a *process-verbal*, akin to a modern affidavit or sworn deposition. Brewer, "Gold, Frankincense and Myrrh," 130. This seems to be exactly what is going on in the documents that were produced for use in Malta; hence my use of the terms "affidavit" and "deposition."

2. In T.A. 2/4 the victims appear to have come directly to Malta.

3. Captains—*patroni*, in Italian—were often but not always the owners of the vessels. In this case Haji Pietro is explicitly identified as the owner. In Italian his name is given as "Cagi Pietro," but this is obviously a corruption of "Haji," which was the designation given to Orthodox Christians who had completed the pilgrimage (that is, the haj) to Jerusalem. T.A. 1/11, 1617, 16v.

4. "Arrubati et spogliati di detta loro mercantia robba, saica, et vestiti insino alle camise loro." T.A. 1/11, 1617, 16r. A saica is a sailing ship that ranged from 40 to 100 tons. Papadopoulos, *The Greek Merchant Marine*, 101, and Krantonelle, Ιστορία της Πειρατείας στους μεσους χρονους της Τουρκοκρατίας, 2:427. For purposes of comparison we may recall that Matthew Vergis's ship was somewhere between 560 and 720 tons. See chapter one, note 101. A saica was also called a saitia, which can lead to some confusion. See Papadopoulos, *The Greek Merchant Marine*, 101.

5. "Alla miseria et misericordia del mare et delli venti." T.A. 1/11, 1617, 17v.

6. A distance of about fifty miles.

7. The description is "licentiato in Iure Advocato consegliaro per detta natione." T.A. 1/11, 1617, 16v. In his study of legal procedure in Castile between 1500 and 1700, Kagan notes there were three different kinds of lawyers: advocates (*abogado*), attorneys (*procurador*), and solicitors (*solicitador*). The advocate was the legal expert. The French "advocato" attached to the French vice-consulate in Saida probably played a role similar to that identified by Kagan. Kagan, *Lawsuits and Litigation*, 52.

8. The phrase is "Bengiamin negrin hebreo residente in questa citta Tarcemano di detta Nacione." T.A. 1/11, 1617, 16v. The chancery official recorded (17v) that Cagi Pietro humbly requested that the tercuman come here—that is, into the chancery—with him.

9. "Ha detto per bocca del detto Negrin Torcemano." T.A. 1/11, 1617, 17r.

10. T.A. 1/11, 1617, 23v.

11. "Il sigillo region di della ma?esta christianissima del re. d. Francia et di Navarra." T.A. 1/11, 1617, 25r.

12. "Per essere presentati a Monsignor Illmo. Gran mastro di Malta." T.A. 1/11, 1617, 25r.

13. T.A. 2/7, 1636, 4r. In the text it is "cugia" rather than "Cugia." The Italian name for Monemvasia, Napoli di Romania, is given.

14. Given his name, the captain must be from Leros, one of the smaller islands of the Dodecanese. It is just south of Patmos. In the text it is "diaco di lero."

15. T.A. 2/7, 1636, 3v. "A pour plus grande Validite nous (?) avons fair appose le seel Royal accoustume."

16. Steensgaard, "Consuls and Nations in the Levant," 26: "The origins of the French consulates and their transition to royal offices are not easily discoverable."

17. Ibid., 21. The Dutch consul recorded that on a 1615 trip to Aleppo, the grand vezir would not allow the consuls to be seated in his presence because he had heard that the French consul had previously been a clerk on board ship. Effective reorganization of the consular service did not take place until the 1660s. Ibid., 28, 30.

18. T.A. 2/2, 1633.

19. In 1633 Crete was still held by Venice. The Maltese use of the relatively unguarded coasts of southern Crete was a constant headache for Venice. It was a Maltese landing there in 1644 that began the long (1645–69) Ottoman-Venetian war over Crete. See my *A Shared World*, chap. 1.

20. T.A. 2/2, 1633, 8v: "doppo haver molto patito in Mare, che per fortuna assalita, si tenevano piu tosto per persi, con l'agiuto di Dio capitorono à Rhodi." Comneno is also known as Georgachi of Mytilene. See chapter four, note 1.

21. The testimony does not comment on this point.

22. And presided over by the *il Mon(sr) Vesvoco di Scio.* The documentation presented in Malta speaks of "il testimoniali fatto nella Corte Vescovale." T.A. 2/2, 1633, 2v.

23. There were Latin bishoprics in Naxos, Syros, and Tinos, and each bishop would have had a court. Frazee, *Catholics and Sultans*, 40. I thank Evdoxios Doxiadis for sharing his wide knowledge of the Cycladic islands with me.

24. Argenti, *The Religious Minorities of Chios*, 206–8. Argenti remains the major authority on the history of Chios under Ottoman rule, as well as the history of the Catholic community on the island.

25. As he had been when the island was under Catholic control. This was unusual; in the Greek islands it was more common for the spiritual rulers to be Italian-born. See Argenti, *Religious Minorities*, 270, and Frazee, *Catholics and Sultans*, 39–40.

26. The copy was, of course, to be taken to Malta.

27. T.A. 2/2, 1633, 13v.

28. T.A. 2/2, 1633, 5r.

29. T.A. 2/5, 1637.

30. Ibid., 4r.

31. Ibid., 5v.: "tre vas(il) Xpriani, uno di Malta, altro di Livorno, et altro si diceva di Sardegna."

32. Ibid.: "ch'erano vas(li) e mercantia di'xpiani, e la Gente tutti xpiani."

33. Ibid.: "puoco riso bagnato."

34. Ibid.: 5r–12v.

35. In the document it is Ioannes.

36. In accounts of these attacks there is often a small boat, in this case identified as a βάρκαν (varka), that is sent out to actually make the seizure.

37. This too was very common. Most attacks took place near land, and some individuals managed to jump ship and flee.

38. T.A. 1/11, 1617.

39. Neither the original Greek nor the Italian translation mentions St. Catherine's by name, instead referring only to Mt. Sinai. But St. Catherine's is certainly what is meant. "λαυρέντιος ελέω(??) Αρχιεπίσκοπος του αγίου και θεοβάδιστου Ορους σινά." "Laurentius misericordia divina Archieposcopus S(o) et theovadisti Montis Sinaii." Ibid., 33r and 34v. The archbishop's statement was translated into Italian in Malta in October 1616.

40. "Insieme con la mia Congregatione di hieromonachi et monach." He makes this declaration in front of "voi giustissimi Sig(ni) et giudici," indicating that the testimony was made at the French consulate in Cairo. Ibid., 34v.

41. There is no Greek document and there is no indication of a translation into Italian in Malta. It would appear that a highly educated man such as Loukaris was able to produce a document in Italian as well as in Greek.

42. "D'un caratto"; literally, "of one share." Ibid., 36r.

43. Efthymiou-Hadzilacou, *Rhodes et sa région élargie*, 289. Vryonis says that in the Aegean most ships were owned by shares. Vryonis, "Local Institutions in the Greek Islands," 123. Konstantinides distinguishes between larger ships, *karavia*, which almost always had multiple owners (the share system), and smaller *caiques*, usually owned by just one person. Konstantinides, Καράβια, Καπετάνιοι και Συντροφοναύται, 73–74. In 1751 the Ottoman authorities in Herakleion (Crete) made a list of the commercial ships belonging to the residents of city. Forty of the forty-eight were owned by one individual. Kremmydas, Καταγραφή των εμπορικών πλοίων του Ηρακλείου, 12–17.

44. In this case and in the other case, T.A. 2/7, involving the French consul in Cairo, the consul is also described as the *consigliere* or *consegliere*. In Saida these are two separate people. The difference must simply reflect different staffing arrangements in the two consulates.

45. Two other individuals are mentioned together with the patriarch: "Pappa Ianna suo Vicario" and "Patri Iasaph caloro dell'ordine Greco." It seems likely that these two clergy members accompanied the patriarch but did not produce separate testimony.

46. "Et Perche detto patron Pietro Inten di partirsi et andare in Chistianita per la recuperatione della detta sua saica et riso." Ibid., 35r.

47. Ibid. The document was written on the June 27, 1616.

48. Krantonelle, Ιστορία της Πειρατείας στους μέσους χρόνους της Τουρκοκρατίας 115–16.

49. Maltezou, "Τα Πλοία της Μονής Πάτμου, 124. I thank Nikos Panou for explaining the meaning of the word Μάσκουλα (mascoula) to me. Μάσκουλα, in this case small canons, are still fired off in Corfu during Easter week celebrations. This commemorates their use during the Venetian period, when they were used to warn against approaching pirate or enemy fleets. See www.corfuvisit.net.

50. T.A. 1/1.

51. In 1669, after a twenty-five-year struggle, the Ottomans would take the island.

52. He is also referred to as Cantanin. At first glance, the name of the ship would seem to indicate that we are speaking here about two ships. The name is *Santa Maria de*

Lindos et Santa Caterina. However, the numerous references throughout the document to "la nave" make it clear that only one ship is being discussed.

53. "Un vassello." T.A. 1/1, 1602, 3v.

54. The document records how the plaintiff and all the sailors were forced to disembark. "feccero sbarcare L'esponente con tutti gl'altri marinari." Ibid., 3v. The island, which is still uninhabited today, is five kilometers long and about one kilometer across. This detail suggests that Cacavo island is somewhere between Egypt and Crete, but I have not been able to identify it.

55. Ibid., 3v: "Dal cui Suprema Tribunale presoro(?)fede, et Testimoniali autentica d'ogni Loro giud-pretensione, La cui copia insieme con l'originale si esebisce alle Si(re)V(re)."

56. Ibid., 5v: "il sugillo col quale viene sugillata et munita la prefata fede et scrittura è del Tribunal del Zante, Governo, Territorio et Giurisditori della S(ria) di Venetia."

57. Ibid.: "impresso in qualsi sia scriturra, et presentato in qualsivoglia tribunale . . . et particolarmente appresso quest'Isola di Malta, in material di chi si sia, et specialmente in caso di verificat(e) confrome al suggetto di chi si tratta, è stato solito, et consueto darli quall piena et indubitata fede, che si deve."

58. Ibid.: "La prova leggitima et giuridica di Sopra d(tti) Tre Capli viene autenticamente provata et approbata dal Tribunale Supremo del Zante."

59. Jal, *Glossaire nautique*, 1139. The entry for "*passeport*" gives the word in various languages. The Genoese term is *patente.* The definition is, "The passport is a permit of free circulation which allows its carrier to approach the port of a city, whether to enter or leave it. By extension from this primitive definition, it is a license delivered to the captain of a boat. By virtue of this document, the boat can freely undertake the voyage for which it has been equipped." At other points in the document the word *passaporto* rather than *patente* is used. The passport in this case was issued for fourteen or fifteen months, according to witness testimony. T.A. 13/10, 1687, 7r. In the document, reis is rendered as "Rayes."

60. T.A. 13/9, 1687, 8r, 9v: "che viagiava nelli antecedenti viagi con un passaporto stante il quale non era molestato da Cap(n) Bavian e de Beberbeia e dalli Corsali Christiani."

61. I have not been able to identify the currency referred to; it is "tumuni." But the rate differential is clear. He testifies that the usual rate is eight tumini for each quintal, whereas the freight on Agostino Plati's boat was eleven tumini for each quintal. T.A. 13/9, 1687, 9v.

62. The plaintiffs were unable to produce the documents in Malta. Ibid., 1r: "li strappo dale mani La patente." And T.A. 13/10, 1687, 1r gives essentially the same account. The two cases concern the same attack but are brought by two different merchants.

63. As we have seen, Venetian consular authority was also called upon on occasion but not nearly to the same extent as the French.

64. Van den Boogert, *The Capitulations and the Ottoman Legal System*, 38.

65. Ibid., 40. As long as they were properly signed and registered.

66. See the case of Athanasio di Pancratio of Thessaloniki, Comneno of Mytilene, and Patron Nikita of Rhodes, discussed above.

67. T.A. 2/4, 1r.

68. T.A. 1/1, 1602, 4r.

69. Devoulx, "La marine de la régence d'Alger," 384–85. Fisher, *Barbary Legend*, 326.

70. See 13/9 and 13/10 above.

71. Fisher, *Barbary Legend*, 326.

72. A 1664 decree prohibited consuls from personally engaging in trade and from charging droits that had not been approved by the crown or the Marseilles Chamber of Commerce. Brewer, "Gold, Frankincense and Myrrh," 97. Predictably, this was not very effective. In the eighteenth century consuls were still ignoring rules against money-lending, trade on their own account, and a host of other risky activities. Van den Boogert, *The Capitulations and the Ottoman Legal System*, 230.

73. This is how we know about his activities. The documents are collected in a volume in the Bibliothèque Nationale and form the basis of Fodor's article, "Piracy, Ransom Slavery and Trade."

74. Fabre was one of the officials who wrote a document in support of the plaintiffs after the attack. See T.A. 13/9, 1687, 2v and 13/10, 1687, 2v. Brewer identifies the Fabre family as one of the dominant families in Levantine trade who often staffed the offices of consul and vice-consul. He writes that Guilhaume Fabre was the vice-consul in "Candie" from 1691 to 1692. Brewer, "Gold, Frankincense and Myrrh," 102. The documents in Malta suggest he was there from at least the middle of the 1680s.

75. Stavrinides, Μεταφράσεις Τουρκικών Ιστορικών Εγγράφων, 2:233, 236. The defterdar was the chief financial officer on the island.

76. Ibid., 2:361, 402, 411.

77. Philipp, *The Syrians in Egypt*, 23.

78. Ginio, "Piracy and Redemption in the Aegean Sea, 145.

79. Ibid., 142.

80. T.A. 1/1, 1602, 4r.

81. Heyberger, "Sécurité et insécurité," 148–49.

82. French influence in the Catholic world radiated out across many centers of power. After Lepanto, most of the Knights of Malta were French. Krantonelle, Ιστορία της Πειρατείας στους μεσους χρονους της Τουρκοκρατίας, 100. In Rome, the French and the Spanish were the main rivals for control of the papacy. See Dandelet, *Spanish Rome*.

83. See 2/2, 1633, 13v; 2/5, 1637, 12v–12r; 13/4, 5v, and 12/11, 1685, 1r.

84. There were three courts on the island in the seventeenth and eighteenth centuries: the bishop's, the kadi's, and the Greek metropolitan's. Argenti, *The Religious Minorities of Chios*, 208.

85. And the exception proves the rule. In his nineteenth-century history, *Ta Meta ten Alosen*, Athanasios Ypselante gives this account of one of the patriarchs of Alexandria. In the year 1747, he writes, Mathaos, a native of Andros, was chosen for the throne of Alexandria. Upon his arrival there he took care concerning the churches in Algeria and Tripoli in North Africa and sent monks (there) "to work for the relief of the Christians enslaved there and the foreign merchants. The Christians and the merchants in Rashid, Pylousion, and Cairo—*seeing Lord Matthew do such unusual things, things that up until now they had never seen* [my emphasis]—each one of them made it a point of honor to approach Lord Matthew and tell him their opinion, that is whether they thought what he was doing was a good idea or not" (355).

86. See the discussion in chapter three.

87. See Heyberger, "Sécurité et insécurité," 147–63.

88. He does present one case that is very similar to what we have been discussing so far in the context of the Greeks. In 1710 a corsair by the name of Antonio Francheschi

seized a ship that belonged to the Greek church in Saida (i.e., a Catholic church following the Greek rite) and took it to Livorno. The Catholic archbishop of Saida, Aftîmyûs Sayfî, promptly sat down and wrote a letter to the grand master in Malta seeking the return of the ship, in much the same way that the archbishop of Karpathos or the metropolitan of Mytilene did in the previous century. Heyberger, "Sécurité et insécurite," 156.

89. Van den Boogert, "Redress for Ottoman Victims of European Privateering," 94. In fact, van den Boogert cites Heyberger when he makes this claim. This is one of the very few studies that exist on the problem of retrieving cargo rather than the much better studied issue of the liberation of slaves.

90. T.A. 1/11, 1617, 17r.

91. T.A. 2/2, 1633, T.A. 2/5, 1637, and T.A. 11/19, 1679.

92. See the *Catholic Encyclopedia*, s.v. "Greek Rite," for a discussion of the term (http://www.newadvent.org/cathen/).

93. The general association of the Greek rite with the East is suggested by other terms that are used, less commonly, to describe it. In his *History of the Popes*, Pastor describes the visit of a priest of the "Bzyantine rite" to Constantinople (29:229). The patriarch of Venice referred to the Greek community there as "Catholics of the Oriental rite." Mavroeide, Συμβολή στην Ιστορία της ελληνικής Αδελφότητας Βενετίας στο ΙΣΤ Αιώνα, 13. The Vatican's willingness to accept the Greek rite does not mean it was neutral on the question of rites. The Latin rite was still considered superior, which is why Latin rite churches were forbidden from going over to another rite. Heyberger, *Les chrétiens du Proche-Orient*, 235.

94. T.A. 11/19, 1679, 5v. "Intende che ogni testimonio si interrogato del Nome, Cognome, Patria etta et sotto qual Ritto e Religione viva."

95. T.A. 13/4, 1686, 4v. An Armenian petitioner is flagged as a "xpriano cattolico" but not as belonging to the Greek rite, which would not make sense in the Armenian case.

96. T.A. 2/2, 1633, and T.A. 2/5, 1637.

97. See the earlier discussion of this case. For reasons that are not clear, the captain, Nikita, did not travel to Chios with the merchants but was content to let them represent him there.

98. T.A. 2/2, 1633, 7r: "intendeno di provar, che tanto loro come d(o) pron Nichita furono et sono xpriani catholici di ritto greco nati di parêti xpiani, e persone di buona, fama, condittione, per talli tenuti, e reputati da tutti."

99. T.A. 2/5, 1637.

100. Ibid., 4r: "Intendeno di provar ch'essi M Duca e M. Nicola furono e sono xpriani catholici di ritto greco, personi d bene, e d honore, nati da parenti xpiani per talli tenutti e reputati da tutti."

101. T.A. 2/2, 1633. Out of the nine witnesses who testified in the bishop's court in Chios, seven affirmed the plaintiffs' religious identity and were asked to explain how they knew. The other two did not affirm and were not asked, meaning they did not consider themselves in a position to know.

102. Ibid., 8r: "he testato, tanto piu, che ha visto e loro, e li parenti d'esso Comneno piu volte confessarsi, e communicarsi."

103. Ibid., 9v: "viver xpianamenti."

104. Ibid., 12v.

105. Ibid., 12r: "confessandosi, e comunicandosi le feste natali (?); e de pasqua della ressurettione del (Christ) e faccendo tutte l'altre attioni, ch'e solito fare un vero e buono xpirano cattolico."

106. T.A. 2/5, 1637, 5r–12v.

107. T.A. 13/4, 1686. Giovanni Marchara di Natione Armeno.

108. The confessional status of Leo Allatius, a Chiot who was the most prominent Greek Catholic intellectual of the seventeenth century, continues to be debated. Karen Hartnup in her study of Allatius writes, "On many Aegean islands, including Chios, the distinction between Catholic and Orthodox was not as significant to the inhabitants as it is today." Hartnup, *On the Beliefs of the Greeks*, 53–54. For more on Allatius, see chapter seven.

109. These are Naxos, Paros, Syros, Tinos, Milos, Argentiera, Mykonos, Andros, Santorini, Chios, and Candia. Steele, *An Account of the State of the Roman-Catholick Religion throughout the World*, 50.

110. See note 22.

111. Heyberger, "Sécurité et insécurité," 160.

112. Cavaliero, "The Decline of the Maltese Corso," 235.

113. This is the subject of Mary Portelli's bachelor's thesis. "Freed in the Name of Christianity," from which this material is drawn.

114. This document is reproduced in Portelli, "Freed in the Name of Christianity," 133–4. The document is in the Archive of the Inquisition (AIM), Correspondence, vol. 28, f. 86.

115. Ware, *Eustratios Argenti*, 20.

116. Ibid., 23.

117. What this does suggest is that there is a whole history of Greek Catholics outside the organized Catholic communities that are already known in the literature. This story has yet to be told.

118. Although his motives may well have been different. Certainly he would have received fees for the services he rendered to the plaintiffs in cases T.A. 2/2 and T.A. 2/5.

119. T.A. 11/19, 1679, 5v.

120. The archbishop's letter provides the only explicit reference to Orthodox Christianity I have seen.

121. In the document it is "Cumneno." T.A. 2/2, 1633, 5v.

122. Ibid., 5r.

Chapter 6
At the Tribunale

1. Graff, "La Valette," 153.

2. Ibid., 157. In 1980 UNESCO declared Valletta a World Heritage Site.

3. The building that stands there now was rebuilt in 1750 and is known as the Palazzo Castellania. It housed all the law courts, including the Tribunale. The building that stood on the site before 1750 was also home to the Tribunale; it was erected during the tenure of Grand Master Jean Levesque de la Cassiere (1572–81). I thank Simon Mercia of the University of Malta for this information on the history of the building.

4. It is the Ministry of Health.

5. Ross, *Blue Guide: Malta and Gozo*, 110.

6. T.A. 2/7, 1636, 14r: "non trova Avocato, ne solicitatore, che lo voglia patrocinare per tanto ricorre da VAS supp: La volersi degniare comandare a un Dottore e solicitatore a patrocinarlo e che uno di essi sappia parlar in Greco et Italiano accio l'ore possa intender a Loro et essi a lui e che siano persone pratiche e sperimentati alle lite e timorosi a Dio."

7. T.A. 1/11, 1617, 16r.

8. "Come persone ricchi, et facoltose et questi poveri; forastieri et miseri per la preda et spoglia di loro fatti." T.A. 1/1, 1602, 13r.

9. Cappello, *Descrittione di Malta*, 54. When he says they are judged by the same shareholders he means that the people who invest in corsairing ventures are the very same people who preside over the cases brought by the Greeks. The officials of the Magistrato were paid through a share (3 percent) of the captured booty. Vella, *The Consolato del Mare* of Malta, 84.

10. Earle, *Corsairs of Malta and Barbary*, 91.

11. Brogini, *Malte*, 373–74.

12. Ibid., 382–83.

13. Ginio, "Piracy and Redemption in the Aegean Sea," 146.

14. Mallia-Milanes, *Venice and Hospitaller Malta*, 226.

15. Victor Mallia-Milanes, personal communication, June 2008.

16. Mallia-Manes, *In the Service of the Venetian Republic*, 5, 28 et passim.

17. The question of Greek consuls in Europe in the seventeenth century, not just in Malta but elsewhere, deserves a study of its own.

18. T.A. 2/4: 1r: "e per li absenti comparisce il Mag(co) Gioseppe Moneglia come procuratore genale della natione e consule."

19. T.A. 13/1, 1684, and T.A.12/11, 1683. The term used was "padrono posticcio." T.A. 13/1, 1684, 99r. Hana's name is spelled a number of different ways in the documents, including Hanna, Ganni, and Ianni. For consistency's sake I use only Hana in the text. T.A. 13/1 and T.A. 12/11 concern the same attack. All of the testimony in T.A. 12/11 dates from 1683. T.A. 13/1 takes up the case again, with proceedings that begin in 1683.

20. In the case his name appears as Haj Mamet filius Ali Reis.

21. The word "false" is unclear, but from the testimony of the next witness is it certain that that is what is meant. T.A. 13/1, 1684, 106r.

22. Ibid., 110v: "da mia picciolta ho havuto la conoscenza del Prod(te) Hana reis questo era molto Amico di Mio padre, é si conferiva spesso in Scio."

23. The rendering of the name is not consistent with previous testimony, but the details recounted make it clear we are speaking about the same person.

24. Ibid., 107v: "della questo non havea nessuna cognittione, havendoli rappresentato esser una cosa da non portar pregiuditio al alcuno."

25. Ibid., 109r: "come Greco ho havuto sua conoscenza."

26. T.A. 11/19, 1679, 3v. Bonici is identified as a "Maltese."

27. Cavaliero, "The Decline of the Maltese Corso," 236.

28. "I Greci sono generalmente di mala fede." Ibid., 235.

29. Presumably he was shown the documents Gioannes had brought from Cairo and that is what he is responding to.

30. T.A. 2/7, 1636, 32r–33v. A Greek from Mytilene, "Manoli de Apostoli grecus de Metelino," also testified as to the authenticity of the royal seal. He does not explain how he knows this. Perhaps because he was from Mytilene and is a merchant, less explanation seemed necessary. Ibid., 33r and 34v.

31. Trivellato, "Sephardic Merchants between Rabbinic and Civil Courts," manuscript, 4; on the proliferation of the tribunals in the early modern period and, at the same time, the lack of studies on the workings of these institutions; ibid., 11. I thank Francesca Trivellato for letting me read a copy of this paper. At this point it is difficult to say whether the establishment of the Tribunale in Malta was connected to the larger Mediterranean-wide proliferation of tribunals. It seems unlikely, given that the latter were equity courts that did not admit the use of lawyers, among other things. Trivellato, *The Familiarity of Strangers*, 158.

32. The representatives correspond to the types of lawyers Kagan identifies in his study of lawsuits in Castille during the same period—advocates, attorneys (procurators), and solicitors. T.A. 2/2, 1633, 42r, and T.A. 2/7, 1638, 14r.

33. Papkonstantinou, "Malta and the Rise of the Greek-Owned Fleet in the Eighteenth Century," 211.

34. T.A. 1/2, 1607, 1v: "et havendo vista in detto galione et sue conserve la bandiera di San. Gio: di questa Sac. Relig(ne) Hyer(ma) portando l'oratore quella di San. Gio: di Pathmos."

35. Gioannes Cugia was sailing on "un vascello di patigne." T.A. 2/7, 1638, 1r. This is an odd spelling, but "Patmiot" must be what is meant because later on Gioannes Cugia speaks of how he loaded his goods onto "il Vassello nominato San Gioanni da Patino, patron et parcenevole D. Nicolo Mata da Patino." Ibid., 4v.

36. *Acta et diplomata Graeca Medii Aevi,* 409.

37. Just four years after Wignacourt's letter the pope wrote to the grand master, warning the knights to stop their attacks on the monastery. Krantonelle, Ιστορία της Πειρατείας στους μεσους χρονους της Τουρκοκρατίας, 2:95.

38. Although the inhabitants of the island submitted to the sultan in 1453, as late as 1508 the grand masters of the Order of St. John, still at this point on Rhodes, ordered their own subjects not to harm the islanders, who should be considered *vassalli* of Rhodes. Zachariadou, "Συμβολή Στην Ιστορία του Νοτιοανατολικού Αιγαίου," 200.

39. Contreras, *The Adventures of Captain Alonso de Contreras*, 48.

40. T.A. 13/9, 1687, 1r, and T.A. 13/10, 1687, 1r.

41. Blunt, *Voyage into the Levant*, 59–60.

42. Contreras, *The Adventures of Captain Alonso de Contreras*, 24.

43. Earle, *Corsairs of Malta and Barbary*, 147. "All ships for their own protection carried a wide selection of flags and pennants and any ship's captain worth his salt would carry papers and letters patent, either real or false, granted by half a dozen potentates."

44. T.A. 2/5, 1637, 4r: "ch'esso riso hano caricato a refuso sopra la saica patrone Iani Zagarachi di Lindo, e lo lino conpartito parte in sei cachi tra grandi, e pic(li) e dui casani, seg(ti) delle marche di fuori." I think Pietro Frassica for identifying the meaning of "a refuso," which is, roughly, loose rather than in identified packages.

45. Since the cargo had been stolen, he must have been shown depictions of these signs or markings.

46. Ibid., 9v: "visit le croce, e segni sop(a) le robbe."

47. T.A. 13/10, 1687, 10r.

48. T.A. 1/1, 1617, 5r.

49. Ibid., 5v: "300 Artepidi sale, che vi è carricato in Nave per Savorra è stato comprato in Alessandria di Egitto, con danari proprii, et speciali di Ant. Cantanin senza compagnia di persona alcuna."

50. T.A. 2/2, 1633, 8r: "tenendo capitale con lui, che? havea da suoi parenti, et ch'egli acquisto con la sua fatica."

51. Ibid., 9r: "si trovo quando con uno, e quando con l'altro in Ales(a), dove ha visto inchetar loro capitali à uso de mercati."

52. Ibid., 10r: "a Scio prego esso test(o) come suo amico, e li salvò in una sua cassa esso danaro, ch'havea toccato dalla vendita d'esso grano." In all, nine witnesses appear in Chios; most make the point that the plaintiffs were trading with their own money.

53. T.A. 13/4, 1686.

54. Ibid., 3r: "non havendo sua conversatione."

55. Ibid. 4r: "habitavano in un vicinato a Rosseta dentro in uno med(mo) Chani, e mangiavano goirnalm(te) insieme, e come paesani e di una stessa natione pratticavano insieme e piu volte ha contato (contasto?) lo suo capitale in sua presenza, e d(to) testimonio e stato in sua stessa habitatione per far imballar esse telle e gl'ha assistito insin all'imbarco."

56. Ibid., 4r: "il padre suo mercante grosso."

57. Ibid., 5v: "che fossero di proprio conto." And he described him as a "mercante non ordinario." It is hard to know what is meant exactly by saying that he is not an ordinary merchant, but given the context, the implication is that he was richer than the average merchant.

58. Heyberger, "Sécurité et insécurité," 151.

59. Ibid., 152.

60. Tenenti relates an incident from 1601 in which a Sevillan and a Frenchman seized a Venetian ship off the shores of Anatolia, saying that all the entries in the name of Christians were false and that the entire cargo really belonged to Turks and Jews. Tenenti, *Piracy and the Decline of Venice*, 48. And see Shmuelevitz, *The Jews of the Ottoman Empire*, 163, where he describes how Jewish merchants often used to register their merchandise in the ship's cargo-book using the name of Christian merchants, precisely to try and protect themselves from Christian (i.e., Catholic) pirates.

61. Masters, *The Origins of Western Economic Dominance*, 63; Heyberger, "Sécurité et insécurité," 151. In the Greek world, too, Muslims and Christians formed business partnerships. Greene, *A Shared World*, 147.

62. Heyberger, "Sécurité et insécurité," 151–52.

63. T.A. 1:11, 1617. See 12:11, 13:9, and 13:10 for references to such a book. In case 13:9, the victimized merchant tells the Tribunale that he doesn't know about Plati (the captain), but the "rest of us have our markings in accordance with what is written down in the scribe's book, which was taken." 10v.

64. Panzac, *La caravane maritime* 11.

65. T.A. 12:11, 1683, 24v. From the context it is clear that by "conventione," Real means a verbal agreement.

66. Ibid., 25r. "Del noleggio io non feci scritura perche si fece il partito inanzi diverso Persone, et il scrivano pur lo noto nel suo libro."

67. Ibid. 25r.

68. T.A. 13:10, 1687, 9r: "non semo soliti fare polizia di Carrigo dal doanero dell nostre mer-cantie ma solo il doanero nota in un pezzo di legna . . . per tal causa gli dico che non havemo fatto poliza di carrigo del d(o) nostro oglio bensi il scrivano del detto sanbichino ho fatta notamento del carrigo nel suo libro il qual libro fu preso dal detto Cap(n) Paolo."

69. T.A. 13:9, 1687, 9r: "perche il Scrivano del sanbichino et il doanere stanno nel magazeno con una taglia di legno."

70. I thank Pietro Frassica for helping me understand the meaning of "*pezzo di legno*" and "*taglia di legno*."

71. Goldie, "The Bill of Lading," 6.

72. *A Collection of Voyages in Four Volumes*, 7:3.

73. Ibid., 7:12.

74. As mentioned in chapter four, fraud was widespread. Thus, any official figures underestimate how lucrative the *corso* was.

75. Eldem, "Strangers in Their Own Seas?," 11. I thank Professor Eldem for letting me read a copy of this work.

76. Blunt, *Voyage into the Levant*, 59–60.

77. Hanley, "Foreignness and Localness in Alexandria, 1880–1914," 352.

78. Harlaftis and Laiou, "Ottoman State Policy," 1. I thank Gelina Harlaftis and Sophia Laiou for sharing an advance copy of their article with me.

79. Cunningham, *Anglo-Ottoman Encounters in the Age of Revolution*, 1:166.

80. Vella, "The *Consolato del Mare* of Malta," 84.

81. See the discussion in chapter two.

82. T.A. 2/4, 1r. "Esso non osservo le legi del Consolato del Mare, conoscendo esser tutti Christiani."

83. T.A. 1/1, 1602, 3v. "Stando li Sudetti parcionevoli con la Lave Loro antedetta in Alessandria di Egitto, furono richiesti d'alcuni mercatanti Turcheschi, chi gli la voles-sero (?) noleggiare per Constantinopoli Onde accordati el prezzo, carricata la nave et finalmente partiti dal porto di Alessandria."

84. Although he does not mention what happened to his Muslim passengers; pre-sumably they were enslaved.

85. T.A. 1/1, 1602, 4r. "Onde essendo La nave di Christiani, li Parcionevoli et Mari-nari battezzati et professati La fede di xpr, nati, vissuti, et allenati in essa non è di giusto che restino defraudati della robba loro, per haver solamentenoleggiato La Nave à Merca-danti Infideli."

86. Kulsrud, *Maritime Neutrality to 1780*, 122.

87. See correspondence between the Vatican and the papal inquisitor on Malta in the case of Gioannes Cugia in chapter seven. More than a month after the inquisitor ex-plained to Rome that the knight in question was away from Malta, he still had not been able to track him down. *Fabio Chigi*, 337.

88. Kagan, *Lawsuits and Litigants in Castile*, 47.

89. T.A. 12/11, 1683.

90. At the time of his testimony he had been a slave, once again, for over a year.

91. T.A. 13/1, 1684, 100v.

92. See chapter five.

93. T.A. 1/11, 1617, 59v. Here Haji Pietro is rendered as Padrone Anzi pietro.

94. T.A. 13/10, 1687, 7r.

95. Ibid., 9v: "subito noi altri havemo arbolato la bandiera bianca sopradetto sanbi-chino, et havemo buttato il Caicco in mare per vender obedienza al Capitano del detto Vascello." I thank Pietro Frassica for discussing this paragraph with me.

96. T.A. 2/5, 1637, 4r: "Secondo, che lori da piu ani in qua furono e sono soliti andar a viaggi in diversi parti per mercatantare."

97. Ibid. See 6v and 6r, where several different witnesses give this type of answer. One says that he himself had traveled with the merchants for trade.

98. T.A. 1/11, 1617, 17v: "Christiani Greci et buoni mercanti non havendo mai fatto altra professione che di traficare et fare commercio."

99. Ibid., 23r and 24v. "Un bon mercadanto non havendo mai visto al detto depo-nente che il detto Cagi habbia mai fatto altra professione che di bon xpan(?) et merca-danto negocianto sopra il mare in molti luochi con vascelli et saichi." Other witnesses said the same and see 2/2 and 11/19 for similar testimony.

100. In 1639 a group of Genoese merchants armed a galley and sent it to Sicily to load raw silk. They found the harbor blocked, so, thwarted in their original intent, they set sail for the eastern Mediterranean in the hopes of capturing Turkish vessels. Kirk, "The Implications of Ceremony at Sea," 3. The important question of the type of weaponry on board Otttoman vessels at this time remains to be explored. The records of the *Tribunale* are not very helpful in this regard as they provide only occasional references on this topic. But see T.A. 12:11, 1683, 26r, where, in response to questioning, a Greek witness says there were two cannons and four *petrieri di ferno* on board the saicha.

101. See chapter four for the statutes.

102. T.A. 12:11, 1683.16v. "non solo a I turchi nemici commun, ma anche ai Chri-stiani Sudditi loro, e vassalli."

103. Ibid., 16v and 16r.

104. See chapter two.

105. T.A. 12/11, 1683. 16r.

106. Cavaliero, "The Decline of the Maltese Corso," 234.

107. The corsairs also had good business reasons for keeping many of their transac-tions in the Ottoman realms hidden. Secrecy allowed them to defraud the investors back in Livorno or Valletta. We have, for example, Roberts's description of how corsairs would land at night along the Syrian coast and kidnap a dozen or so Turks. Then they would "sail away to those places where the Turks live (viz) to Tripoly-Soria, Joppa, Caipha, St. John de Acres, Sidon or Barute. There they come to an anchor w.o. Gunshot, they hoist a white Ensign, and fire a Gun. Hereupon the Turks will come off and Treat with them, for the Redemption of their Slaves." Roberts, *Adventures*, 9.

108. T.A. 1/1, 1602, 12v. "Non si devosi ammettere alla testimonienza persone, quali vivono sotto il Tyrano dominio di Mahometto, da quali posson venire forzati a furia di bastonati a testificar cio che egli vogliono."

109. Ibid., 13v.

110. Ibid., 29v–r.

111. T.A. 2/7, 1638, 30r.

112. Ibid., 33r.

113. "Greci Levantini o da loro dependeno."

114. One witness from Venice said he was born in Venice and "non dependo da greci da Levante." Another said said "sono greco nato in Metelino, sono greco levantino." T.A. 2:7, 1638, 33r.

115. Earle, *Corsairs of Malta and Barbary*, 115.

116. Earle mentions that in the eighteenth century the Greeks "had ceased to attempt the farce of prosecuting them [the corsairs] in the courts of Florence or Spain" (ibid., 119). H.J.A. Sire mentions the prize court of Leghorn (the Order of St. Stephen) without giving any further details. Sire, *The Knights of Malta*, 90–91.

117. Dokos, "Μια Υπόθεσις Πειρατείας, 36–62. Very interestingly, and exceptionally, Dokos characterizes the problems that arose from Christians attacking Christians as problems of "a legal type" (37).

118. Evidently Mellos was the only person still on board at the time of the attack. It was very common for merchants and crew to flee onto land if they were close enough at the time of the attack and it seems that had happened in this instance as well. Dokos, "Μια Υπόθεσις Πειρατείας," 38.

119. The exact nature of the forum in which Mellos's case was heard is unclear. The Duchess of Savoy did involve herself directly, in that she ordered three individuals— Blancardi, Pallavicino, and Frichignono—to hear the case. Ibid., 50. The diploma that authorized the corsairing expedition was issued in 1670 by Carlo Emanuel II, Duke of Savoy, 1638–75. It was drawn up in the *Consolato del Mare*. Ibid., 62.

120. Ibid., 51.

121. As previously discussed, the convention in Europe was to refer to the Ottomans, and to Muslims more generally, as Turks. My use of the term "Turk" in the discussion of this case simply follows the text.

122. "Greçe iuxta ritum ecclesie." Dokos, "Μια Υπόθεσις Πειρατείας," 51.

123. That is my translation of the term "βαρβαρικάς θάλασσας."

124. From Ottoman attack, presumably, although he does not say this. Mellos never says what flag he was flying under. From the earlier discussion it is possible that he was not flying any flag.

125. This is a remarkably speedy decision. Francesca Trivellato has noted that we lack studies of the length of litigation in European commercial tribunals in the early modern period. But she does draw our attention to one study of the Chancery of London, where most lawsuits lasted three years in the second half of the sixteenth century. Trivellato, "Sephardic Merchants between Rabbinic and Civil Courts," 11. It is difficult to know whether the Mellos case represents an efficient court or summary justice.

126. Dokos, "Μια Υπόθεσις Πειρατείας," 47.

127. A *çavuş* was a messenger. Possibly they simply mean to indicate that the Turks were officials of some sort.

128. Unfortunately, we must rely on Dokos's Greek translation, which is, roughly, "both canon and municipal law" (νόμοι κανονικοι και Αστικοί). He does not reproduce the original Latin or Italian. Ibid., 53.

129. Krantonelle, Ιστορία της Πειρατείας στους μεσους χρονους της Τουρκοκρατίας, 166.

130. Characteristically, the instructions specifically excluded Greeks who were Venetian subjects. The Knights of St. Stephen tried to avoid tangling with Venice.

131. Earle, *Corsairs of Malta and Barbary*, 112. This distinction must also be at play in Robert Cavaliero's remarks about French consuls in the Levant in this period. He writes, without providing a source, that "Turkish" *caravaneurs* were entitled to patents from the French consuls for cargo that was destined for France. Cavaliero, "The Decline of the Maltese Corso," 228.

132. I thank Professor Nicholas Rodger at the University of Essex in the United Kingdom for alerting me to this aspect of maritime law. My application of this rule to Tuscan and courts of Savoy is my own.

133. See http://specialcollections.wichita.edu/collections/ms/82–04/82–4–A.html.

134. Earle, *Corsairs of Malta and Barbary*, 118.

135. Mavroeide, Συμβολή στην Ιστορία της ελληνικής Αδελφότητας Βενετίας στο ΙΣΤ Αιώνα, 12. Leo Allatius, the most prominent Greek Catholic intellectual of the seventeenth century, was born an Orthodox Christian in Chios but converted to Catholicism and spent most of his career in Rome. At the Vatican he argued that the Orthodox were "really just misguided Catholics." Hartnup, *On the Beliefs of the Greeks*, 69. For more on Allatius, see chapter seven.

136. See http://specialcollections.wichita.edu/collections/ms/82–04/82–4–A.html.

137. Oikonomou, "Όψεις της Ελληνικής Ναυτιλίας κατά το 17ο αιώνα," 405.

Chapter 7
The Turn toward Rome

1. "The other lethal factor operating against the Corso, and this was to make recovery from French displeasure quite impossible, was support in the Roman Curia for Schismatic Greeks. The claims of Greek traders that they had been depredated by Maltese armateurs first became insistent in 1702." He goes on to say that volume of cases being heard in the Holy See increased after 1713. Cavaliero, "The Decline of the Maltese Corso," 233, 234.

2. Similar to what Bernard Heyberger has done for the Arab Christians in his *Les chrétiens du Proche-Orient*.

3. He was deposed and reinstated seven times between 1620 and his death, at the hands of Ottoman authorities, in 1638. See Pastor, *The History of the Popes*, 29:233.

4. Loukaris and his views have been the subject of great debate. For a brief summary, see Ware, *Eustratios Argenti*, 8–11. His *Confession* was condemned by no less than six councils during the half century following his death.

5. Ibid., 10. Césy began serving in 1619 and, except for a brief period in the early 1630s, remained at his post until 1639. Ware, *Eustratios Argenti*, 96–97.

6. Ibid., 24.

7. See chapter five.

8. Pastor, *The History of the Popes*, 29:227.

9. See the description in Herring for an attempt by the Propaganda to cultivate its own channels of communication with the patriarch, independent of the French. Herring, Οικουμενικό Πατριαρχείο, 125.

10. Ibid., 138. See Herring both for the declaration itself and for the circumstances surrounding the November 1627 meeting. The document itself, in the original Latin, is reproduced in Georg Hofmann, "S. I. Patriarch Kyrillos Lukaris und die römische Kirche," 57. I thank Michelle Garceau for translating the Latin. "Mercatores graecos, qui in urbibus christianorum negotiantur, admonendosesse, ut Cyrilli patriarchae haeretici eiectionem e sede patriarchali moliantur, curentque alium, qui occidentales haereses

abominetur, substitui: alioquin eorum navigia et merces a militibus christianis non erunt, sicut hactenus fuerent, salvae, sed in eorum praedam cedent."

11. Herring, Οικουμενικό Πατριαρχείο και Ευρωπαϊκή Πολιτική, 138–39. Pastor also discusses these proceedings in *The History of the Popes*, 29:236.

12. Frazee, *Catholics and Sultans*, 147, and 145–48 for other struggles in Palestine at this time.

13. Steele, *An Account of the State of the Roman-Catholick Religion*, 51. The power of the Orthodox Church in Jerusalem in the seventeenth century is suggested by the name that the Franciscans gave the Orthodox patriarch of the city, Dositheos, who served from 1669 to 1707. They called him *infensissimus Latinae ecclesiae hostis*, "the scourge of the Latins." Ware, *Eustratios Argenti*, 31.

14. See chapter four.

15. Tsirpanles, Στη Ρόδο του 16ου–17ου Αιώνα, 46.

16. Efthymiou-Hadzilacou, *Rhodes et sa région élargie*, 20. Given this very long history it is striking that no one has written a history of exiles on the island.

17. See Tsirpanles, Στη Ρόδο του 16ου–17ου Αιώνα, 57–59, for information on these various metropolitans.

18. Ibid., 46.

19. Ibid., 72.

20. "Και παλιν ο Καλβινισμός σωρηδόν εις το τρισάθλιον πατριαρχείον Κωνσταντινουπόλεως." This letter is published, in both Greek and Italian, by Georg Hofmann in *Griechische Patriarchen und römische Päpste*, 18–20.

21. For the Greek text, see Hofmann, *Griechische Patriarchen und römische Päpste*, 18.

22. Argenti, *The Religious Minorities of Chios*, 262.

23. See chapter five.

24. *Fabio Chigi*, 242. Fabio Chigi went on to become Pope Alexander VII (1655–67).

25. See AOM 1416.

26. See Pastor, *The History of the Popes*, 29:157, for the appointment date.

27. Hartnup, *On the Beliefs of the Greeks*, 62.

28. Tsirpanles, Το Ελληνικό Κολλέγιο της Ρώμης, 42. I thank Liam Brockey for explaining to me the duty of the cardinal protector to intervene with the Vatican on behalf of his client.

29. See Argenti, *The Religious Minorities of Chios*, chap. 3, part 2, for an extensive discussion of his life and works. Argenti writes, "The most notable of the Chian Catholics of the seventeenth century and the only one to take an active part in the intellectual life of the Vatican was the polymath Leo Allatius" (233).

30. See ibid. for details on the relationship between Allatius and Barberini.

31. Nussdorfer, *Civic Politics in the Rome of Urban VIII*, 34–36.

32. *Fabio Chigi*, 3. This account also draws on Bonnici, *Medieval and Roman Inquisition in Malta*. Despite the dual mission, I refer to him as simply the inquisitor. According to Bonnici, it was as "the Inquisitor" that this official was always known, and it was in this area that his powers were greatest (ibid., 32). Brogini, whose study includes an extended discussion of Malta as a frontier, points out that increasing economic activity on the island—with all the cultural contact that involved—was accompanied by ever greater attempts at religious and ideological policing. The office of the inquisitor, which was established in 1574, was part of this effort. Brogini, *Malte*, 229, 233.

33. *Fabio Chigi*, 9. In 1600 the chronicler of the order, Abbé de Vertot, made his sympathies clear: "The inquisitors, to make their court to the pope, are continually making encroachments on the authority of the grand master and council, and make themselves odious and insupportable to the knights." Vertot, *The History of the Knights Hospitallers of St. John of Jerusalem*, 5:83.

34. Bonnici, *Medieval and Roman Inquisition*, 199. And inquisitors did not serve very long. There were thirty inquisitors over the course of the seventeenth century, with tenures ranging from one to seven years. Ibid., chap. 5.

35. Mallia-Milanes, *In the Service of the Venetian Republic*, 15. I thank Professor Mallia-Milanes for explaining to me, in a conversation in October 2007, the unique position of the inquisitor as the only official on the island who was not appointed by the grand master.

36. Bonnici, *Medieval and Roman Inquisition*, 47.

37. *Fabio Chigi*, appendix B, 500: "Sarnno raccomandati a V.S. Ill.ma. I poveri greci christiani che sono depradati da vascelli armati in malta, a fine che li sollevi dalla potentai de loro avversarii, facendo dal G.M. dar loro avvocato, e procuratore precettato, poi che altrimenti bene spesso non ardiscono, per la paura de cavalieri, e procurando che l'Amamento faccia loro buona giustitia."

38. See chapter five.

39. Bonnici, *Medieval and Roman Inquisitiona*, 46. The slaves "often begged for clemency on the grounds that their having become Muslim was only the result of the unbearable ill treatment meted out to them during the time they had spent in slavery. Such cases were frequent during the term of office of each Inquisitor."

40. Mallia-Milanes "From Valona to Crete," 161.

41. Barberini gave Mangiaco his "*raccomandazione*." *Fabio Chigi*, 122.

42. AOM 1413, letter dated September 30, 1634. *Registro delle Lettere Italiane Spedite ai Vari Sovrani, Ambasciatori ed Altri Personaggi dal Gran Maestro de Paula.*

43. *Fabio Chigi*, 123. In this case as in several others, the individuals are described only as "Greci." They must have been merchants, since they all complain of the loss of merchandise (*mercantie*). The name Giovanni Mercurio also appears in one of the cases before the Tribunale in Malta. T.A. 2/7. Identified as a merchant from Monemvasia, he testified on behalf of the victim, Gioannes Cugia. It is difficult to know if this is the same person who applied to Barberini for justice on his own behalf. In any event, it is not the same case, as Gioannes Cugia was attacked in April 1636 and the Barberini letter was written almost two years earlier.

44. *Fabio Chigi*. See the letters on 157, 165, 174, and 178.

45. Loukaris would have just commenced his exile on Rhodes, in May 1635.

46. "Il breve de' I Micheli, mercanti Greci, ha fatto rumor grande, ma non è stato male il fare far all Religione questa paura, perché tanto più procuraranno quelli dell'Armamento di far la giustitia." *Fabio Chigi*, 174.

47. *Fabio Chigi*, 178. This correspondence is not part of the Chigi archive. It is to be found in the Archive of the Order of St. John in Valletta, which Borg also consulted.

48. Ibid. Although Borg doesn't say where the appeal was lodged, it must have been the Tribunale dell'Udienza, which was the court of appeal in Malta. Vella, "The Consolato del Mare of Malta," 7. And Giacomo Cappello describes the system in *Descrittione di Malta*, 70.

49. "Vi acceniamo bene, che molte volte questi greci vengono qui fraudolentemnete a pretendere robbe di turchi imbarcate sotto loro nome, assicurati forse dall'animo pietoso di molti." *Fabio Chigi*, 242.

50. See chapters five and six for more information on his case.

51. *Fabio Chigi*, 296.

52. See chapter six.

53. *Fabio Chigi*, 323. Chigi says that he received the letter from Cuia himself. The timing would seem to make it impossible for Cuia to have brought the letter from Rome. Possibly an intermediary was involved.

54. Ibid., 337.

55. *Fabio Chigi*, 447. The island was under Ottoman control.

56. Ibid., 461.

57. Chigi Archives, Vatican Library A.II.37. 207r.

58. *Fabio Chigi*, 303.

59. Cavaliero, "The Decline of the Maltese Corso," 233.

60. Grand Master Wignacourt had instituted the Tribunale in his capacity as the head of a religious order; therefore appeals to Rome were always possible. Ibid. In this article Cavaliero also describes the inquisitor as "the champion of the Greeks" (232). And see Barberini's letter to Chigi, dated November 17, 1635, in which he points out that the Micheli brothers could launch appeals against the decisions of the Tribunale in Rome. *Fabio Chigi*, 178.

61. Cavaliero, "The Decline of the Maltese Corso," 233.

62. Ibid., 235.

63. Vertot, *The History of the Knights Hospitallers of St. John of Jerusalem*, 5:107. The reference to "Catholic princes" is very reminiscent of the 1627 declaration of the Propaganda Fide. Dal Pozzo discusses the 1635 events as well. Dal Pozzo, *Historia della sacra religione*, 1:832–33.

64. Dal Pozzo, *Historia della sacra guerra*, 1:833. Later on he described the Greeks as "enemies of the good and true Christians."

65. Ibid., 1:833–34.

66. "Per un saggio dell'empieta de Greci Levantini." Ibid., 1:834.

67. Ibid. Paoli, *Codice Diplomatico del Sacro Militare Ordine Gerosolimitano oggi di Malta*, 324–25, also gives an account of this correspondence between the grand master and Cardinal Antonio Barberini.

68. *Fabio Chigi*, 348.

69. Ibid., 372.

70. Cavaliero, "The Decline of the Maltese Corso," 234.

71. Ibid., 235.

72. Their names were Νικολις Απεργης (Nicolis Aperges) and Ασκανιος Μαρκης (Askanios Markes). Dokos, "Μια Υπόθεσις Πειρατείας," 43. The account that follows is based on the information provided in Dokos's article.

73. Ιωαννος and Αργυρος Μπεναλδης.

74. Unfortunately, Dokos does not give the names of the other officials.

75. Dokos, "Μια Υπόθεσις Πειρατείας," 48. "Frank" was the term used to refer to Western, and especially Catholic, Christians.

76. Evidently he was working for the Propaganda but was still Greek Orthodox.

77. Heyberger, *Les chrétiens du Proche-Orient*, 259–60.

78. In eighteenth-century Aleppo too, the right to wear a wig was claimed by the Sephardim, who were under French protection. Trivellato, *The Familiarity of Strangers*, 129.

79. Dokos, "Μια Υπόθεσις Πειρατείας," 49.

80. Dokos says only that he was in Spain for "many years" without giving further details. Even this information, however, is once again a striking reminder of the great lengths to which litigants would go to try and obtain justice.

81. The letter is reproduced in Dokos, "Μια Υπόθεσις Πειρατείας," 54–55.

82. At some point after his death his personal papers, including the records of this failed lawsuit, came into the possession of the Greek Institute of Venice. Ibid., 53.

83. See the numerous cases, from both the seventeenth and the eighteenth centuries, in Cavaliero. And Benaldes, in his letter to Mellos, talks about the number of times that the Greeks have received justice in Rome.

Conclusion

1. An account of this case can be found in Krantonelle, Ιστορία της Πειρατείας στους μέσους χρόνους της Τουρκοκρατίας, 167–72. My discussion of the case draws exclusively on Krantonelle. The documents of the case can be found in the Florentine State Archives.

2. The silver coin of Venice.

3. Krantonelle, Ιστορία της Πειρατείας στους μέσους χρόνους της Τουρκοκρατίας, 167.

4. Krantonelle describes them as pirates. Given the opprobrium attached to the term, I doubt that this word is used in the original documents.

5. Vella, "The Bureaucracy of the *Consolato del Mare*," 69.

6. Gonzaga, *In the Service of the Venetian Republic*, 62.

7. Heyberger, "Sécurité et insécurité," 158.

8. Ibid. This is Heyberger's translation of the original Italian, which he gives: "che li franchi sono cani, che non cercono cattolici in Levante, che per mangiarli, e tenerli come schiavi della loro giuriditione, senza portar loro nissun sollievo nella dura schiavitú in qual si ritovano."

9. Breik, *Documents inédits*, 43. The word used for corsairs is قرصان. For the Greeks, the traditional term *Rum* (روم) is used. I thank Karam Nachar for helping me read this passage.

10. Ware, *Eustratios Argenti*, 65–107. I thank Bruce Masters for drawing my attention to the connection between Breik's chronicle and the events in Istanbul.

11. Van den Boogert, "Redress for Ottoman Victims of European Privateering."

12. Van den Boogert notes that we see only "occasional" instances of victims complaining to the Porte. At this point we do not know why and when victims decided to seek redress and when they decided to let it go. He also points out that the Ottoman government did complain frequently to European ambassadors in a general way about attacks by European corsairs, "but these generally seem to have had little result." Ibid., 92.

13. Van den Boogert uses the terms "corsair" and "privateer" interchangeably, which seems problematic in light of the special meaning of "corsair" and "*corso*" I laid out in

chapter two and elsewhere. If in fact the word corsair was used, this would be evidence of the fuzzy line between those states that had diplomatic relations with the Ottoman Empire and those that did not. I use the term "privateer" in discussing the Dutch, as it seems more accurate.

14. This is the exact reversal of the Maltese practice of torturing people to get them to admit to being Ottoman subjects.

15. Research would be needed to discover whether Ottoman Christians were swept up in these attacks.

16. Van den Boogert, "Redress for Ottoman Victims of European Privateering," 104.

17. Ibid, 99.

18. Ibid., 94.

19. See Kulsrud, *Maritime Neutrality to 1780*, 109.

Bibliography

● ○ ●

Archival Sources

Archives of the Order of St. John (AOM) and Archives of the Cathedral of Malta (ACM), Malta Study Center, Hill Museum and Manuscript Library, Saint John's University, Collegeville, Minnesota. Online address: http://www.hmml.org/centers/malta/malta_start.html.

Tribunal Armamentor (TA), Law Court Records, National Archives of Malta, Banca Giuratale, Mdina, Malta. Online address: www.libraries-archives.gov.mt/nam/ser_law_courts.htm.

Chigi Archives, Vatican Library, Rome.

Published Sources

Acta et Diplomata Graeca Medii Aevi: Sacra et Profana, Collecta et Edita. Vol. 6, *Acta et Diplomata Monasteriorium et Ecclesiarum Orientis,* edited by Franz Miklosich and Joseph Muller. Aalen, Germany: Scientia Verlag, 1968.

Ahrweiler, Hélène. "Course et piraterie dans la Méditerranée orientale aux XIVème–XVème siècles." In *Course et piraterie: Études presentées à la Commission internationale d'histoire maritime à l'occasion de son XVè colloque international pendant le XIVè Congres international des sciences historiques,* edited by Michel Mollat, 3 vols. Paris: Centre national de la recherche scientifique, 1975.

Aksan, Virginia H. *An Ottoman Statesman in War and Peace: Ahmed Resmi Efendi 1700–1783.* Leiden: Brill, 1995.

Alexandrowicz, Charles Henry. *The European-African Confrontation: A Study in Treaty-Making.* Leiden: Sijthoff, 1973.

D'Angelo, Michale, and M. Elisabetta Tonizzi. "Recent Maritime Historiography on Italy." In *Research in Maritime History New Directions in Mediterranean Maritime History,* vol. 28, edited by Carmel Vassallo and Gelina Harlaftis. St. John's, Newfoundland: International Maritime Economic History Association, 2004.

Angiolini, Franco. *I cavalierie e il principe: L'ordine di Santo Stefano e la società toscana in età moderna.* Florence: Edifir, 1996.

Arbel, Benjamin. "Roman Catholics and Greek Orthodox in the Early Modern Venetian State." In *The Three Religions,* edited by Nili Cohen and Andreas Heldrich. Munich: Herbert Utz Verlag, 2002.

———. *Trading Nations: Jews and Venetians in the Early Modern Mediterranean.* New York: Brill, 1995.

Argenti, Philip P. *The Religious Minorities of Chios: Jews and Roman Catholics.* Cambridge: Cambridge University Press, 1970.

Bargrave, Robert. *The Travel Diary of Robert, Levant Merchant, 1647–1656.* London: Hakluyt Society, 1999.

Barkan, O. L. "Essai sur les données statistiques des registres de recensement dans l'empire ottoman aux Xve et XVIe siècles." *Journal of the Economic and Social History of the Orient* 1 (1958): 9–36.

Baruchello, M. *Livorno e il suo porto: Origini, caratteristiche e vicende dei traffici livornesi.* Livorno, 1932.

Baumer, Franklin L. "England, the Turk and the Common Corps of Christendom." *American Historical Review* 50, no. 1 (October 1944): 26–48.

Benton, Lauren. "Legal Spaces of Empire: Piracy and the Origins of Ocean Regionalism." *Comparative Studies in Society and History* 47 (2005): 700–724.

———. *Law and Colonial Cultures: Legal Regimes in World History 1400–1900.* Cambridge: Cambridge University Press, 2002.

Blunt, Henry. *Voyage into the Levant.* London, 1636.

Bonnici, Alexander. *Medieval and Roman Inquisition in Malta.* Malta: Rabat, 1998.

Bono, Salvatore. *Schiavi Musulmani nell'Italia moderna.* Napoli: Edizioni scientifiche italiane, 1999.

Braude, Benjamin. "Venture and Faith in the Commercial Life of the Ottoman Balkans." *International History Review* 7, no. 4 (1985): 519–42.

Braudel, Fernand. *The Mediterranean and the Mediterranean World in the Age of Philip II.* New York, 1973.

Breik, Michel. *Documents inédits pour server L'Histoire du Pays de Damas de 1720 à 1782.* Hariss, 1930.

Brewer, M. Jonah. "Gold, Frankincense and Myrrh: French Consuls and Commercial Diplomacy in the Ottoman Levant 1660–1699." PhD diss., Georgetown University, 2002.

Brogini, Anne. *Malte: Frontiere de chrétienté (1530–1670).* Rome: École française du Rome, 2006.

Brummett, Palmira. "Imagining the Early Modern Ottoman Space, from World History to Piri Reis." In *The Early Modern Ottomans: Remapping the Empire,* edited by Virginia H. Aksan and Daniel Goffman. Cambridge: Cambridge University Press, 2007.

Burke, Ersie. "'Your Humble and Devoted Servants': Greco-Venetian Views of the Serenissima." In *Street Noises, Civic Spaces and Urban Identities in Italian Renaissance Cities,* edited by F. W. Kent. *Monash Publications in History* 34 (2000):10–16.

Camerani, S. "Contributo alla storia dei trattati commerciali fra la Toscana e i Turchi." *Archivio Storico Italiano* 97, no. 2 (1939): 83–101.

Cappello, G. *Descrittione di Malta, anno 1716.* Edited and with introduction and notes by Victor Mallia-Milanes. Malta, 1988.

Cassar, Paul. "The Maltese Corsairs and the Order of St. John of Jerusalem." *Catholic Historical Review* 46, no. 2 (July 1960): 137–56.

Castignoli, Paolo. "La tolleranza enunciazione e prassi di una regola di convivenza." In *Studi di storia: Livorno. Dagli archivi alla citta.* Livorno: Mondadori, 2001.

Cavaliero, Robert. "The Decline of the Maltese Corso in the 18th Century: A Study in Maritime History." *Melita Historica* 2 (1959): 224–38.

Celumeau, J. "Un ponte fra Oriente e Occidente: Ancona nel cinquecento." *Quaderni Storici* 5 (1970).

Clissold, St. *The Barbary Slaves.* London: P. Elek, 1977.

Cochrane, E. *Florence in the Forgotten Centuries 1527–1800: A History of Florence and the Florentines in the Age of the Grand Dukes.* Chicago: University of Chicago Press, 1973.

A Collection of Voyages in Four Volumes. Vol. 7, *Mr. Robert's adventures and sufferings amongst the corsairs of the Levant; his description of the Archipelago islands, &c.* London, 1729.

Collins, James B. *The State in Early Modern France.* Cambridge: Cambridge University Press, 1995.

Contreras, Alonso de. *The Adventures of Captain Alonso de Contreras: A 17th Century Journey,* translated by Philip Dallas. New York: Paragon, 1989.

Cooperman, B. D. "Venetian Policy Towards Levantine Jews in Its Broader Italian Context." In *Gli ebrei e Venezia,* edited by G. Cozzi. Milan: Edizione di Comunità, 1987.

Crecelius, Daniel, and Abd al-Aziz Badr. "French Ships and Their Cargoes Sailing between Damiette and Ottoman ports (1777–1781)." *Journal of the Economic and Social History of the Orient* 37 (1994): 251–86.

Cunningham, Allan. *Collected Essays.* Vol. 1, *Anglo-Ottoman Encounters in the Age of Revolution,* edited by Edward Ingram. London: Frank Cass, 1993.

Cutajar, Dominic, and Carmel Cassar. "Malta's Role in Mediterranean Affairs: 1530–1699." In *Mid Med Bank, Reports and Accounts* (1984).

dal Pozzo, B. *Historia della sacra religione militare di S. Giovanni Gerosolimitano detta di Malta.* Verona, 1703.

Dandelet, T. *Spanish Rome 1500–1700.* New Haven: Yale University Press, 2001.

Davis, R. "The Geography of Slaving in the Early Modern Mediterranean 1500–1800." *Journal of Medieval and Early Modern Studies* 37, no. 1 (Winter 2007).

de Bruyn, Cornelis. *Voyage au Levant.* Delft, 1700.

Devoulx, A. "La marine de la regence d'Alger." *Revue Africaine* 13 (1869): 384–420.

Dokos, K. "Μια Υπόθεσις Πειρατείας κατά τον 17ον Αιώνα (1678–1680)" (A Case of Piracy in the Seventeenth Century 1678–1680). Thesaurismata 2 (1963).

Domenico, Roy. *The Regions of Italy: A Reference Guide to History and Culture.* Westport, CT: Greenwood Press, 2002.

Dritto Municipale di Malta: Compilato sotto de Rohan G.M. or Nuovamente Corredato di Annotazioni. Malta, 1843.

Dursteler, Eric. *The Venetians in Constantinople: Nation, Identity and Coexistence in the Early Modern Mediterranean.* Baltimore: Johns Hopkins University Press, 2006.

Earle, Peter. *The Pirate Wars.* London: Methuen, 2003.

———. *Corsairs of Malta and Barbary.* London: Sidgwick and Jackson, 1970.

———. "The Commercial Development of Ancona 1479–1551." *Economic History Review,* n.s., 22, no. 1 (1969).

Efthymiou-Hadzilacou, M. *Rhodes et sa région élargie au 18ème siècle: Les activités portuaires.* Athens, 1988.

Eldem, Edhem. "Strangers in Their Own Seas? The Ottomans in the Eastern Mediterranean Basin in the Second Half of the Eighteenth Century." Unpublished manuscript, Department of History, Boğaziçi University.

Engels, Marie-Christine. *Merchants, Interlopers, Seamen and Corsairs: The "Flemish" Community in Livorno and Genoa (1615–1635)*. Hilversum: Verloren, 1997.

Evelyn, John. *The Diary of John Evelyn*, vol. 2. Oxford, 1955.

Fabio Chigi, Apostolic Delegate in Malta (1634–1639): An Edition of His Official Correspondence. Edited by Vincent Borg. Vatican City: Biblioteca Apostòlica Vaticana, 1967.

Fedalto, Giorgio. *Ricerche storiche sulla posizione giuridica ed ecclesiastica dei greci a Venezia nei secoli XV e XVI*. Florence: Leo S. Olschki, 1967.

Fisher, Godfrey. *Barbary Legend: War, Trade and Piracy in North Africa 1415–1830*. Oxford: Clarendon Press, 1957.

Fodor, Pál. "Piracy, Ransom Slavery and Trade: French Participation in the Liberation of Ottoman Slaves from Malta during the 1620s." *Turcica* 33 (2001): 141–90.

Fontenay, Michel. "Corsaires de la foi ou rentiers du sol? Les chevaliers de Malte dans le corso mediterraneen." *Revue d'Histoire Moderne et Contemporaine* 35 (Juillet–Septembre 1988): 361–84.

Fontenay, Michel, and Alberto Tenenti. "Course et piraterie mediterranée de la fin du moyen-âge au début du XIXè siècle." In *Course et piraterie: Etudes présentées à la Commission internationale d'histoire maritime a l'occasion de son XVe colloque international pendant le XIVe Congrès international des sciences historiques*, edited by Michel Mollat, 78–136. Paris: Centre national de la recherche scientifique.

Frattarelli Fischer, Lucia. "Alle radici di una identita composita: La 'nazione' Greca a Livorno," in *Le iconostasi di Livorno: Patrimonio iconografico post-bizantino*, edited by Gaetano Passarelli. Livorno, 2001.

———. "Merci e mercanti nella Livorno seicentesca, 'magazzino d'Italia e del Mediterraneo.'" In *Merci e monete a Livorno in età granducale / a cura di Silvana Balbi di Caro*. Milano, 1997.

Frazee, Ch. *Catholics and Sultans: The Church and the Ottoman Empire 1453–1923*. Cambridge: Cambridge University Press, 1983.

Freller, T. "Adversus Infideles: Some Notes on the Cavalier's Tour of St. John and the Maltese Corsairs." *Journal of Early Modern History* (Netherlands), 4, nos. 3–4 (2000): 405–30.

Fusaro, Maria. "Coping with Transition: Greek Merchants and Shipowners between Venice and England in the Late Sixteenth Century." In *Diaspora Entrepreneurial Networks: Four Centuries of History*, edited by Ina Baghdiantz McCabe, Gelina Harlaftis, and Ioanna Pepelasis Minoglu, 95–123. Oxford: Berg, 2005.

———. "Un reseau de cooperation commerciale en Mediterranne venitienne: Les Anglais et les Grecs." *Annales ESC* 58, no. 3 (2003): 605–25.

———. *Uva passa: Una guerra commerciale tra Venezia e l'Inghilterra 1540–1640*. Venice: University of Venice Press, 1996.

Ganshof, François L. *The Middle Ages: A History of International Relations*. New York, 1970.

Ginio, Eyal. "When Coffee Brought About Wealth and Prestige: The Impact of Egyptian Trade on Salonica." *Oriente Moderno*, n.s., 25 (2006): 93–107.

———. "Piracy and Redemption in the Aegean Sea." *Turcica* 33 (2001): 135–47.

Goffman, Daniel. *Izmir and the Levantine World 1550–1650*. Seattle: University of Washington Press, 1990.

Goitein, S. D. *A Mediterranean Society: The Jewish Communities of the Arab World as Portrayed in the Documents of the Cairo Geniza.* 6 vols. Berkeley and Los Angeles: University of California Press, 1967–93.

Goldie, Charles. "The Bill of Lading: Then and Now." In *Consolati di Mare and Chambers of Commerce: Proceedings of a Conference Held at the Foundation for International Studies*, edited by Carmel Vassallo. Valletta, 2000.

Gonzaga, Massimiliano Buzzaccarini. *In the Service of the Venetian Republic: Massimiliano Buzzaccarini Gonzaga's Letters from Malta to Venice's Magistracy of Trade 1754–177*, edited by Victor Mallia-Milanes. Malta, 2008.

Graff, Philippe. "La Valette: Une ville nouvelle du XVI siècle et son evolution jusqu'à nos jours." *Revue du Monde Musulman et de la Mediterranee* 71, no.1 (1994): 151–65.

Greene, Molly. The Mediterranean Basin." In *Europe 1450 to 1789: Encyclopedia of the Early Modern World*, edited by Jonathan Dewald. New York: Charles Scribner's Sons, 2003.

———. "Beyond the Northern Invasion: The Mediterranean in the Seventeenth Century." *Past and Present* 174 (2002): 40–72.

———. *A Shared World: Christians and Muslims in the Early Modern Mediterranean.* Princeton: Princeton University Press, 2000.

Grotius. *De jure praedae commentarius: Commentary on the Law of Prize and Booty.* Vol. 1 of The Classics of International Law. Oxford: Oxford University Press, 1950.

Haddad, Robert. *Syrian Christians in Muslim Society.* Princeton: Princeton University Press, 1970.

Hanley, Will. "Foreignness and Localness in Alexandria, 1880–1914." PhD diss., Princeton University, 2007.

Hanna, Nelly. *Making Big Money in 1600: The Life and Times of an Egyptian Merchant.* Syracuse: Syracuse University Press, 1998.

Harlaftis, Gelina, and Sophia Laiou. "Ottoman State Policy in Mediterranean Trade and Shipping, c.1780–c.1820: The Rise of the Greek-Owned Ottoman Merchant Fleet." In *Networks of Power in Modern Greece*, edited by Mark Mazower. New York: Columbia University Press/Hurst, 2008.

Hartnup, Karen. *On the Beliefs of the Greeks: Leo Allatius and Popular Orthodoxy.* Leiden: Brill, 2004.

Heberer, J. M. *Voyages en Egypte de Michael Heberer von Bretten, 1585–1586.* Cairo: American University in Cairo Press, 1976.

Herring, G. Οικουμενικό Πατριαρχείο και Ευρωπαϊκή Πολιτική 1620–1638 (The Ecumenical Patriarchate and European Politics 1620–1638). Athens, 1992.

Hess, Andrew. *The Forgotten Frontier: A History of the Sixteenth Century Ibero-African Frontier.* Chicago: University of Chicago Press, 1978.

———. "The Evolution of the Ottoman Seaborne Empire in the Age of the Oceanic Discoveries, 1453–1525." *American Historical Review* 75, no. 7 (1969–70): 1892–1919.

Heyberger, Bernard. "Sécurité et insécurité: Les chrétians de Syria dans l'espace méditerranéen (17th–18th centuries)." In *Figures anonymes, figures d'elite: Pour une anatomie de l'Homo ottomanicus*, edited by Meropi Anastassiadou and Bernard Heyberger. Istanbul: Isis, 1999.

Heyberger, Bernard. *Les chrétiens du Proche-Orient au temps de la Réforme catholique: Syrie, Liban, Palestine, XVIIIe siècle.* Rome: École française de Rome, 1994.

Hofmann, Georg. *Griechische Patriarchen und römische Päpste: Untersuchungen and Texte.* Orientalia Christiana Periodica. Rome: Pontificium Institutum Orientalium Studiorum, 1929.

———. "S. I. Patriarch Kyrillos Lukaris und die römische Kirche." *Orientalia Christiana* 15–1, no. 52 (May 1929).

Inalcık, Halil. "Ottoman Galata, 1453–1553." In *Prèmiere rencontre internationale sur l'Empire ottoman et la Turquie moderne,* edited by Edhem Eldem. Istanbul, 1991.

———. "The Policy of Mehmed II Toward the Greek Population of Istanbul and the Byzantine Buildings of the City." *Dumbarton Oaks Papers* 23–25 (1969–70): 229–49.

Inalcık, Halil, and D. Quataert, eds. *An Economic and Social History of the Ottoman Empire.* Cambridge: Cambridge University Press, 1994.

Iorga, N. *Byzance après Byzance: Continuation de l' "Histoire de la vie byzantine."* Bucharest: Institute d'Études Byzantines, 1935.

Jal, A. *Glossaire nautique: Répertoire polyglotte de termes de marine anciens et modernes.* Paris, 1848.

Julien, Charles-André. *History of North Africa: Tunisia, Algeria, Morocco. From the Arab Conquests to 1830,* edited and revised by R. Le Tourneau (1952), translated by John Petrie; English edition edited by C. C. Stewart. New York: Praeger, 1970.

Kafadar, Cemal. "A Death in Venice: Anatolian Muslim Merchants Trading in the Serenissima." *Journal of Turkish Studies* 10 (1987): 191–218.

Kagan, Richard L. *Lawsuits and Litigation in Castile 1500–1700.* Chapel Hill: University of North Carolina Press, 1981.

Kahane, H., and A. Tietze. *The Lingua Franca in the Levant: Turkish Nautical Terms of Italian and Greek Origin.* Urbana: University of Illinois Press, 1958.

Kaklamanes, Stefanos. "Μάρκος Δεφαράνας (1503–1575), Ζακύνθιος Στιχουργός του 16ου Αιώνα" (Markos Defaranas: A Sixteenth-Century Poet from Zakynthos). Thesaurismata 21 (1991).

Khalilieh, Hassan S. *Admiralty and Maritime Laws in the Mediterranean Sea (ca. 800–1050): The Kitab Akriyat al-Sufun vis-à-vis the Nomos Rhodion Nautikos.* Leiden: Brill, 2006.

Kirk, Thomas. "Genoa and Livorno: Sixteenth and Seventeenth Century Commercial Rivalry as a Stimulus to Policy Development." *History* 86 (281) (2002): 3–17.

———. "The Implications of Ceremony at Sea: Some Examples from the Republic of Genoa (16th and 17th Centuries)." *Australian Association for Maritime History* 18, no. 1 (1996): 1–13.

Konstantinides. Καράβια, Καπετάνιοι και Συντροφοναύται, 1800–1830 (Ships, Captains and Shareowners). Athens, 1954.

Krantonelle, A. Ιστορία της Πειρατείας στους μεσους χρονους της Τουρκοκρατίας 1538–1699 (Piracy in the Middle Years of Turkish Rule 1538–1699). Athens, 1991.

Kremmydas, V. "Καταγραφή των εμπορικών πλοίν του Ηρακλείου το 1751" (Register of Commercial Ships of Herakleion in 1751). Mnēmon 7 (1978).

Kulischer, J. M. *Storia economica del medio eveo e dell'epoca moderna*, vol. 2, Italian translation. Florence, 1964.

Kulsrud, Carl J. *Maritime Neutrality to 1780: A History of the Main Principles Governing Neutrality and Belligerency to 1780*. Boston: Little, Brown, 1936.

Lane, Frederic. *Venice: A Maritime Republic*. Baltimore: Johns Hopkins University Press, 1973.

———. "Venetian Bankers, 1496–1533." In *Venice and History: The Collected Papers of Frederic C. Lane*, edited by a committee of colleagues and former students, foreword by Fernand Braudel. Baltimore: Johns Hopkins University Press, 1966.

——— "Tonnages, Medieval and Modern." *Economic History Review* 17 (1964–65): 213–33.

Leon, George. "The Greek Merchant Marine (1453–1850)." In *The Greek Merchant Marine*, edited by Stelios A. Papadopoulos. Athens: National Bank of Greece, 1972.

Lézine, A., and A. R. Abdul Tawab. "Introduction a l'étude des maisons anciennes de Rosette." *Annales Islamologiques* 10 (1972).

Luppé du Garrané, Jean-Bertran de. *Mémoires d'un chevalier de Malte au XVIIe siècle: Suivi des mémoires de son neveu Jean-Bertrand de Larrocan d'Aiguebère*; introduction and notes by Claude Petiet. Paris, 2001.

Luttrell, Anthony. "The Earliest Documents on the Hospitaller *Corso* on Rhodes: 1413 and 1416." In *The Hospitaller State on Rhodes and Its Western Provinces, 1306–1462*, 195–212 Aldershot, Hampshire, UK: Ashgate Variorum, 1999.

———. "Venice and the Knights Hospitallers of Rhodes in the Fourteenth Century." In *Papers of the British School at Rome* 26 (n.s. 13) (1958).

Makuscev, V., ed. *Monumenta Historica Slavorum Meridionalium*, vol. 1. Warsaw, 1874.

Mallia-Milanes, Victor, ed. *In the Service of the Venetian Republic: Massimiliano Buzzaccarini Gonzaga's Letters from Malta to Venice's Magistracy of Trade 1754–1776*. Malta, 2008,

———. *Venice and Hospitaller Malta*. Malta: Publishers Enterprises Group, 1992.

——— "From Valona to Crete: Veneto-Maltese Relations from the Late 1630s to the Outbreak of the Cretan War." In *Malta: A Case Study in International Cross-Currents*, edited by Stanley Fiorini and Victor Mallia-Milanes. Malta: University of Malta, 1991.

Maltezou, Chryssa A. "The Historical and Social Context." In *Literature and Society in Renaissance Crete*, edited by D. Holton. Cambridge: Cambridge University Press, 1991.

———. "Τα Πλοία της μονής Πάτμου (16th–17th αι)" (The Ships of the Monastery of Patmos, 16th–17th Centuries). In *Praktika diethnous symposiou: Hi mone hag. Ioannou tou theologou: 900 Chronia historikes martyrias (1088–1988)*, Patmos, September 1988.

Manousakas, M. I. Επισκόπηση της ιστορίας της Ελληνικής Ορθόδοξης Αδελφότητας της Βενετίας 1498–1953 (An Overview of the History of the Greek Fraternity in Venice 1498–1953). *Ta Historika* 6, no. 11 (1989).

———. "Η εν Βενετία Ελληνική Κοινότης και οι Μητροπολίται Φιλαδελφείας» (The Greek Community of Venice and the Metropolitans of Philadelphia). *Epeteris Etaireia Byzantinon Spoudon* 37 (1969–70).

Martini, A. *Manuale di metrologia*. Turin, 1883.

Masters, Bruce. *The Origins of Western Economic Dominance in the Middle East: Mercantilism and the Islamic Economy in Aleppo, 1600–1750*. New York, 1988.

———. "Trading Diasporas and 'Nations': The Genesis of National Identities in Ottoman Aleppo." *International History Review* 9, no. 3 (1987): 345.

Matar, Nabil. *Britain and Barbary, 1589–1689*. Gainesville: University of Florida Press, 2005.

———. Introduction to *Piracy, Slavery and Redemption: Barbary Captivity Narratives from Early Modern England*, edited by Daniel J. Vitkus. New York: Columbia University Press, 2001.

———. *Turks, Moors, and Englishmen in the Age of Discovery*. New York: Columbia University Press, 1999.

Mavroeide, Phane. Ο Ελληνισμός στο Γαλατά (1453–1600) (Hellenism in Galata 1453–1600). Ioannina, 1992.

———. Συμβολή στην Ιστορία της ελληνικής Αδελφότητας Βενετίας στο ΙΣΤ Αιώνα (Introduction to the History of the Greek Fraternity in Venice in the 16th Century 1533–1562). Athens, 1976.

Mitler, Louis. "The Genoese in Galata: 1453–1682." *International Journal of Middle East Studies* 10 (1979): 71–91.

Mueller, Reinhold. "Greeks in Venice and 'Venetians' in Greece." In *Ricchi e poveri nella società dell'oriente grecolatino*, edited by Chryssa A. Maltezou, 167–80. Biblioteca dell'Istituto ellenico di Studi Bizantini e postbizantini di Venezia, no. 19. Venice, 1998.

Muscat, Joseph. *The Maltese Galley*. Malta, 1998.

Natalucci, M. *Ancona attraverso i secoli*. Città di Castello, Italy: Unione arti grafiche, 1960.

Necipoğlu, N. "Byzantium between the Ottomans and the Latins: A Study of Political Attitudes in the Late Palaiologan Period, 1370–1460." PhD diss., Harvard University, 1990.

Nicol, Donald M. *The Last Centuries of Byzantium, 1261–1453*. Cambridge: Cambridge University Press, 1993.

Nussdorfer, Laurie. *Civic Politics in the Rome of Urban VIII*. Princeton: Princeton University Press, 1992.

Oikonomou, M. "Όψεις της Ελληνικής Ναυτιλίας κατά το 17ο αιωνα: Ο θεσμος του Εμπορικου Προξενείου των Ελλήνων Εμπόρων Οθωμανών υπηκοων στον Χάνδακα" (Aspects of Greek commercial shipping in the 17th and 18th century: the office of the commercial consul and the consulate of Greek merchants of Ottoman citizenship in Candia). *Paroussia* 10 (1994).

Pagano de Divitiis, Gigliola. *Mercanti Inglesi nell'Italia dei seicento: Navi, traffici, egemonie*. Venice, 1990.

Pamuk, Şevket. "Money in the Ottoman Empire." In Inalcık and Quataert, *An Economic and Social History of the Ottoman Empire*.

Panayiotopoulos, Kristas. "Έλληνες Ναυτικοί και Πλοικτήτες από τα παλαιότερα Οικονομικά Βιβλία της ελληνικής Αδελφότητας Βενετίας (1536–1576)" (Greek Sailors and Shipowners according to the Oldest Registers of the Greek Fraternity in Venice 1536–1576). *Thesaurismata* 11 (1974).

Pangrates, G. *Chiesa Latina e missionari Francescani Conventuali nelle Isole Venete del Mare Ionio: Documenti dall'archivio della sacra Congregazione di Propaganda Fide (17 se)*. Padua: Centro Studi Antoniani, 2009.

——. "Sources for the Maritime History of Greece." In *Research in Maritime History: New Directions in Mediterranean Maritime History*, edited by Carmel Vassallo and Gelina Harlaftis, vol. 28. St. John's, Newfoundland: International Maritime Economic History Association, 2004.

——. "Γιαννιώτες Έμποροι στη Βενετία στα μεσα του 16ου Αιώνα 1550–1567" (Merchants of Ioannina in Venice in the Middle of the Sixteenth Century 1550–1567). *Thesaurismata* 28 (1998).

Panopoulou, A. "Συντροφιές και Ναυλώσεις Πλοίων στο Χάνδακα (1635–1661)" (Partnerships and the Hiring of Boats in Chandaka 1635–1661). Pepragmena tou Ektou Diethnous Krētologikou Synedriou Chania, 1991.

Panzac, D. *La caravane maritime: Marins européens et marchands ottomans en Méditerranée (1680–1830)*. Paris, 2004.

Paoli, S. *Codice Diplomatico del Sacro Militare Ordine Gerosolimitano oggi di Malta Raccolto da Vari Documenti di Quell'Archivio per Servire alla Storia dello Stesso Ordin*. Lucca, 1737.

Papadopoulos, Stelios, ed. *The Greek Merchant Marine*. Athens, 1972.

Papkonstantinou, Katerina. "Malta and the Rise of the Greek-Owned Fleet in the Eighteenth Century." *Journal of Mediterranean Studies* 16, nos. 1–2 (2006): 199–217.

Pashley, Robert. *Travels in Crete*, vol. 2. Athens, 1989.

Pastor, Ludwig. *The History of the Popes from the Close of the Middle Ages, Drawn from the Secret Archives of the Vatican and Other Original Sources*, edited by R. F. Kerr. 40 vols. London, 1891–1953.

Philipp, Thomas. *The Syrians in Egypt: 1725–1975*. Stuttgart: Steiner Verlag, 1985.

Pia Pendani, M. *In nome del Gran Signore: Inviati Ottomani a Venezia dalla caduta di Costantinopoli alla guerra di Candia*. Venice, 1994.

Ploumides, G. Αιτήματα και πραγματικότητες των Ελλήνων της Βενετοκρατίας (1554–1600) (Demands and Realities of the Greeks under Venetian Rule, 1554–1600). Ioannina, 1985.

——. "Considerazioni sulla popolazione greca a Venezia nella seconda meta del 1500." *Studi Veneziani* 14 (1972): 219–26.

Portelli, M. "Freed in the Name of Christianity." Bachelor's thesis, University of Malta, 1988.

Postan, M. M., and H. J. Habakkuk, eds. *Cambridge Economic History of Europe*. 2nd ed. Vol. 2, *Trade and Industry in the Middle Ages*. Cambridge: Cambridge University Press, 1966–89.

Pullan, Brian, ed. *Crisis and Change in the Venetian Economy in the Seventeenth Centuries*. London: Mathews and Co., 1968.

Rambert, Gaston, ed. *Histoire du commerce de Marseille*. Vol. 5, *De 1660 à 1789: Le Levant*, edited by Robert Paris. Paris: Chambre de commerce et d'industrie de Marseille, 1957.

Randolph, Bernard. *The Present State of the Islands in the Archipelago*. Oxford: printed at the Theatre, 1687.

Ravid, Benjamin. "A Tale of Three Cities and Their Raison d'Etat: Ancona, Venice, and Livorno and the Competition for Jewish Merchants in the Sixteenth Century." *Mediterranean Historical Review* 6, no. 2 (1991–92): 138–62.

Raymond, André. *Artisans et commerçants au Caire au XVIIIe siècle*. Vol. I. Damascus, 1973.

Rediker, Marcus. *Villains of All Nations: Atlantic Pirates in the Golden Age*. Boston: Beacon Press, 2004.

———. *Between the Devil and the Deep Blue Sea: Merchant Seamen, Pirates, and the Anglo-American Maritime World, 1700–1750*. Cambridge: Cambridge University Press, 1987.

Ross, Geoffrey Aquilina. *Blue Guide: Malta and Gozo*. 5th ed. London: 2000.

Rothman, E. Natalie. *Between Venice and Istanbul: Trans-Imperial Subjects and Cultural Mediation in the Early Modern Mediterranean*. PhD diss., University of Michigan, 2006.

Sanudo, Marino. *I diarii*. Venice, 1880–87.

Saracini, G. *Notitie historiche della citta' d'Ancona*. Bologna, 1968.

Sathas, Constantine N. Μνημεία της Ελληνικής Ιστορίας, *Documents inédits relatifs à l'histoire de la Grèce au moyen âge, publiés sous les auspices de la Chambre de deputes de Grèce*, 9 vols. Paris: 1883.

Setton, Kenneth M. *The Papacy and the Levant 1204–1571*. Vol. 4, *The Sixteenth Century to the Rule of Julius III*. Philadelphia: American Philosophical Society, 1980.

Shaw, Stanford J. *The Financial and Administrative Organization and Development of Ottoman Egypt, 1517–1798*. Princeton: Princeton University Press, 1962.

Shmuelevitz, Aryeh. *The Jews of the Ottoman Empire in the Late Fifteenth and the Sixteenth Centuries: Administrative, Economic, Legal and Social Relations as Reflected in the Responsa*. Leiden: Brill, 1984.

Sire, H.J.A. *The Knights of Malta*. New Haven: Yale University Press, 1994.

Slot, B. J. *Archipelagus Turbatus: Les Cylades entre colonisation latine et occupation ottomane c. 1500–1718*. Istanbul, 1982.

Spanakes, Stergios. "Relatione dell Sr. Benetto Moro ritornato provveditore generale del regno di Candia, letta in pregadi a 25 giugno 1602." In Mnēmeia tēs Krētikēs Istorias (Monuments of Cretan History), vol. 4. Herakleion, Greece, 1960.

———. "Η Εκθεση του Δούκα της Κρήτης" (The Report of the Duke of Crete). Krētika Chronika 3 (1949).

———. "Relazione del Nobil Huomo Zuanne Mocenigo ritornato provveditore generale del regno di Candia presentata nell'eccellentissimo consillio 17 Aprile 1589." Mnēmeia tēs Krētikēs Istorias (Monuments of Cretan History). Herakleion, 1940.

Stavrinides, N. Μεταφράσεις Τουρκικών Ιστορικών Εγγράφων (Translations of Turkish Historical Documents). 5 vols. Herakleion, 1984–87.

Steele, Richard, ed. *An Account of the State of the Roman-Catholick Religion throughout the World. Written for the use of Pope Innocent XI., by Monsignor Cerri . . . Now first translated from an authentick Italian ms. never publish'd. To which is added, a discourse concerning the state of religion in England. Written in French, in the time of K. Charles I. and now first translated. With a large dedication to the present pope; giving him a very particular account of the state of religion amongst*

Protestants; and of several other matters of importance relating to Great-Britain, by Urban Cerri. London: 1715.

Steensgaard, N. "Consuls and Nations in the Levant from 1570 to 1650." *Scandinavian Economic History Review* 15 (1967): 13–55.

Stoianovich, Traian. "The Conquering Balkan Orthodox Merchant." *Journal of Economic History* 20, no. 2 (1960).

Struys, John. *The Voiages of John Struys.* London, 1684.

Tai, E. S. "Restitution and the Definition of a Pirate: The Case of Sologrus de Nigro." *Mediterranean Historical Review* 19, no. 2 (December 2004).

Tenenti, Alberto. *Piracy and the Decline of Venice, 1580–1615.* Translated and with an introduction by Janet and Brian Pullan. Berkeley and Los Angeles: University of California Press, 1967.

———. *Cristoforo Da Canal: La marine vénitienne avant Lépante.* Paris: SEVPEN, 1962.

———. *Naufrages, corsaires et assurances maritimes à Venise, 1592–1609.* Paris: SEVPEN, 1959.

Theiner, T. *Annales Ecclesiastici* iii. Rome, 1856.

Theunissen, H. "Ottoman-Venetian Diplomatics: The Ahd-Names." *Electronic Journal of Oriental Studies* 1, no. 2 (1998).

Thiriet, F. "La vie des hommes de les rapports des collectivités." In *La Romanie vénitienne au Moyen Âge: Le développement et l'exploitation du domaine colonial vénitien (XIIe–XVe siecles).* Paris: 1959.

Trivellato, Francesca. *The Familiarity of Strangers: The Sephardic Diaspora, Livorno and Cross-Cultural Trade in the Early Modern Period.* New Haven: Yale University Press, 2009.

———. "Sephardic Merchants between Rabbinic and Civil Courts: Probing Property Rights and Contesting Authority in the Eighteenth Century Mediterranean." Forthcoming.

Tsirpanles, Z. N. Στη Ρόδο του 16ου–17ου Αιώνα: Από τους Ιωαννίτες στους Οθωμανούς Τούρκους (Rhodes in the 16th and 17th Centuries: From the Knights to the Ottoman Turks). Rhodes, 2002.

———. Το Ελληνικό Κολλέγιο της Ρώμης και οι Μαθητές του (1576–1700): Συμβολή στη Μελέτη της μορφωτικής πολιτικής του Βατικανού (The Greek College of Rome and Its Students [1576–1700]: A Study of Vatican Cultural Policy). Thessaloniki, 1980.

Tucci, Ugo. "Un problem di metrologia navale: La botte veneziana." *Studi Veneziani* 9 (1967): 201–46.

Turan, S. "Venedik'te Türk Ticaret Merkezi." *Belleten* 32 (1968).

Tzamtizis, A. I. "Ships, Ports and Sailors." In Papadopoulos, *The Greek Merchant Marine.* Athens, 1972,

van den Boogert, Maurits H. *The Capitulations and the Ottoman Legal System: Qadis, Consuls and Beratlis in the 18th Century.* Leiden: Brill, 2005.

———. "Redress for Ottoman Victims of European Privateering: A Case Against the Dutch in the Divan-I Hümayun (1708–1715)." *Turcica* 33 (2001): 91–117.

Vansleb, F. *The Present State of Egypt.* London, 1678.

Vatin, N. *L'ordre de Saint-Jean-de Jérusalem, l'Empire ottoman et la Méditerranée orientale entre les deux sièges de Rhodes, 1480–1522.* Paris, 1994.

Vella, Sebastian. "The *Consolato del Mare* of Malta: A Study of an Institution 1697–1725." Bachelor's thesis, University of Malta, 1998.

———. "The Bureaucracy of the *Consolato del Mare* in Malta (1697–1724)." In *Consolati di Mare and Chambers of Commerce: Proceedings of a Conference Held at the Foundation for International Studies*, edited by C. Vassallo. Valletta, 2000.

Vertot, Abbé de. *The History of the Knights Hospitallers of St. John of Jerusalem, styled afterwards, the Knights of Rhodes, and at present, the Knights of Malta. Translated from the French of Mons. l'Abbé de Vertot.* 5 vols. Edinburgh, 1757.

Vlame, D. Το Φιορίνι, το σιτάρι και η οδός του Κήπου: Ελληνες έμποροι στο Λιβόρνο 1750–1868 (The Florin, Grain and Garden Street: Greek Merchants in Livorno 1750–1868). Foreword by Spyros Asdrachas. Athens: 2000.

Vlassopoulos, Nikos St. Ιόνιοι Εμποροι και Καραβοκύρηδες στη Μεσόγειο, 16ος–18ος Αιώνας (Ionian Merchants and Shipowners in the Mediterranean, 16th–18th Centuries). Athens, 2001.

Vryonis, Sp. "Local Institutions in the Greek Islands and Elements of Byzantine Continuity during Ottoman Rule," *Annuaire de L'Universite de Sofia: Centre de Recherches Slavo-Byzantines Ivan Dujčev* 83, no. 3 (1989).

Ware, Timothy. *Eustratios Argenti: A Study of the Greek Church under Turkish Rule*. Oxford: Clarendon Press, 1964.

Winter, Michael. "A Statute for the Mercantile Fleet." *Mediterranean Historical Review* 3, no. 2 (1988).

Wright, A. D. *The Early Modern Papacy: From the Council of Trent to the French Revolution 1564–1789*. Harlow, UK: Longman, 2000.

Ypselante, Athanasios Komnenou. *Ta meta ten alosen.* Constantinople, 1870.

Zachariadou, E. "Συμβολή Στην Ιστορία του Νοτιοανατολικού Αιγαίου" (A Contribution to the History of the southeastern Aegean). *Symmikta* (Athens) 1 (1966).

Zupko, Ronald Edward. *Italian Weights and Measures from the Middle Ages to the Nineteenth Century*. Philadelphia: American Philosophical Society, 1981.

Index

● ○ ●

Made in the USA
Middletown, DE
10 October 2020